Dyad Leadership in Healthcare:

When One Plus One *is* Greater than Two

Dyad Leadership in Healthcare:
When One Plus One
is Greater than Two

Kathleen D. Sanford, DBA, RN, CENP, FACHE
Senior Vice President and Chief Nursing Officer
Catholic Health Initiatives
Englewood, Colorado

Stephen L. Moore, MD
Senior Vice President and Chief Medical Officer
Catholic Health Initiatives
Englewood, Colorado

. Wolters Kluwer

Philadelphia · Baltimore · New York · London
Buenos Aires · Hong Kong · Sydney · Tokyo

Acquisitions Editor: Shannon W. Magee
Product Development Editor: Maria M. McAvey
Developmental Editor: Lisa Marshall
Senior Marketing Manager: Mark Wiragh
Editorial Assistant: Zachary Shapiro
Production Project Manager: Marian Bellus
Design Coordinator: Stephen Druding
Manufacturing Coordinator: Kathleen Brown
Prepress Vendor: SPi Global

Copyright © 2015 Wolters Kluwer.

9 8 7 6 5 4 3 2

Printed in China

Library of Congress Cataloging-in-Publication Data
Sanford, Kathleen, author.
  Dyad leadership in healthcare : when one plus one is greater than two / Kathleen D. Sanford, Stephen L. Moore.
       p. ; cm.
  Includes bibliographical references and index.
  ISBN 978-1-4511-9334-3 (paperback : alk. paper)
  I. Moore, Stephen L. (Stephen Lee), 1954- , author. II. Title.
  [DNLM: 1. Hospital Administration—methods. 2. Interprofessional Relations. 3. Leadership. 4. Models, Organizational. 5. Organizational Culture. WX 150.1]
  RA971
  362.11068—dc23
                                                                                    2014038709

LWW.com

DEDICATION

To the most important Dyads of our lives, the two who have been there for us through every challenge and joy. With love and gratitude to our life mates, William (Bill) Mack Sanford and Karen Elizabeth Moore.

KS and SM

Contributors

Renae N. Battié, MN, RN, CNOR
is the associate vice president for perioperative and GI services for CHI Franciscan Health System, responsible for coordinating the perioperative, GI, and sterile processing departments at their five hospitals in the greater Tacoma, Washington area. Her previous roles were in academic and private nonprofit multicampus systems. She has experience in OR design/construction, surgical information system implementations, specialty team development, and just culture. Renae was honored to receive the AORN Award for Outstanding Achievement in Perioperative Nursing Management in 2010. She is a member of the Seattle Chapter, Washington State Council, and currently serves as the national AORN President-Elect.

Judith Sims Billings, RN, PhD
is a retired nursing school administrator. She has a bachelor's degree from Fort Hays Kansas State University and master's degree and PhD from the University of Minnesota. In 1965, she began her career in nursing as a staff nurse at Good Samaritan Hospital. Judy began teaching nursing in 1968; she taught at St. Francis School of Nursing in Grand Island, Nebraska, and South Dakota State University. In 1976, she returned to Kearney to develop the nursing program at the University of Nebraska Kearney (aka Kearney State College), which she administered for 25 of the next 29 years. She retired from University of Nebraska Medical Center College of Nursing Kearney as the assistant administrator.

Since retirement, Judy has volunteered in several positions in Good Samaritan Health Systems.

Kimber Bonner, RN, MSN, BSN
is the director of Intensive Care Unit and Neuro Trauma at Good Samaritan Hospital (GSH). Kimber received her bachelor of science in nursing from the University of Nebraska Medical Center and masters in nursing with emphasis in management and leadership through Walden University. She has been employed at GSH since 1997.

Larry E. Bragg, MD
is a member of the Good Samaritan Hospital (GSH) medical staff, providing general surgery services to the region since 1991. Dr. Bragg has provided strong medical staff leadership by serving in various offices, including medical staff president and as chairman of the following: Credentials Committee, Critical Care Committee, Medical Executive Committee, Performance Improvement Council, Surgery Department, and Bylaws/Accreditation Committee. Dr. Bragg currently serves as the trauma medical director and trauma committee chair for GSH's level II trauma center. He is also a physician member of GSH's Integrated Leadership Team.

Sam Brandt, MD, DABFP
is the CMIO for Catholic Health Initiatives (CHI). His healthcare career began as a family practice physician, followed by a hospital medical director position. He has worked in the

informatics world for 15 years, serving as CMIO for a clinical systems vendor immediately prior to joining CHI.

Jennifer (Jenni) Bringardner, RN, MHA, FACHE

is the administrative vice president of the CHI National Cardiovascular Service. With over 30 years of healthcare experience, her background includes cardiovascular nursing, cardiac business development, strategy, marketing, and service line growth and development. In addition to a nursing degree, Ms. Bringardner holds a bachelor of arts in organizational management and a master of health administration. She is a member of the American College of Cardiovascular Administrators and is a fellow of the American College of Healthcare Executives.

F. Peter Buckley, MD

is currently employed as an anesthesiologist by the University of Washington Medical Center, in Seattle, Washington. His clinical interests include pain management and regional anesthesia for operative and postoperative pain control. Peter attended the Medical College of St. Bartholomew's Hospital in the United Kingdom. He has developed and managed acute pain services at both a trauma center and cancer center. His patient care philosophy is to bring to patient care the most recent knowledge and skills and to integrate these into a patient-acceptable and friendly management plan.

Dennis Edwards, MD

has been vice president of medical affairs at Good Samaritan Hospital (GSH) since May 2011. Dr. Edwards first joined the medical staff of GSH in 1980 as a pediatrician, then left to become an anesthesiologist, and returned to Good Samaritan in August 1985. He is a respected physician leader and has served in many capacities during his tenure including medical staff president.

Thomas W. Frederickson, MD, FACP, SFHM, MBA

is the medical director for Hospital Medicine at Alegent Creighton Health in Omaha, Nebraska. Since completing his residency in internal medicine in 1998, Tom has been dedicated to the field of hospital medicine and making hospitals safer places for patients. He perused medicine as a second career. After working in corporate finance for a number of years, he attended medical school at the University of Minnesota and then completed internal medicine residency at the University of Missouri, Kansas City. Tom is active in the Society of Hospital Medicine where he currently serves on multiple committees. He served on the board of Overland Park Regional Medical Center and has held many positions in medical staff leadership. His professional interests include delivery of value-based care, patient safety, evidenced-based care, clinical process improvement, hospice care, and medical leadership.

Ellen Gitt, BS, MT (ASCP)

is the director of service quality, patient advocate, and Planetree coordinator at Good Samaritan Hospital in Kearney, Nebraska. Ellen graduated from Kearney (Nebraska) State College with a degree in medical technology.

Jerome (Jerry) Granato, MD, FACC

is the vice president and medical director of the CHI National Cardiovascular Service. Prior to joining CHI, Dr. Granato was the senior vice president and chief medical officer at Excela Health System in Pittsburgh, Pennsylvania. He has a wide range of expertise and experience involving the full spectrum of cardiovascular care. Dr. Granato obtained an undergraduate degree in engineering from the Stevens Institute of Technology in Hoboken, New Jersey; his medical degree and internal medicine residency training from Johns Hopkins Medical School in Baltimore, Maryland; and postdoctoral fellowship in Cardiovascular Disease from the University of Virginia Medical Center in Charlottesville, Virginia. He has a master of business administration from the Kellogg School of Management–Northwestern University in Evanston, Illinois.

Michael S. Hein, MD, MS, MHCM, FACP

is the vice president of Medical Affairs at St. Francis Medical Center (SFMC) in Grand Island, Nebraska. He joined the hospital in October 2011. Trained as an internal medicine physician, he practiced in Holdrege, Nebraska; Yankton, South Dakota; and at the Grand Island Veterans Health Administration before coming to SFMC. He received his medical degree from the Sanford School of Medicine at the University of South Dakota and completed his residency in internal medicine at Gundersen/Lutheran Medical Center in La Crosse, Wisconsin. Dr. Hein also has two master's degrees. The first is in exercise physiology from St. Cloud State University and the second is in healthcare management from Harvard University, School of Public Health.

Deborah Hood, MBA

is a Dyad leader of the National Oncology Service Line for Catholic Health Initiatives (CHI) with Dax Kurbegov, MD. Together, they lead teams for 45 CHI cancer centers in 21 markets in 13 states. Deb has a bachelor of science in biology from the University of Wisconsin–Green Bay and a master's in business administration from the University of Colorado–Colorado Springs. She has worked in the healthcare industry for more than 35 years. Her previous work includes clinical laboratory administration; healthcare strategic planning and marketing and communications; cancer center administration; and Oncology Service Line development.

Dax Kurbegov, MD

is a Dyad leader of the National Oncology Service Line for Catholic Health Initiatives (CHI) with Deborah Hood, MBA. Together, they lead teams for 45 CHI cancer centers in 21 markets in 13 states. Max joined CHI in December 2012. His experience includes serving as chief fellow at MD Anderson Cancer Center and faculty positions with the University of Miami Miller School of Medicine and the University of Colorado School of Medicine. Throughout a decade of medical oncology clinical practice, most recently as director of Memorial Health Systems in Colorado Springs, he has developed innovative models of multidisciplinary care. Dax completed medical school at Baylor College of Medicine and residency at the University of Colorado Health Sciences Center.

Jeanie Mamula, MSHA, MT, CPHQ

has worked in healthcare for over 30 years, with 20+ years' experience in both quality and risk management. As the vice president of Clinical Quality Improvement for Catholic Health Initiatives (CHI), she has led many performance improvement initiatives and most recently is partnering with risk management to lead CHI's High Reliability initiative. This initiative focuses on changing the culture to one in which patient and staff safety is our first priority.

Joe Mangiameli, RN, MSN

is the senior director for Hospital Medicine, Neurology, and Medical Specialties for Alegent Creighton Clinic. He has been in healthcare since 1997, having worked in a number of areas to include cardiovascular, intensive care, and emergency department. He holds a bachelor's degree in business administration and nursing, as well as master's degrees in nursing and healthcare administration. Joe has worked with Alegent Creighton Health since 2004. In addition to his civilian career, he also serves in the Nebraska Army National Guard at the rank of Major. He has deployed multiple times to Iraq and Afghanistan in the capacity as a nurse, educator, and healthcare administrator.

Diane S. Menendez, PhD, MCC

is the director, Organizational Talent Management for CHI. In this role, she leads system-wide coaching and mentoring initiatives and coaches clinical and operational leaders in the Transformational Leadership Development Program. Prior to joining Catholic Health Initiatives, she held leadership roles at AT&T, Macy's, and Convergys. She also ran a leadership practice coaching firm for 15+ years. Her first private coaching client was a frustrated physician, and she learned from that experience the power of coaching clinical leaders. She has a doctorate from Indiana University and substantial postdoctoral work applying research in Positive Psychology to coaching practice. Diane was one of the first International Coach Federation's Master Certified Coaches. She has developed a practical, spiritual, and compassionate approach to coaching leaders. Her approach to coaching for transformation focuses on wholeness, integrating mind, body, emotion, and spirit. Diane believes that coaching Dyad leaders can bring about the positive relationships and results that can transform our healthcare system.

Stephen L. Moore, MD

joined Catholic Health Initiatives (CHI) in March 2009 as a senior vice president and chief medical officer. In this role, he has executive responsibility for quality and safety, electronic health records (including HIE, clinical informatics, and analytics), telemedicine and telehealth business lines, physician leadership development, and clinical resource utilization across 19 states, 82 hospitals, 3500 employed providers, and 40 nursing homes. For 14 years, Dr. Moore was a practicing family physician in rural Maine and Virginia. Prior to CHI, Dr. Moore also served as the chief medical officer at Bon Secours Health System, Hampton Roads, Carolinas Healthcare System, and Inova Health System. Dr. Moore earned his bachelor's degree from University of Maine and his medical degree from Tufts University School of Medicine, Boston, Massachusetts.

Pat Patton, MSN, RN, FCN

is the vice president of Nursing Operations, Acute Care at CHI National in Denver. Pat is responsible for system-wide inpatient nursing models, the national clinical competency program, development of Magnet and Pathway to Excellence programs, Faith Community Nursing, and clinical innovation. Mr. Patton has over two decades of nursing experience. Previously, he has served as a chief nursing officer, a house administrator, a nursing manager, and staff nurse. In addition, past responsibility has included home health administration.

Manoj Pawar, MD, MMM

is the vice president, Clinical Operations & Physician Leadership Development at Catholic Health Initiatives, where he is involved in foundational work that will ultimately reduce variation in costs and improve outcomes. In addition, he is responsible for building individual and collective leadership capacity among the system's senior-level physician executives. Dr. Pawar is a seasoned physician executive, with experience in leading hospitals, medical groups, and integrated health systems on journeys that involved clinical, operational, strategic, and cultural transformation.

Richard L. Oken, MD

was the president and chairman of the board of directors for Alta Bates Medical Group from 1999 to 2014. He has practiced pediatric medicine in private practice in the East Bay area of San Francisco since 1974 and has been the managing partner of East Bay Pediatrics Medical Group for 25 years. He is a graduate of the medical school of the University of California at San Francisco (UCSF) with a subsequent 3-year residency including chief resident. Dr. Oken continues as a clinical professor of pediatrics at UCSF. Dr. Oken has been involved in HMO, IPA, and health plan governance; is a former president of the medical staff and chairman of the board at Alta Bates Medical Center in Berkeley, California; and currently serves on the board of directors of Brown and Toland Medical Group.

Libby Raetz, RN, MSN, MS, CEN

earned a BSN from the University of Nebraska Medical Center. At Clarkson College in Omaha, Nebraska, she obtained a master of science in nursing administration as well as a master's in health services management. She is a certified emergency nurse. Ms. Raetz has been with CHI Saint Elizabeth for 26 years. In 1995, she became the director of Emergency Services and Ambulatory Care; in November 2011, she was named vice president of nursing and chief nursing officer. Ms. Raetz has also chaired many internal committees and councils at CHI Saint Elizabeth. She serves on various board of directors in the Lincoln community. She has provided strong leadership for Embrace the Spirit—a value-based, customer service program—which inspires a system-wide focus on excellent care.

Robert (Bob) Ritz, MHA, FACHE

is the president of Mercy Medical Center in Des Moines, Iowa. He has been president and CEO at Saint Mary's Health System in Waterbury, Connecticut, and president and CEO for the Monongalia Health System in Morgantown, West Virginia. His position prior to joining Mercy was with Hospital Sisters Health System where he helped to develop strategic alignments with area hospitals and physician practices. Bob's bachelor of science degree in business administration is from Wheeling Jesuit University. He earned his master's in health administration from the Sloan Program in Health Services Administration at Cornell University.

Kathleen D. Sanford, DBA, RN, CENP, FACHE

joined Catholic Health Initiatives (CHI) in November 2006 as the senior vice president and chief nursing officer. She has responsibility for quality and patient safety, clinical operating improvement, leadership development of clinicians, and clinical information technology. She also leads evidenced-based practice initiatives and the practice of nursing across CHI's continuum of care. Dr. Sanford has more than 40 years of experience in healthcare, including staff nursing, middle management, chief nurse executive, and hospital administrator roles. A former Army nurse, she has served in leadership positions for multiple community and charitable organizations. She is a past president of the American Organization of Nurse Executives (AONE). She is a past board member of several healthcare organizations including the American Hospital Association (AHA), Washington State Hospital Association (WSHA), and Nursing Organizations Alliance (NOA). She is currently Editor-in-Chief of Nursing Administration Quarterly. As a newspaper healthcare columnist and author for a variety of publications, she has published numerous articles and the management book, *Leading With Love*. Dr. Sanford's education includes a bachelor's degree in nursing from the University of Maryland/Walter Reed Army Institute of Nursing, a master's degree in human resources management from Pepperdine University, a master's degree in business administration from Pacific Lutheran University, and a doctorate in business from Nova Southeastern University.

Michael Schnieders, MBA, FACHE

was named president of Good Samaritan Hospital in June 2010. A native of Iowa, Michael earned his masters in business administration from The University of Iowa and has worked in healthcare management for more than 25 years. He is a member of the American College of Healthcare Executives and of the Healthcare Financial Management Association. He has a strong background in strategic development, finance, and physician relations, as well as extensive experience in nonprofit Catholic healthcare and the for-profit health sector.

Ann Shepard, RN-BC, MSN

serves as the CNIO for Catholic Health Initiatives (CHI). She worked as a critical care nurse and nurse manager in Des Moines, Iowa, at one of the CHI hospitals before joining the national office as part of the IT informatics team. Ann is the first person to serve in this system nursing informatics executive position. Her responsibilities include leadership for all regional CNIOs, the system's informatics department, and (in partnership with her Dyad CMIO) the implementation of clinical IT systems across 18 States.

James Slaggert, MBA

is the vice president of Integrated Health Networks at Englewood, Colorado-based Catholic Health Initiatives (CHI), the nation's third-largest faith-based health system. In this role, he provides leadership to the executive management of CHI's clinically integrated networks across all market-based organizations. Before joining CHI,

Mr. Slaggert served as the chief executive officer for the Alta Bates Medical Group, a 600-physician independent practice association in Berkeley, California. He holds a bachelor of science degree from Rochester Institute of Technology, Rochester, New York, and a master of business administration degree from the University of Cincinnati.

Francine Sparby, MS, BSN

has more than 25 years of nursing leadership experience with responsibility for nursing and support services in both academic and community medical centers. During her career, Francine has successfully implemented new nursing leadership models, quality and patient safety initiatives, and improvements in patient experience. She has extensive experience in developing collaborative practice models with physicians, nurses, and other healthcare team members. Currently, Francine is the vice president for Patient Care Services at Creighton University Medical Center at Catholic Health Initiatives Alegent Creighton Health.

Amanda Trask, MBA, MHA, FACHE, CMPE

is the vice president for CHI's National Hospital Medicine Service Line. Amanda is developing the national hospital medicine service line, with her physician Dyad partner. Their focus is on improving clinical and business outcomes through enhanced collaboration, improved processes, and optimized practices of the nearly 900 hospitalist providers practicing in CHI hospitals. Amanda holds a master's of business administration and master's of health administration from Georgia State University, as well as bachelor of arts from Converse College in Spartanburg, South Carolina. She is a fellow with the American College of Healthcare Executives, as well as a Certified Medical Practice Executive from the American College of Medical Practice Executives. In 2013, she was named as one of Becker's Hospital Review *Top 25 Healthcare Leaders Under 40*.

Carol Wahl, RN, MSN, MBA

is the vice president of Patient Care Services at Good Samaritan Hospital in Kearney, Nebraska. Good Samaritan is a 287-bed regional level II trauma healthcare facility located in central Nebraska and is a member of Catholic Health Initiatives. Carol earned her MBA from the University of Nebraska at Omaha and her MSN from the College of St. Mary, Omaha. Among her many accomplishments was leading Good Samaritan to become the system's first Planetree organization.

Cary Ward, MD, CMO, FACP

earned his medical degree at the University of Texas, Southwestern Medical School, Dallas, and completed his internship and residency at Washington University in St. Louis, Missouri. He practiced internal medicine in Lincoln until 1998 when he started and directed the hospitalist program, Inpatient Medical Services, at CHI Saint Elizabeth Regional Medical Center. He has also served as the director of hospitalist operations for the other CHI hospitalist programs. Dr. Ward was named the chief medical officer

of CHI St. Elizabeth Regional Medical Center in 2002 and serves as the physician lead on the executive committee for CHI Nebraska.

Randy Wick, CPHRM, CIC, ARM, CPCU, CCLA

is a graduate of the University of South Dakota. He has been with Catholic Health Initiatives (CHI) since 1992 and is currently vice president, Risk Management Operations. He is responsible for the overall direction and oversight of patient, employee, and environmental risk management and safety programs. With his quality Dyad partner, Mr. Wick has led the system-wide program to enhance a culture of partnership and safety among all stakeholders.

Foreword

At first glance upon reading the title or a synopsis of *Dyad Clinical Leadership*, it might seem to be a book about physician and nurse relationships and how to develop a more collaborative working relationship between the two. However, I see a book about some of the first important steps in the new world order evolving in the system of healthcare delivery. The new world order is the shift in how hospital systems, which serve as the foundation of healthcare delivery, reinvent themselves to address the three-pronged challenge that faces our nation's healthcare industry. This challenge includes improving the quality of care delivered to those who are ill; reducing the cost of providing that care; and finally, morphing from hospital systems to health systems that work with individuals to maintain their healthy state and to avoid the physical, psychological, and economic perils of becoming ill.

I describe the lessons of this book as the first steps in the new world order, because creating collaborative working relationships between practicing clinicians from different disciplines is the first step in eliminating the fragmented care common in this country. The lack of collaboration and integration between the work of different clinicians, all treating the same patient, is the source of much of the poor clinical quality and inappropriately expensive care that individuals experience on a daily basis. If the United States is to ever improve the costs and the outcomes of our healthcare system, it will be because our clinical leaders from different disciplines have learned to work collaboratively as a team. An integrated team that weaves together complementary skills and uses data-driven decision and design development tools, such as lean process improvement techniques, is the first step in the process of creating a more effective and efficient healthcare system.

Dyad Clinical Leadership, and the first step that it represents, is not just about the clinical side of healthcare delivery but also about the leadership required to oversee and manage the large and complex organizations that have been formed to deliver care. Large health systems and their many component institutions, departments, and functions require a new philosophy of leadership and management to chart a more person-centered system of care. This book helps to outline a path that veers from the traditional methods of management and decision making in healthcare delivery organizations. I applaud the work of authors Steve Moore and Kathy Sanford, not just in outlining this path forward but also for the difficult and tireless work involved in being a successful example of a dyad model within their own organization, Catholic Health Initiatives.

Michael Rowan, FACHE
President and Chief Operating Officer, Healthcare Delivery
Catholic Health Initiatives
Denver, Colorado

Preface

T he concept of pairing two leaders to accomplish organizational goals is not new. Many of our colleagues can point to projects they have co-led in the past, sometimes even in the distant past. However, the development of a model of leadership in which two leaders from differing professional backgrounds are placed in formal management positions, as a strategy for moving into the next era of healthcare, is new.

Our current world is largely centered around acute care hospitals. Single or small (not affiliated with a large system) institutions have been able to thrive in the past. There has been little financial reward for quality outcomes, and we still receive quite a bit of fee-for-service reimbursement for care to individuals. In the next era, stand-alone organizations will need to unite with others, because scale will be more important. Revenue will be based on provision of value, defined as efficiency *and* quality, delivered to populations. The next era of healthcare is already beginning, and leaders are planning how to best manage the evolution into the future.

Another important change for hospitals and physicians is that past regulations which have hindered our collaboration are being replaced with aligned incentives and government encouragement to coordinate care. This has been a major impetus to the development of co-management models, including the development of Dyads. Our book is for executives considering the implementation of this type of leadership. It is also intended for leaders who are new or experienced Dyads, as a guide for becoming true partners.

We wrote this book because we see great promise in this new model of leadership. It has the potential to bring professionals who have traditionally not "played well together" into high-performing teams who will perform an essential role in effectively transforming healthcare in America. Our organization, Catholic Health Initiatives (CHI), is investing in and implementing this way of leading as part of our commitment to healthier communities, users of healthcare, our employees, and other existing or future partners. We know that healthcare must change, and we believe the adage "doing things the same way and expecting different results is madness." The future requires innovation, which is a strong CHI value. Development of high-functioning, multidisciplinary teams, led by Dyad leaders, is one of our innovations for the future.

Others are beginning to utilize this leadership model, but we are alarmed by the number of our colleagues who, perceiving its value, are naming two individuals from diverse professions as co-leaders of departments or programs without thoughtful, deliberate planning and development of these leaders' management, partnership, and team skills. As with any major change, the implementation of formal leadership partnerships requires an understanding of benefits and costs, along with executive commitment to development of something that is new to healthcare, unfamiliar to existing "single" leaders, and alien in an industry where most of us have grown up in professional silos. Without deep understanding and an exploration of what Dyad leadership is and needs to be, we fear these early experiments in partnering will fail, or at the very least, not reach their potential for excellent leadership in the next era.

We (Steve and Kathy) are a functioning CMO–CNO Dyad team for one of the largest healthcare systems in America. As coauthors and editors, we are sharing our learnings in our Dyad development. In addition, this book includes a variety of personal experience stories by different Dyad partners, as well as contributions from participants in the development of our Dyad leaders, at the end of each chapter. From their accounts, executives considering this model, as well as potential Dyad leaders, will get a flavor of the challenges and rewards experienced on the road to a new way of leading.

As clinicians, we strongly believe in evidence-based practice, whether it is for clinical care or management. Throughout this book, we will reference management studies and leadership literature that have led us to our model. We are not including detailed information about the studies themselves, but if readers are interested in the background management science, our references will lead you to appropriate sources. We will be studying the success of our organization's Dyads, because of our strong commitment to ensuring that all innovation or planned change is evaluated over time, so that they can be modified appropriately, or even abandoned if they do not support the organization's vision, mission, and values in the best way to meet our goals. We don't think this will be the case with Dyads, but *only* if they are planned, initiated, and maintained with a deliberate, competent approach.

We believe that there will be unintended consequences that could result from inadequate preparation or development of partners and their leadership skills. These include hierarchal dysfunction, professional clashes, active and passive resistance to change, gender bias issues, and lack of clarity surrounding leadership accountability and responsibility. While difficult enough for the Dyad partnership to navigate, the organizational view of these issues could be confusing and potentially destructive to the strategic and operational direction.

We hope you are reading this book because you know our healthcare organizations must, and will, require new ways to lead and to partner. If you are intrigued by the idea of formal Dyad leadership, please take time to understand and plan it well for your organization. We believe this is a model that is sorely needed if we are to overcome a history of competition, siloism, and misunderstanding between professions and healthcare organizations. It is only by coming together that we can truly transform healthcare for the good of all.

Kathleen D. Sanford
Stephen L. Moore

Acknowledgments

We were only able to write this book because of the generosity of others who contributed their stories and their talents. Most of the authors share with us the good fortune of working for an innovative, strategic, mission driven, faith-based organization. We are blessed to be part of Catholic Health Initiatives. We are also lucky to have the support of two remarkable women, Linda Pickett and Karen Moses, who worked long hours to help us with editing, typing, and reference checking. We are thankful for them and for our families, who were understanding and supportive when we said we needed to write this book.

In addition, we want to acknowledge our book team at Wolters Kluwer, especially, Shannon Magee, Maria McAvey, and Lisa Marshall.

Contents

Chapter 1

An Introduction to a New Leadership Model

Some years ago, one of us (the nurse in our CMO–CNO Dyad partnership, Kathy) was enjoying a day off with a ferry boat ride in Washington State when she heard an announcement over the boat's PA system. The voice was calm but emphatic: "Any medical personnel on board please report to the dining area right away for a medical emergency."

As a nurse in executive practice, she was well aware that her clinical skills were not as sharp as they once were, but she responded to the call anyway. After all, the boat was in the middle of the Puget Sound, with 15 minutes left before it would dock, so any passenger needing assistance could only get help from someone on board. As a military reservist, she was still certified in cardiopulmonary resuscitation (CPR) and had been teaching nursing courses for the Washington Army National Guard's 91C (LPN) course. Also, there was a good chance there were other clinicians on board, so she would probably be part of a team.

She was right. Three people showed up to see what they could do for the obviously pregnant young woman who had asked the ferry boat crew for help. As the CNO in the sole community hospital where the ferry originated, she knew both of the others. One was a respiratory therapist, who would have been of great help if the emergency had been of the respiratory or cardiac variety. The other was a banker who served on the hospital board. He came because he also had some training in CPR, from the local YMCA.

The mother-to-be, with help from her excited and slightly stressed husband, explained that they were on their way to become parents at a Seattle hospital. She thought there was plenty of time for the 1-hour over-water trip but was now regretting her decision. "The labor is so intense," she said, as the nurse assessed her, timed the contractions and listened to the patient (how quickly the CNO thought of herself as a nurse and the young woman as a patient!) describe sensations that sounded very much like the instinct to push.

The respiratory therapist and board member were still willing to help, but were open about not having any experience in the birthing of babies. They were visibly relieved when the nurse told them that she had noticed something they had not on her way to the dining area.

"Go and get Doctor X," she said, "He is sitting in the stern. He's in the third booth on the right after you pass the vending machines. Please tell him we need his help."

When the respiratory therapist returned with the physician, the young couple was also visibly relieved. As the doctor introduced himself, the CNO could tell they knew everything was going to be all right, even though their firstborn might be born on a boat. After all, they now had a white-haired (as in obviously experienced) doctor and a nurse in attendance. The physician had an impeccable bedside manner. He politely introduced himself, and then drew the nurse aside. "I'm afraid I can't be of much help here," he said. "I'm a gerontologist. I haven't even examined a pregnant woman since medical school."

"That's okay," the nurse said. "I know what to do … but you are the clinician with the highest level of medical licensure on this ferry, so we need you to stay here and work with us. Just having you here has reassured these kids. There's a good chance we will be delivering a baby, and we can do it together."

It turned out that the baby didn't actually arrive until moments after the Mom-to-Be arrived in the hospital lobby, after transport from the ferry dock via the waiting ambulance. But for months afterward, whenever Dr. X and the CNO met in the hospital corridors, they talked about their "ferry adventure." They were both delighted with the letters of gratitude and baby pictures from the family.

The CNO was also pleased with the "bonus" learning she got from sharing this experience. She had gained a new admiration for this physician colleague because she learned something new about him. He was humble enough to admit what he did not know and had self-esteem strong enough to allow him to follow the lead of a non-MD team member who had more experience in a particular situation. His actions were not about the clinicians or hierarchy; he wanted to do what was best for the patient.

Dr. X was long retired when the model of management known as Dyad Leadership began to take hold in healthcare. He would have been a natural at it, had he chosen to be a manager. He shared the same short-term goal as his "temporary" Dyad partner (the CNO): the safe delivery of a baby, with the best possible outcomes for both the mother and child. The two of them (doctor and nurse) had out-of-the ordinary challenges to meeting this goal (e.g., the delivery would have taken place on a crew cabin table rather than a specially designed delivery bed). Neither partner was as experienced as they would have liked to have been in this particular situation, but together they made good decisions. And each contributed his or her own experience, pursuing their goal as partners.

There's a good chance, though, that Dr. X would not have had any interest in being a manager of any kind. He loved his older patients. As their primary care physician, he had personal, long-term relationships with them. He might not have been quite as happy with the challenges of management as he was with clinical issues. And he might have blanched at the idea of "leaving" his profession to become one of "those people."

THE "SUITS" AND THE "COATS"

"Those people" are the nonclinicians who attend to the business side of healthcare. They are also clinicians who once cared directly for patients before exchanging their hands-on patient care work for jobs on the management "side" of the workforce. For years, clinicians (and in particular, physicians) have described the formal leaders in their organizations as "the suits," while those who deliver direct care are called "coats" (as in lab coats). Stephen Klasko, a practicing OB-GYN physician, and Gregory Shea, a university professor and healthcare consultant, describe this labeling and what it represents in their 1999 book, *The Phantom Stethoscope: A Field Manual for Finding an Optimistic Future in Healthcare*. They share that "a physician who begins to collaborate with administration excites, among other physicians, tremendous suspicion and a presumption of betrayal." The physician is portrayed as betraying the "coats" and in danger of becoming a "suit" (1).

Klasko and Shea state that each group judges the other based on its own group culture and norms and that those cultures and norms are very different. Physicians and healthcare managers have different values and socialization, leadership, and organizational forms and collective decision making (Table 1-1). All of these work to make it very challenging to develop trust between the two groups.

Cultural differences are not new between the two groups. As a result, interdiscipline relationship problems and conflicts have been documented for at least the past 100 years. Power struggles between managers and physicians are historical. Management professors Margarete Arndt and Barbara Bigelow have combed through early 20th century articles from the American Hospital Association's first journal, *Modern Hospital*, as part of their research. They found letters to the editor about problems with "difficult" physicians, and articles written by hospital leaders who reported business (financial) challenges caused by the hospital's dependence on doctors for admissions, the costs of providing facilities and opportunities for physicians, and

| Table 1-1   The Very Real Differences between Administrator and Physician Culture ||
Physician	Administrator
Values autonomy	Values interdependence of bureaucratic structures
Advocates for his or her "own" patients	Advocates for hospital as a whole, patients as a group
Focuses on finance of own area	Focuses on finance for entire organization
Thinks timely response means immediate	Thinks timely response is limited by use of systems
Is primarily loyal to the medical profession	Is primarily loyal to the organization
Does not view others (even elected peers) as speaking for the individual physician	Believes elected physician leaders can speak for the medical staff as a whole

Adapted from Klasko, S., & Shea, G. (1999). The Phantom Stethoscope. Franklin, TN: Hillsboro Press.

the ability of medical staff members to adversely influence public perceptions about hospital quality if the organization did not purchase technology that the doctor wanted for his use (2).

In more modern times, authors of healthcare books speak of problems caused in hospitals by inappropriate medical staff involvement in some hospital issues and lack of physician involvement in other, appropriate issues. Frontline staff have opinions about the relationship of administrators and doctors. Nurses have mentioned their perception to Kathy (our nurse Dyad author) that there is a general disdain that physicians feel for hospital administration. Klasko and Shea would probably not be surprised at these sentiments, as they note that neither physicians nor hospital leaders recognize that their views are culturally biased, and, because of this, each group judges members of the other group by their own norms (1).

Clinicians view managers as bureaucrats (sometimes helpful but often roadblocks to what the providers want to accomplish). Managers, while recognizing the importance of the clinical caregivers to the success of organizations, complain that some clinicians are "difficult to work with," or describe them as being "not team players." Members of both groups sometimes express feeling that individuals in the other group don't respect them, are inflexible, and are more interested in the money to be made in healthcare than in providing the best possible care to patients. Each group wonders if members of the other group recognize the value of their expertise to the organization. Sometimes the actions or words of individual managers or clinicians reinforce these perceptions. Individuals who have had even a short career in healthcare have probably heard statements similar to the quotes gathered from our colleagues when we asked them to give examples of when they heard statements that they perceived as an indication of a lack of respect for particular roles (or former roles) in healthcare:

- "Don't those administrators realize they wouldn't have a hospital … or jobs … if it wasn't for us?"
- "Those bureaucrats in the administration don't know a thing about the real work we do in this hospital. All they know how to do is throw out red tape and make it hard to get anything done."
- "Docs always say they are about ethics and what is best for patients. I think I'll write a book about physician ethics. It will be 450 pages with only one thing printed on each page … a big dollar sign."
- "No, I don't want any physicians on the committee. We'll waste all our time trying to educate them on the ramifications of what they think is best for this organization and why what they want to do is illegal or will cause us compliance problems."
- "Oh, and I don't want any nurses there either … they will waste our time talking about quality and staffing. This needs to be a business decision."
- "Well, you know the problem with pharmacists is they all wanted to be doctors but didn't have the smarts to get into medical school."
- "One reason we have trouble with the hospital executives is that they were all the "C" students in school and we (physicians) were the "A" students. Of course we have trouble communicating."
- "I really resent the big salaries those administrators rake in. They don't make the money for this place. We physicians do."
- "When I became a CEO, I stopped using my RN credential. You know, the other administrators just wouldn't respect me as much if they were reminded that I was a nurse."
- "These employed physicians want a say in how we manage? Don't they realize they are employees? Employees don't get to vote on everything we do!"
- "Don't those doctors realize they wouldn't have this hospital and the expensive equipment we provide if it wasn't for us administrators?"

Of course, there are many professionals in every role who act and speak respectfully about other team members. However, traditional definitions of work and the greater community's thoughts about that work has produced widely accepted stereotypes of individuals who perform different work in our society, along with beliefs about their intelligence and relative value to society. For example, the definition of a profession was once mainly limited to only three occupational fields: law, theology, and medicine. It's only been in recent decades that other careers have been recognized as meeting the definition of a profession, which is "a field that requires extensive study and mastery of specialized knowledge, such as law, medicine, the military, nursing, the clergy, or engineering," and which is "held by an individual who is usually licensed, is regulated by a quasi-governmental organization, must complete certain courses of education, pass further examinations, and are subject to disciplinary action, including revocation of a license" (3).

While who is designated as a professional may not seem significant today (when many career areas call themselves professions), this history of a premium label for only some members of the healthcare team has affected the collective consciousness about which work is "most significant." It has also contributed to historical challenges to true teamwork among physicians, other clinicians, and "administrators." It has the potential of making the development of true partnerships between healthcare leaders even more difficult, because change can occur only when people are willing to acknowledge that what may have been true in the past (i.e., only a few professions actually met the definition of a profession) or was *perceived* to be true in the past (those with higher education in one field are superior in all ways to those with *lesser* educations) is not absolute truth today.

Slightly derisive labeling (suits vs. coats) and philosophical arguments about who is a professional aside, there is another question for *clinicians* who choose formal leadership positions. Are they managers with a clinical background or clinicians with a management job? That question has more than one answer and differs for individuals both in how they identify themselves and how others describe them. For example, physicians who become managers or executives universally maintain "MD" or "DO" as part of their signature, expect to be called "Doctor," and identify themselves as physicians, even if it has been decades since they performed any type of patient care. Nurses more often drop the "RN" immediately when they move into administrative roles that don't require them to be an RN, such as COO or CEO positions. (Other clinicians, like pharmacists, who move into top roles seem to follow the same convention of "not advertising their clinical backgrounds" as the RNs). Without dwelling on the cultural, psychological, or societal reasons for this difference, it appears that physicians identify with their profession regardless of their particular job, are proud of their clinical background, and believe it is value added to their management/leadership role while many other clinicians do not.

The premise of this book is that both extensive clinical and business backgrounds/educations are essential for competent leadership of a healthcare organization. You will notice we did not say both are essential for *a* leader of a healthcare organization. It would be wonderful for an organization if it could boast of having individual leaders at every level who are interested in maintaining expertise in both the clinical and business world. However, as organizations enter the next era of healthcare, our very complex industry is becoming even more complicated, and there will be fewer individuals who can claim expertise in two specialties. (Peter Drucker has been widely credited with saying many years ago that healthcare is the most complex business of all. He should see us now!) Knowledge of two or more specialties is possible and preferable (a clinical leader needs an understanding of finance), but expertise (having as much financial education and knowledge as the CFO) is unlikely.

Leaders have always had to depend on their teams to supply expertise they lack, and the need for this will continue. In addition, some components of our new systems require leadership from both clinicians and business professionals. That's why a variety of healthcare organizations are implementing a formal leadership structure referred to as Dyad Management.

A NEW MODEL FOR LEADERSHIP: THE DYAD

Many leadership theorists and practitioners have recognized the values of teams in decision making and in accomplishing the work of the organization. Thompson and Strickland noted in 1999 (and organizations have only become more complex since then!) that this is true in all American organizations. They stated, "Not only are many strategic issues too big or complex for a single manager to handle, but they are often cross-functional and cross departmental in nature" (4). John Maxwell agrees in *Teamwork 101*. He says, "I assert that one is too small a number to achieve greatness. You cannot do anything of real value alone" (5). His writing is about teams in general, but the thoughts he expressed support the development of a leadership team model, such as the dyadic model of management.

Dyads are, as the name implies, mini-teams of two people who work together as coleaders of a specific system, division, clinical service line, or project. They may also consist of two leaders from different departments or service lines whose work is so interdependent that the organization's goals can best be accomplished when they consistently and continually partner to meet those goals. Dyad management is a model of formal leadership in which two individuals with different skill sets, education, and backgrounds are paired to better fulfill the mission of the organization. The two partners have different job descriptions, and different duties that complement each other. When combined, their skills complete a set of management competencies needed for accomplishing particular clinical, business, and strategic goals of the organization. In the best *pairings*, the Dyad provides synergy. In other words, they create a team in which one leader plus one leader equals more than two leaders. By working together, Dyad partners can accomplish (along with their larger teams) what three or more managers accomplish working in individual silos.

Often (but not always) one Healthcare Dyad partner is a business and/or operations expert, and the other is a physician. The number of designated Dyads that includes a physician is growing because the model is recognized as a way for healthcare operations leaders and medical leaders to comanage a department, service line, or project. As the healthcare system evolves to meet the new world that is projected to constitute the next era of healthcare, the need for the business/operations side to merge with the clinical delivery side is intuitively superior to past models where there was greater (or at least perceived) division between them. Accountable care, bundled payments, pay for performance (or pay for value) all require operations/ business leaders and physicians to work together on the development and implementation of new strategies. Both types of expertise are needed to work hand in hand for this to occur. A bonus to this new paradigm is that Dyad leadership increases the understanding of other team member's contributions to the organization's (and even other profession's) success. Through these partnerships, organizations can begin to bring the two cultures (clinical and administrative) together to develop a blended culture for success in the new era. With new models of teamwork and Dyad management, there is an energy for development of new understanding of and respect for others.

In a permanent Dyad (identified on an enterprise's organizational chart), one partner does not *report* to, or *work for*, the other. The boss–subordinate role implies that one profession is more important than the other, which perpetuates the age old perceived lack of (or at least lesser) respect for the skills of one of the leaders. It has the potential of setting up a less than open and transparent relationship between two people. (Whether we like to admit this or not, it is much more difficult to disagree with the person who evaluates you and has influence on your pay and future with the company. Respectful disagreement, or ability to openly state different thoughts on any issue, is important for the due diligence that all decisions should be subject to.) The success of the Dyad and of the organization requires a system that supports decision making that balances clinical and operational/business needs.

The partners often both report to the same executive, but in the increasingly matrixed world of healthcare systems, this might not be true. The essential tenet, wherever the individuals report, is that Dyad partners are perceived (and perceive themselves) to manage as equals. Even if the two partners report to different people, they should be positioned on the same level of the organizational chart. (If one reports to an executive VP, the other should report to an executive VP. If one reports to the CEO, the other should report to the CEO, etc.) Neither delegates to the other, because each has his or her own responsibilities for the management work they colead. However, each partner does have an accountability, not only to the organization but to the other Dyad partner, because they both "own" the department, service line, project, or other entity and have a shared responsibility for its success.

There is no limit to the variations of Dyad partnerships. Organizations can, and will, develop them to effectively work toward the accomplishment of the enterprise vision. Some examples of "permanent" Dyad partnerships (identified on the enterprise organization chart) include the following:

▶ A physician and nonphysician operations manager for a clinical service line (such as cardiology or oncology)
▶ The organization's CMO and CNO
▶ A nursing manager (for the management of staff) and a clinical nurse leader (CNL) or advance practice nurse (APN) (for nursing clinical/nursing quality leadership of patient care) on an individual inpatient nursing unit

▶ The organization's identified quality executive and the safety executive
▶ A physician and nurse comanaging an inpatient unit (critical care, orthopedics, etc.)
▶ A physician and nurse comanaging the organization's perioperative services
▶ A physician and business manager comanaging an individual physician office or clinic
▶ The organization's chief nursing informatics officer (CNIO) and chief medical informatics officer (CMIO)

The larger part of this book concerns these permanent Dyads. However, there are organizations that have found it to be effective to utilize temporary Dyad partnerships as a tactic for accomplishing projects that support their strategy. Examples of these types of "project" or "short-term Dyads" include the following:

▶ A nurse leader and a physician leader assigned to colead a building project for the company
▶ A nurse *champion* and a physician *champion* for a major change in the organization, such as implementation of evidence-based practices, installation of a new clinical information technology system, a new care model, or an LEAN process
▶ A nurse leader and a pharmacist leader to implement and enforce the appropriate use of bar-coding or smart pump technology
▶ A clinical leader and a financial leader to plan the clinical budget for a specified period of time or a particular set of goals

Whether the Dyad is permanent or temporary, the partners who make up this model of management are accountable to the organization as well as each other, to lead in a manner that honors the mission of the organization, supports advancement to the vision of the organization, and utilizes tactics that will fulfill both short- and long-term goals of the organization.

The mission of an enterprise is simply what the company seeks to provide, or do, for its customers. Mission statements are similar between healthcare organizations, although some are *bigger* or broader than others because of who the organization defines as its customers. The customers could be whole countries or communities or specific subsets of a population defined by criteria that segments individuals into groups that the organization serves.

Healthcare organizations do not have missions to "make money" (regardless of their for-profit or not-for-profit status), provide employment for healthcare providers (or anyone else), or serve as "workshops" for clinicians. They may do all of these things, but they are not the reason the organization exists.

The vision for the organization is where the enterprise is headed or wants to go. It is a picture of what its leaders (including the Board) see as its future. Strategy is the game plan for reaching that future. Tactics are the specific actions that managers utilize at every level in the organization to ensure that the goals that support the organizational strategy are being pursued and met. Dyad partners, like all organizational leaders, have a responsibility to understand the vision, contribute to strategy, and utilize tactics in pursuit of the organization's goals.

As stated earlier in this chapter, the skills and responsibilities of Dyad partners will probably overlap, but they should not have identical job descriptions, and each should have identified primary accountabilities that are complementary to the other's duties. In addition, when one leader has a primary role identified in his or her job description, this should not prevent the other partner from "stepping in" to help with that role. This can be tricky because it calls for exquisite communication skills and trust between the partners. The success of the Dyad depends on this.

An example of this need for complementary roles with specific accountabilities is the CMO and CNO Dyad partnership. The job description for the CMO may include a responsibility for leading all things involved with the practice of medicine across the continuum in the organization. The CNO's job description will include leading all things involved with the practice of nursing across the continuum in the organization. Of course, medical care and nursing care cannot be that neatly divided; the two professions depend on each other, just as patients (or, in more modern parlance, the consumers of healthcare) depend on both professions. They overlap, which is why Dyad leadership is especially suited to these two positions.

When Dyads work well, their constituents (direct reports or members of the individual Dyad leader's profession) feel comfortable approaching either Dyad leader for direction, advice, and guidance or to provide opinions and input to the leadership team. One example of this is when a physician has a concern about a new hospital policy or a medical best practice the organization is contemplating and just happens to run into the CNO before she sees the CMO. She can give her input to the CNO Dyad member, confident that the Dyad will consider it together. Conversely, a nurse who would like more information about a new nursing procedure should feel free to ask the CMO for assistance. When either the physician or nurse waits to speak to the leader of his or her profession, he or she is contributing to the "lack of nimbleness" frequently attributed to hospital leaders. Waiting to talk to someone from one's own profession is undermining the ability of the Dyad to cover more ground and deliver on the promise that one plus one equals more than two.

This ability to back each other up requires regular, deliberate, and transparent communication between the Dyad partners. It requires each educating the other about his or her profession and informing the other about current profession-specific issues. It requires humility from each partner that allows him or her to realize that he or she doesn't know what he or she doesn't know. It requires a deliberate image campaign (discussed later in this book) that visibly demonstrates the partnership to all constituents and other stakeholders, such as patient populations and the community. It requires an understanding between the partners that each will strive to represent accurately the other's thoughts and guidance to third parties. It requires trust that the partner respects and believes fully that this is a Dyad of Equals.

Traditional professional images (and, sometimes, gender images) present challenges to Dyads getting to equality. (Because the physician has traditionally been labeled the *captain of the ship* in patient care/clinical work, some assume he or she should also be *the boss* in operations and management/financial arenas even when he or she is the less experienced or educated manager.) However, there is another challenge that needs to be acknowledged and addressed in the development of successful, healthy Dyads. When one or both of the Dyad leaders is a clinician, his or her profession may have inculcated him or her with a conscious or unconscious disdain for the field of management. Conversely, a successful premanagement clinical career may have instilled a belief that formal leadership roles are a natural for people of advanced clinical skills, requiring no special education or preparation.

The latter conviction has caused problems in healthcare leadership for multiple decades. Many clinical leaders have been promoted into management positions because of their superior clinical skill. Unfortunately, because the skills of a clinician (even a leader in the provision of clinical interventions) are not the same as the skills of a manager, many fail to develop into superior leaders. Some fail and leave their formal leadership positions. Some succeed, but only after untold damage may have been inflicted on the organization or individuals while the new manager learned, by trial and error, his or her new (and foreign) role. Most frontline clinical leaders, regardless of clinical specialty, can relate horror stories from personal history with uneducated, untrained, or inexperienced managers. (Some can relate similar sagas even when managers were educated in management, but that is a competence issue, and is covered later.)

The study of management (with a brief history presented in Chapter 2) indicates that there are theories and research-supported best practices for those who occupy formal management positions. Like medicine, management is both an art and a science. Based on this, our premise is that clinical enterprise management is a specialty. A specialty requires specialized education, experience, and residencies (or on-the-job mentoring by an experienced professional manager.)

Acknowledgement that clinical management is a specialty helps explain many of the issues for which new clinical managers are not prepared. Clinicians beginning to practice a new specialty within their broader profession would never be expected to perform flawlessly, regardless of their previous competence in another specialty. For example, a physician whose specialty is medical cardiology could not perform cardiac surgery without additional training as a surgeon. A psychiatric nurse could not float to the operating room to scrub (or circulate) for an orthopedic surgical procedure without surgical nursing (and, even further, *orthopedic* surgical nursing!) specialty training.

Yet clinical leaders are placed in management jobs without any management education (and then are criticized for making errors that experienced leaders consider basic "Management 101") that even a brand new leader should have learned in school or along the way somewhere.

When organizations or individuals do not understand that management is a specialty, they are taking risks with the organization's and individual's success every time a clinician who is not prepared for the specialty of management is placed in a formal leadership position. Healthcare organizations are no exception. Outstanding medical or nursing care alone will not ensure that the organization will thrive or even survive. An enterprise needs competent leadership and competent management, too.

LEADERSHIP AND MANAGEMENT

There has been quite a bit of discussion about the difference between leadership and management. Various academics, consultants, authors, and other "experts" have defined the two words with their own emphasis on differences between their meanings and their practical application. Some examples of management definitions are as follows:

▶ Management is the organization and coordination of the activities of a business in order to achieve defined objectives. Management consists of interlocking functions of creating corporate policy, and organizing, planning, controlling, and directing an organization's resources in order to achieve the objectives (www.BusinessDictionary.com).

▶ Management is both an art and a science. It is the art of making people more effective than they would have been without you. The science is how you do that. There are four basic pillars: planning, organizing, directing, and monitoring (www.About.com/management).

▶ Management is achieving goals in a way that makes the best use of all resources (www.leadershipdirect.com).

▶ Management is, above all, a practice where art, science, and craft meet—Henry Mintzberg.

Leadership is usually defined with less granularity than management. It's one of those elusive qualities that people just seem to know when they see it! However, many people have their own opinions of what leadership is. Some quotes on leadership come from well-known leaders:

▶ Leadership is the art of getting someone else to do something you want done because he wants to do it—Dwight Eisenhower.

▶ Leadership is intentional influence—Michael McKinney.

▶ Leadership is getting people to work for you when they are not obligated—Fred Smith.

▶ If your actions inspire others to dream more, learn more, do more, and become more, you are a leader—John Quincy Adams.

▶ Leaders conceive and articulate goals that lift people out of their petty preoccupations and unite the in pursuit of objectives worthy of their best efforts—John Gardner.

The difference between leadership and management has been defined by a variety of people, as well:

▶ Effective management is putting first things first. While leadership decides what "first things" are, it is management that puts them first, day by day, moment by moment. Management is a discipline, carrying it out—Steven Covey.

▶ Management is efficiency in climbing the ladder of success. Leadership determines whether the ladder is leaning against the right wall—Stephen Covey.

▶ In contrast to management, leadership is about influencing people to change (http://www.leadersdirect.com).

▶ Management is doing things right. Leadership is doing the right things—Peter Drucker.

If we simply accept Drucker's definition of management versus leadership, we would be hard pressed to say which is most important to the long-term success of organizations. There seems to be a preference for being a leader, though. Each of us (authors) has met various people who work in healthcare who have proudly announced, "I am not a Manager. I am a Leader!" We can almost hear the slight sneer underlining *manager* in contrast to the pride of being a *leader*. We believe that both excellent leadership and excellent management are essential for the excellent organization.

Clinicians should be able to understand the difference and the importance of both doing the right thing and doing a thing right. A medical example that is currently making headlines in the United States comes from interventional cardiology. Some physicians have been accused of placing stents in patients who do not have a medical need for them. They are being censured for not doing the right thing, even if they flawlessly placed the stent. On the other hand, other clinicians might do a poor job of placing a stent that is medically indicated. From a patient's point of view, which is more important? Would you say you received better care if you received an unnecessary intervention, done with great competence? Or would you prefer to need the stent and have the procedure done poorly (with adverse outcomes of some sort?)

The patient is better served by a physician who both does the right thing and does the thing right. Organizations are better served by people in power positions who both do the right thing (lead) and do things right (manage). In some situations, one individual is competent at both leadership and management. In Dyads, both partners should be leaders. At least one must be a professional manager. Dyad leadership is a model that supports the development of both leadership and management for a particular unit, program, service line, or project; *because it leverages different skills of two leaders, and only one must be a management specialist.* The other partner must have education and current knowledge about appropriate and competent performance of their professional specialty. *In healthcare organizations, that partner is most often skilled in a clinical profession.*

A strong Dyad has two leaders from different professional backgrounds who combine their experience and intelligence to make decisions about what is right to do. However, only one of the partners may be a professional manager, with the training, temperament, and experience that it takes to "do things right in an organization." The other may not initially need to learn everything about "Management 101" because he or she brings more value to the Dyad by continuing to be an expert in his or her original professional specialty. For example, the physician member of a Dyad in healthcare today brings most value to the organization as the partner with medical, not management, expertise. He or she comes from the physician culture, which gives him or her credibility with medical colleagues along with knowledge of current best practice of medicine. (When he or she *does* have management experience and expertise, it is a bonus for the Dyad and the organization.)

MANAGEMENT 101: DOING THINGS RIGHT

Either as a primarily business profession or as a specialty of a clinical profession, management is a field populated with individuals of varied skill. Anyone who has worked for more than one boss has determined that there are differences between the abilities of individuals who are positioned to manage projects or people. Some of these management variations may be due to perceptions of the formal leader's charisma, or chemistry with people on his or her team. Others are due to very real variations in manager competency.

Clinicians understand that there are certain science-based core competencies that providers of care must possess to produce the best possible clinical outcomes for patients. There are also core competencies for managers. Some of these are the basics that make up the science side of management. Core competencies of management science include the ability to plan, organize, direct, and evaluate (or monitor) projects or ongoing operations.

Planning involves assessing a current state versus a desired state, setting a goal to reduce the gap between them, and then figuring out what resources are needed to accomplish that goal. Organizing is combining these resources in a way that will make the plan happen. Directing is telling people what to do. Evaluating is making sure they are following these directions in a way that ensures the plan is being carried out.

Plan, organize, direct, and evaluate—voila, you are a manager! How hard can that be, especially if you have been a successful clinician? The steps don't sound all that different from the scientific method (based on the same steps used in research) learned in medical or nursing school and applied to the diagnosis and treatment of disease. This simplification of management to scientific competencies, of course, does not illustrate the total picture of this field, just as scientific knowledge (even when combined with technical proficiencies) does not constitute the total set of competencies for a clinician.

While the sciences of all three endeavors (research, medicine, and management) are similar, both clinicians and managers know that those who are really great at the practice of their respective crafts are also masters at the art of their profession, which is much more complex than the science. Art is the ability to use knowledge and specialty education in real-life situations. It is perfected with experience, involves creativity, and personal skill. Sometimes called the soft skills of a profession, the components of a professional's art may seem intangible to those who are not members of that profession. That's because it is much harder to describe, quantify, or prove than is science. Yet it is the art of each Dyad member's specialty that brings the greatest value to this model of leadership.

It is art when a physician's hunch results in a correct diagnosis that the evidence doesn't make obvious. It is art when a nurse, consciously or subconsciously, is able to sense, feel, perceive, and know how to deliver the type of individualized care most likely to promote healing in his or her patient. It is art when a manager applies management theory and research differently in different situations. Since art is perfected with practice, it's important that at least one member of the Dyad is an experienced, successful manager. In addition, part of his or her value-added expertise is knowing how to get things done in the organization, through an understanding of how the bureaucracy works, relationships with key organizational members, policies, and procedures.

In emerging healthcare Dyads, where a physician is partnered with a clinical operations professional or business manager, the nonphysician is usually the primary partner accountable for management of areas such as supply chain, human resources and labor, finance and budget, competition strategy and market share, the metrics, and performance scorecards. The physician partner is accountable for working closely with other physicians, with specific responsibilities such as managing physician productivity (particularly as this relates to the organization's compensation model), establishing new models of care (such as medical homes or team-based care in primary care offices), managing physician driven use of resources, and decreasing inappropriate variation in physician clinical practice.

Both Dyad leaders are managers. They both need to do things right. To do things right requires communication skills, organizational knowledge, strategic thinking, and skill at implementing tactics. Each partner has different primary accountabilities, based on his or her expertise, experience, and influence derived from identification with a specific profession and culture. A Dyad's influence on an organization, or individuals, is a combination of both partner's influence on organizational stakeholders. In times of change, such as now, one of biggest benefits of Dyad leadership is this greater span of influence that comes from a leadership team with partners from two different professions and professional cultures.

Influence comes from power. Formal leaders in an organization have legitimate power, which means it is derived from the job and where it is positioned in the organizational hierarchy. Designated Dyad leaders have legitimate (or positional) power to perform their management work. They can hire, fire, and direct people to perform certain duties. In addition, each partner has personal power derived from expertise in his or her profession. Each has connection power as a result of networking with colleagues inside and outside the organization and information power based on knowing what is going on. One or both leaders may add referent power to the mix, a result of personal charisma that creates loyalty and admiration from others. In healthcare organizations, expertise, connection, information, and referent power can be closely tied to the leader's profession and professional culture. So, it makes intuitive sense that power and influence of a Dyad team is multiplied when the two partners come from different professions.

Of course, the influence of the Dyad will not be effective if the two professionals do not come together as true partners or do not agree on their vision or goals. The promise of this type of leadership will only be fulfilled when this occurs, when the partners learn to lead together by doing the right things and to manage together by doing things right. The following chapters, along with stories about actual Dyad models and experiences are presented as a guide for leaders contemplating this type of leadership in their organizations and for potential and actual leaders who aspire to maximize the effectiveness of their unique partnership as a healthcare Dyad for the next era of healthcare.

CHAPTER SUMMARY

The world of healthcare is becoming even more complex. As healthcare organizations move into the next era, leaders are implementing new management models. One of these, the Dyad, is envisioned as a way to manage complex systems while increasing partnerships between groups that have previously operated in silos. When two leaders are assigned to lead together each brings abilities and distinct competencies that complement the other's skills. It is only when the partners respect each other as skilled professionals that they can learn to lead together.

Dyads in Action

THE DYAD LEADERSHIP MODEL AS A STRATEGIC INITIATIVE
Bob Ritz

The U.S. healthcare industry is experiencing an unprecedented sea change. The culprits behind this include the shifting demographics of the U.S. population, rising federal deficits, consumer demands for higher value, federal healthcare policies, an unsustainable appetite for new technologies, and general market dynamics caused by reduced third party payments. While the forces behind the change are not unique, response in today's healthcare organizations appears to be very different from past experiences. Perhaps one of the most exciting results of this changing climate is the interest in adopting new delivery system models with physician alignment and clinical integration at the top of the priority list. Today's healthcare organizations can either embrace this growing movement or they can take a "sit and wait" posture to see if these new emerging delivery system models actually succeed and make a difference in the long-term outlook and success for their organizations.

As we face these changing times with a different perspective, there is an opportunity to seize the moment and transform old models of working side by side, but not integrated, to true partnership. Mercy Medical Center in Des Moines, Iowa (MMC-DM), recognized the opportunity to change how it provides services by adopting a philosophy of integrating providers to redefine the delivery of its healthcare services. MMC-DM is one of several market-based organizations in Catholic Health Initiatives (CHI).

CHI is based in Englewood, Colorado; is one of the largest health systems in the U.S. MMC-DM, founded by the Sisters of Mercy in 1893; and is an 802-bed medical center providing a full range of services ranging from major tertiary care to primary care services. MMC-DM is composed of three hospital campuses, a highly integrated multispecialty clinic with more than 500 providers, and over 50 locations of physician clinics and outpatient care centers. MMC-DM operates an Accountable Care Organization with more than 100,000 enrolled members to date. MMC-DM is also a member of the Mercy Health Network, a multihospital network of 39 hospitals in Iowa operating under a Joint Operating Agreement between CHI and Catholic Health East/Trinity.

INDUSTRY AT A GLANCE

The U.S. healthcare system is clearly taking on a different look today with growing regional and national health systems, the rapid fading of the private practice model, an increasing number of physicians aligned with and/or employed by healthcare systems, adoption of electronic medical records, and new partnerships emerging with historically competing organizations. Perhaps the general public believes these changes are the direct result of President Obama's signature Affordable Care Act (ACA) passed in March 2010. We in the industry know the move to clinically integrated organizations and delivery systems was well underway long before the federal legislation took shape. In fact, the industry was under a self-imposed move toward integration based on the recognition that our traditionally fragmented healthcare system was not providing the value required by the Federal Government, commercial insurers, American businesses, or individual consumers. There was a clear recognition that the increasing cost of healthcare was unsustainable while, at the same time, the U.S. healthcare system ranked low in clinical outcomes and vital sign indicators when compared to other developed nations. As far back as the early 1980s, when the diagnostic-related grouping (DRG) payment methodology was implemented by Medicare to pay for inpatient care services, our healthcare leaders have been deploying new models of delivery systems and payment models. The passage of the ACA simply formalized and popularized the public spotlight on some of the changing models that were already under development. Regardless of the cause or need for change, one of the outcomes of this shift has been the coming together of historically separated parts of the healthcare system. The recognition and gradual fusion of physicians and hospitals working to become one clinically integrated delivery system has been an important operational and strategic step taken by numerous healthcare organizations. Alignment of providers has taken center stage for success for today's healthcare systems, given the shared incentives emerging with the transformation of the healthcare system.

THE MOVE TO DYAD LEADERSHIP

One of the changes healthcare organizations have undertaken to prepare for the future is a new leadership model—the Physician Dyadic (Dyad) Leadership model. The "Dyad" assigns the dual responsibility to a physician and nonphysician leader, who assumes accountability for a clinical service, department, strategic initiative, or operating department within a healthcare organization's structure for the entire organization. As the industry transforms to a shared and aligned operating agenda, the Dyad leadership model can be a complementary structural change to facilitate the development of an aligned organization. In its sociological roots, a Dyad can be defined as two persons involved in an ongoing relationship or intervention (6). As healthcare organizations embrace the opportunity for systemic change, the Dyad model is growing in popularity. We have all heard the old phrase, "a physician's pen accounts for the majority of the cost of care." Regardless of whether this is accurate or not, it is symbolic of the traditional model of care in which the physician directs the care provided to a patient while the hospital staff delivers the care based on a physician's directions. It has also long been believed that this traditional payment model resulted in conflicting incentives between physicians and healthcare organizations, yet the new emerging model of accountable care and value-based payment systems are quickly fading any gap in incentives between physicians and healthcare organizations. The effective deployment of a Dyad leadership model in today's healthcare organization can offer numerous benefits to drive the value agenda, while systemically creating an aligned culture for the organization to remove the separateness we have operated with in the past.

THE DYAD LEADERSHIP MODEL REQUIRES A SUPPORTIVE CULTURE

While on the surface, it may seem simple to adopt a Dyad leadership model to assist an organization in navigating the churning waters of healthcare reform, it is clearly more than just a plug and play strategy. The effective emergence of a new leadership model requires a supportive culture to succeed. An organization's culture can best be described as "how things really happen around here" or "the collective personality of the organization." Regardless of the description of culture, it is imperative that an organization's culture embrace the adoption of the Dyad leadership model. The culture needs to recognize the need for alignment and the shared physician role. It also must acknowledge the need for change to optimize the value of care, and service healthcare organizations must deliver to achieve accountable and cost-effective healthcare objectives.

Recognizing the culture imperative, MMC-DM's board of directors, medical staff leaders, and administrative team implemented a "game changer" process to explore the best way to prepare for a new delivery system for the future. One of the most strategically and operationally important conclusions was the recommendation to adopt a Dyad Leadership Model in 2011. Essentially, MMC-DM understood the challenges of achieving a high-value delivery system using the traditional functional hierarchical and separated model of leadership and care delivery. To address both the challenge and opportunity to transform the organization's operation and strategic direction, MMC-DM selected eight physician leaders to be paired with eight nonphysician leaders. These teams of two were designated to lead the organizations' operational and strategic plans.

While MMC-DM was going through the "Game Changer" process, it was effectively shaping the culture to accept this change in the leadership model. For many years, MMC-DM maintained a vision for an aligned and integrated delivery system. It invested millions in developing an integrated multispecialty medical group to be relevant in an integrated model of care. MMC-DM had already initiated the path to an aligned future of physicians with the medical center through strategic initiatives for more than 20 years. The move to the Dyad was a natural extension of MMC-DM's past philosophy to involve physicians in every possible area of the medical center's operations. The culture at MMC-DM was ready to support the move to a Dyad in 2011. (As other healthcare organizations consider the Dyad model of leadership, it is very important that they assess the readiness of the culture before modifying the organization chart.)

THE PATH TO VALUE-BASED CARE

The Dyad leadership model is also a prerequisite to truly building a higher value healthcare operation and system. There are numerous reasons why our health-care system in the United States needs to move to a value-based healthcare system. Providers were historically paid for the volume of care provided; today's move is to pay for value. The federal government's Value-Based Performance (VBP) Program is a clear example of this transition. While we are likely in the early phase-in of moving to a completely value-based payment model, under the VBP, hospitals are subject to a loss of payment for inpatient care provided to Medicare beneficiaries based on per-formance for specific outcomes, patient experience, and process measures.

While the VBP is in a phased-in status, we can assume the healthcare payment system in the future will be almost entirely based on the value of the care and service provided. As a hospital executive, I have to ask: Why shouldn't this be the case? We all, as consumers, use Internet-based search engines to find a value buy. In addition, based on tremendous variation and inconsistent clinical outcomes our traditional volume-based system has produced when compared to other industrialized nations, the move to a value-based system appears absolutely essential.

A value-based system of care design and delivery is completely complementary to the Dyad model. This is a topic of greatest interest and focus in our healthcare system today. The Robert Wood Johnson Foundation, in its November 2008 paper, *From Volume to Value; Transforming Healthcare Payment and Delivery Systems*, indicates that a major problem with the U.S. healthcare system is the payment system built to reward quantity of treatment, not the quality of care (7).

In addition, Oliver Wyman, a well-established global management firm, recently published a White Paper, *The Volume to Value Revolution*, in which it states that the U.S. healthcare system has not competed on value historically but that it is ready to change (8). Our literature is replete with papers and articles on the need to improve the value of our healthcare system in the United States. As the saying goes, we are perfectly positioned to get the results we are getting. If we are not achieving the value-based results we need in order to compete and sustain our missions, then we must address the structural changes needed to improve performance. Engaging and align-ing physicians through a Dyad leadership model is the perfect structure change to achieve improved results and higher value outcomes. This opinion is backed up by statistics: a review of 300 top-ranking American hospitals found overall quality scores were about 25% higher when doctors ran the hospital compared to other hospitals (9).

THE AFFORDABLE CARE ACT

The Dyad model of leadership has been used in some healthcare organizations for more than 25 years. Today's adoption of the model seems to be growing with the trend toward integrated delivery systems and value-based and accountable care. These organizational changes preceded the passage of the Affordability Act, but they are certainly consistent with the broader goals to reform healthcare and improve value. President Obama signed the Affordable Care Act (ACA) into law on March 23, 2010. This sweeping legislation brought the debate on the organization and financing of healthcare in the United States into everyone's living room, office, and locker room. While there continues to be open debate over the merit of the law and the likely chance for the successful attainment of the goals of the Act, it is now the law and we need to move to implement it accordingly.

MMC-DM's strategic agenda to develop a highly integrated, high-quality, and cost-effective delivery system was in place long before the ACA, which provided some real head winds for us. Section III of the ACA: "Improving the Quality and Efficiency of Healthcare" is perhaps the most important and influential section of the ACA on the organization, delivery and financing of healthcare services. MMC-DM's move to engage physicians in a Dyad model is directly consistent with the tenets of the Section III of the ACA. These include Transforming the Healthcare Delivery System, Linking Payment to Quality Outcomes, Hospital Value–Based Purchasing Program, and Medical Shared Savings Program.

These are just a few of the highlights of the key objectives under Section III of the ACA, but they certainly reinforce the need to actively engage physicians in the leadership of today's healthcare organizations. We need our medical colleagues to help us achieve the objectives of transforming the healthcare marketplace while meeting the obligations of the ACA for providers. MMC-DM's "Game Changers" were perfectly timed to seize the opportunity to restructure the organization for success in a rapidly changing environment.

GAME CHANGER: FROM THEORY TO PRACTICE

As previously mentioned, MMC-DM has a long history of physician alignment initiatives. In the early 1990s, we initiated two major Dyad models of leadership. These were established to lead two high volume, high impact clinical service lines. The first model emerged as a coleadership partnership for cardiovascular care. This was followed by the creation of a jointly led orthopedic specialty hospital arrangement. Figures 1-1 and 1-2 represent the organizational structures of MMC-DM's two initial Dyad-led clinical service lines. In both cases, the system engaged and embraced a physician Dyad model to lead these important game changing initiatives.

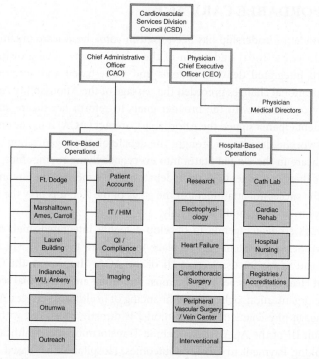

FIGURE 1-1 Mercy Medical Center/Iowa Heart Center organizational chart.

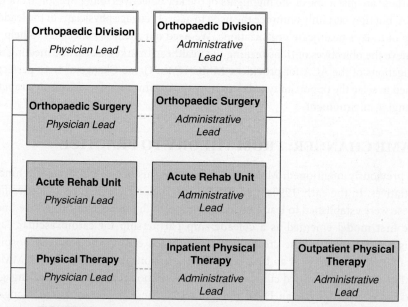

FIGURE 1-2 Mercy Medical Center Orthopaedic Division organizational chart.

There were several compelling reasons to start with these two clinically integrated models of specialty care services. In both cases, the goal was to improve clinical outcomes, reduce the cost of care, and achieve regional growth strategies. In 2011, MMC-DM board of directors, medical staff leadership, and administrative staff recognized the need to take the existing aligned Dyad model to a much broader approach in order to move the value dial to a higher level. The end result was a completely redesigned coleadership model to oversee the general direction and operational management of the medical center. Figure 1-3 displays MMC-DM's organization chart depicting the integration of the Dyad into the overall organizational structure.

This newly designed dyad organizational structure outlined a new model for accountability in which the coleaders are organized under a clinical Dyad framework. The purpose of this new structure was to adopt a model of leadership and care delivery to achieve the broader Game Changer objectives. These objectives included: improve physician and clinical integration, improve physician engagement, increase teamwork among the medical staff and leadership team, create innovative solutions to drive improved clinical outcomes and value, reduce the cost of delivering high-value care and services, position the organization for success under the ACA, develop an operating structure to complement the needs of the ACO and Shared Savings Programs, and embrace new models of leadership and care while increasing market share in the regional service area. These are essentially the same outcomes MMC-DM had experienced with the long-standing Dyads in cardiovascular and orthopedic clinical service lines. To date, the results of the structure are already demonstrating progress toward our goals.

MMC-DM's experience with the cardiovascular and orthopedic service lines has been very positive. Results of adopting a service line approach for these two service lines show steadily improving performance. Both service lines are governed by a formal process including representatives from MMC-DM and the two physician groups involved in these service lines. While both service lines employ Dyad coleadership, the models differ slightly. Each includes a highly engaged physician leader along with a strong content expert as the nonphysician leader. Tables 1-2 and 1-3 show the actual results achieved from these early adopter service lines at MMC-DM.

PRIORITIZING THE SELECTION OF DYAD SERVICE LINES

Healthcare organizations must carefully consider the process of selection of the initial Dyad service lines, based on the organization's goals for this type of change. There are a number of factors to consider when transitioning an organization to a Dyad structure. These factors or influences will change based on broader changes in the healthcare industry. Today, with the evolution of the VBP payment system

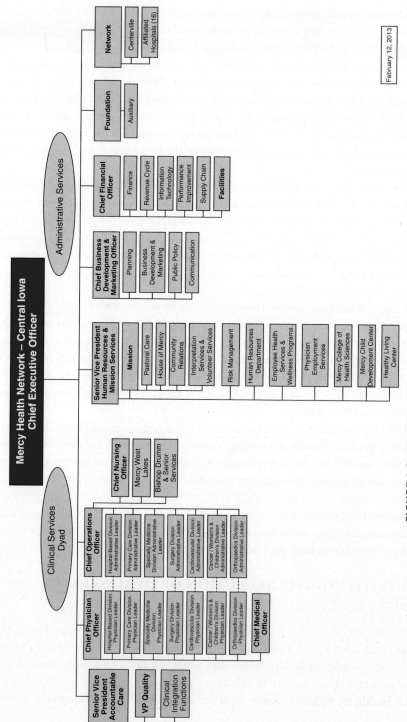

FIGURE 1-3 Mercy Health Network-Central Iowa organizational chart.

Table 1-2 Mercy/Iowa Heart Center Cardiovascular Service Line Performance FY 2011–FY 2013

Volumes	2011	2012	2013
Cath Lab Cases	4513	4634	4863
Cardiac surgery cases	966	1008	1046
Mercy-based office consults and visits	48,839	53,426	54,091
Mercy-based hospital admits and daily visits	22,759	23,926	23,231
Total office procedures	145,963	143,814	139,416
Market Share			
IP cardiac nine county market share	41.62%	43.70%	49.30%
Cardiothoracic surgery nine county market share	58.38%	59.60%	63.50%
Rhythm management nine county market share	46.87%	47.90%	53.50%
Contribution Margin (Direct)	$ 29,995,883	$ 28,503,033	$ 35,341,685
Quality Metrics			
AMI 30-d mortality (survival rate)	85%	85%	84%
Heart failure 30-d mortality rate (survival rate)	88%	88%	88%
Primary PCI received within 90 min of hospital arrival	99%	99%	98%

IP - In Patient
AMI - Acute Myocardial Infarction
PCI - Percutaneous Coronary Intervention

Table 1-3 Mercy Medical Center–Des Moines Orthopedics Service Line FY 2011–FY 2013

Volumes	2011	2012	2013
Inpatient cases	3745	3526	3619
Outpatient cases	672	692	770
Market Share			
Nine county service area market share	22.60%	23.00%	29.00%
Three county service area market share	40.34%	40.92%	39.65%
Contribution Margin (Direct)	$ 26,128,175	$ 24,313,723	$ 20,743,165
Quality Metrics			
First case on-time start rate main, AMS & MWL	74%	88%	91%
Fx Hips to OR: 24 h or less from admission	75%	83%	78%
Length of stay—DRG 470—joint replacement	86%	88%	79%

AMS - Ambulatory Surgery Center
MWL - Mercy West Lake Facility
OR - Operating Room
DRG - Diagnostic Related Group

under Medicare, the move from volume to value may be the primary consideration in selecting the leaders and the areas to be led didactically.

Perhaps the greatest benefit of the use of the Dyad to improve value is the growing fusion between the physicians and the organization in operating a higher-value, more accountable model of care delivery. In addition, if an organization has a clear strategic plan to create centers of excellence (neurosciences, pediatrics, emergency medicine, etc.), these service lines will be the initial areas to organize as Dyad led. Organizations focused on improving profitability as a driving influence for the Dyad must carefully analyze the contribution margin of each service line to select the first series of lines to be organized under a Dyad, using a service line structure.

Two diagrams (Figs. 1-4 and 1-5) show MMC-DM's analysis of the contribution margin for each service line based on our actual performance. These charts were developed to show MMC-DM's leaders the importance of a service line for reduction of cost and achievement of growth. These were important considerations in selecting our service line models.

It is important for an organization moving to a Dyad service line model to realize the benefit of a phased-in approach to this new and often complicated model for leadership. To be successful, the building of operational relationships with support departments and detailed performance reporting are essential. That's why selecting just two or three service lines of Dyad leadership is often a good first step.

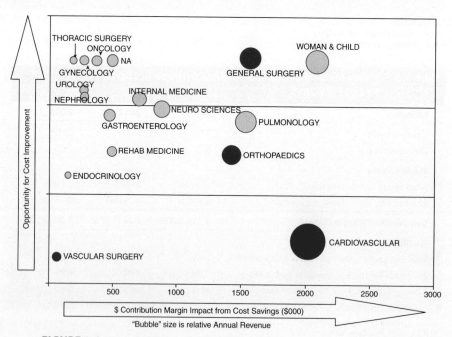

FIGURE 1-4   Mercy Medical Center contribution margin impact of 10% cost reduction.

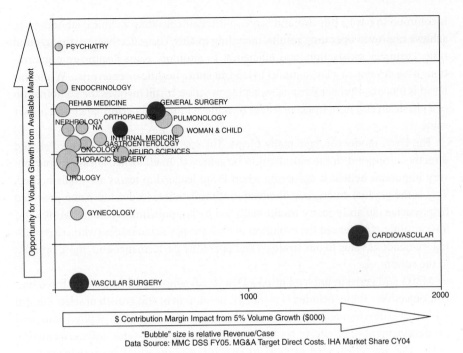

FIGURE 1-5 Mercy Medical Center contribution margin impact of 5% volume growth.

DYADS MAY BE ORGANIZED IN SEVERAL WAYS TO ACHIEVE DIFFERENT OBJECTIVES

As an organization considers moving to a Dyad leadership model, it is important to clearly articulate the objectives for the transition. While improvement in clinical and operational results will likely be achieved in different Dyad models, the model implemented should be designed in direct relation to the objectives to be achieved.

The manufacturing industry has traditionally used product line leadership models to produce products through accountable and focused factory-based processes. For example, a team approach to manufacturing a product may be used on a production line to assemble a product from its many parts. In this model, the product line leader has total responsibility to oversee the production, marketing, sales, and financial performance for a discrete product. Focused factories are also used in manufacturing to standardize the task of producing a high volume of products with consistently high-quality results.

In healthcare, a Dyad service line leader model typically involves a physician and nonphysician leader to oversee the organization and delivery of a clinical service designed to meet the needs of a homogenous group of patients with a clinical need (such as cardiovascular care). Other models of Dyad leadership may be designed to provide overall leadership to a functional department in a hospital. For example, it is common to have a director and medical director coleading a clinical laboratory to achieve improved operating results, including quality, cost-effectiveness, turnaround time, customer satisfaction, and efficiency. In addition, some healthcare organizations have developed a Dyad model to lead an entire healthcare enterprise. While this Dyad is more comprehensive and sweeping in scope, it still involves the combination of a physician and nonphysician leader to achieve improved performance and higher value.

The Dyad model can take many forms. The specific partnership selected should directly correspond to the objectives to be achieved. In all forms, a less obvious but very important benefit is occurring when Dyad leadership teams are implemented. This is the gradual emergence of effective administrative leadership being provided by physicians in an industry traditionally led by lay, nonclinical leaders. MMC-DM has certainly experienced the evolution of multiple physician leaders who are providing tremendous value to our strategic and operating performance and, more broadly, to the culture.

MMC-DM's goal in implementing a Dyad leadership model focused on three specific objectives. These included (1) strategic development and growth of select clinical services, (2) development of a culture of alignment and integration of physicians, and (3) development of physician leaders to improve long-term value and performance. MMC-DM was challenged by how to structure the organization to achieve these complementary, yet somewhat different objectives. With a history of two mature clinical service line models already in place, we recognized the need to fuse the leadership model with physicians and administrative functions at the highest level of the organization. The board and leadership team recognized the challenge of combining the new structure with the traditional clinical service line model.

We knew we would not be successful without an infrastructure to support this cultural change. As a result, a Physician Leadership Council (PLC) was developed to provide the executive leadership with an appropriate team to achieve the goal of Dyad leadership over the entire organization. Figure 1-6 shows how this global leadership dyad model and governance structure was organized. Display 1-1 provides a summary of the PLC Charter.

MMC-DM selected Dyad physician leaders based on their skills, fit, content expertise, interest, and organizational impact. We entered into contractual agreements with the physicians in which 25% of their time was allocated to serve on the PLC. The two established models remained in place, with the coleadership models leading the cardiovascular and orthopedics service lines. Maintaining two scopes of Dyad leaders (global vs. service line) required MMC-DM to clearly define and articulate the different roles, scope of authority, and general purpose.

In contrast, St. John's Hospital (SJS) in Springfield, Illinois, chose a different approach to accomplish its goal to engage physicians in leadership positions. SJS completely reorganized the hospital's structure to operate with a complete clinical

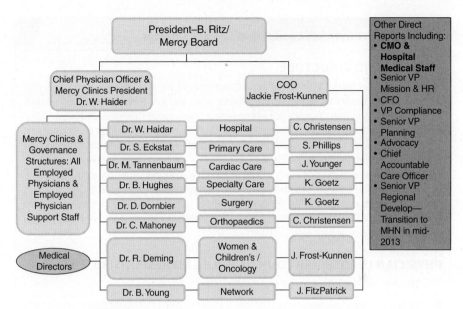

FIGURE 1-6 Mercy Medical Center physician–administrator dyads.

service line model. SJS effectively turned the organization into a Dyad leadership model by reorganizing the entire hospital operations around 13 clinical service lines with Dyad leaders. Most of these leaders were engaged contractually for 50% of their time as service line leaders.

There are numerous other examples of how healthcare organizations have integrated physicians into leadership utilizing Dyads. Alberta Health, located in Edmonton, Canada, has one of the most integrated structures to involve physicians in leading and operating the organization. Alberta established Strategic Clinical Networks (SCNs) comprising Clinical and Strategy Codirectors to lead their clinical networks. They refer to their approach as a management model in which the SCNs have a much "broader mandate" for system leadership than their previous managers did (10).

Regardless of how an organization adopts the Dyad model, it is critical to have the model directly aligned with the goals to be achieved, no matter how broad (new culture) or how specific (improve service line performance; Fig. 1-7).

HOW TO SELECT THE PHYSICIAN DYAD LEADERS

The selection of physicians to serve as a Dyad leader requires careful consideration. At MMC-DM, our selection process included an evaluation of the individual's:

1. Emotional intelligence, including the ability to assess and evaluate others
2. Communication skills, including knowledge of focused and broad-based messaging

---

Display 1-1 Physician Leadership Council Charter

PURPOSE AND STRUCTURE

Mercy Medical Center (MMC) is designing a closer relationship with its physician community to transform our healthcare system with significant input and influence from the Medical Staff. The Physician Leadership Council (PLC) will provide a collaborative mechanism to improve the health of our patients. The Council's mission is to improve healthcare, clinical quality, systems and processes, and importantly Medical Staff satisfaction by enhancing relationships among physicians, administration, staff, and patients.

The PLC meets at least once every month. The PLC will consider issues deemed appropriate by a majority of the Council's members and make recommendations, as appropriate, to MMC's Administration. Following each PLC meeting, a meeting summary, including recommendations considered by the Council and resulting actions, will be developed and shared with the Medical Executive Committee and the Hospital Board.

PHYSICIAN LEADERSHIP COUNCIL ROLE AND RESPONSIBILITIES

The PLC (shall have the following role and responsibilities):

▶ Advise on the development, design, content, and distribution of relevant projects or programs
▶ Assist in the development of a Physician Engagement Plan
▶ Assist in the development of a structured Physician Communication Plan
▶ Provide an opportunity to develop a new coleadership model with MMC
▶ Identify specific strategic and/or operational issues that need to be addressed to improve performance and physician engagement
▶ Provide oversight to MMC's Administrative Staff to ensure a healthy work environment between MMC and the Medical Staff
▶ Provide for physician leadership on all key strategic, clinical, operational, and financial matters
▶ Provide support and guidance for MMC to provide a positive Mercy Experience for all served
▶ Provide a vehicle for physicians to communicate changes to the Medical Staff

---

3. Commitment to continuous learning, including leadership development
4. Diplomacy: ability to navigate and manage organizational processes, politics, and relationships
5. Team skills, including the ability to lead a team while also being a team member
6. Medical content expertise, or the ability to maintain and provide content expertise from a medical perspective
7. Alignment with the organization's mission, values, people, and culture
8. Charisma or the ability to inspire all stakeholders to achieve the desired destiny
9. Balance or the ability to maintain a perspective, which always considers the needs of the patient, organization, and clinical specialty

Physicians are very intelligent and motivated individuals. They have committed their lives to helping people during their greatest time of need, while committing to a life of learning and continuous service. While these are important traits for

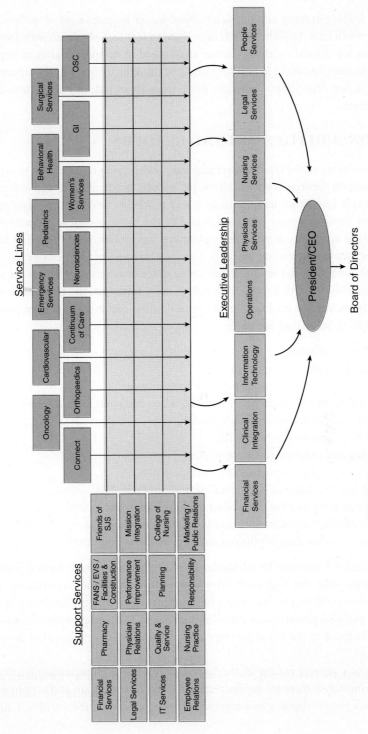

FIGURE 1-7   Mercy Medical Center service line organizational chart.

effective leaders, serving as a physician Dyad leader requires a set of skills not all physicians will have. In addition, it is important to realize, a physician with a superb reputation for clinical excellence is not guaranteed to be successful in an organizational leadership role. It is also important to think broadly about the future and to seek the "up and comers" who can drive value in an industry characterized by rapid change.

RESPONSIBILITIES OF DYAD LEADERS

The responsibility of the Dyad leaders may vary widely from organization to organization based on the organization's culture, philosophy, needs, abilities, and objectives. It's important to partner these duos in a way that adds value to the organization because of complementary expertise. Some of the more common responsibilities for the Dyad are policy development, planning, operations, marketing, and financial management. Depending on the use of the Dyad model (service line vs. organizational oversight), the responsibilities may differ in function or scope, yet some core responsibilities will be common across most organizations with this leadership model. Below is a brief outline of responsibilities commonly found in position descriptions of both Dyad members:

1. Support the mission
2. Advance a vision for the future
3. Embrace and emulate the values of the organization
4. Foster a culture of collaboration, quality, safety, and continuous improvement
5. Improve physician and staff engagement
6. Achieve patient satisfaction goals
7. Develop and implement a strategic plan
8. Achieve annual performance and strategic goals
9. Develop and achieve annual operating and capital budget
10. Define and improve the value of services provided
11. Adopt effective use of information and clinical technologies
12. Improve market share for the organization and/or service line

To ensure an effective Dyad model, it is important to have formal position descriptions with the responsibilities clearly identified and understood. It is equally important to monitor and assess performance at least quarterly and to formally evaluate performance on an annual basis. This will provide an opportunity for feedback to the Dyad partners and promote the development of development plans.

Below is a general outline of the responsibilities of a physician/administrative Dyad. As indicated, there are unique responsibilities of a physician and nonphysician leader while the overlapping area represents the shared responsibilities (Fig. 1-8).

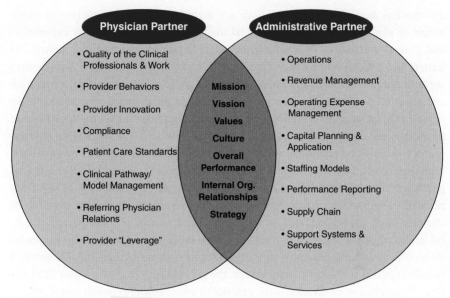

FIGURE 1-8   Dyad management responsibilities.

VALUE OF THE DYAD

The value of Dyad leadership depends on the design, scope, use, and organizational embrace of the model. Healthcare organizations are using the Dyad leadership model in a variety of ways. Regardless of the specific use, the Dyad can produce significant short-term and long-term performance results. Here is a summary of the some of the more common short-term and long-term benefits of effective deployment of a Dyad model:

1. Improved culture of physician engagement
2. Improved clinical outcomes
3. Improved market share
4. Improved financial performance
5. Improved strategic agility
6. Improved efficiency of leadership process
7. Improved communication among the staff and medical staff
8. Improved attractiveness for recruiting physicians
9. Improved culture of innovation
10. Improved capital investment decisions

MMC-DM has used the Dyad model to lead clinical service lines. The model serves as team infrastructure, combining eight physicians and an equal number of administrative staff to populate a leadership team (Physician Leadership Council) to improve the medical center's performance. We are actively involving physicians in every aspect of planning, operations, financial management, quality, patient experience, and general oversight of the organization. We also pair physicians and nonphysician leaders to lead clinical ancillary departments, including the laboratory, emergency services, surgical services, and imaging departments. Results are tracked, monitored, and reported on a monthly basis, using traditional operation reports, responsibility reports, and balanced scorecards. In every case, we are convinced the move to pair physicians and nonphysicians has paid clear dividends. In fact, the emerging philosophy of engaging physicians in leadership has created a culture of greater transparency, improved communication, improved quality and safety, improved stronger financial performance, and improved planning and market strategy. Moreover, MMC-DM's physician alignment structure over the past 20 years set the stage for a more robust strategic plan. This culminated in the development of a large multispecialty medical group, regional strategic partnerships with other providers, and the successful development of an accountable care organization with more than 100,000 enrolled members in just two short years. Perhaps, the greatest benefit of this legacy of physician alignment and integration is the practice of systematically considering physician involvement in all decisions concerning operations, strategic initiatives, and long-term vision. Our culture of physician alignment has taken hold at MMC-DM to the point where we do not set future strategies without including medical staff members at the table. Most importantly, the alignment of physicians through Dyad management has focused everything we do on the patient experience.

DYAD LEADERSHIP AS A STRATEGIC INITIATIVE

The development of a Dyad model can also serve as an important strategic initiative. Healthcare organizations today are faced with the daunting task of improving the value of core operations while developing a new business model (accountable care organization) to assume performance and insurance risk and to manage the health of a defined population. An organization with a history of Dyad leadership will be better positioned to navigate this challenging balancing act for several reasons.

An organization with a history of physician leadership will have better performance results. There are some who believe organizations with physician CEOs have improved performance over their nonphysician counterparts. We are all familiar with highly reputable healthcare organizations with physician leaders known for their performance including Mayo Clinic, Cleveland Clinic, and Geisinger Health System.

Organizations with a track record of physician alignment and involvement will have cultures in place to be more strategically agile when transforming their business models for the future. Organizations with little history of active physician leadership will be required to build the culture first to embrace the physician leadership model step by step. This can be a long and difficult process.

Engaged physicians have the ability to influence their peers. As organizations migrate to a new model of combined delivery and financing systems, broad physician support and involvement are critical. Healthcare organizations with a history of Dyad leadership models in place will find it easier to engage more physicians in a more expeditious manner.

Dyad organizations have a better opportunity to transform care from the pay-for-volume to pay-for-value model. Physician leaders can help improve quality and safety thereby reducing the cost of care by working on reducing the variation of care. These engaged physicians can also help reduce waste by working on evidenced-based protocols, improving supply chain standardization and garnering support from their physician peers to support these changes.

Organizations with Dyad physician leaders can also help make improvements in staff and patient satisfaction. Based on their proximity to the patient care process, physician Dyad leaders can help focus the organization on the pressing issues impacting staff and patient satisfaction. (One of the considerations an organization will need to contemplate is how much of a clinical practice the physician Dyad leader should continue in order to maintain their clinical credibility through this proximity.)

In addition to the five points listed above, the adoption of a Dyad model with physicians and nonphysician leaders can maneuver the organization to continuously improve its strategic position. Table 1-4 is a visual representation of the Strategic Plan of our Cardiovascular Service Line. This plan represents a matrix of goals and objectives for service line leaders preparing for the change in design and framework of cardiovascular care consistent with broad industry trends in payment models.

Organizations that do not have Dyad or physician leaders engaged in operations or strategy will find it more difficult to transform their organizations for accountable and risk-based care delivery and financing in time to take advantage of the changes coming in both.

THE METRICS COUNT WITH THE DYAD MODEL

Healthcare, as an industry, uses data for almost everything in the care delivery process. Without metrics, one cannot truly assess the added value of any decision. Consistent with value-based purchasing initiatives, healthcare organizations need to establish, measure, and report metrics to assess performance. MMC-DM's Dyad model uses a balanced scorecard approach to track performance on a monthly basis. Specific metrics include volume of services provided, market share, clinical quality outcomes, financial performance, patient experience scores, and physician and staff engagement scores. The contractual agreement with the Dyad leadership team typically includes incentive compensation for specific results and improved performance.

Figure 1-9 represents a standard balanced scorecard used at MMC-DM to focus the Dyad on achieving performance goals according to the goal performance categories.

Table 1-4   New Cardiovascular Service Line Product Portfolio

Disease	Primary Prevention	Chronic Disease Management	Preventive Diagnostics and Procedures	Minimally Invasive Procedures	Inpatient Services	Post-Acute Care	Secondary Prevention
Coronary artery disease	Smoking cessation Weight management Exercise Stress tests	Antihypertensives Statins	CCTA Chest pain observation	PCI	CABG	Cardiac Rehab	Smoking cessation Weight management Exercise Pharma management
Heart failure	Smoking cessation Weight management Exercise Echo EF screening	Diuretics Ace inhibitors Beta-blockers Remote monitoring	Observation Aquapheresis Regenerative medicine (stem cells)		Aquapheresis ICDs CRT-Ds VADs Transplants	Home health Palliative care	Heart failure clinic Remote monitoring Pharma management
Vascular disease	Smoking cessation Weight management Exercise PAD/AAA screening	Statins Antihypertensives Antiplatelets	Compression stockings	Interventional vascular therapies	Open surgery		Smoking cessation Weight management Exercise Pharma management
Atrial fibrillation	Smoking cessation Weight management Exercise Holter monitoring	Rate and rhythm control Anti-coagulation	EP studies	Catheter ablation Balloon catheters	Surgical ablation		Anti-coagulation

Current fee-for-service focus

Expanded focus under bundled payments

Prevention and disease management focus under shared savings

CCTA - Cardiac Computed Tomography Angiography
PCI - Percutaneous Coronary Intervention
CABG - Coronary Artery Bypass Graft
EF - Ejection Fraction
ICD - Implantable Cardiac Device
CRT-D - Cardiac Resynchronization Therapy Device
VAD - Ventricular Assist Device
PAD - Peripheral Arterial Disease
AAA - Abdominal Aortic Aneurysm
EP - Electro-physiology

	MEASURE	FY 13 Result	FY 14 Target	July 13	Aug 13	Sept 13	Oct 13	Nov 13	Dec 13
People	# RN terminations (voluntary/reason)								
	# of Proc. Tech/Clerk; Clerk; LPN; Surgical Tech								
	Vacancy rate of RN's (filled and functioning)								
	Vacancy rate of Proc. Tech/Clerk; Clerk; LPN; Surgical Tech								
Operational Indicators	LOS								
	C/S								
	Vaginal								
	Antenatal (IMC)								
	GYN pts.								
Quality	Birth Trauma Events								
	Neonatal Deaths								
	NICU Transfer NB								
	Injury to brachial Plexus								
	Elective Ind. resulting in C/S								
	Elective Ind. prior to 39 wks								
	Elective C/S prior to 39 wks								
	Peri Lac 4th deg for vag del								
	Cesarean Deliveries (#/%)								
	Live Births								
	HCAHPS Pain (% rank)								
	PPcomp								
Service	HCAHPS Communication with Nurses (% rank)								
	HCAHPS Communication with MDs (% rank)								
	Overall Rating of Care (% rank)								
Growth	Monthly volume (deliveries)								
	Monthly volume (triage pts)								
	Monthly volume (gyne)								
	Women Service's Market Share								
Finance	Total cost/unit								
	Actual								
	Budgeted-static								

FIGURE 1-9   MMC sample women's service line performance-based scorecard.

During the past 25 years, I have had the opportunity to work with healthcare organizations where we embraced the Dyad coleadership model. In each case, the coleadership model was organized as clinical service line teams. (The range of service lines varied from 5 to 13 in three different organizations.) Typically, a service line steering committee is established to assist the coleaders achieve their respective goals. Each month, a scorecard is used to report progress and drive improved performance while ensuring a model of accountability. The steering committee initially serves to help organize the service line while fostering a new culture of physician leadership. As the new model matures, the steering committee is used to assess performance and suggests changes to optimize the service line performance. In some situations, the steering committee is a very formal structure established by a Joint Operating Agreement or Joint Venture organized to establish the service line goals. In other

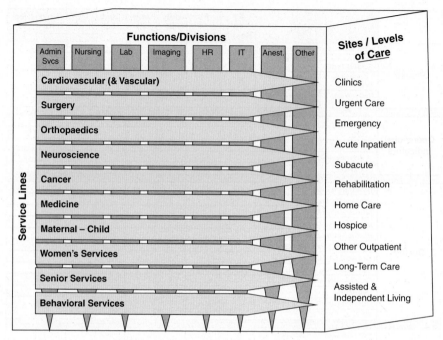

FIGURE 1-10   MMC-Des Moines service line framework.

cases, the steering committees are committee structures formed by the coleaders to involve the discrete clinical and support functions servicing the clinical service line patient cohorts. Regardless of the structure (formal legal organization vs. informal committee structure), the steering committees play a significant oversight and guidance role for the Dyad and clinical service line team members.

Figure 1-10 shows some common features of service line structures, including clinical areas and departments. This diagram helps to determine which departments/functions should serve on the Steering Committee.

SCOPE OF INFLUENCE OF DYAD MODELS AND STRUCTURAL DESIGN IMPLICATIONS

Scope of influence and authority can vary with each Dyad model. Regardless of the specific scope of authority, it is critical to provide enough authority and responsibility for the model to produce the desired results. A typical scope of responsibility includes planning, strategic initiatives, marketing, operations, financial performance, and clinical care systems. In order for Dyads to fulfill their roles, the organization's leadership philosophy must support the transfer of administrative power and influence from traditional managers to the Dyad. This is one of the greatest challenges of implementing this model.

Organizations have historically organized leadership along the traditional functional silos. Accountability and authority have been divided between clinical nursing, clinical ancillaries, and support departments. The art of the Dyad leadership model is to identify how to succeed with a new leadership model that breaks down and cuts across these silo functions. This is where the organization's executive leadership must support this transformational change. If a Dyad is to be successful, it is imperative for the organization to embrace the need for a new way to manage. Leaders of these traditional functional departments will often experience the transition as organizational and leadership ambiguity. While this is a common side effect of a move to a Dyad model, it is essential for the leadership team to clearly articulate the need for change and communicate a shared vision. It is also important to articulate how the Dyad will help advance the vision and outline how the traditional functional departments should work with and support the service line models.

In a very mature Dyad service line model, some organizations will completely change the organization structure to make supporting roles clear. Due to its management history, the move to the Dyad model can truly challenge leaders to question their personal fit in this new structure. This adoption of a Dyad can be traumatic for many long-term leaders who only know one way to organize and deliver care and service.

After several months of constant communication and discussion after the decision to implement Dyads, a new structure can began to take hold. One word of caution: it may be necessary to remove the traditional leadership structure when moving to a new, clinical service line model with Dyad leaders. It is not unusual for the traditional single leaders to assume an ownership mentality after having served in a role for several years. If an organization does not remove the old model, there could be a dysfunctional block between the old culture and the new. Each organization contemplating a move to a Dyad model to lead clinical service lines must closely consider this reality when designing the new organization structure. It can also be too costly to maintain both old and new management models. (As a simple analogy, if you build a new bridge over water to replace an existing one, and you don't remove the old bridge, both bridges will be used.) A transformational change will probably be necessary to help the organization with the transition.

POTENTIAL PITFALLS OF THE DYAD MODEL

While the Dyad model offers numerous benefits, there are also some common pitfalls that should be anticipated. These challenges should not deter interest in developing this transformational leadership model. They will, however, need to be considered and managed. Perhaps the most challenging issue is the risk of reactions to perceptions of inclusion versus exclusion. Healthcare organizations are filled with many different professionals who constitute the healthcare team. Selecting certain physicians to serve as Dyad leaders can create a "we/they" perspective among the medical staff. This can be overcome with significant communication on the need to develop Dyad leaders to improve value, to improve a physician practice experience, and to elevate the voice of physicians in the organization.

When a nonphysician leader is paired with a physician leader, there can be a fear the physician will dominate the leadership relationship. This is due to the historical level of importance placed on the physician as a customer. To foster teamwork of a Dyad, it is important to position both leaders as equals and to manage the leadership process accordingly.

A possible pitfall for successful Dyad implementation is a lack of cultural alignment with the new model. If the organization's culture is not ready to support this transformation, both Dyad leaders may feel unsupported in their roles. The physician leader may find it difficult to transition his or her thinking as he or she transitions from the autonomy of clinical practice to an organizational team-based perspective. (This is why the selection of the physician leaders is so critical.) Some physician leaders will require transitional support to make this change in alignment. Others may not be able to make the transition to this new perspective.

The organization will need to make some broad changes to support the Dyad model. The concept of sharing leadership is not generally natural to those who aspired to leadership positions. It's important that CEOs and other executives who have determined to implement this model support its success by:

1. Clearly defining the scope and limits of Dyad and individual authority
2. Serving as a supporting sponsor to this model and resource
3. Coaching and inspiring the team to excel
4. Giving power and influence to the Dyad
5. Creating a culture of innovation and creativity
6. Treating the Dyad as equals, with no special authority for one over the other
7. Constantly communicating about the role and value of the Dyad to all audiences
8. Changing the organization chart; removing structural barriers to aid in clarity of roles
9. Articulating the role of support departments (which could begin to feel less important)
10. Realizing the Dyad team will face challenges and some resistance (They will need support in overcoming these.)

CONCLUSION

Mercy Medical Center–Des Moines, like numerous other healthcare organizations, recognizes the need for alignment and integration among physicians and the medical center. We are embracing the Dyad leadership model (Display 1-2).

Display 1-2 **Members of the Physician Leadership Council and Administrative Council Agree This is a Model for our Future**

"Serving as the Chair of the Physician Leadership Council, it strikes me that this Council provides a unique opportunity to address physician-related issues at a high level. Ideally, the group functions as a cabinet to the President of Mercy Medical Center. Not only can we direct policy to improve patient care, but doctors now also have an avenue to directly influence the requests and allocation of resources."

—William C. Young, M.D., Chair of Physician Leadership Council

"The Dyad structure within a cardiovascular service line has optimized the managerial functions of our organization and facilitated execution of our strategy by leveraging the complementary skill sets of our administrative and physician leaders. Each of these individuals brings to their role a different kind of knowledge and set of experiences. Together they create a whole that is ultimately greater than the sum of their parts."

—Mark Tannenbaum, M.D., Leader of Cardiovascular Service Line

"Healthcare today, now more than ever, requires the integration of physicians into the decision-making processes that used to be confined to hospital administrators. The dyad model allows physician leaders to partner with experienced administrators to create a leadership team that utilizes the physician's clinical expertise with the administrator's more traditional business talents. At its best, it works like a peanut butter and jelly sandwich! One of the potential pitfalls of the Dyad model of leadership is that it can create uncertainty regarding the line of authority. There needs to be a clear understanding of how differences of opinion between the two Dyad leaders are dealt with. There also needs to be a clear channel of communication to and from those individuals that report to the Dyad. With the advent of ACOs and bundled payments, physician integration into the administrative suite is not a luxury; it is a necessity. It's only by collaborating on decision-making throughout all levels of a healthcare organization that progress will be made in achieving high quality of care, patient satisfaction, and cost reductions."

—Richard L. Deming, M.D., Medical Director of Mercy Cancer Center

"As an Orthopaedic Surgeon, it is essential to have an open and transparent relationship with hospital administration. The Dyad Leadership Model facilitates that relationship by creating a formal body that benefits both sides. Physicians are empowered to take greater responsibility in hospital success and will gain a deeper understanding of health system operations by participating. Administrators benefit by gaining physician advocates through the Dyad relationship who are involved in ground level activities. The one-to-one communication also allows administrators greater insights into the needs of physicians."

—Craig Mahoney, M.D., Leader of Orthopaedic Service Line

"The Dyad model facilitates prioritization and alignment of work to improve growth, quality, and efficient resource utilization. The partnership between operations and physicians enhances mutual understanding, common goals, and working together to benefit patients, physicians, and the community. The Dyad leadership model improves our collective strength in meeting the turbulent challenges of today's healthcare environment. We can hold ourselves mutually accountable to determined metrics."

—Jackie Frost-Kunnen, Chief Operations Officer and Member of the Physician Leadership Council Dyad Model

(Continued)

"For many years, Mercy Medical Center and its Medical Staff have worked together to build a better system for ensuring quality of care and service to our patients. Through careful deliberation Mercy and the Medical Staff leadership worked on a plan for completely integrating how we serve our patients in the future in recognition of broad trends. The dyad model quickly emerged as a natural first step in forging a collaborative relationship consistent with providing predictable and high-value quality of care and service."

—*David H. Vellinga, President & CEO, Mercy Health Network*

The growing emergence of the Dyad leadership model is truly a positive step for a healthcare organization. Dyads support the probability of success in the rapidly transforming healthcare industry. The need for the alignment and integration of healthcare providers has never been greater so that we can provide a quality, cost-effective healthcare system. A leadership model that fuses the alignment of the historically separated roles of physicians and nonphysicians into a leadership Dyad will help an organization drive value with improved quality and better service at a reduced cost. A Dyad model will help position an organization for success amidst the radical reform underway in our U.S. healthcare system.

Organizations looking ahead should consider the Dyad leadership model as an important strategic, operational, and systemic step to prepare for the future. There are numerous considerations, challenges, and pitfalls to effectively adopt this leadership model. However, if done correctly, a Dyad model will truly shape future opportunities to succeed by combining the energy, commitment, talents, and mission-based work of physicians and healthcare organizations in our rapidly changing and value-focused healthcare industry.

INTO THE NEXT ERA
Camille Haycock and Xavier Sevilla

Traditional hospital organizations are evolving into systems of care that include the entire continuum. Relationships between physicians, traditional hospital hierarchies, and nurse leaders are changing to create models of leadership that support this evolution. This essay, from the viewpoints of a physician leader and nurse leader tasked with planning for this next era, together explore where we've come from and where we need to go.

FROM A PHYSICIAN PERSPECTIVE

"You are the captain of the ship. You are responsible and accountable for everything that happens to your patients; you better check and make sure things get done." This is the very familiar statement that most physicians heard again and again during medical school and residency education. It is an underpinning to our old model of hierarchical medical system that teaches physicians that the doctor is at the "top," isolated, and solely responsible and accountable for providing most of the care that occurs inside a hospital or in the physician office setting.

As a by-product of this out dated model, I have come to recognize some of the short comings this education has produced for leaders in the new world of healthcare. The old model created physicians who think in a vertical, pyramidal way. The doctor diagnoses and treats conditions and gives "orders" to the staff. Communication is mainly unidirectional with short data reports as the only feedback expected from the rest of the care team. This has made physicians skilled at complex decision making but not very proficient in the art of executing plans and projects. It also reinforces a very strong independent streak that most physicians possessed even before going to medical school. This educational model makes it very difficult for physicians to trust and rely on other care team members who could contribute to improved care in many efficient and effective ways. The role of the physician in the future healthcare system is not at the top, acting alone, but as a full member of a team, and in some cases as a leader who shares a leadership role.

The hierarchal model is still very much practiced in most medical groups as well as in hospitals in the United States. In fact, this was the unspoken rule of engagement in the previous organization where I spent the first 13 years of my career in medicine, before coming to CHI. After finishing my pediatric residency, I joined an ambulatory community health center in rural Florida. Six months into my new professional life, I realized that there were some serious operational problems at this practice. These impaired my ability to deliver excellent clinical care. I started to inquire about the operational tactics and how we could improve them. This inquisitiveness, plus a good reputation as a clinician, was enough to propel me into the role of medical director for the clinic.

I think my experience follows a very similar course for most physicians in health-care organizations. As they are recognized for their clinical work, they are "saddled" with more managerial duties, without necessarily being provided with any training on the different capabilities needed for leadership roles. After I successfully implemented a quality improvement initiative to improve access and efficiency in my clinic, I was promoted to Chief Quality Officer for the whole ambulatory medical group. This became a pivotal moment. I could no longer actually do the work myself but had to collaborate with other managers in the organization to get things done. Here, the culture was very much consistent with that classic structure where physicians, nurses, and operations leaders work in silos. As a result, it was very difficult to get projects executed on the ground.

While I was struggling with trying to accomplish transformation with a team that wasn't a team, Catholic Health Initiatives, the healthcare system, was rapidly changing its composition. The organization was acquiring physician practices and venturing more and more into the continuum of care. I learned about this, left my clinic work, and was hired as part of a physician enterprise leadership team to provide a structure for quality in the new ambulatory world of CHI.

Even before my interview at CHI, I was surprised to learn that the system had a CMO and a CNO that worked as a dyad and were considered equal in "status" by the organization. I was also surprised to learn that among the many National Vice Presidents in the corporate office, there were nurses and/or administrators who were on equal footing with vice presidents who had a medical background. This was not how business was conducted in the hospitals and healthcare organizations that I had worked with since entering medical school!

I was introduced to the concept of dyad leadership and learned how each profession has unique skill-sets that can complement other's professional perspectives and abilities. I learned, and continue to grow in understanding, that as physicians, my peers and I can contribute to the vision of a better healthcare environment, as well as work out the causes of current problems along with possible solutions. Our dyad partners are very helpful in complementing the "diagnostic" view of a problem, but more importantly, they are expert in getting a solution implemented.

FROM A NURSING PERSPECTIVE

"A good nurse is efficient, smart, can critically think, and is the quintessential multitasker." These are the words from a nursing preceptor and mentor that I had the privilege of working with early in my nursing career. These skills, in fact, are learned very early in nursing and are valued by other team members and employers.

A typical first position that a nurse may assume in a hospital includes an assignment on a busy medical/surgical unit or a busy telemetry unit. It is not uncommon that this new graduate will discharge and admit upward of three to four patients per shift, while assuming the care of another four or five patients. This new nurse quickly learns to prioritize and create processes and organizational structures to accomplish the many demands of patients, physicians, family members, and administrators. The nurse also learns very quickly how to optimize the talents of those around her or him to accomplish the many details of personalized patient care. For example, a unit clerk may be mobilized to assist a family in need, while a nursing assistant can quickly respond to a call light or personal patient need. Therapy services can be called upon to assist with patient mobility. A nurse learns how to mobilize resources, prioritize, organize, and build efficient processes and structures to get things done.

I remember as a new nurse in a busy ICU, evaluating the success of my day by whether or not my patient's lives were improved because I was there. I also learned early to evaluate my success as a nurse through quality patient outcomes, and patient/family satisfaction. I realized that this could not be accomplished without the help of a lot of other people and required near "obsessive" organizational skills. Later as a flight nurse in a helicopter, I learned that teamwork and reliance on work partners could be the difference between your own (*or your patient's*) life and death. These early career experiences not only built confidence in my own abilities, they taught me the necessity of trusting team mates and relying on the skills and abilities of others to get things done.

In leadership positions, these early learned nursing characteristics and skills are very transferrable to business acumen and critical to organizational success. Nurses are exceptionally skilled at building processes and structures, while focusing on patient outcomes and measurement. Nurses are also extremely adept at working in teams and can quickly assess the skills of others and how these skills can be leveraged toward improving patient care. Further, nurses are typically very relationship oriented, have the trust of patients and families, and can identify the "*how*" for getting things done.

As a nurse, I was hired by CHI to reduce clinical variation through the implementation of evidence-based practice in acute care settings. Over the past 5 years, we have successfully reduced hospital-acquired conditions and cost of care by implementing standardized evidence-based practices in all of our markets. As we prepare for the next era of healthcare, and prepare for payment reform, it is an imperative that clinical variation be reduced across the care continuum, with standardized processes utilizing evidence-based practice. These practices have been "hard-wired" in acute care and have become the practice norm. As CHI expands its ministries, it is imperative that processes that have achieved results, in acute care, be duplicated and expanded into ambulatory settings and across the care continuum. Having this perspective, my scope was expanded from acute care services to the care continuum. While I have had some experience as a nurse practitioner in a cardiology practice, I was not familiar with care practices and processes in primary care and how primary care was undergoing significant transformation across CHI. I needed to rely heavily on the expertise and vision of Dr. Xavier Sevilla. I realized that he brings great skill at understanding and thinking through complex issues. I learned that primary care transformation needed to become a core competency for CHI, as the company continued to acquire primary care practices, and that physicians are essential partners to help lead this transformation.

DYAD LEADERSHIP ACROSS THE CARE CONTINUUM

The experience of our patients and customers is not neatly divided into ambulatory, acute, and postacute occurrences. Their experience is longitudinal, across all care settings. Population health management requires these "artificial" silos to be merged together into a comprehensive, coordinated care delivery model. Working within this dyad leadership structure, we have been able to share resources that also have unique expertise and knowledge that can be transferable to other care settings. We have set about to begin breaking down silos and working in a synergistic fashion.

We have learned that we are "better together" and have several accomplishments working within this dyad relationship. One accomplishment is the development and implementation of standardized and evidence-based diabetes and hypertension management toolkits that were built by a multiprofessional representative group from across CHI. A glycemic control toolkit had already been built for acute care using a multidisciplinary approach. We utilized this same methodology to expand this set of practices to ambulatory care and in order to bridge the care of the patient from acute care to the care continuum.

WHAT WE HAVE LEARNED FROM EACH OTHER

From this dyadic relationship, we have learned that each member of the team brings important skill sets that are crucial to the outcome of any project. We also have learned the importance of respecting the skills of others and allowing each member of the team the autonomy to contribute his or her respective skills and opinions to project development, from inception to outcome. We have learned to have trust and respect for each other's abilities and insights, while maintaining the values of an organization that is steeped in tradition and mission. We have also learned that to achieve quality and evidence-based practice within an ambulatory setting, we have to embed these standards into essential work flows and record keeping. We have also learned that not all acute care processes are easily transferable to primary care. Each care setting has unique variables and resources that make transferring processes from one care setting to another very difficult. Also, when building resources to be used in primary care, one has to focus on a wellness perspective and not the acute care mindset of intervention and stabilization. This is a complete paradigm shift from the admission/discharge mentality of acute care. We have also learned that a clear vision is extremely important. Of equal importance are the processes, structures, and measurable outcomes that are requisite to deployment of any project.

CHANGING THE HEALTHCARE LANDSCAPE

As our Catholic ministries expand from a hospital centric organization to a continuum-based system, it will take the skills of all disciplines to effect this change and be successful in the next era of healthcare. We also need to shift our paradigm to thinking about a "wellness" model instead of a "sick" model but not just because payment reform will reward keeping populations healthy, rather than paying the costs for interventional and episodic care in acute care settings. This new model resonates with both nurses and physicians. It aligns with the reason we all went into healthcare. We want people to be well and to live their lives in as healthy a status as possible. Both physicians and nurses share unwavering commitment to the patient's well-being. We have unique and different leadership qualities that complement each other.

Most leaders need a range of leadership behaviors to be truly effective. Dyad leadership provides a vehicle for deploying a complementary range of leadership behaviors, because two individuals contribute to that range. The model allows each member of the dyad to learn from the other and to become truly transformational leaders in the process.

Healthcare, now and in the future, will be a team sport. Nurses, doctors, administrators, and patients will need to work together to truly improve health. Dyad leadership can help us model these desirable behaviors in our respective organizations. Dyads can be an example of the value of teamwork to our doctors and nurses at the point of care. When we work together as a team, we add up to so much more than merely the sum of the components of the team.

REFERENCES

1. Klasko, S., & Shea, G. (1999). *The phantom stethoscope*. Franklin, TN: Hillsboro Press.
2. Arndt, M., & Bigelow, B. (2007). Hospital administration in the early 1900s: Visions for the future and the reality of daily practice. *Journal of Healthcare Management, 52*(1): 34–37.
3. Khurana, R., Nohria, N., & Penrice, D. (February 21, 2005). Is business management a profession? *Working Knowledge*. Harvard Business School. Retrieved from http://hbswk.hbs.edu/item/4650.html
4. Thompson, A. A., & Strickland, A. J. (1999). *Strategic management: Concepts and cases*. Boston, MA: Irwin McGraw-Hill.
5. Maxwell, J. (2008). *Teamwork 101: What every leader needs to know*. Nashville, TN: Thomas Nelson.
6. Zismer, D. K., & Brueggeman, J. (2010). Examining the dyad as a management model in integrated health systems. *Physician Executive, 36*(1): 14–19.
7. Corporate author. (November 1, 2008). From volume to value; transforming healthcare payment and delivery systems. *Research and publications*. Princeton, New Jersey: Robert Wood Johnson Foundation.
8. Main, T., & Slywotzky, A. (2012). *The volume-to-value revolution: Rebuilding the DNA of health from the patient in*. New York: Oliver Wyman Group.
9. Goodall, A. (July 21, 2011). Physician-leaders and hospital performance: Is there an association? *VOX, CEPR's Policy Portal: Research Based Policy Analysis and Commentary from Leading Economists. accessed at: http://www.voxeu.org/article/should-physicians-manage-hospitals*
10. Corporate author. (October 11, 2011) FAQ: Strategic Clinical Networks. *AHS Team Today and Tomorrow*. Edmonton, Alberta, Canada: Alberta Health Services.

Chapter 2

How Did We Get Here and What Do We Need to Get Out of Here?

The chief medical officer in our Dyad partnership (Steve) didn't plan a career in management when he went to medical school. He didn't expect to need to develop formal leadership skills, except, maybe, those needed to ensure a smooth operation in his clinical office. He discovered that his career wasn't exactly what he trained for when his first position out of a family practice residency included duties as the medical director of a Community Health Center in the New England area. In addition to his office practice of medicine, he found himself with responsibilities that included federal submission of quality paperwork, evaluation of clinical performance at the Health Center (every third weekend), and sole coverage of a 45-bed inpatient facility 30 miles from the office! His duties included primary care, obstetrics, pediatrics, and emergency medicine. He made hospital inpatient rounding that included care in an intensive care unit. Patient care circumstances frequently made his presence necessary in multiple areas of the hospital as the covering physician.

Within a matter of weeks of arriving in his new practice location, it became clear that neither medical school nor residency training curriculum covered the management and leadership skills required to appropriately delegate, create patient-centered care teams, defer care based on triage, and balance the needs of patients through use of the skills and competency of the staff assembled to care for them. He had experienced no education on the business and paperwork side of healthcare. It also became abundantly obvious that there wasn't enough time for one person to manage both direct care and operations.

The physician was appropriately overwhelmed and unable to rely on education or experience to address all of the patient clinical needs and the supervisory responsibilities of management. The work could only be done with an organized team in which nurses worked at the top of their licenses and administrative personnel took on the accountability for operations. Only teamwork and division of labor made it possible for the Community Health Center to function and fulfill its mission. Different members of the team possessed different skills, and often, none really understood what the others did. There were communication and interpersonal challenges as a result. The team made this system work, but even then, the physician thought that there had to be a better way.

As a microcosm of the national healthcare scene, this young doctor's personal experience led him to examine the phenomena of the parallel but separate professional development of nurses, physicians, and administrators. He realized that the complex set of isolated business relationships had the potential to impair the effectiveness of any one of the participants in their short- and long-term roles. In addition, he noted that frustration and misunderstandings occurred between well-meaning team members, even though each thought he or she was doing what was right for patients and the organization. Over the course of his career, the physician learned that his experience was viewed through the lens of a professional trained within his own medical silo. Part of his personal growth was realizing that other team members also had their own lenses in place when they worked in a group.

Somehow, healthcare professionals have managed to coexist in a conglomeration of care sites with business objectives that don't always match. Hospitals have needed physicians to supply them with customers (patients). Physicians have needed hospitals as workshops that could provide 24-hour nursing care and that could afford new technology. Hospitals depended on nurses to provide that care, just as the physicians did. Nurses depended on hospitals as places of employment and on physicians to provide the medical portion of care. In spite of all of this mutual dependency, the relationship has been uneasy. Sometimes it seems like we are speaking different languages, and, in a way, that's true. It seems to clinicians that healthcare administrators have a "clinical competence gap." For their part, executives occasionally complain that clinicians simply do not understand realities of healthcare as a business. The challenges in today's environment dictate an urgent need to develop stronger understanding between clinical and administrative leaders.

Getting to a new relationship requires knowledge about how we got to the current state of affairs. Some answers to this lie with the development of our professions, including the following:

▶ Physician skill and competency training following the Flexner report of 1912
▶ Modern nursing training and development originating in the Florence Nightingale era of the 19th century
▶ The evolution of the fairly new profession of hospital administration
▶ Financial reimbursement models

The parallel development of physician education, nursing education, and hospital administrator education is a significant factor in why very different ways of thinking have led to difficulties in understanding each other.

MEDICAL STAFF HISTORICAL DEVELOPMENT AND THE IMPACT OF THE FLEXNER REPORT

In 1910, Abraham Flexner published his now famous review of medical education in the United States. He lambasted the variation in quality and educational content of the more than 500 medical schools of various sizes and diversity. As a result, more than a third of the studied colleges were closed, because of what the report said was suboptimal medical education. This was good for the development of the medical profession and for the patients who would receive medical care from better prepared practitioners. On the flip side, Flexner's lack of knowledge in medical practice and his endearment for the German educational model resulted in recommendations for medical education that created a foundation for American medicine based upon scientific research and education. Some physicians point to this change as the beginning of an era where the patient–physician relationship took on less importance to their healing bond. The eminent physician, according to these educational tracks, was one who did research, spent little time in educational pursuit, and approached patients as subjects serving medical, academic, and research interests, rather than being the center of a "beneficent healing" relationship. The model for care that came out of Flexner's report mirrored programs at Johns Hopkins (Flexner's alma mater) and Yale (1).

According to T. Duffy, of Yale, this "single model of medical education required large sums to support the scientific focus at its core." While no one could object to medicine becoming more scientific, Sir William Osler bemoaned that "a generation of clinical prigs would be created; individuals who were removed from the realities and messy details of their patient's lives." Osler believed that the Flexnerians (those who believed as Flexner did) had their priorities wrong because they situated the advancement of knowledge as the overriding aspiration of the academic physician. Osler placed the welfare of patients and the education of students as more important priorities, although he reverenced the "centrality of scientific knowledge in that regard" (2).

This standardization of scientific research, along with academic and research training, affected the development of the medical educational process. Case studies became the core of mortality and morbidity conferences, as educational discourse for professors, students, fellows, and residents. Diagnostic pathways and differential diagnosis, diagnostic tools, procedure techniques, and literature reviews became the definitions of the informed and educated clinician.

Epidemiological and population health implications, including costs for evaluative workups in pursuit of differentials, never entered the realm of these conferences, even peripherally. The patient herself represented an aggregate of symptoms in this process, which was a sterile depiction of a body to be healed and cared for.

Physicians were educated to be identifiers of problems, with a mission to fix the problems they found.

As medical education and research foundations changed, hospitals implemented formal medical staff structures. As early as 1910, numerous academic centers created leadership responsibility roles, predominately led by a chair or chief of service. The structure supported research and education while further segmenting the staff through medical professional competition for residents, dollars, and resources. Community hospitals duplicated these structures. With the advent of government payment for hospital services in the 1960s, the medical staff, complete with this formalized structure, became a regulatory requirement for participation in Medicare and Medicaid programs. The responsibility for quality was delegated by hospital boards to the medical staff structure. Unfortunately, many of these delegations failed to include a quality role and responsibility for nursing management or administration.

The organizational management and operational inefficiency of the medical staff structure have partly been to blame for the less than optimal quality of peer review, the cost and complications associated for patient care, and the inability to create multidisciplinary teams of physicians, nurses, administrators, and other clinicians in the care of the patient. Peer review is frequently disconnected from quality improvement committee work. Often, when deficits in patient care are present outside of the medical staff, there are few formal connections so that the medical staff can work with colleagues to make improvement interventions. As a result, many quality improvement or root cause analyses, as well as requests for peer review, fall into a chasm of inefficiency and indeterminism.

NURSING STAFF HISTORICAL DEVELOPMENT

Florence Nightingale is widely recognized as the founder of modern nursing (although both Catholic and Protestant religious orders of women were among her teachers in care of the sick). In her *Notes on Nursing*, published in 1859, Nightingale clearly separated the practice of nursing from the practice of medicine. She stated, "every day sanitary knowledge or the knowledge of nursing, or in other words, of how to put the constitution in such a state as that it will have no disease, or that it will recover from disease, takes a higher place (in professional nursing). It is recognized as the knowledge that everyone ought to have, *distinct from medical knowledge*, which only a profession can have" (3).

Nightingale was not the only leader who insisted that nursing is a separate profession from medicine. Sarah Hale, a nonnurse editor of a popular 19th century women's magazine, *Godey's Ladies Book and Magazine*, wrote, "there can be no doubt that the duties of the sick nurse, to be properly performed, require an education and training, little, if at all, inferior to those possessed by those of the medical profession … every medical college should have a course of study adapted for ladies who desire to qualify for the profession of nurse. Graduate nurses would be as much above ordinary nurses of the present day as the professional surgeon is above the barber-surgeon of the last century" (4). Levinia Lloyd Dock, who wrote some of the earliest professional nursing text books, was another early advocate for nursing to be a separate but equal profession to medicine (5).

Other nurse leaders have felt strongly that nurses and physicians should be educated separately. As a consequence, the development of the nursing profession within hospitals took a path along areas such as pain and pain relief, comforting, infection and other disease prevention, fall and complication reduction, as well as physical care. University education of nurses is partially about the science and evidence behind effective hands-on care of those who are injured or ill. It is also largely based on the maintenance of the highest possible physical, emotional, and spiritual health attainable *for the individual.* In other words, nursing goals for even a terminal patient include helping him to be as physically, emotionally, and spiritually healthy as *possible* even though there will be no cure. Nurses have been trained to be systems thinkers, by looking at the human not only as a "whole" but as part of a larger environmental system that a person interacts with. While the profession has many theories of nursing (each one vigorously defended by its academic proponents), all of these sets of ideas about what nursing is (and should be) include the need for holistic views of people. They also emphasize the importance of keeping individuals and families well, rather than discovering how to heal them when they become sick. For a variety of reasons, both individual and societal, theories are not always put into practice by every member of a profession. However, a number of notable nurses have demonstrated practices that have either informed or followed these tenets of holistic and "wellness" care. For example, Mary Breckenridge founded the Kentucky Frontier Nursing Service (KFNS) in 1925, which started out as a midwife service but was organized later as a public health service. KFNS district nurses were responsible for the total health of populations within a geographical grid. They contacted physicians for complicated cases when members of the "community" did get sick (6).

Lillian Wald, another American nurse, has been recognized as the founder of public health. She insisted that, "patients must have direct access to nurses and nurses must have direct access to patients without the intervention of medical men." Her work was again much broader than was hospital care. She believed that health and nursing, in order to be holistic, included building playgrounds, helping people find employment, preventing under age children from working, and assisting new immigrants become part of the society. She believed that schools were an important place for health habits to be taught and founded public school nursing in 1902 (7).

The unintended consequences of Nightingale's and others' distinct professional creation separate from "medical" knowledge has probably contributed to nursing and medical disparate approaches to patient care. In addition, the historical gender difference between the two professions has contributed to different approaches to patient care as well as friction between the two groups.

Until recent times, physicians have predominantly been male, while nurses have mostly been female. (In fact, women were barred from "modern" medical schools until Elizabeth Blackwell was admitted to Geneva Medical College in 1847. When she graduated, she couldn't obtain a hospital staff appointment and had to establish her own women's infirmary and medical college). While a growing number of men have chosen nursing as a career, nurse historian M. Patricia Donahue points out that "the history of nursing is essentially the story of women." Women's lack of power in society translated to resistance against their autonomy or leadership in hospitals. Lavinia Dock believed that "male dominance in the health field was the major problem confronting the nursing profession" (6). Nurse historians credit gender discrimination (women couldn't even vote until 1920) and politics with the eventual laws and regulations that limited much of nursing practice. Gender politics is not a comfortable conversation for many people, but we can't have an honest discussion about the history of interprofessional relationships and the parallel development of each profession without acknowledging the influence gender has played on how each evolved.

In spite of professional differences and frictions (some of which continue today), physicians and nurses have historically (and continue to) work closely together. In 1875, the first annual report of St. Catherine's General and Marine Hospital in Ontario, Canada, noted, "the vocation of nursing goes hand in hand with that of the physician and surgeon, and they are absolutely indispensable to each other" (8).

HOSPITAL ADMINISTRATION DEVELOPMENT

The formal history of Hospital Administration as a distinct profession is much shorter than those of medicine and nursing. Unlike Medicine, historically practiced by men, *or* nursing, historically practiced by women, this field *was* predominately female and clinical until the profession was "masculinized."

Early hospital administrators were called superintendents. The majority were nurses who took on leadership positions. Others were physicians (mostly in academic institutions) and Catholic sisters. The first formal hospital administration educational program, in health economies, was established at Columbia Teachers College in 1900. It was developed at the urging of superintendents seeking to add business acumen to their nursing knowledge.

In 1929, the book, *Hospital Administration a Career: The Need for Trained Executives for a Billion Dollar Business, and How They May Be Trained*, was published. The author suggested a 2-year graduate curriculum for hospital executives to include accounting, statistics, management, economics, social sciences, history of hospitals, business policy, public health, and labor relations (9). In 1934, the University of Chicago established the first graduate program in hospital administration. Michael Davis, the aforementioned author, was named to lead the program. In the 1940s, 8 other universities began to offer this degree, with 9 more in the 1950s and 15 additional programs in the 1960s.

Margarete Arndt, who teaches at the Clark University Graduate School of Management in Worcester, Massachusetts, has extensively studied the evolution of hospital administration. She reports that once the MHA programs were established, hospitals who wanted educated administrators could only hire men because the university graduate programs admitted *virtually no female students* (10).

Arndt also described the problems faced by female hospital superintendents before the move to leadership by men educated in business. They included less-than-ideal relationships with physicians, the need to find funds for new technology, and the increasing costs of healthcare, which alarmed community businessmen (11). These business leaders, from outside healthcare, felt that if businessmen educated to lead hospitals were put in charge, they would be able to solve the problems, particularly the rising costs of providing care. Unfortunately, although business skills are very important to healthcare organizations, the problems listed in the early 1900s have not been solved and have become even bigger challenges. Healthcare is more complex than non–healthcare business leaders realized. Simply replacing female clinicians with male executives did not solve the problems.

Most healthcare executives serving today in hospital system CEO or COO roles pursued the MHA or MBA in healthcare graduate education. Current curricula are diverse, multidisciplinary, and consistent with a balanced management program (Display 2-1).

The different cultural conditioning of physicians and administrators discussed in Chapter 1 can be understood more clearly when the histories of medicine, nursing,

---

Display 2-1 **Example of Master of Health Administration Curriculum**

Required core courses

    Intersectoral Leadership (PPD 500)
    Economics for Policy, Planning and Development (PPD 501a)
    Problems and Issues in the Health Field (PPD 509)
    Financial Management of Health Services (PPD 510a)
    Health Information Systems (PPD 511)
    Legal Issues in Healthcare Delivery (PPD 513)
    Economic Concepts Applied to Health (PPD 514)
    Strategic Management of Health Organizations (PPD 515)
    Financial Accounting for Healthcare Organizations (PPD 516)
    Concepts and Practices in Managing Healthcare Organizations (PPD 517)
    Quality of Care Concepts (PPD 518)
    Human Behavior in Public Organizations (PPD 545)
    Modeling and Operations Research (PPD 557)

From the University of Southern California Sol Price School of Public Policy. (http://priceschool.usc.edu/programs/masters/mha/curriculum/)

and hospital administration are explored. Of course, this trio of professionals is not the only healthcare groups with their own cultures. Various specialties bring even more complexity to the caregiving world. Some identify more closely with Medicine (such as radiology technicians); some have evolved and then separated from nursing (such as respiratory therapy); some are considered subcultures of administration (such as finance). Those that are branches of business often know very little about the day-to-day work challenges of the clinicians. To complicate matters, physicians and nurses who are promoted into management are given leadership positions based primarily on success as clinicians. Their caregiving skills do not translate directly into the complex and broad world of business management.

An excellent nurse has often been placed in a unit management positions with little or no education in finance, leadership, or even the organization's mission. The newly appointed physician medical director, well respected by colleagues, assumes a position that includes operational responsibilities for which she knows little or nothing. Without appropriate education, her default position within the leadership milieu is to defend the medical staff's need for autonomy! Given responsibility for "quality," she may place narrow parameters around safety and quality based on her medical experience only. In other words, she may have no context for understanding the importance of efficiency, reduction in variation, systems thinking, and relationship management as they relate to her accountabilities.

We *are* increasing the number of clinical leaders, particularly physicians, into the formal management ranks. Whether they are promoted as "single" leaders, as Dyad partners, or in some other team leadership structure, there must be purposeful examination of their knowledge gaps. There must also be plans for education to fill these gaps.

We feel the need to make an important point here: Sometimes conversations among administrators seem to take on a flavor of superiority when discussing clinician ignorance of business or management. Since they are "moving into" management (a different culture), clinicians are the one with knowledge deficits. Professional executives are not transferring to clinical roles, so may believe they have no need for clinical education. It's important to remember that all groups have gaps in understanding of others. Everyone needs to learn new things if we are to become a high-functioning team. If that wasn't true, we wouldn't be in the situation we are today—scrambling to figure out new relationships *and management models* that will make us successful in the next era of healthcare.

An outsider observing the uneasy relationships among healthcare professionals would be justified in asking, "How have you been able to exist with these dysfunctional relationships for so long?" (The same question is posed by people observing unhealthy relationships within families. They can't comprehend why physically abused partners remain in marriage; emotionally abused children remain attached to the parents who abuse them; spouses support or even abet the behavior of alcoholic husbands or wives.) Why do relationships continue when they are uncomfortable, stressful, and where distrust is high? How do groups with what seems to be poor esteem for others continue to work together and accomplish anything, particularly when members of the group aren't even family (if "family" in the business world can be stretched to mean those who are all employed by the same organization)?

Dysfunctional relationships continue for a variety of reasons, such as:

▶ An inability to visualize or imagine any different way of relating
▶ An inability to figure out how to change or extricate oneself from the relationship
▶ Codependency
▶ Perceived or real financial dependencies

While some brilliant thinkers have visualized better systems, as a country and as an industry, we've been unable (so far) to extricate ourselves from what we have become. We've maintained our fragmented, multicultural systems because we've been dependent on each other to practice our various professions. That dependence has been strengthened by regulatory and reimbursement systems. Complicating this dependency has been the ability of one group (medical doctors) to control where the customers (patients) are admitted for care, practice his craft (and direct patients) at multiple competing hospitals, and even own or control organizations that compete with the hospital for certain types of care or services.

Our complicated financial relationships have changed over time. The first hospitals were "cash" businesses that relied a great deal on philanthropy. Today, very few people pay 100% for their care. The biggest payer category is government (national and state), followed by private insurance companies. The Centers for Medicare and Medicaid Services (CMS), formerly known as the Healthcare Financing Administration (HCFA), is a major promulgator of regulations around how healthcare entities are paid. Frequently, private insurers mimic CMS practices and requirements. Table 2-1 provides a brief history of hospital payment system and some of the ramification of that evolution.

When payment models have changed, healthcare providers (hospitals, private physicians, and others) have adjusted their practices to maximize payments *like any rational business would do*. The regulatory "strings" that come with payments have contributed to both interdependencies among providers *and* areas of friction and competition.

The next era is bringing more payment reform. We are moving away from fee-for-service to outcome-based payment systems. Hospitals and physicians will be paid for value (lower cost for high quality) rather than volume (number of patients, visits, interventions, diagnostic tests, etc.). Instead of being reimbursed for episodic interventions (mostly sick care), it's envisioned that we'll be paid as a system for care provided to defined populations. If the future unfolds as planned (and none of us can guarantee that!), keeping people well will be more profitable than treating them when they are sick. Charges for services will become more transparent to customers

Table 2-1   History and Evolution of Hospital Payment Systems

When (Time Period)	What (New Payment Systems)	How (System Worked)	Ramifications
Prior to 1966	Fee for service	Most individuals and insurance companies paid charges to hospitals and physicians Charges were not regulated Some charity care was provided	Many people died without care because they could not afford it
1966	Medicare (for older individuals) and Medicaid (for the poor) programs initiated	Health services for older people and the poor were paid by government Medicare became the largest payer for most hospitals and other providers Hospitals were required by law to take part in programs and were required to accept the payment rates provided. Medicare originally reimbursed hospitals for "reasonable costs" Physicians were required to participate in Medicare but did not have to accept payment rate. Physicians were not required to participate in Medicaid. Medicare originally paid physicians reasonable and customary charges, based on location	With cost reimbursement, higher costs led to higher revenues Reducing costs of care led to lower revenues. There was little incentive to reduce costs Providers learned to maximize Medicare revenues by allocating overhead costs among revenue-producing departments and utilizing most favorable statistics to split overhead allocations between Medicare and other payers
1970s	Nongovernmental payers begin trying to control their healthcare costs	Competitive healthcare bidding by business coalitions was initiated Managed care plans and Health Maintenance Organizations were started Per Diem and per case payments became a practice	Healthcare organizations offered discounts
1982	TEFRA (The Tax Equity and Fiscal Responsibility Act) implemented	Per Diem limits were imposed; the cost per patient day was reimbursed only to the per diem rate limits for routine and intensive nursing care Payments could still be increased by provision of other ancillary services (such as physical therapy)	Some patient care previously performed by nurses was transferred to ancillary departments Nursing care was emphasized as a major *cost* rather than revenue enhancer

Table 2-1	History and Evolution of Hospital Payment Systems (*Continued*)		
When (Time Period)	**What (New Payment Systems)**	**How (System Worked)**	**Ramifications**
1983	PPS (The Prospective Payment System) announced as Medicare's new inpatient payment methodology	Each Medicare inpatient was classified into one DRG (Diagnostic Related Group) as part of a per case payment rate. Payment rates for inpatient services were established in advance of care. PPS was phased in over 4 y	Hospitals treating more complex DRGs were paid more than those providing less complex care (as determined by case mix)
			If a hospital kept costs lower than payment rate, it kept the "profit." If hospital costs were higher than the rate, the hospital lost money
			Hospitals were incentivized to reduce costs, through a reduction of length of stay, reduction of ancillary use, and control of nursing care costs
			Hospitals "cost shifted" by increasing charges to the fee-for-service payers (private insurance and individuals)
1983–1997	PPS refined every year. Nongovernment payers continued to seek relief from high healthcare costs. Some capitation payment plans implemented	Some insurance companies adopted DRG-based payment rates. Managed Care Plans contracted with providers to care for defined populations, paying a monthly premium per person	Providers continued to try controlling costs per patient but had no incentive to reduce the number of inpatients. (Revenues were driven by volume)
			Because of the incentive to avoid unnecessary utilization of care, overall health costs *should* have been reduced
1997	Balanced Budget Act of 1997	A plan implemented to limit funding for Medicare and Medicaid. More cost controls were implemented by government and others; these include preapproval for healthcare services, limits on lengths of stay, long-term contracts with locked-in payment rates	The *rate* of increase in funding was cut, not the actual funding so overall cost of Medicare and Medicaid continued to rise
			Hospitals attempted to diversify, merge, and develop integrated systems

(Continued)

Table 2-1	History and Evolution of Hospital Payment Systems (*Continued*)		
When (Time Period)	What (New Payment Systems)	How (System Worked)	Ramifications
2010	The Patient Protection and Affordable Care Act (ACA)	The ACA protected rights to insurance for those with preexisting conditions Established minimum standards for health insurance policies Established an individual mandate to maintain health insurance Restructured payment (moving to bundled payments) Established an employer mandate for employee healthcare Expanded Medicaid eligibility	Hospitals have begun pursuing clinically integrated networks, while increasing partnerships with physicians and others Healthcare organizations have begun establishing wellness programs for staff and customers Health systems are employing more physicians

Adapted from Whetsell, G. (1999). The history and evolution of hospital payment systems: How did we get here? Nursing Administration Quarterly, 23(4), 1–15.

(who will become more and more the actual users of healthcare and payers). Some leaders believe charges will become much more regulated. (So we won't find, e.g., the "list price" for an appendectomy ranging from $1529 to $183,000 in the same community.) (12) Bundled payments (that all providers within an integrated network *share*) will become the common way to pay for healthcare.

Healthcare systems have already begun to respond to these payment changes as we always have—*as rational economic entities*. We'll do what we need to be paid for our services. *This time*, we believe incremental tweaking won't be enough to change what must be changed if we are to exist through the coming decades.

Nobody knows with certainty what a reformed healthcare system will eventually become. Most of us are convinced we must try new models, in which clinicians and business leaders work closer together to implement coordinated systems. The Dyad leadership model is one strategy to work toward this future.

DYADS AND MANAGEMENT THEORY

The emergence of Dyads is conceived as a way to manage that will help align the clinical and business side of healthcare. It might also contribute to development of a management theory centered on shared formal leadership.

Bernard Bass, author of a book every graduate student of management should recognize (*The Bass Handbook of Leadership*), says that "good theories start from one idea or a small set of ideas." In developing them, "There is a convergence of several interests and activities at the same time … conventional wisdom may be revised or rebased. Research is restated in alternative ways. Established value judgments are challenged. Above all, to be good, theories need to be grounded in assumptions that fit the facts." In addition, he adds that in theory development, "Intuition and feelings supplement logical analysis" (13).

The development of leadership *shared* by *paired* managers from different professions is certainly one intuitive solution for bridging healthcare's cultural gaps, combining different skills and knowledge for greater problem solving and increasing the span of control and influence of leadership. Two can "cover more territory" than one. Is it also a model supported by previous research? Can it be grounded in assumptions that fit the facts?

Our interest in these questions isn't because we want to participate in an academic exercise. (We're a working-more-than-full-time CMO and CNO. We don't have time for academic exercises or esoteric research). Our purpose is to help organizations who are contemplating the Dyad model determine whether or not it's a good fit for them. Some might be tempted to say, "These are desperate times that call for desperate measures. Let's try it and see if it works." They might find the model intuitively appealing ("Why didn't we think of this before?") Or, they might believe that if other organizations are doing this, we should follow suit. ("If it's good enough for CHI, it's good enough for us!")

We believe healthcare systems should answer three major questions before embarking on a Dyad leadership model. Actually, they're the same questions for every system or process change: Why? What? and How? (After those are answered, of course, the Who? needs to be addressed as well.)

Each of these questions will be answered differently depending on the organization and the management issue to be addressed. (Although much of this book and interest in this model are around Dyads in which one partner is a physician, there are reasons to partner two nonphysician leaders.) The macro *"why,"* which we assume is predominant for most providers, is the need to align the business (operational) and medical (or clinical) sides of our organizations so we are better partners for the next era of healthcare. The *"what"* is an implementation of Dyad partnerships. The *"how"* is the subject threaded throughout this book, including real-life experiences shared in the Dyads-In-Action stories at the end of each chapter.

In this chapter, we are primarily concerned with the *"why."* Why are you considering this model? It's important that you have a problem or issue you really believe will be better addressed by two coleaders rather than one. It cannot be because of a need to pander to the medical staff. ("Look, physicians! You are now in charge, so bring us your patients. You don't really have to do any managing.") It cannot be to manipulate. ("Let's get a doctor coleader in here to help us get those doctors to do what *we* want.") If those are the underlying reasons for implementing Dyads, they won't succeed.

It *is* true that members of a culture identify with, communicate better with, and trust sooner, someone from their own culture. There is credibility between people who have shared socialization. For clinicians, this is even truer between the subcultures known as "specialists." Surgeons mostly identify only with other surgeons, for example. A physician dyad member from a specialty that matches her leadership with doctors from the *same* specialty is a smart hire. For example, an orthopedic surgeon hired as the Dyad physician for the orthopedic service line makes more sense than an ophthalmologist or a general surgeon even though all are physicians who practice surgery.

The "*why*" for implementing Dyads must include the need to improve value for the organizations. Value is both quality (including safety) and financial success. In addition, organizations will only succeed in bringing cultures together when the objective is a true *partnership* or uniting of missions and goals. In other words, the Dyad leads a "merger" not a "takeover" of another specialty.

Dyad leadership is not easy. It requires massive change. The successful Dyads, and organizations who implement them, believe in its promise as a true shared leadership. We feel it is the right thing to do in preparation for the next era of healthcare. We also believe that an examination of management theories and research provides some support for the implementation and development of this type of leadership for healthcare.

Dyads are put in place largely (at least this is *our* assumption) to help bridge the cultural differences between business or operational leaders and clinical leaders. They are contemplated by leaders who believe, as early management educator Chester Barnard did, that "cooperation is essential for an organization's survival" (14). Their emergence in healthcare, as we are entering an era when we must bring competitive groups together, is validated by research on who can influence others.

Robert Cialdini's work on influence stresses that "we most prefer to say yes to requests from people we know and like" (15). Who are we most inclined to like? Those who are most similar to us! According to research, including the work of D. Byrne, we like people who share our opinions, personalities, backgrounds, and lifestyle (16). We are most inclined to like (and therefore be influenced by) leaders from our own professional cultures. This is as true for nurses and hospital executives, as it is for physicians. Partnered leaders from different professional backgrounds will have more influences on members of their culture and can help bring their constituents into a new multidisciplinary group, which is better able to cooperate.

Of course, this presumes that the Dyad leaders themselves are able to straddle the gap between two cultures. Can, for example, a strong, respected clinician maintain credibility with his or her medical colleagues while "serving" the goals of a healthcare organization? (This question brings to mind the suit vs. coat discussion in Chapter 1.) Some management research indicates that this *is* possible and that the most successful leaders are both competent in the eyes of *their* supervisors *and* are able to fulfill the expectations of those they lead (17). In fact, as Bass points out "potential conflict may be reduced, avoided, and even resolved because people, who are *members of both groups*, which have conflicting interests, may consider themselves *loyal to both*" (13). In other words, clinicians who have been socialized in one culture *can* learn to be part of another culture and to support both. When they do this, they help both groups cooperate.

Nurse executives have long demonstrated this ability. They balance the organization's business (financial) needs with quality and safety and the system's goals with *patient and caregiver* needs. Physician executives are now being asked to do this, too. Because their relationship and culture have been less aligned with the hospital, there appears to be more trepidation about how well they will be able to do this (Display 2-2).

We already know physicians who are successfully bridging the gap between the clinician and administrative world. We believe many more can, and will, do this with appropriate management models in place, as well as careful hiring of individuals who will be asked to adopt a second culture.

Who are appropriate individuals? Some leaders may make the mistake of assuming that they are simply those clinicians who have gone back to school to obtain business education. A growing number of physicians and nurses are obtaining MBAs and MHAs. This business education is wonderful for clinicians and should improve their understanding of the "business tools" side of healthcare leadership. They will be better able to communicate in the language of business and probably have increased expertise in the numerous

---

Display 2-2 **A Cultural Phenomenon: Are Physicians Really That Different from Everyone Else?**

There are differences in professional cultures, which need to be understood as we learn to work more closely together. However, we hypothesize some differences may be exaggerated. The possibility that some people believe executives think physicians and others are not psychologically similar was brought home to us recently.

Our company hired an expert (from a well-known consulting firm) for education purported to help us better understand physicians as they migrate into employee and employed leadership positions. His presentation title, power point slides, and words all implied that he was imparting information based on research specific to medical doctors. We heard from him that physicians:

1. Must have basic safety needs met before they can become self-actualized.
2. Are not motivated by money. While they are dissatisfied if their pay is not as high as they believe it should be, more money will not motivate them to become team players. They can only be motivated if they feel they are achieving something important.
3. Have four separate areas of self-knowledge. They have traits of which they (and others) are unaware; information about themselves that they know about but others don't; traits people see in them of which they're blind; and areas where both they and others are conscious of their traits.
4. Desire to be self-directed and want to exercise their own initiative and responsibility. (Hospitals want to structure physician's roles and control their actions in order to meet hospital objectives. This causes conflict between physicians and hospitals.)

As each power point displayed on screen, the speaker stated, "Research has shown that physicians … (followed by the points above)." Never was a particular physician-centric study cited.

(Continued)

Unfortunately, neither was attribution given to any theorist or researcher, other than recognition that Abraham Maslow is identified with Point 1. We recognized other people's work though the following:

#1 is the work of Abraham Maslow and his "Hierarchy of Needs" theory (18).

#2 sounds suspiciously like Frederick Herzberg's Two Factor Hygiene and Motivation theory, in which money (and other work factors) must be present to keep a worker satisfied but only achievement, recognition, growth, and interest in the job motivates him to do more (or change) (19).

#3 is a description of the Johari window developed by Joseph Luft and Harrington Ingham (that's where "Johari" comes from—their first names). It's been widely used to help people from all walks of life understand their relationships, both with themselves and others. Labeled by Luft and Ingham as "Quadrants", the first (as listed by our speaker) is called to the "Unknown," the second is the "Façade," the third is the "Blindspot," and the fourth is the "Open Arena" (20).

#4 Chris Argyris put forward this theory (the Maturity–Immaturity theory) over 50 years ago! He saw a natural conflict between employees and organizations as a result of this difference in control needs (21).

After the presentation, we puzzled over what we had just heard. Aside from our incredulity that he didn't appear to think any of the executives in his audience would recognize classic management theories (with the exception of Maslow's work), the consultant's "class" left us curious. Why was the speaker hesitant to inform us about the authors of the theories he shared? Why did he appear to want us to believe there is a large body of research specific to the psychology of physicians, as if it differs from research on other employees? Did he believe that executives would not accept anything other than physician-specific behavioral research as credible when applied to medical doctors?

As we pondered these issues, we realized that each of us had been in multiple meetings or discussions in which individuals (both physicians and nonphysicians) *have* implied that they might believe the last point. They might not accept that research done with factory workers, office workers, or nonphysician leaders could be applied to medical staff members.

As more clinicians become employees and formal leaders, there will be opportunities for research on their behaviors and comparisons with other employees or leaders.

We may be proven right or wrong by these studies, but our belief is, that in spite of professional conditioning, we are more alike than different. Education and increased interprofessional understanding *will* bridge cultural gaps.

---

financial transactions of healthcare. However, business education isn't enough to ensure outstanding leadership performance by clinicians (or nonclinicians for that matter!) as we move into the next era of healthcare. If we agree that we are in need of *transformation*, as a system, we need to seek *transformative* leaders to populate our Dyads (Display 2-3).

Transformational leadership is practiced by leaders who create visions, shape values, and empower their colleagues to change. Since the 1970s, management researchers and theorists have studied the characteristics of these successful agents of transformative change (Display 2-4).

Much of the literature of transformational leadership contrasts this type of management with "transactional" leadership. Transactional leaders are described as managers who consider their relationships with subordinates or team members as

---

Display 2-3 **Researcher and Management Expert Descriptions of Transformative Leaders**

"A transforming leader raises other's level of consciousness about the value of goals and the importance of reaching them; gets followers to move beyond self-interest for the sake of the team, organization, or greater good; raises team member's needs from safety and security to self-actualization."

—Burnes, J. M. (22)

"Transforming leaders are optimistic."

—Berson, Y. (23)

"Transforming leaders are not bound by today's solutions and create visions of possibilities."

—Brown, D. (24)

"Transformational leaders practice individual consideration for each member of the team. They do this by "telling the truth with compassion, looking for others loving intentions, disagreeing with others without making them feel wrong, and recognizing contributions of each individual regardless of cultural differences.""

—Bracey, H.; Rosenbaum, J.; Sanford, A., et al. (25)

"They've been shown to raise consciousness of those around them while providing realistic but optimistic views of the future."

—Bennis, W.; Nanus, B. (26)

"They possess six transformational attributes: articulating a vision, providing an appropriate model, fostering acceptance of goals, setting high-performance expectations, providing support, and giving consideration to individuals."

—Podsakoff, P.; MacKenzie, S.; Moorman, R., et al. (27)

"They are inspirational networkers, encouragers of critical and strategic thinking, developers of potential, and are genuinely concerned about others, while being approachable, accessible, decisive, self-confident, honest, and trustworthy."

—Alimo-Metcalfe, B.; Alban-Metcalfe, A. (28)

"Charismatic leaders are likely to be transformational, but it is possible—although unlikely—to be transformational without being charismatic."

"Transformational leaders raise follower's level of maturity, ideals, and concerns for the well-being of others, the organization, and society."

"They stimulate others, think through problems, and teach the skills to do this. They help followers become "more innovative and creative" because they question assumptions and help the team look at old problems through new eyes."

"They clarify the mission, generate excitement about the work, and show empathy for others."

—Bass, B. (13)

"Transformational leaders articulate and use visions more than transactional leaders do."

—Judge, T.; Bono, J. (29)

(Continued)

"They have the motivation to lead, self-efficacy, and the capacity to relate to others."

—Popper, M.; Mayseless, O.; Castelnovo, O. (30)

"They are more likely to use rational discussion for upward influence rather than ingratiating behavior or strong emotion."

—Deluga, R.; Sousa, J. (31)

a continual series of transactions. Leaders and "followers" agree on objectives (or leaders solely determine objectives and communicate them). When these objectives are met, team members are rewarded. When they are not met, or standards are not followed, the leader metes out psychological or material "punishment."

Both types of leadership can be practiced for legitimate reasons even by the same individuals. There are situations when transactions meet the organization's needs—as when employed physicians are paid by RVUS (Relative Value Units), productivity, or quality standards. However, Bernard Bass, as a compiler of leadership research, points out, "Considerable evidence has accumulated on the greater effectiveness of transformational leadership of politicians, public officials, nonprofit agency leaders, religious leaders, educators, military officers, business managers, and *healthcare directors*" (13).

Transformational leaders ask others to transcend their self-interests for the good of the organization or society. Bringing together our disparate healthcare cultures will require all of us to put comfort with how things are now (or have been) second to a healthcare system that is better at keeping our communities healthy.

Transformational leaders encourage critical and strategic thinking. We'll need this as we undertake the next era's challenge of changing the healthcare system for the entire country!

Display 2-4 Competencies and Behaviors that Correlate Positively with Transformational Leaders

1. Superior cognitive ability or intelligence (Wofford, J.; Goodwin, V.) (32)
2. Good sense (or use of) humor (Avolio, B.; Howell, J.; Sosik, J.) (33)
3. Eloquence (persuasiveness and social sensitivity) (Bass, B.) (13)
4. Superior communication skills (Hater, J.; Bass, B.) (34)
5. Emotional intelligence (Dasborough, M.; Ashkanasy, N.) (35)
6. Intended focus and control (Shostrum, E.) (36)
7. Self-acceptance (Gibbons, T.) (37)
8. Hardness (Kobasa, S.; Maddi, S.; Kahn, S.) (38)
9. Optimism, positive thinking, feeling over thinking (Atwater, L.; Yammarino.) (39)
10. Risk taking (Hater, J.; Bass, B.) (34)
11. Awareness of own emotions (Ashkanasy, N.; Tse, B.) (40)

Transformational leaders develop the potential of team members and genuinely care about individuals. Clinicians, as well as business leaders, need this kind of support to make the kind of change they will personally need to make.

Just as we espouse using clinically evidence-based practices for patient care, it certainly seems we should seek Dyad leaders with either a track record or ability to develop transformational leadership. In Chapter 7, we present methods for identifying who these leaders are. Their job will be to help transform the organization while many must simultaneously transform *themselves* from membership in a single clinical culture to participation in a dual culture (clinical and system), while learning to colead with a Dyad partner!

It can be done. If you understand our healthcare multicultural history and believe we need to bridge cultural gaps in order to thrive in the future, you are right to consider Dyad management for yourself or your organization.

CHAPTER SUMMARY

As we move into the next era of healthcare, it's helpful to review a few points in the history of our professions. This can help us better understand why clinicians (particularly physicians and nurses) and hospital executives have developed differing views of healthcare. For leaders considering the Dyad model, we've also presented a rational for why this type of leadership can help move us into the future if we choose the right Dyad partners. We believe these new leaders need to be transformational.

Dyads in Action

LEVERAGING OUR SKILLS FOR THE NEXT ERA
Deborah D. Hood and Dax Kurbegov

Service lines are becoming more common as an infrastructure for business and quality provision of a healthcare system's care. We manage a national oncology service line (NOSL) as a Dyad. Here is our story from the MBA-educated business partner (Deb) perspective and the physician partner (Dax) viewpoint:

MBA: The NOSL was created as an outgrowth of Catholic Health Initiatives' (CHI's) participation in the National Cancer Institute's Community Cancer Centers Program (NCCCP) at the end of 2009. The NCCCP was a pilot program that started in 2007 with the participation of five CHI cancer centers. CHI found this program to be invaluable to the participating cancer centers and wanted to internally extend these learnings to more of their sites.

One of the recommendations that came from the NCCCP was to have full-time physician leadership at participating sites—something that none of the original pilot sites had. Community cancer centers typically have medical directors who provide clinical guidance ranging from a few hours per month to 0.25 FTE, but very few utilize full-time physician leaders. In the case of CHI, this physician leadership came from a practicing MD who dedicated 0.25 FTE to CHI for national leadership of the NCCCP and 0.25 FTE as medical director at one of CHI's participating cancer centers. This arrangement was in place from 2007 to 2010, but it was particularly difficult for this surgeon to operate and manage surgical patients 50% of the time, while working in an administrative capacity for two different entities the remaining 50%. After the launch of the NOSL, this balancing act proved even more difficult. When the surgeon decided to take another position out of the area, CHI began to consider other alternatives.

When it was implemented, the National Oncology Service consisted of 10 cancer centers in 8 states, 1 director (me), and an administrative assistant. We received physician guidance through a clinical advisory board of 8 to 10 physician leaders from the system's markets. They met once a month. This arrangement seemed workable between 2010 and 2012, while the service line grew in size and participation. Physician champions from each site were enlisted for all major initiatives. CHI was lucky to have experienced and knowledgeable physicians from all disciplines who were willing to volunteer their time to champion new programs, such as our Breast and Lung Centers of Excellence. There were many others who joined various work groups to develop policies or adopt new techniques and technology, such as universal screening of colorectal cancers for Lynch syndrome. All of these were valuable contributions but typically involved a defined issue. There was no consistent medical leader considering long-range strategies and overall philosophies of care. As the service line matured, it became evident that an even broader array of clinical standardization and quality initiatives required greater physician involvement on a daily basis.

It became clear that the service line needed a physician as part of our daily leadership. There was a lot of work to be done and we were making good progress, but as time went on, we seemed to be calling for medical leadership more and more from the same group of physicians. I was facilitating physician work groups, but I certainly didn't have the clinical expertise or the inside knowledge to best address difficult, new areas that we were considering. Something was missing and the more our team looked at our work, the more we realized we needed a physician as part of our team.

CHI already had a dyad partnership at the national level with our CMO and CNO. So we considered: Why not utilize this model in the service line? CHI leadership was supportive of the concept, but the first question raised was whether or not we really needed a full-time physician. Some leaders were concerned that a physician responsible for a service line would need to maintain clinical expertise in order to be relevant and respected by peer oncology providers. Shouldn't the candidate be expected to practice some of the time and thus maintain his or her licensure? During these discussions, I argued that part-time physician support could no longer be effective for a national service line of our size. During my career, I'd already seen the challenges part-time medical directorships posed for oncologists who tried to practice clinically and also provide administrative leadership. It was very difficult for these leaders to compartmentalize their work day with administrative duties when they were caring for very sick patients. This is a challenge at the community cancer center level, but it becomes an even greater challenge at the national level. Is it fair for a surgeon to operate on a patient and then turn that patient over to his or her partner for follow-up care because he or she needs to get on a plane the next day for a meeting in one of our markets? The issue is equally problematic for a radiation or medical oncologist. Patients who are undergoing treatment for a life-threatening illness want their doctor to be there for them.

There were multiple times that physician champions facilitating a national meeting had to break away from the discussion to deal with an acute patient care issue. Putting the patient first is absolutely the right priority, but we needed someone whose role was to focus completely on the leadership side of cancer. I realized that it would be a challenge for physicians to stop practicing and still maintain their clinical expertise. In fact, all the physician candidates for the new position expressed this same concern. CHI was open to looking at opportunities to develop a solution with our final candidate for my full-time Dyad partner. However, in the year since Dax joined us, no workable solution for staying current in practice while leading the service line has been found, other than attendance at national clinical conferences. To date, the concern about maintaining clinical expertise for our nonpracticing physician leader has not been an issue. He is effective as a service line leader without current patient care practice.

By mid-2012, CHI leadership approved this full-time Dyad leadership approach and posted a position for a 1.0 FTE Physician Vice President for the NOSL who would partner with me in my new role as service line Administrative Vice President. The approval process for this approach turned out to be the easy part. More challenging was finding the right candidate for the job.

Although various physician disciplines could be considered for the position (i.e., pathologist, radiologist, urologist), we were really hoping to find a medical oncologist, surgeon, or radiation oncologist. The service line team felt strongly that the ideal candidate needed to be located in Colorado Springs with the rest of the team … or at least in Denver with the larger national office leadership. In a national organization as large as CHI, many employees and team members work very successfully from remote locations. In this case, however, we felt that in order to build a strong dyad partnership, the two vice presidents (VPs) needed to be able to have face time and in-person working sessions on a more regular basis.

I was nervous that we would have difficulty finding the right candidate. My previous experience as a cancer leader with part-time medical directors was that the physicians provided their input or vision, but I was expected to take complete responsibility for the implementation of those ideas and changes. Part-time medical directors didn't have time to dedicate to the development of strategies and policies. I was looking for a partner who would not only propose new structures or programs but would also lead clinical teams to make these ideas real. I didn't want to be someone's assistant. I wanted a partner and to be half of a team whose skills complemented each other. I already had more work on my plate than I could handle with tons of ideas and opportunities that our limited resources could not address fast enough. I needed someone who would dive in and do the hard work of building programs with me.

MD: Sometimes opportunity knocks when you least expect it. Certainly that was the case for me as I made the leap from bedside doctor to office-based "physician leader." My decision to pursue a career in medical oncology many years before had been driven by two key observations: (i) the science of cancer medicine was exploding in terms of molecular insights that would radically improve the prognosis for the world's most dreaded disease and (ii) nowhere in the landscape of healthcare are relationships between doctors and patients more intense or more meaningful than in the field of oncology. With those beliefs in my heart, I completed my hematology and oncology fellowships and enthusiastically entered clinical practice as an employed oncologist in a large community hospital in South Florida. Perhaps without realizing it, I had already made a significant decision that would impact my long-term career trajectory—to be employed by a large institution with a diverse peer group rather than enter private practice. Though economic pressures were already mounting on the traditional independent physician model, that aspect was not a critical factor for me. In fact, there were clearly more lucrative financial opportunities available to me in private practice at the time. I suppose that a part of me already understood that my aspirations were to build a model of cancer care that would require the resources of a health system—a collection of providers, administrators, and others with a shared purpose that went beyond themselves.

As my confidence grew in my ability to connect with and care for patients, so did my need to confront what appeared to be systemic barriers to delivering good care—poor alignment between physicians and health systems, challenges around electronic records that fell well short of their promises, pressure to spend my time almost anywhere except with the patient. Thus, in 2006, I accepted an opportunity to lead the development and expansion of a municipal health system's cancer program in Colorado Springs, Colorado. In this role, I continued to manage a heavy clinical load but also enjoyed expanded opportunities to materially influence program development, to bring together physicians who shared a common vision, and to advance initiatives that addressed some of the barriers I saw. It was during this period that I was introduced to the model of dyad leadership. We didn't call it that. It wasn't a formal structure within the organization. However, the director of the cancer center invited my participation and input in almost all cancer program decision making from day one. That dyad relationship saw unprecedented change and growth in the cancer program through the complementary efforts of physician and administrator. Still, there were challenges. Even as I saw the potential for making even greater impacts on community cancer services, I grew increasingly challenged to give enough to those efforts while meeting the needs of an ever-increasing patient population that needed and deserved my full attention. I could provide vision and some clinical insights but ultimately needed my administrative partner to do much of the ground work. It wasn't a true partnership.

Enter CHI, a large faith-based healthcare organization undergoing a radical transformation in which true physician–administrative partnerships were being heralded as the model that could meet the needs of the "Next Era" of healthcare. It sounded too good to be true. But as I met with physician after physician within the organization and as I came to understand the resources that were being deployed to develop physicians as leaders, not to turn them into administrators; the more I was intrigued by the opportunity to join this effort. Within CHI, the NOSL was led by Deb Hood, a highly experienced cancer program leader. For the past 3 years, Deb had led a small team that had accomplished extraordinary things across broad geographies: (i) defining a common vision for cancer care across historically distinct and different programs, (ii) mobilization of multidisciplinary care providers to explore and share better ways of caring for patients, and (iii) implementation of IT platforms that would enhance the understanding of the quality and cost of care being delivered. CHI was an organization that was 100% committed to preparing itself to deliver value-based care and manage populations by harnessing the shared skills of administrators and physicians. I found a partner who was accomplished, but genuine in her desire to share leadership with a physician. It still sounded too good to be true. But by this time, I knew that I would have to find out for myself.

MBA: Dr. Dax Kurbegov, a medical oncologist practicing in Colorado Springs, started as the Physician VP for the national service line on December 12, 2012. We wanted a hands-on leader with other skills that would be needed in oncology as health systems transitioned into the next era of population health management. The top five skills (which are likely applicable to other areas) that I wanted for our oncology dyad include the following.

COLLABORATIVE BUT DECISIVE LEADERSHIP

In order to be effective today, leaders need to seek input from experts of all relevant disciplines at the operational level and get buy-in. But, in large organizations, it's unlikely that there will be 100% agreement and support. Someone needs to make a decision and lead through the ramifications that follow. In a dyad partnership, there are some decisions that clearly belong to either the MD or the MBA; but often times the leadership lines are blurred. Partners need to be comfortable expressing their opinions to each other and determining whether one member compromises or yields to the decision of the other. Once a decision is reached, both members need to be comfortable in supporting that decision and the actions that follow. In order to be effective, a united front is important.

PROBLEM SOLVING AND CONSTRUCTIVE CONFLICT RESOLUTION

The oncology world today is filled with conflict and opportunities to solve problems. There are plenty of issues where both the MBA and the MD need to exercise their skills in conflict resolution. While I have no problem with addressing these issues, I absolutely do not want to always be the bad guy. I need a strong partner who is comfortable in dealing with difficult physician issues. My past experience included physicians who willingly dealt strongly with issues but alienated others through the process. Other physicians wanted to maintain the peace and hoped the problem went away on its own. It rarely did. (Luckily for me, Dax is very pragmatic but extremely skilled in handling these situations. He looks for the mutual win and tries to find common ground. And, when someone is being unreasonable, he doesn't hesitate to point that out, albeit very diplomatically.)

INNOVATION

Innovation is prized by all leaders, but national service line leaders need to be open to and actively seeking new ways of doing business. While interviewing for a physician leader, some applicants gave the impression that they were interested in a position where they could comfortably finish out their career. Many did not seem hungry or visionary about what could be accomplished. (Dax was younger than most applicants and had not been practicing as long as others, but he clearly articulated his drive and excitement for what the future could hold.)

LIFELONG LEARNING AND TEACHING

These skills go hand in hand with "Innovation" above. In order to anticipate future needs, it's important for dyad leaders to keep abreast of changes in their specialty through articles, conferences, and networking. Many applicants for the physician leader position were clinical experts in their field but had little to no knowledge about changing market forces and trends. While this information could be learned in a new position, it clearly made some candidates stand out from others because they were aware of challenges that they could be expected to deal with. Likewise, a willingness to educate other health providers about these issues in a nonjudgmental manner is key to effective collaborations.

TEAMWORK

Very few decisions in the oncology service line have been made unilaterally. Teamwork has been the hallmark of our best initiatives. Strong egos on the part of either partner could interfere with effective team participation and leadership. Although the dyad partners are often the team leaders, they also need to know when to listen to the ideas and advice of others, creating truly synergistic collaborations that lead to paradigm shifts in business.

MD: Given the rapidly changing landscape of healthcare, it still remains a great challenge to predict the skill set that will be required to succeed in the future. As I migrated into the role of the physician dyad partner for the NOSL, I spent considerable time reflecting on how I might leverage my clinical experience and background to support our ongoing efforts. I am, after all, who I was trained to be. When confronted by a diagnostic or therapeutic dilemma, I meticulously gather data from as many sources as possible, request additional studies or information to either confirm or refute my clinical suspicions, synthesize that information into a coherent diagnosis, communicate my impressions in a way that is understandable to my audience, and then take definitive action as a partner with my patient. I am and always will be a doc, no matter my title.

While considering what I brought to the table, I also began to appreciate the strengths and success factors that my administrative partner demonstrates each day. Foremost among these is an unwavering commitment to *collaborative* decision making. Deb's ability to engage and empower stakeholders is an essential asset in a leader who is guiding others through uncharted territory. Related to this is a focus on *teamwork*—Deb effectively identifies the strengths of those around her and creates opportunities for them to succeed and grow. But perhaps, the skill I admire the most in Deb is her ability to eloquently articulate a vision that is compelling to others. Inherent in this skill is the ability to understand what matters to the audience in front of her. I have observed Deb in our small NOSL group distill longwinded and sometimes tangential conversations into actionable and straightforward action steps. She is equally adept in large group settings. Early in my CHI career, I had the luxury of appreciating Deb's ability to reach a diverse group of physicians who had little track record of meaningful cooperation and unify them around a vision of coming together to do cancer research in a novel and integrated way. To paint a picture compelling enough to move physicians out of the comfortable fiefdoms that they are used to operating within is a significant accomplishment.

MBA: Soon after starting with CHI, Dax scheduled visits to many sites to meet key physicians. One of the things I've been so impressed with is his ability to develop positive working relationships with so many physicians in a short time. That early work laid the foundation for difficult decisions and tough conversations in later months. Dax is able to pick up the phone and have very frank and supportive conversations about complicated subjects. He is able to positively work toward a conclusion without alienating anyone. I also think that of the two of us, he is much more the diplomat. I'm not saying we play "good-cop/bad-cop" roles, but when I've been fired up about something, he has a great way of stepping in, calming everyone down, and refocusing us on the big picture.

One of the challenges with dyad leadership is determining whether one or both of us need to be involved. Constant communication is key. It's easy to include the dyad partner in all e-mail communications on critical subjects although this can lead to an enormous number of e-mails that are tangential to the work at hand. While both parties want to stay aware of the key issues, it's also important to communicate with each other if someone wants to step out of the loop and let the other take the lead. Dyad leadership communication can also be a challenge for our widespread facilities sites and departments. Sometimes they are not sure if they should communicate with one or both parties. We've tried to keep each other in the loop without overloading the other but we also try to decide and articulate up front which of us will take the lead.

It's important to be cognizant of whether both parties or just one of us needs to be present at meetings and phone calls. It's neither cost- nor time-effective to always have two people covering the same issue. But, there are many situations where each leader brings a unique set of skills to the discussion and both should be present. The only way to address this is to constantly be aware of the need for efficiency and effectiveness. This model will be most successful if each leader uses his or her skills to cover a large territory of work while maintaining strong communication with his or her partner.

The right partnership means that both leaders truly act as a one. Each covers different areas based on the individual's interest and/or expertise, but the service line goals remain the top priority. A true partnership means supporting each other's decisions, consulting constantly with one another, having each other's back, and trusting that both are acting in the best interest of the organization.

MD: As I entered the equation, the NOSL had been in place for several years working on an array of initiatives ranging from quality metrics to physician alignment to information technology infrastructure. To join this group, which had long track record of working effectively with one another and with cancer program leaders around the country, posed a number of challenges. How does accountability change within the team when a new dyad partner is introduced? How do stakeholders outside of the immediate team come to understand to whom they should direct queries? How would I effectively support Deb and the team when I had such a profound deficit around organizational intelligence compared to the rest of the group? The key to successful integration rested in frequent and effective communication between Deb, myself, and other key leaders within CHI as well as the development of a learning plan that offered me the opportunity to gradually expand the scope and depth of my involvement in service line initiatives.

Like many coming into a new leadership role, I was challenged to temper my intrinsic desire to be immediately impactful. Considerable discipline was required to recognize that our NOSL had been performing at a high level under Deb's leadership for an extended period of time and that if I attempted to alter internal team dynamics or external team dynamics too quickly I risked disrupting ongoing priorities and introducing confusion where previously there had been clarity. Thus, in the first few months with CHI, my attentions were most clearly focused on those activities where clinical insights were critical for success. Prior to my arrival, this role had been filled by our physician advisory group that met monthly. However, clinical questions frequently arose that required immediate answers to keep the project progressing. Providing timely clinical insight and assisting the NOSL team in prioritizing clinical projects based on potential impact allowed me not only to make contributions from the start but also to begin to understand how roles and responsibilities had evolved within the team. A critical aspect of this work was that it allowed me to begin piecing together how individual projects supported a long-term, larger vision and how I could add my own ideas to that vision. As I became more familiar with the projects, I also had the opportunity to better understand how our NOSL team interfaced with other national leadership groups at CHI and with our cancer program leaders out in the markets. In parallel with this effort, I began to establish and develop relationships with physician leaders across CHI through a series of purposeful and coordinated site visits. Recognizing that a critical success factor for me would be the ability to credibly relate to and represent our cancer physician leaders, Deb and I identified specific markets and program leaders for early contact. This element of my learning plan provided key contact points across the organization and also provided me with an outside perspective on the perceived value and effectiveness of the NOSL group.

Organizational IQ was another important focus of learning. Rather than detailed explorations of every individual active initiative, Deb and I scheduled a series of conversations around CHI structures and processes as well as around current major challenges for cancer care providers in each market. Key leaders at the national level were identified for extended dialogues, providing greater clarity to me about their roles and priorities as well as creating a peer group of both physician and administrative leaders on whom I could call if I had need. Of course, Deb's 35 years of experience within the organization has always made her an ideal partner to whom I could direct organizational questions. One example of where such interdependence is vital involves our exploration of decision support tools. As the amount and complexity of data that oncologists must process to make the best decisions for patients increases, a number of third party tools are being developed to help streamline decision making. Whereas my background made me well suited to evaluate the utility of such clinical pathways, I was equally ill-equipped to navigate CHI's multifaceted information technology groups, governance groups, project management resources, and processes for evaluating such applications. Through frequent and targeted communication with Deb, I could move the project forward while receiving timely guidance on how best to mobilize national resources to support the effort. After a year in my role, I have much greater command of how to get things done within CHI. However, given the size and complexity of the organization, I continue to rely on my dyad partner as a key source of organizational insight.

For dyad partners to effectively lead, it is essential that both partners commit not only to frequent communication but also to investing the time to better understand each other's communication styles and needs. I have always admired Deb's ability to move quickly and confidently from discussion to action. However, in my early days with CHI, I sometimes felt that we were making the transition from exploration to implementation without all of the data. I sometimes found myself deferring to others within our group out of respect for their experience within the organization. Sometimes this felt more like we had moved on before I had made my contribution. It caused me distress because I felt I had more to offer and I believe it may have caused distress to others, as they might misinterpret my lack of passionate discourse as ambivalence. We were communicating openly, we had a shared vision of where we were going, and we had a great deal of trust. But still, something was off. For me, the light went on during a 3-day conference where both NOSL leaders and our oncology dyad leaders from the markets participated in a leadership seminar focused specifically on the dyad model. Though this was originally intended to be primarily of value to the market dyads, the focused time dedicated to communication and leadership styles provided valuable insights that would enhance my ability to work with Deb and other NOSL members. These insights were about me—my need to diligently collect data and differing viewpoints, my desire to process that internally before rendering judgment, and my preference to move slowly but without error. They were also about my dyad partner—Deb's ability to offer strong input early in conversations, her desire to drive action, and her willingness to course-correct on the fly. Without an understanding of our innate styles, I believe there would have been opportunity for friction and frustration. By moving through this purposeful exercise, we took an important step to a better understanding of how our styles could be complementary. This type of leadership exercise may be extremely valuable in the context of the dyad leadership model, especially if early endeavors don't meet expectations.

MBA: Dax's insights about different leadership and communication styles are spot on. Finding out about these similarities and differences between dyad leaders is an important exercise that should be explored early in the partnership. We are fortunate that our styles are very different. If my partner worked in a style identical to mine, we may not be as successful as partners. Because we are different, we provide different perspectives, varied decision-making styles, and different analyses of situations. Whatever the similarities or differences within the dyad partnership, awareness and balancing the strengths, challenges, and workplace preferences of each other is critically important.

MD: At this time, I find my dyad leadership role to be among the most professionally satisfying of my career. While there are still many opportunities for improvement, I have not felt my independence or autonomy compromised; a fear common among physicians asked to share in leadership roles. To trust and collaborate with another who brings a unique perspective and different set of skills can be immensely rewarding. The model lends itself to lifelong learning because we can safely and collegially challenge one another on a range of topics. It is quite clear to me that this partnership creates an opportunity to accomplish together more than either of us would achieve on our own.

MBA: Dax has been a Godsend, and everything that I wished for in a physician leader. I truly didn't know what we were missing and how much more effective our team could be until he joined our group. My fears around the dyad leadership model have been unfounded. I am amazed at the positive impact that Dax made to the NOSL in a very short period of time. Several difficult initiatives that had been stalled have been completed or are well on their way. There are so many changes occurring today with initiatives that require clinical AND business leadership. In my mind, this is the only way to create significant and sustainable change across the cancer world.

KEY SUCCESS STORIES

The following five topics are a sample of areas where we, as the oncology dyad, have realized the benefits of each other's unique skills and focus. Each leader contributes our own strengths, which provide a better overall picture of the situation along with ways to address challenges.

Physician Alignment and Engagement

The benefits of physician leadership in this arena are a "no brainer." Physicians often relate one to one with their peers more effectively with nonphysician healthcare administrators. A physician leader understands intimately the clinical and business challenges of running a practice. Dax is able to call and reach physicians quickly to discuss various issues. It's much more common for Dax than for Deb to receive a timely call back from a physician that he has never spoken with before. (Deb needs to explain in more detail who she is, the organization she is calling from, and what she is calling about, not only to peak the physician's interest but also to keep staff gatekeepers from interpreting this as a "sales call.")

Over the past year, we've been involved in various discussions on new physician models in our communities. Because Deb has been with the organization longer and knows more of the history in the facility/physician relationship, she often knows the key CHI players who need to be involved, as well as some of the contractual, financial, and legal aspects of various models. Dax is able to provide the physician perspective and connect more effectively with physicians in discussions. Together, we've been able to propose win–win situations for all parties.

Clinical Research

The National Cancer Institute announced formation of a new program, NCORP (National Cancer Institute Community Oncology Research Program), at about the time Dax joined the service line. CHI began investigating facility interest in developing a CHI national research structure that would meet the NCORP requirements. Conference calls and meetings were held to determine interest, and as a team, we were immediately able to engage and organize physicians in each market. Dax's interest and experience as a physician conducting research was key to developing a physician work group that defined the physician's role in this large national network and determined work flow for selecting clinical trials, developing a robust portfolio of studies, and identifying physician experts and leaders who could interface across the network, with research bases and academic medical centers. Dax and other physicians developed the physician conditions of participation for this network, which defined research expectations of participating physicians. Similar documents have been developed in the past for other areas in Oncology, but administrative leaders found that implementing these types of documents took months to years of work before physicians agreed to the format and content. With a physician leader, these documents were quickly agreed to and implemented across the network.

Quality Initiatives

Dax's presence on the NOSL team has provided stability for the team regarding clinical guidance, overall strategy and philosophy related to oncology quality initiatives. While physician champions are still needed, because a single physician cannot lead all the initiatives CHI currently has in play, Dax is instrumental in the long-range planning and organization of major initiatives. Since the inception of the service line, nonphysician team members have successfully implemented numerous quality initiatives. Discussions of clinical standardization and pathway development were postponed, however, as team members didn't feel they had the appropriate skill level to make these decisions. A single physician champion from one market would also have a difficult time, on a part-time basis, leading a complicated initiative such as this. It requires focused attention and a great deal of ongoing work over an extended timeframe. Although this type of work is still difficult and quite time consuming, Dax has successfully moved the organization ahead in these areas.

Electronic Health Records/IT

The NOSL is implementing an oncology-specific electronic health record (EHR) in our outpatient medical and radiation oncology practices. Deb has led this initiative since 2010. At every implementation, physicians have felt very challenged with the workflow changes they encounter as well as the increased time required from them to input data. The changes have been most profoundly felt in practices moving from paper records to their first EHR. Dax's presence on the team doesn't change the situation itself, but he has invested the time to talk individually with physicians and listen to their concerns. Often, he is able to provide insights to the applications team that can help with the difficult transition.

Data Analytics and Management

This is an area where together, both leaders have contributed toward a better, combined understanding of what is needed. Dax has greater depth in the clinical aspect of DRGs, CPT codes, and procedural parameters along with a quality tracking focus. Deb's focus, on the other hand, is on the business, acquisition or infrastructure of the data. The level of data management and analytics required today in oncology is beyond what either leader has experienced in the past. Together, along with other team experts, we're finding our way forward in building oncology data marts, pulling structured and unstructured data into meaningful information, and gathering vastly improved information that can drive quality decisions and outcomes. This is uncharted territory where two heads and two different perspectives can propel the organization forward.

Our Dyad is a true leveraging of two sets of skills. We're believers in this model of management. We also believe we are making a difference for patients and those who care for them in a time of great change. We are fortunate to be part of a transformational era and to be leading together.

REFERENCES

1. Flexner, A. (1910). *Medical education in the United States and Canada*. Washington, DC: Science and Health Publications, Inc.
2. Duffy, T. (September 2011). The Flexner Report-100 Years Later. *Yale Journal of Biology and Medicine*, *84*(3), 269–276.
3. Nightingale, F. (1859). Preface. *Notes on Nursing: What it is and what it is not*. Glasgow and London, UK: Blackie and Son, Ltd.
4. Hale, S. (1871). Lady nurses. *The Godey's Lady's Book and Magazine*, 188–189.
5. Ashley, J. (September 1975). Nursing and early feminism. *American Journal of Nursing, 75*, 1465.
6. Donahue, M. P. (1985). *Nursing, the finest art: An illustrated history*. St. Louis, MO: The CV Mosby Company.
7. Woolf, S. J. (March 7, 1937). Miss Wald at 70 sees her dreams realized. New york: *New York Times Magazine*.
8. Gibbon, J. M., & Mathewson, M. S. (1947). *Three centuries of Canadian nursing*. Toronto, ON: The MacMillan Company of Canada.
9. Haddock, C., McLean, R., & Chapman, R. (2002). *Careers in healthcare management: How to find your pat and follow it*. Chicago, IL: Health Administration Press.
10. Arndt, M. (2010). Education and the masculinization of hospital administration. *Journal of Management History, 16*(1), 75–89.
11. Arndt, M. (2007). Hospital administration in the early 1900's: Visions for the future and the reality of daily practice. *Journal of Healthcare Management, 2*(1), 34.
12. Staff (May 2012). Castlight wins a whopping $100 million dollar round to bring transparency to healthcare. Website: techcrunch.com; Retrieved from http://techcrunch.com/2012/05/01/castlight-100m/
13. Bass, B. (2008). *The bass book of leadership: Theory, research and managerial applications*. New York, NY: The Free Press.
14. Barnard, C. (1938). *Functions of the executive*. Cambridge, MA: Harvard University Press.
15. Cialdini, R. (1993). *Influence*. New York, NY: Harper-Collins College Publishers.
16. Byrne, D. (1971). *The attraction paradigm*. New York, NY: Academic Press.
17. Sarbin, T. R., & Jones, D. S. (1955). The assessment of role expectations in the selection of supervisory personnel. *Educational and Psychological Measurement, 15*, 236–239.
18. Maslow, A. (1954). *Motivation and personality*. New York, NY: Harper and Row.
19. Herzberg, F. (1966). *Working and the nature of man*. New York, NY: Crowell.
20. Luft, J., & Ingham, H. (1955). The Johari window, a graphic model of interpersonal awareness. *Proceedings of the Western training laboratory in group development*. Los Angeles, CA: UCLA.

21. Argyris, C. (1964). *Integrating the individual and the organization.* New York, NY: Wiley.
22. Burnes, J. M. (1978). *Leadership.* New York, NY: Harper and Row.
23. Berson, Y., Shamir, R., Avolio, B., et al. (2001). The relationship between vision, strength, leadership style and context. *Leadership Quarterly, 12,* 55–73.
24. Brown, D. (1987). *Leadership and organization transformation: A competency model.* Doctoral dissertation. Santa Barbara, CA: Fielding Institute.
25. Bracey, H., Rosenbaum, J., Sanford, A., et al. (1990). *Managing from the heart.* New York, NY: Delacorte Press.
26. Bennis, W., & Nanus, B. (1985). *Leaders: The strategies for taking charge.* New York, NY: Harper and Row.
27. Podsakoff, P., MacKenzie, S., Moorman, R., et al. (1990). Transformational leader behaviors and their effects on followers trust in the leader, satisfaction, and organizational citizenship behaviors. *Leadership Quality, 1,* 177–192.
28. Alimo-Metcalfe, B., & Alban-Metcalfe, A. (1999). *The development of a new transformational leadership questionnaire.* Leeds, UK: University of Leeds, Nuffield Institute Centre for Leadership.
29. Judge, T., & Bono, J. (2000). Five-factor model of personality and transformational leadership. *Journal of Applied Psychology, 85,* 751–765.
30. Popper, M., Mayseless, O., & Castelnovo, O. (2000). Attachment and transformational leadership. *Leadership Quarterly, 11,* 267–289.
31. Deluga, R. J., & Sousa, J. (1990–1991). The effects of transformational and transactional leadership styles on the influencing behavior of subordinate police officers. *Journal of Occupational Psychology, 64*(1), 49–55.
32. Wofford, J., & Goodwin, V. (1998). *Toward a cognitive process model of leadership behavior.* Paper. San Francisco, CA: Academy of Management.
33. Avolio, B., Howell, J., & Sosik, J. (1999). A funny thing happened on the way to the bottom line: Humor as a moderator of leadership style effects. *Academy of Management Journal, 42,* 219–227.
34. Hater, J. J., & Bass, B. M. (1988). Supervisors' evaluations and subordinates' perceptions of transformational and transactional leadership. *Journal of Applied Psychology, 73,* 695–702.
35. Dasborough, M. T., & Ashkanasy, N. M. (2002). Emotion and attribution of intentionality in leader-member relations. *Leadership Quarterly, 13,* 615–634.
36. Shostrum, E. I. (1974). *POI manual: An inventory for the measurement of self-actualization.* San Diego, CA: Educational and Industrial Testing Service.
37. Gibbons, T. (1986). *Revisiting the question born vs. made: Toward a theory of development of transformational leaders.* Doctoral dissertation. Santa Barbara, CA: Fielding Institute.
38. Kobasa, S., Maddi, S., & Kahn, S. (1982). Hardness and health; a prospective study. *Journal of Personality and Social Psychology, 42,* 168–177.
39. Atwater, L., & Yammarino, F. J. (1989). *Predictors of military leadership. A study of midshipmen leaders at USNA* (ONR Tech. Rep. 7), Binghamton, NY: State University of New York, Center for Leadership Studies.
40. Ashkanasy, N. M., & Tse, B. (2000). Transformational leadership as a management of emotion: A conceptual review. In N. Ashkanasy, C. E. J. Hirtel, & W. J. Zerbe (Eds.), *Emotions in the workplace: Research, theory and practice.* Westport, CT: Quorum Books.

Chapter 3

Developing a Dyad

A few years ago, a medical colleague and his long-time fiancée celebrated their marriage. The wedding was an intimate affair, with only family and a few close friends in attendance. But the reception was a joyous, raucous, bountiful extravaganza. There were hundreds of guests, who came to congratulate the couple, enjoy music and decorations from two different continents, and feast on both typical "American" wedding dinner food and exotic, delicious food from the groom's native country. The music and food were very different, but both types were enjoyable.

Both extended families were present, of course. Both sets of parents were gracious and appeared pleased to greet their children's various friends and acquaintances. The groom's parents, who had flown in from their home in India, were more reserved than the bride's Italian-American family, but that could have been because of a difference in culture. Some of us wondered about how accepting they really were of this union, though. We had been privy to the angst our friend had experienced as he wavered (and the decision took years) between whether to bow to his parents' insistence that he marry the bride his parents had selected for him or to break with family tradition and marry the woman he chose.

Some of our friends couldn't believe that this highly educated man, who had been living in the United States for nearly two decades, would even consider accepting an arranged marriage. One thoughtful nurse from yet another culture had a different take.

"Well," she said, "Arranged marriages can actually turn out better than so-called love matches. People learn to love each other as mates—it's just that this happens after the wedding, not before."

The same point can be made about Dyad partners. Some leadership duos may actually choose their work partner, but many find themselves working in arranged partnerships. They need to learn about each other at the same time they are learning a new model of leadership.

Dyads and marriages aren't the same thing, of course. For one thing, Dyad leaders don't commit to working together for a lifetime! Most of us would agree that the person we marry is the individual who is most important to our overall life happiness. However, the relationship with a Dyad partner has a great deal of influence on job success and satisfaction. Your partner's competencies and skills are essential to what you will be able to achieve. Your ability to meet goals depends on how well you work together. Even your personal recognition, compensation, and advancement in the organization will be overtly or less openly tied to the abilities of your partner, and what you are able to accomplish together.

Together is the important word here. Dyads are formed in organizations because someone (like the CEO) or multiple individuals (like the Leadership team) has determined that there is value in bringing together professionals from two different cultures, with two complementary but different skill sets, to lead together. The assumption behind that decision is that this partnership will actually function *as a partnership*. Sometimes, Dyads are put together based on positions that are already filled by individuals who are accustomed to leading solo. Sometimes, especially when the model is new to an organization, partners get to select each other. Sometimes one position is vacant, and the incumbent gets to choose (or at least be part of the hiring decision) his partner. The first example resembles an arranged marriage; the last two are more like a marriage of choice.

THE ARRANGED DYAD VERSUS THE SELECTED PARTNER

Most of us would probably prefer to choose the partner who will work closely with us. We'd like to know that we are compatible, that we share a vision of what we want to accomplish, and that we have the same work ethic. We'd like to be assured that the person we are tying our professional future to is competent in the areas *we* think he should be. Certainly, our work lives would be more pleasant if our partners are like-minded, with harmonious personalities well-suited to us! If we already share the same vision, we won't have to work hard to understand our partner's view of the world. (Even better, we *think* we won't have to compromise or change our vision in any way.) If we know that our potential work mates are competent, especially in areas in which we ourselves might be weak (or would simply prefer not to do), and that they will work as hard as we do, we can feel better about this new model. So, choosing our partners is preferable to us. Unfortunately, because Dyads are formed by organizations for particular business reasons, this isn't always possible.

It is likely that Dyad partners will be more like the arranged marriage my physician friend decided to reject. His intended bride was selected because of position and culture (same caste and a particular family his family wanted to align with). He did not really know her. In organizations, Dyad partners are also selected because of position, or job, not because of individual choice of who they want to work with.

As our Asian colleague explained, arranged marriages can, and do, become strong and successful. Dyad partnerships can also become strong and successful, even when partners do not choose each other. The Indian arranged marriage has an advantage that the arranged Dyad does not, though. The marriage partners come from similar backgrounds and the same culture. The Dyad members, as discussed in Chapter 1, often come from different professional cultures and backgrounds. They are actually placed in the Dyad because of this. The rationale for (and the strength of) the Dyad model can also be a challenge to a harmonious partnership. In other words, the very thing that has the potential of making this sort of leadership model most value added to the organization (the melding of two professional cultures to accomplish common goals) may be the biggest challenge to its success.

The individuals who do get to select the partners with whom they will colead may be surprised that they have the same issues becoming true team mates as those who do not. Professional cultural issues can cause difficulties in getting to a complementary equality. In addition, even colleagues who believe they know each other well will find that becoming accountable for managing as a pair does not change the dynamics between the two. This closer working relationship may uncover differences and incompatibilities that weren't recognized (or considered important) when the two did not share the same accountabilities. In addition, selecting a partner based on vetting and interviewing is not a fail-safe method for finding the best match for your Dyad. Any manager with long experience in a leadership role can tell you that sometimes the person you interview is not the same person who shows up for work. Who people say they are, or even who their references say they are, does not always match on-the-job behavior.

When people marry by choice, they sometimes find that the marriage is not what they expected, or that the person is not exactly who she or he was perceived to be before marriage. This is true even when a couple thinks they really know each other well. When marriages don't work out, they can devolve into what is commonly known as dysfunctional relationships, which are big contributors to dysfunctional families. Often, they end in divorce. Similarly, when Dyads don't work out as successful leadership partnerships, they have the potential of causing or enhancing the dysfunctions of the team they colead. Team members may be confused by leaders who aren't partners. Some may choose loyalty to one leader and not the other, which splits the team that is supposed to be working together toward common goals. The partners may eventually split up (divorce), but in the meantime, they can cause harm to the organization through their dysfunctional relationship and their dysfunctional team.

If it bothers you that we are comparing a Dyad to a marriage, please understand that we do not think that this relationship is as important to individuals as their life mate partnerships are. We explained this earlier in the chapter. However, multiple leadership and management consultants and writers draw out the parallels between business partners and marriage partners. One example is Forbes Magazine writer Amanda Neville, who often compares business partners to marriage. She says this is because both require "mutual trust and respect, involve money, and require a conscious choice, every day, to continue working toward a common goal with someone other than yourself" (1).

SUCCESSFUL DYADS

While most of these experts are comparing marriage to partnerships in which two or more individuals actually own an enterprise together, their thoughts on the similarities are just as appropriate for comanagers within an enterprise. Dyad leaders own departments, goals, and organizational responsibilities together. Comparison of the literature and research on what makes marriages successful and what makes partnerships *or teams* successful can only lead to one conclusion: with a few differences based on the nature of the relationship, partnerships of any kind share qualities that make them successful.

Success may be defined differently for various types of partnerships. In addition to the generic, simplistic definition of success (the accomplishment of defined goals), numerous management and leadership researchers have proposed their own definitions. These are based on their descriptions of what leaders (or managers) should do.

There are a number of definitions or descriptions from management and leadership theorists on what managers or leaders do. Managers "work through others in order to achieve organizational objectives in an efficient manner" (2). Their functional responsibilities are to plan, organize, and control the work plan of a group (3). They initiate change, support others, inform others, and evaluate group members (4). They serve as linchpins to connect a larger group of managers, supervisors, and peers with a group that consists of the manager and his subordinates (5). Leaders resolve conflicts, mediate, compromise, and build coalitions and trust (6). They facilitate interpersonal interaction and positive working relations while structuring tasks and work to be accomplished (7). They analyze problems, make decisions, and communicate (8).

We could write a whole book (and multiple books *have* been written) on the numerous descriptions of what managers and leaders do. Leadership jobs are complex and diverse, both between organizations and within single organizations. Dyad leadership adds complexity, so we've looked at definitions that could help simplify the description of functions that are enhanced by this model.

We especially like a description of what organizational leaders do derived from the work of T.B. Roby, who developed a mathematical model of leadership functions based on his research. His use of science to model leadership isn't why we like it (although, as clinicians, it does appeal to our scientific side). We think it is a good definition for success in today's healthcare world because of the reasons Dyads are being formed.

Roby identified four major leadership functions: to bring about congruence of goals between members of an organization, to balance group resources and capabilities with environmental demands, to provide group structure that will focus information effectively upon problem solutions, and to make certain that all information is available to decision makers when required (9). Completing these functions successfully means the individual leader (or the Dyad) is successful.

BRINGING CONGRUENCE TO GOALS OF DIFFERENT MEMBERS OF THE ORGANIZATION

The rationale for the development of many Dyad leadership teams is based on the historical divergence of goals between major players in a hospital's success, namely clinicians and administrators. While it can be argued that the two groups have always shared the same *really* important goal, which is to deliver quality care to the people we both serve (patients), the difference in values pointed out in Chapter 1 have not led to a commonly stated vision nor objectives that need to be completed to get to that vision.

For a number of reasons, including the need to increase our collective (institutions and providers) value (defined as higher quality for lower cost), we recognize the need to transform healthcare delivery in this country. Physicians, hospitals, and a variety of providers of care in the entire continuum of care are trying to become an integrated system. Organizations and physicians are coming together to form clinically integrated networks. Healthcare systems are pursuing a new iteration of accountable care networks that emphasize keeping people as healthy as possible rather than just treating them when they are sick. Physicians are becoming employees. Both they and the organizations that have hired them struggle with what that means, and how it does or should change the relationship between them. The amount of change occurring in organizations and to individuals is staggering. This would be difficult to handle even if we had all been closely aligned in the past. It's overwhelming because we were not.

A major reason Dyads are being formed is to bring leaders from two different cultures together to bring congruence to the goals of both cultures. To unite goals of differing groups requires leaders with personal (influential) power from each group. In other words, Dyads are a new healthcare leadership model to meet Roby's first tenet of what leaders must do.

BALANCING GROUP RESOURCES AND CAPABILITIES WITH ENVIRONMENTAL DEMANDS

Those who have been in healthcare leadership for any period of time have lived through almost constant incremental change. Most are saying the same thing about the current environment for providers: The changes we are facing now are, or will be, more disruptive than anything we've experienced in multiple decades. Some would like to blame the transformation that's coming on political maneuvering that is causing our need to transform the system through both legislation and regulation. But, many years before the Affordable Care Act (ACA), pundits within and outside the federal government were predicting major change in how we provide and pay for healthcare, based on prognostications that what we have now (and have had previously) is not a sustainable system. We can't afford it.

Facts about the cost of care (and the less than optimal health results purchased by that care) have been recognized and published long before the 44th president was elected in 2008. While the percent of the gross domestic product spend on healthcare is, and has been for some time, significantly higher in the United States than in other industrialized nations, our performance on measures such as infant mortality, life expectancy, and premature or preventable deaths is below par. According to studies of quality, the care across the country is uneven, with "a large share of patients not receiving clinically proven, effective treatments" (10).

Whether or not we agree with the details of healthcare legislation, or the way our government implements it, we should not be surprised that the environment in which healthcare must function is defined by a shift from our largely fee for service system to a value-based system (where both cost and quality must be balanced.) Strategies to accomplish the shift include minimizing core operating costs, correlating the cost of various treatments to the efficacy of the treatments, and standardizing care as well as equipment/supplies used for that care if there is evidence that supports standardization. Hospital executives and clinicians need to come together to determine which clinical procedures will be performed in their organizations and what evidence of effectiveness and appropriateness will be used to justify them. This is an especially important question for new and emerging technologies that have no evidence, pro or con. Most of us have heard various reports that a significant proportion of healthcare expenditures are directed to care that has not been shown to be effective and may cause harm (11). We must agree on what our standards of quality and safety will be, how these will be measured, and what the rewards and consequences will be for clinicians who cannot, or will not, meet those standards.

Leadership also has to determine the appropriate cost of the procedures and treatments that an organization has agreed to provide. Different physicians caring for patients with the same diagnoses may order very different diagnostic tests, specialty units, drugs, and use of expensive equipment for their patients. An individual patient could be the recipient of widely varying care and costs depending on where he is geographically located in the country, what facility he is admitted to, or who his physician is. Given the limitations on healthcare dollars and resources, leaders have to determine the value of allowing an individual practitioner to use a product he prefers versus a less expensive product that evidence shows to be equally effective for the patient.

The current movement to encourage clinicians to practice at the top of their licenses is another way to balance group resources through utilization of different caregivers. This is true when the evidence supports various clinicians' capabilities to deliver care with outcomes equal to those of more expensive caregivers, and when changing care models helps the organization respond to the environmental demand for lower costs (12). However, professional loyalty or beliefs may cause individual clinicians or professional groups to take actions that block the ability of organizations to make rational evidence-based change.

One reason for a physician member to be included in a Dyad is to add the influence she has with her colleagues to the leadership partnership. She is more likely to be able to educate and convince them that standardization of care based on evidence, along with better utilization of the skills of different team members, is the right thing to do. The successful Dyad would meet Roby's leadership definition of balancing resources with environmental demands.

PROVIDING GROUP STRUCTURE THAT WILL FOCUS INFORMATION UPON PROBLEM SOLUTIONS

Roby wrote his explanation of what leadership should do long before healthcare systems were widely promoting the development and adoption of evidence-based practices (EBPs), but we think he would be a supporter of this trend. EBPs, after all, are based on evidence (also known as verified information) that they are effective because they have driven the attainment of superior results. Increasingly, they are labeled EBPs when they not only result in high quality but are shown to be cost-effective. A successful Dyad partnership is one whose expert power (clinical and business) can be used to lead others to understand and use EBPs to increase the value equation for patients.

Two leaders, with complementary skills, have combined knowledge (information), and when they bring their separate professions together as a team, they have access to even more specialized information. This multiplied expertise can be brought to bear on solving organizational problems. As members of separate professional cultures, they have access to more of the opinions, thoughts, issues, and even rumors that could be important for leaders to know, particularly in a rapidly changing environment. In addition, successful Dyads (just like successful single leaders) are those who structure their teams so that communication is open and transparent, and where all members of the team feel respected and safe (both necessary environmental factors for a free exchange of information). According to John Maxwell, communication is one of the foundational qualities of an effective team. Without communication, team members will work against each other rather than tackling issues together (13).

ENSURING ALL INFORMATION IS AVAILABLE TO DECISION MAKERS WHEN NEEDED

Roby knew that information is not useful if it is not available when it could aid in fully informing decision makers about the pros and cons of potential directions. Good leaders not only seek out as much information as they can for their own decision making, but they keep everyone around them informed, too. This includes those they report to, those who report to them, and anyone else who needs to make informed decisions. That's just about everyone.

It isn't just formal leaders who need information in order to make decisions that affect the success of organizations. Without the latest lab results for their patients, physicians might prescribe the wrong treatments. Without clear and accurate information, employees may resist changes they don't understand. Without supporting data, clinicians might choose not to follow procedures deemed "best practice" by the hospital.

Some of us have had the misfortune of working with others, including leaders, who are information hoarders. They seem to have interpreted the Francis Bacon quote that "Knowledge is power" to mean that they lose power if others have the same information they do. They may justify their stinginess by saying, "There's need to know and there's nice to know. I only share what people need to know." The problem with that attitude is none of us really know what others need to know in order make the best possible decisions for their jobs. (We don't know what we don't know!) So, in line with Roby's thoughts, we believe that successful Dyad leaders are generous with data and actively work to share information with everyone.

Roby's four functions of leadership are a good start for evaluating the success of a Dyad leadership *team*. But before the Dyad can succeed, the two leaders must bond. They must become a cohesive duo, operating as, and perceived by others as, true partners.

DEVELOPING THE DYAD PARTNERSHIP

Bonding as Dyad leaders is based on the same skills and processes for bonding as partners in *any* human endeavor, because it is based on the basics of human relations. Research on relationships tends to be done for very specific groups. As a result we have experts and data on what makes successful marriages, productive business partnerships, good parent–child dynamics, and bonded teams. Each group of experts report identical or nearly identical factors for success. (If you doubt our conclusion, try this fun exercise: Do a literature search for articles on relationship building in each of the groups we list here. Remove anything that identifies the specific population that was studied. Then guess which teams or partnerships they were.) Based on the similar results in each of these specific arenas, we are confident that future long-term research on Dyads will produce the same important relationship components as other partnerships need.

We've already pointed out that Dyad leaders from different professional cultures may have significant challenges bonding as true partners. However, our experience in a large system that has implemented this model of leadership is that *it can be done*. Development of leadership teams of two requires three major, heavily related relationship reinforcements that form the foundation of the partnership. These are **communication, trust, and respect**.

COMMUNICATION: THE FIRST RELATIONSHIP REINFORCER

Communication is usually the first thing (or among the first things) mentioned in any literature search about human relations. The ability to utilize language creatively, imaginatively, verbally, or in written form is pointed to as a major difference between people and animals. In fact, sociologists claim that verbal communication is a condition of the existence of human society. Communication competencies are basic to leadership (14).

It may seem odd that something so inherent to our existence would need to be defined, but numerous definitions of communication exist. So do abundant examples of how communication failures can cause harm to individuals, organizations, communities, or countries. Anyone who has ever watched a soap opera (those serial radio or television dramas originally sponsored by soap companies) knows that the shows were only able to keep their story lines going week after week (and year after year) because the characters involved didn't communicate well. The melodramatic results of deliberately not sharing information, or misunderstandings caused when information was not perceived by its receiver (the person or persons for whom the message is intended) the way the sender (the person transmitting the information as a message to another or others) intended it, kept viewers coming back. The audience just wanted to see what terrible thing would happen next. (What happened next was more poor communication!) Poor communication may make for entertaining fictional stories, but in the real world, it can lead to unhappy, or even tragic, results (Display 3-1).

The vast majority of miscommunications do not result in catastrophes. However, miscommunication is almost always present when catastrophes do occur, as anyone who has performed a deep dive root cause analysis of clinical, or business, disasters can attest.

Poor communication is blamed for failures in personal connections as well as organizations' ability to meet goals. Articles and books are written to inform people about how to communicate with others. Educators and coaches are able to make

---

Display 3-1 Examples of Miscommunication and Harm

▶ When a military Captain commanded his British Cavalry Brigade to attack, he was so excited that he misstated the orders. As a result, all 670 men were killed on October 25, 1854, in what is now known as the Charge of Light Brigade.

▶ General Johann Rall received a note from a spy that was written in English. Because he could only read German, he put it in his pocket. That's why he did not know that enemy troops were approaching from the north. Consequently, those soldiers, commanded by General George Washington, defeated Rall's Hessians at the 1776 Battle of Trenton (15).

▶ On October 8, 2001, a Cessna Citation business jet was given clearance to taxi to its takeoff point on a route that would avoid the main runway (where large commercial jets took off). The Cessna crew misinterpreted the air traffic control message, and turned the wrong way. They found themselves in the path of a commercial jet. As a result, 118 people died (16).

▶ An American Marine and a Navy medic were killed in Afghanistan in April 2011 when the US crew guiding the drone that hit them was not informed that another department was watching live videos and had doubts that the two were actually enemy targets (17).

▶ The FDA has reported that children and adults have died when mistakenly given edetate disodium instead of edetate calcium disodium. Not only do they have similar names, but both are commonly referred to as EDTA (18).

---

a living just teaching or helping others learn how to express their ideas or how to really hear what others are saying. There are courses on listening, writing well, public speaking, concise messaging, nonverbal communication, intercultural communication differences, and even specific education on the use of diplomacy and tact. One organization that has taught courses like these since 1912 (Dale Carnegie) is still presenting them to individuals and organizations that have self-assessed problems with getting their messages across to internal or external audiences!

Humans know communication is important. We teach it and even grant college degrees in it. Our children learn it from birth, progressing quickly to use spoken and then written words. We've organized the English language so concisely that we can even diagram sentences to identify subjects, verbs, direct objects, adjectives and adverbs. We know about clauses and complex sentence structures. Why, then, are communication problems so frequent, even when individuals share a native language? Of course the reason is that language is not exactly the same thing as communication. If we were to attempt to diagram a human interaction (the way we diagram a sentence), we would quickly see how challenging it really is. We would have to include all of the following (and more):

▶ The words used, and their various, possible meanings (which may slightly differ depending on whatever is our favorite dictionary)

▶ Punctuation or variation of emphasis on certain words, as well as speaking cadence and speed

▶ Body language and facial expressions of both sender and receiver

▶ The ability of both sender and receiver to interpret body language correctly

▶ A message sender's intent

▶ A receiver's understanding of the language and vocabulary words used

▶ The sender's cultures (including professional)

▶ The receiver's cultures (including professional)

▶ The receiver's understanding of the sender's use of acronyms and abbreviations

▶ The sender's and the receiver's equal understanding of abstract versus concrete thought (such as simile, metaphor, allegory, idiomatic expression, rhetorical expression)

▶ The sender's and the receiver's psychological health

▶ The sender's and the receiver's self-esteem, as well as esteem for the other

So, what are some of the definitions of this thing that is so crucial to human endeavors but can cause such problems when it doesn't work well? The U.S. Army defines it simply as "the exchange and flow of information and ideas from one person to another." It involves a sender transmitting an idea, information, or feeling to a receiver (19). Others expand on this by defining effective communication as occurring only when the receiver understands the exact information or idea that the sender intended to transmit. We think that Dyad leaders are best served with the even further clarified definition shared in the 1991 book, *Empowered Teams*. Authors Wellins, Byham, and Wilson's definition is "The style and extent of interactions both among members and between members and those outside the team. It also refers to the way that members handle conflict, decision making, and day-to-day interactions" (20).

Dyad partners need to be aware that communication is not communication if the receiver does not understand the message. Partners will be frustrated (not to mention upset and even angry) and attainment of organizational goals will be hindered if they do not learn how to transmit information and thoughts to each other. Each requires assurance that these have been decoded or translated the way they were meant to be. One technique that is often taught to ensure this occurs is to practice this style of verbal communication: Person A speaks. Person B listens carefully. Person B repeats what he thinks Person A meant to communicate. If Person A agrees that Person B "got it," they can agree they have communicated successfully. If not, Person A will need to restate his thoughts, and the process is reiterated until they are in agreement on the message.

Sounds simple, right? It isn't always. In our busy healthcare world, taking time to repeat messages and meanings to each other can seem burdensome. It can even aggravate those senders who think that any misunderstanding on the receiver's part is solely the receiver's problem, not theirs! Once, one of us tried to use this technique with a colleague when his message wasn't quite clear. She started, "I want to be sure

I am understanding you. I believe I heard you say ....." He interrupted her with, "Don't you give me any of your MBA psycho-babble. You heard me ... just do what I said," before he stormed away.

The colleague in this story was perceived as disrespectful and dismissive of the receiver of his communication. He refused to clarify his statements. We share this story to underscore that, as Dyad leaders, you will not be able to communicate with honesty and transparency if there are trust or respect issues (discussed later in this chapter) between you. You will not be able to correct miscommunications if you aren't willing to try new ways of learning to understand each other, including those that might seem onerous.

Good communicators have learned to listen. They pay full attention to what is being said to them, rather than thinking about what they want to say when it is their turn to talk. They don't finish other people's sentences, don't let their minds wander during a conversation, and don't dominate a conversation. They ask clarifying questions to be sure they understand the message.

Great communicators do all of this, and, in addition, are aware of their own biases. They consciously work to keep an open mind in spite of these. They are able to tailor their communication techniques to their audience, whether that is a group or an individual. When they are the sender of information, either verbally or in writing, they state facts objectively. They are also the masters of gentle persuasion.

All of us have biases, which can be positive or negative. We have ways of thinking about things based on our family backgrounds, past experiences, and cultures, *including professional cultures*. These biases include stereotypes about people from other races, religions, political affiliations, cultures, genders, professions, jobs, or any other differentials that group people into "silos." They cause us to make assumptions about others that may hinder effective communication or cause incorrect interpretations of messages. They also can be beliefs about our own race, religion, political party, culture, gender, or profession. Some of these are conscious thoughts, but others may influence our perceptions without us even realizing it (Display 3-2).

What we believe about ourselves as members of our culture or group, or as an individual, can hinder or help us communicate with others. In a rigorous 10-year study, David Logan, John King, and Halee Fischer-Wright studied 24,000 people in two dozen corporations. In their book, *Tribal Leadership*, they describe groups of people (tribes) that exist in five stages of development. Each stage involves a prevailing view that influences how members of the tribe view life, themselves and others. The view at stage one is that life is bad (the authors use a more modern euphemism, i.e., "life sucks"). Individuals who belong to groups at stage two believe that "my life" is bad. People in stage three groups believe that "I'm great, you're not." At stage four, the prevailing thought is "we (the group) are great." Stage five tribes are described as those whose mantra is "Life is Great." Groups at stage five are those who are motivated to change the world for the benefit of all (21).

Display 3-2 **Assumptions that Block Communication**

Assumption of Superiority. When the sender believes he is superior to the receiver (or of more value), he may use an imperious tone, project arrogance, or appear to "talk down" to others. As a result, the receiver may respond by not listening or shutting down (not engaging in the conversation). When the receiver believes she is superior to the sender, she may not listen, may disregard the message as inconsequential, or interrupt the sender before the message is complete.

Assumption of Inferiority. When the sender believes he is inferior to the receiver, he might withhold information because he assumes the receiver already knows it or wouldn't want it. When the receiver believes she is inferior to the sender, she might also withhold important information if it contradicts or is not the same as what the sender has stated, because she assumes the sender must be right.

Assumptions About Knowledge. When the sender assumes the receiver knows everything he knows, he may not share information. When the receiver assumes the sender knows everything she knows, she might not respond with data that were missing in the sender's message. When the sender assumes the receiver does not have knowledge she actually has, he might be perceived as arrogant (or ignorant) if she perceives he is trying to educate her (especially if the subject is within her expertise).

Assumptions About Group Membership. When either sender or receiver assumes an individual is "a perfect specimen" of what he or she has learned about tendencies of certain groups (through experience or published research reports) he or she might make communication errors.

Assumptions About the Universality of Our Own Cultural Lens. When either sender or receiver fails to perceive that differences in culture could be causing misunderstandings, interpersonal relationships can be damaged.

The authors' research shows that 45% of all professionals belong to tribes in stage three. (In fact, they list some healthcare professionals as being especially prone to this stage, due to the educational system that rewards them for competing with other individuals for grades and prestige). Unfortunately, communication (and partnerships) suffer when one or both partner has been enculturated with a belief that he or she is superior, smarter, and of more value than other people, whether those are their Dyad partners or members of their multidisciplinary teams. Feelings of superiority or the need to compete for power or recognition (also listed by Logan, King, and Fischer-Wright as part of stage three cultures) make it difficult to listen and learn, both essential to great communication.

While feelings of superiority can hinder the listening side of communication, the opposite is true for the sending side. If one person in the Dyad believes himself to be less competent, even in the areas in which he has more expertise, he is more likely not to communicate or bring up facts or issues important to the Dyad's success, believing that his partner must know more than he does! Or, if he does not see himself as "inferior" to his colleague, he still might make the mistake that many bright, but humble, people do. They assume that, if they know something (from reading, education, or experience) their colleagues must surely know it as well, and therefore, don't need to be told about it.

When a sender does not know a receiver well or does not have an understanding of the receiver's professional education and expertise, he might offend the receiver while trying to be a good communicator. It is not uncommon that a clinician, who, excited by what she has just learned about management theory in a 2-hour class, generously decides to share her new knowledge with a professional administrator. Without considering her colleagues graduate degree (or degrees) in management (as well as his experience), she "educates" him on a management theory that is brand new to her, even though he has been acquainted with it for 20 years. The manager may see this sharing of information as a lack of respect for the knowledge that is common in his profession or might choose to find it amusing. One of our administration colleagues shared that this sort of tutelage was offered to him after the organization offered classes on business techniques to physicians. "Imagine," he said, "if I need an article on new surgical techniques for aortic stenosis and then proceeded to lecture my vascular surgeon friend about it, as if he didn't have a clue about his own specialty."

Even when senders and receivers know quite a bit about each other's cultures and educational backgrounds, they can miscommunicate when they view and individual as a stereotype. While there are descriptions of people born in the 1960s and 1970s as cynical and disaffected (22), an individual might not conform to this label. Similarly, the widely reported "truth" that all surgeons are cantankerous, dominant, arrogant people with poor communication skills is not true of every person who happens to be a surgeon! Understanding generalizations about group cultures is helpful when communicating with group members but each individual should be judged by his or her behavior.

Most of the misconceptions about others that can result in communication problems are caused by our own cultural conditioning. As Klasko and Shea state in *The Phantom Stethoscope*, "The considerable differences between physician and administrator culture mean that even when members of the two groups try to work together, mutual misinterpretation abounds. Neither group questions the universality of its views nor recognizes its views are culturally based. Each group, then, judges the behavior of individuals—even of individuals of other groups—by its own norms" (23).

Stereotypes, biases, and our own cultural and conditioning can lead to poor communication skills that get in the way of organization success. They can also retard an individual's personal growth and ability to learn and evolve as individuals and leaders. As writer Johann Wolfgang Von Goethe has been quoted, "No one would talk much in society if they knew how often they misunderstood others." We address the importance of understanding both your own and your partner's beliefs in Chapter 5. In Chapter 7, we describe ways to learn about yourself, and how personal coaching and other personal development techniques can be utilized to help you and your partner become more effective as a Dyad, and as leaders of multidisciplinary (multicultural) teams.

Display 3-3 **Public Speaking: A Dyad Leadership Skill**

Are you expert enough in public speaking to make cogent, understandable presentations to a variety of audiences? It's OK if this type of communication isn't your favorite. Fear of public speaking is common. However, in today's world, more and more leadership job descriptions include speaking to audiences of various sizes as part of the requirement for leaders to have "excellent verbal and written communication skills," whether this is explicitly spelled out or assumed as part of the "verbal" abilities.

Most healthcare leaders will need to do this in order to be effective during these times of change. Even if you feel you do this well, what do written evaluations or trusted, honest colleagues tell you after a presentation?

This competency isn't just about knowing your subject and imparting it to an audience. It includes being able to "read" the room, gauge whether people are understanding or still paying attention to you, and changing speaking tactics if they appear to be disengaged. It also incorporates the skill of tailoring language and concepts to the audience. (The vocabulary used when addressing a group of cardiothoracic surgeons about cardiac surgery is probably not appropriate when explaining the same procedures to a community of lay people.)

As a CNO and CMO Dyad, we have found one method of public presentation especially effective. Whenever possible, we share our public speaking opportunities. We stand on the stage together and we present together. (That doesn't mean that one talks for the first half of the presentation, and then the other ends the talk the last half. If we have a set of slides, we alternate speaking, slide by slide. Most of the time, we don't even decide ahead of time who will present each power point slide.) The result is a visual example to others that we are partners. In addition, since we plan the presentation together, without a plan of who will speak to which slides, we learn more about the other's area of expertise.

Besides knowing yourself and your partner as individuals with biases and cultural backgrounds that might need to be addressed to improve communication, it is important to understand your personal strengths as a communicator (Display 3-3). As a sender, are your messages concise, and to the point? (Even as expert listener might find her mind wandering if the sender drones on and on, or seems "enamored" of his own voice.)

Do you send concise messages? Are they accurate, objective, and inclusive of appropriate attribution? These qualities are important in communication, whether it is verbal or written. This may seem far too elemental to even mention in a book for and about leaders, but even brilliant professionals can lose sight of how important they are in building trust between partners, teams, or any other individuals or groups. When a partner is habitually incorrect about "facts" she shares, others learn not to trust what she says. When he implies that what he has to say is undisputed fact, but it is actually just his opinion, he teaches others to doubt his credibility. This is also true if she repeats factual information but does not attribute them to their source. When he states or writes secondhand information about something that he did not personally observe, he may be perceived as deliberately telling an untruth. None of these actions are likely to engender the trust needed between leadership partners.

Dyad bonding can be prevented by inaccurate, nonobjective, nonattributed communication, even though the sender of this communication did not intend her message to be any of these things! As basic and required as these communication components may seem to some people, they may not even be recognized as being absent by others. The dynamic causing what may seem to be dishonest, even unethical, communication isn't usually the result of an intent to mislead. In Dyads where the partners come from different cultures, genders, or professions, the underlying issue that may make communication difficult is the variance in socialization of different groups. Professionals from two different backgrounds may not only have different vocabularies, they may have been socialized to view a certain way of communicating as acceptable, when other individuals do not agree. They may have developed habits that get in the way of their messaging, even though those habits were appropriate or at least worked well in a former, nonmanagement role.

TRUST-BUSTING COMMUNICATION HABITS

Of course when there *is* evidence to back up statements, it should be shared. It should also be attributed to its source. When this does not happen in papers or documents, the veracity of the written words are (at the least) questioned. At a more serious level, written nonattribution is called plagiarism.

Great managers who wish to be trusted and known as accurate speak with attribution when it is appropriate, just like competent, ethical writers do. (They don't practice "verbal plagiarism," which might be a habit developed by clinicians because of the need to instill faith and hope in others that there is "someone who is infallible and will cure me.") They are also careful not to report *as fact* occurrences not witnessed, but *reported* to them.

The act of reporting (verbally or in writing) nonwitnessed events as facts is a common communication error. For clinicians, this may be a habit because of the norm in clinical practice of accepting past diagnoses and past medical records from other trusted clinicians as fact. When this practice is carried over to other circumstances, erroneous information might be perpetuated as factual (Table **3-1**).

In Table **3-1**, the difference between the communications in column 2 (what was reported) and those in the third column (what a factual report would have been) may seem subtle, but they are hugely impactful to each of these situations. In column 2, the manager reported *what was reported to him or her*, as fact. Had the communication been passed on as portrayed in column 3, the factual information was about the *report* of an incident, not the assumption of the truth from that report. (If you doubt the importance of this difference, ask either an attorney or an ethicist which is the least risky, most accurate, most ethical way to pass on information, especially information that will result in a manager or other person taking some sort of action).

Table 3-1	Examples of Perceived/Reported Circumstances as Fact	
Perceived Event	**Nonfactual Report of Event**	**Factual Report of Event**
Mary stated to her colleague John that a third colleague, Jim, had "yelled at her during a meeting" when she disagreed with him.	John e-mailed his Dyad Partner Liz (Jim's direct supervisor): "Jim is out of control. He yelled at Mary in a meeting."	E-mail from John: "Mary reported to me that Jim yelled at her during the team meeting on Wednesday."
A patient's letter to a hospital executive stated "My call light was not answered for 20 minutes!"	The hospital executive told the unit where the patient had been admitted, "This patient's call light was not answered for 20 minutes!"	Report from the executive to the nurse manager: "I received a letter from a patient who stated that his call light was not answered for 20 minutes."
An independent physician called a Physician Dyad Partner to tell him that he was informed by the hospital Finance VP that he was no longer welcome to practice at the hospital because he cost the organization too much money.	The Physician Dyad Partner called his management partner and relayed that, "The VP of Finance said Dr. X is costing the hospital too much money, so he can't practice here."	Report from the first Dyad Partner to the second: "Dr. X called me and stated that the VP for Finance told him he is no longer welcome to practice here."

All of the reports in column 1 *could* have been 100% accurate. Or, they could have been inaccurate, either because of a deliberate (for whatever reason) bending of the truth *or* misperceptions of the original reporter. Good managers continually remind themselves that perceptions are often at the root of communication problems.

All three of the incidents listed in Table **3-1**, column 1, are real issues that occurred in a community hospital where one of us worked. All three of the responses in column 2 were communications that resulted from them. When they were investigated, it was discovered that:

1. Jim had disagreed with Mary at a meeting where an entire group was voicing opinions about what their strategy should be. The other six people at the meeting stated that Jim never raised his voice but he did state he thought she was wrong. Mary was the only person who perceived him as "yelling" at her.
2. There was no way to verify the time it took to answer the patient's call light. The time could have been more or less than the patient perceived it to be.
3. The Vice President for Finance did not have the same recollection of his conversation with the physician as the physician did. His memory of the hallway discussion was that the physician approached him and stated he was unhappy with the hospital's decision not to buy another DaVinci Robot. The VP recalled stating that the hospital had determined that the return on investment for a third robot was negative and couldn't justify buying another one, especially when capital is limited.

By accepting and reporting perceptions as fact, the individuals involved lost credibility when the circumstances were investigated. Their ability to communicate factually and fairly appeared to be impaired. (We are not implying that any of these three incidents should not be investigated for potential interpersonal, patient service, or relationship interventions. The issue here is appropriate reporting of nonwitnessed or verified information.)

It's important that partners understand how each of them communicates. If one feels the other is not clearly and objectively communicating, he must be able to discuss this with him or her *for the good of the partnership, the team, and the organization.* Failing to address communication issues with a partner leads to more miscommunication. In fact, failure to communicate about any issue, misunderstanding, or disagreement is a mistake. Partners, whether they are marriage partners or business Dyad partners, cannot lead together without honestly addressing what they perceive to be blocking their mutual success. This includes open dialogue in areas where their thoughts are divergent. Healthy Dyad Partnerships require the ability of the partners to recognize and work through areas of conflict.

Conflict is not considered to be particularly desirable among people. The word may even conjure a vision of violence. (After all, we sometimes euphemistically label military actions that cost soldiers their lives conflicts rather than wars.) For many of us, conflict is unpleasant, and uncomfortable. We often choose to avoid it.

Sometimes we may not want to risk facing even the short-term discomfort that open disagreement brings. We might fear that arguing with our partner could cause long-term harm to our relationship. (This may be true if we have not established bonds that are strong enough to remain intact during less-than-harmonious times *or* our differences are so great that we cannot compromise *or* one or both of us lacks the skill or emotional maturity to negotiate constructively) Any of these situations has the potential of being fatal to a Dyad. (Marriages faced with these types of challenges have been known to end in divorce.)

Hopefully, most individuals promoted into management will not be fatally traumatized by the latter two problems. They will have consciously worked to build a mutually respectful bond as partners. That's important, because conflict should be expected between them. Two leaders have been paired to bring two skill sets together for the creation of a synergy needed in the next era of healthcare. They come from different professional cultures, and maybe other different cultures due to ethnicity, gender, or family background.

While Dyad Partners share interdependent goals, performance criteria and activities, each has his own behavioral preferences for performance of joint activities. In order to bring their model of leadership up to its full potential, they *should* sometimes disagree. Working through their differing points of view (also called conflict resolution) is healthy for organizations and groups. It can help both individuals, and the Dyad Partnership, grow stronger. In addition, it helps organizations avoid a phenomenon known as groupthink (Display 3-4).

Display 3-4 **Groupthink**

Groupthink is "the pressure to achieve a unanimous decision, which overwhelms individual group members' motivation to weigh alternatives realistically." As a result, individuals neglect critical thought and the need to weigh pros and cons.

Groupthink occurs when group members want to achieve consensus, maintain good feelings among group members, and appease leaders.

Groupthink occurs most often in crisis, among tight-knit groups and where members are insulated from criticisms of qualified outsiders or when powerful leaders promote his or her favored solution.

Adapted from Newman, D. (2000). Sociology: Exploring the architecture of everyday life. *Thousand Oakes, CA: Pine Forge Press.*

A Dyad Partnership could fall victim to the same groupthink problems if one or both partners is more concerned about the relationship than to the organization's success. It can occur if one leader feels "less than" the other in any way. Their entire team could also get stuck in this mode if they observe the leaders struggling with power or with one continually acquiescing to the other without an observable (but civil) weighing of options. If a partner leader continually and aggressively promotes (or demands) his solution as *the only* solution, the entire group may stop thinking critically.

At a time when healthcare organizations need innovation, successful Dyads understand that failing to acknowledge conflict can have serious ramifications for their success. They understand, too, that confronting conflict is not only desirable, it is indicative of engagement with the organization *and* Dyad partners.

David Augsburger recognized this when he wrote, *Caring Enough to Confront*, in 1983. He pointed out that people who choose not to address their conflicts because of discomfort or perceived risk to the relationship are choosing *their* comfort over the health of the relationship. It is those who truly care about the organization, and in our case, the success of their Dyad partnership, who will choose confrontation over conflict avoidance. Confronting misalignments, disagreements, or divergent goals is honest. Augsburger points out that selective honesty is not honesty at all—and that good relationships require honesty in two way communications. Augsburger doesn't advocate war-like, no holds barred, winner take all conflict. In fact, he talks about confrontation where, "truth told with love brings healing, enables us to grow and produces change." His underlying tenet is that "truth and love are the two necessary impediments for any relationship with integrity" (24).

If you're uncomfortable with the word "love" for your business partner, just substitute "care" or "concern." The point is that all human interactions are about relationships. All relationships are interpersonal, and that must be considered when working with a partner on how you will manage together. When working on conflict resolution it's important to remember this. The best Dyad partners, like the best

---

Display 3-5 **When Dyads Can't Succeed/Resolve Conflict**

We are champions for Dyad leadership because of its benefits …

But, we have a note of caution for executives who implement the model. Not every individual is able to overcome cultural conditioning or personal proclivities. Some may not be able to learn how to work in a partnership. Some will be unable to share power and accountability.

Their styles in managing conflict may never evolve beyond forcing (utilizing position power to bend others to their will).

The thoughtful executive will observe how individual Dyad leaders deal (or refuse to deal) with conflict. This is a strong indicator of whether he or she can succeed in this type of relationship.

As leaders, we sometimes make hiring mistakes but because we care about our organizations, we must correct these. Dyads aren't for everyone. Leadership positions aren't for everyone. When a partner doesn't fit as a Dyad leader, it's time for a separation—or divorce. (Those who cannot manage together are unlikely to be good leaders even as single leaders in an era where team skills and a need to decrease silo thinking is essential for an organization's success.)

---

marriage partners are fair, reasonable, kind, compassionate and empathetic, even during conflict.

Dyad partners may face conflicts caused by intellectual differences, beliefs about shared issues, or struggles for power and resources (Display 3-5). Comanagement may be difficult because of differences in managerial style. Perceived or real differences in status of two who are supposed to be equal partners can add to conflict, because "conflict is less and performance is more effective when there is a congruence of status" (25).

Role ambiguity, different perspectives, overlapping duties, and dual loyalties (to both a profession and an organization) are all potential areas of conflict that are especially likely in the Dyad Management Model. When healthy Dyad relationships exist (where both leaders are emotionally healthy and share mutual respect and trust) individuals are able to resolve their conflicts through productive problem solving techniques. Having agreed on priorities, expectations, goals, formal operating guidelines (how we will make decisions) and basic methods for work, they can collaborate and redefine their conflicts as problems to solve together.

Dyad leaders who can resolve conflict are skilled in interpersonal negotiations. They listen before they talk and they explore options together. They have patience and integrity. They avoid the presumption of ill intention on the part of their partners. They focus on the issues, breaking big issues into smaller issues and discuss them, while controlling their emotions. They don't threaten or manipulate. They are invested in reaching understanding, resolving points of differences, and focusing on problems. They also don't waste time trying to negotiate what can't be negotiated: Core values, integrity, emotions, attitudes and trust. Instead, they concentrate on things their partners and they can change together: Behavior and organizational decisions.

Healthcare leadership Dyads are established to bring together two managers with different skills and abilities. They are paired because they have different professional backgrounds. They come from different cultures. Conflict is to be expected. In fact, it is desired, because the strength of this leadership model does not stem from how much the two think identically. The theory behind Dyad leadership is that the quality of decision making will be enhanced when two leaders are able to constructively bring their differences to their mutual work. Their success depends on their ability to recognize, acknowledge, discuss and manage their conflict. Each must understand and deploy the art of persuasion. Each must be graced with the ability to compromise and/or change.

Early in their partnership, Dyad leaders will need to determine how they can most effectively communicate on a day-to-day basis. They have different responsibilities, and may go days without face-to-face time. One of the strengths of this model is that two leaders can "cover" more territory and attend different meetings. However, this increases the challenge of keeping each other informed. A plan for a regular information exchange (calls, e-mails, scheduled meetings), along with an agreement of what information each needs or wants to know, is an important part of the individuals' shared responsibility. This will save the time that would have been used to correct possible misinformation or misunderstandings. Because they are mutually accountable for leading a department, project or operational area, it cannot be assumed that any information that one has isn't important to the other. Only by talking about what method each prefers for keeping informed, and what information should be shared, can the two leaders really know the best way to communicate with each other.

It is equally important to agree on a methodology for decision making. Strategic decisions (or those that will materially affect the Dyad's success at meeting their mutual goals) require partners to discuss and decide together. Many of day-to-day decisions fall into the exclusive job description of one partner. Some of these may not be of importance to the other partner (or they may be of importance, but the individual trusts his dyad partner is taking care of these details and does not feel the need to be informed of these). Others might be helpful for him or her to know. It's a mistake for either partner to assume the other automatically knows which decisions are strategic and need to be made together, which are the purview of only one partner but should be shared with his partner after the decision has been made, and which don't need to be communicated to the partners at all.

Explicit advice on what teams must agree on is included in a classic book on team-building by Dyer, Dyer and Dyer, now in its 5th edition. The authors state that a team must agree on priorities, share expectations, clarify goals, formulate operational guidelines (including how decisions are made), agree on basic work methods, and determined how differences will be resolved (26). This is as true for a Dyad partnership as it is for a larger team.

Table 3-2   Example of a Dyad Decision-Making Discussion Grid

Decision Type (Each partnership lists what decisions are specific to their Dyad)	Made Together	Made by Partner A Reported to Partner B	Made by Partner A and Not Reported	Made by Partner B Reported to Partner A	Made by Partner B and Not Reported
aaaaaaaaaaaa	X				
bbbbbbbbbbb			X		
ccccccccccccccc					X
dddddddddd		X			
eeeeeeeeeee				X	

Different Dyads will determine which decisions fall into which category for them and their unique partnership. They may or may not even document their decision making plan on a decision grid (Table **3-2**), although most professionals won't do this, and prefer a verbal discussion only. However they choose to address it, a determination of how decisions will be made, early in the relationship, will increase the speed of their bonding with trust.

TRUST: THE SECOND RELATIONSHIP REINFORCER

Trust has been defined as "an assured reliance on the character, ability, strength, or truth of someone" (27). It isn't automatic just because two leaders have been placed in comanagement jobs, with the same goals and accountabilities. In most Dyad relationships, because of differing cultures, it will take time to establish a level of trust that ensures the individuals success as partners. Each has to demonstrate to the other she is capable and competent to perform her job. In addition, he must earn confidence that he has integrity, communication skills, respect for others, and commitment. This commitment is to the organization and its mission as well as to the success of the Dyad partnership and team.

Writer SM Covey describes trust as "the one thing, if developed and leveraged, has the potential to develop unparalleled success and prosperity" (28). In his book on the subject, he makes the point that what inspires the greatest trust is seeking mutual benefit. For a Dyad, the mutual benefit would be the success of both partners, which leads to success for the organization. In other words, the organization's goals are best met when individual partners work so that both are successful leaders. Neither has a self-serving agenda in which only one wins as the recognized superior leader.

This is difficult if either (or both) originate from what Logan, King, and Fischer-Wright describe as a Tribe in Stage 3—Their research indicated that those who soak long enough in that stage, where "I'm great, you're not," and "in order for me to win, you must lose," become ambassadors for that way of behaving, even when moved to another environment (29). Some leaders from such cultures *can* become partners, though, especially when they realize that both of them are needed to meet goals that one could not do alone.

To create credibility with each other, and to inspire trust, Dyad leaders must behave in a way that demonstrates a concern for the best interests of their partners, as well as the organization. Besides communication and the skills previously described, there are certain actions that build trust. These include giving credit where credit is due, showing loyalty, and holding yourself and each other accountable.

GIVING CREDIT WHERE IT IS DUE

In a previous book (30), Kathy described surveys of staff members in which they were asked to describe traits of the best and the worst bosses they had ever reported to. Best bosses were described as giving credit to others for their work. Worst bosses were seen as taking credit for the work and ideas of others.

This shouldn't come as a surprise to anyone who has ever had the misfortune of working for someone (or working with someone) who habitually represents other people's work ideas as his own. It's a disheartening, demotivating experience for any employee and one way to ensure a dysfunctional Dyad.

At its worst, credit taking for what someone else did is lying. At its best, it's an ignorance of what others contribute to your personal success or the group's success.

If a Dyad partner is guilty of not attributing credit to her partner because of the latter, education and learning about each other's work should change this behavior. As the partners bond, if one feels she has not been recognized for her contributions, she can discuss this with her partner because of their ability to communicate honestly. If the root problem for not giving credit is deliberate prevarication, the partnership is doomed because integrity can't be negotiated or learned.

It's a good practice in any relationship to look for ways to recognize your partner for his contributions. (Of course, this is true for all members of your team.) Everyone appreciates recognition. It strengthens bonds and increases motivation to perform well.

SHOWING LOYALTY

Partnerships require loyalty. While Dyad leaders may not agree, they need to know they are supported in spite of these. In marriages, there are times when a spouse must choose between family and friends and husband or wife. The same will probably be true with Dyad partners from different professional or cultural families. Recognizing relationship imperfections and working on them to improve partnership is not the same thing as complaining about your partner to your professional colleagues.

For example, the administrator Dyad partner may hear culturally based criticism of her physician partner. Another executive might say, "It must be a real problem working with a doctor—the arrogance must get under your skin." Loyalty to her partner prevents her from either staying silent or agreeing. A loyal partner would counter with statements about why she enjoys working with her partner or how she hasn't found him to be arrogant at all. This loyalty teaches others they cannot "divide and conquer" a leadership team. It enforces the partnership bond.

HOLDING YOURSELF AND EACH OTHER ACCOUNTABLE

Dyad leadership is about each partner contributing his unique skills. Shared success is only possible if each knows what her responsibilities are, what her partner's responsibilities are, and that both will be accountable to complete the tasks assigned to their roles (completely, accurately, and within a defined time span). Written job descriptions are a must and may have to be continually refined for increased clarity around roles and responsibilities.

Mature employees hold themselves accountable for the completion of their specific jobs. They monitor their own quality and self-correct when necessary. Mature managers do the same thing in their roles. Mature Dyad leaders do this, and they hold their partners accountable, too. Trust is built when each individual does what he says he will do and completes his part of the Dyad work.

Accountability is about more than responsibility for individual or joint task completion. It is about an attentiveness to the actions that strengthen the partnership bond. In other words, each individual should consciously consider how his or her behavior adds to the success of the management duo. They should both learn to be comfortable with actions that demonstrate they care about their organization, teams, customers, and Dyad partners enough to confront each other about anything that could interfere with this. Each should hold the other accountable for his or her communications, actions that increase or endanger trust, and respectful interactions, even when disagreeing.

RESPECT: THE THIRD RELATIONSHIP REINFORCER

In an on-line article on relationships, author R. Graf asks, "In all honesty, do you want to be around anyone who does not respect you? In other words, thinks that you are meaningless, and not worth the time?" (31) Graf is writing about the necessity of respect for communication in marriage but indicated that respect is a simple basic necessity for all human relationships. Families, friends, and work teams function best when respect is part of the culture.

Display 3-6 **Respect**

The 1913 Webster's Dictionary defined respect as "to take notice of, to regard with specific attention, to care for, to heed, to consider worthy of esteem, to regard with honor."

The 2014 Wikipedia definition of respect is "a positive feeling of esteem or deference for a person or other entity, *and also* specific actions and conduct representative of that esteem."

The definitions are 100 years apart. Both refer to feelings but the modern, online version goes further: it adds actions and conduct.

For Dyads, actions and conduct not only signal respect to each other, they model for others and signal to others, that the partners hold each other in high regard, both as individual people and as representatives of different professional cultures.

Many healthcare organizations include respect in their core values. Sometimes they spell out what they mean by the "R" word as it relates to customers (patients), visitors, or work associates (Display 3-6). Often it is assumed that everyone knows what respect means or looks like. It is something that we know when we see it. We perceive attitudes of individuals toward ourselves or others as respectful (or not). Sometimes this needs to be spelled out between partners, whether these are spouses or Dyad leaders.

For Dyad partners, the underlying premise of respect is a belief that each is a specialist in his or her profession and that each is equally important to a mutual success as leaders. As we discussed in Chapter 1, that requires an understanding that both sets of skills brought to the partnership are essential for the accomplishment of goals.

Respectful people can disagree and are comfortable with disagreement. They can, and should be, frank with each other. They can be passionate about their own beliefs and will negotiate for these with team members, but their negotiations are fair and reasonable.

CHAPTER SUMMARY

In Dyads, two people with different but complementary skill sets are teamed to lead together. They are responsible for bringing congruence to goals of at least two different groups within an organization. Their responsibilities include balancing resources with what the organization needs for success in the current environment and what it will need to succeed in the next era of healthcare. Together they provide a new team/group structure to do this, and they make sure that decision makers have information from multiple professional viewpoints.

To form the partnerships necessary for success, individuals in Dyads strengthen their leadership teamwork by concentrating on communication skills, trust, and respect. These are the same underpinnings of all successful relationships.

Dyads in Action

A CLINICAL IT PARTNERSHIP
Ann Shepard and and Sam Brandt

Healthcare professionals have worked side by side throughout their careers. However, the development of Dyad leadership as a management model, where responsibility and accountability are shared is a novel idea to many. It was a foreign concept to us, too. In fact, we believe we were the first chief medical informatics officer (CMIO) and chief nursing informatics officer (CNIO) to be paired formally as coleaders of clinical information technology for a multistate, large healthcare system!

A CLINICAL IT JOURNEY

In early 2009, the clinical IT journey at Catholic Health Initiatives (CHI) was accelerated following the signing of the Health Information Technology for Economic and Clinical Health (HITECH) Act, which requires and rewards organizations for implementing and using electronic health records (EHRs) in a meaningful way. The act got everyone's attention because it outlined penalties for organizations who failed to comply with the new law and regulations by specified due dates. While we were already implementing IT systems, CHI began the expedited process of planning a long and complicated path to a fully electronic health record that would include appropriate tools for our clinicians. For many of our 87 hospital locations, this move from pen and paper recording of clinical events to electronic capture of data elements portended dramatic change. Additionally, it shifted our process from traditional local implementations to a shared national implementation. That meant that we needed to coordinate with all of our sites to design and build the best possible clinical electronic health environment.

Our plan, which was simultaneously aggressive and expensive, would impact all hospital staff as well as physicians. It included the installation of clinical applications such as documentation tools for nurses, physicians, and ancillary staff; electronic order entry for providers; bar-scanning of patients and medications; and a new financial system for revenue and admission information. Some of our locations had no clinical IT systems. Others had legacy applications that would need to be replaced with standardized products.

We knew that a change of this magnitude would require strong leadership. We believe that the best model for this would be to utilize multidisciplinary teams, including the two-person management teams that CHI called Dyads. Although our clinicians and providers understood the necessity of changes to their practices, our executives were concerned about the magnitude of change required for success. They knew that such a transformation would require cooperation from departments that previously worked in silos. Therefore, they created a management structure to establish a partnership to include both clinical and technology leaders. These leaders would share responsibility for oversight and governance of the system IT program, which was dubbed *OneCare* to symbolize our dedication to the development of a national IT product that would be used to decrease clinical variance through widespread adoption of best practices. The system chief nursing officer (CNO), chief medical officer (CMO), and chief information officer (CIO) were named as joint executive sponsors of the initiative. Other leaders from finance, compliance, communication, and other departments were tapped to provide support. In partnership with external vendors, a governance structure was designed to include national, regional, and local oversight of the program, with final decision-making authority resting at the national level.

National systems have multiple priorities. If specific leaders aren't assigned accountabilities for important priorities, they may not be pursued. It was clear that this large program's success required a strong informatics leadership infrastructure in addition to the existing executive leadership. We needed leaders who would concentrate on OneCare. We had IT leaders, but we needed clinical executives. CHI had prior experience with the CMIO but that position had been vacant for several years. The executive sponsors know that clinical IT is broader than medical IT, so when it was determined that the CMIO job should be filled, a CNIO position was added. These clinical leaders would be part of a team that included the vice president of clinical IT and the vice president of applications, who both reported to the CIO. However, they would be a special miniteam as a subset of the larger group: a national clinical IT leadership Dyad.

THE ARRANGED MARRIAGE

Some Dyad leaders have the opportunity to select their partners. Because we were hired into our positions at the same time, our partnership is more like an arranged marriage! The Oxford University Press (2007) defines arranged marriage as "a marriage planned and agreed to by the families or guardians of the couple concerned, who have little or no say in the matter themselves." In our case, it was our CHI family (with the CHI CNO and CMO as surrogate parents) who determined who we would partner with.

Candidates for our jobs were interviewed separately by national interdisciplinary groups. Memberships of the groups overlapped, and colleagues who interviewed us say that they considered personalities and probabilities of successful bonding of the various candidates as one of the criteria for hire. With this parallel path of selection, we didn't get to meet each other until our "marriage day."

What we discovered quickly is that our experience and skills are quite different, but they are highly complementary. The CNIO has a background in nursing, administration, and clinical IT leadership. The CMIO's experience includes private primary care, medical informatics, and physician leadership in a large capitated managed care organization. He had also worked for a healthcare IT vendor. These backgrounds underscore our different perspectives as we approach problems together. They also are the root cause of some of our more spirited debates! Even when we don't completely see eye to eye, we have discovered that frequently the combination of our two ways of looking at the world is frequently necessary to provide a more complete picture for making better decisions.

COMING TOGETHER DURING CHALLENGING TIMES

Marriages that are started in stressful circumstances probably have greater challenges than those where there is plenty of money and support for the couple. The same thing is true for partnerships. We were hired to take leadership roles when the system was on a fast track to massive change. We've been told by outside consultants that our OneCare program is among the most complex and challenging to implement. So our "marriage" started in more of a stressful environment than a calm one. How stressful? We were tasked with putting IT technology into hundreds of sites (this includes our acute care hospitals, physician offices, clinics, and other continuum locations). We needed to do this within a time frame that would help each of these entities reach meaningful use and get ready for the new ICD-10 payment system. We were responsible for adding technology beyond what many people consider to be IT. (We weren't just putting in computers. We were initiating Smart Pump technology and bar-code medication scanning technology.) We were determining appropriate work flows for a variety of infrastructures. We were part of the teams responsible for making cultural changes in every one of those organizations (and no two organizations were the same). Holy Computers, Batman! As we write this, we wonder if either one of us was sane when we accepted our jobs.

A clinical technology implementation program has multiple concurrent streams of work even when only one system is being implemented. While we would have liked to implement one product, for various system reasons we started out with three major vendors. Over time, as the system (CHI) has acquired new markets and facilities, we have added additional vendors, programs, and IT activities. This strategic initiative has become complicated, to say the least. We think of it like the construction of a building: there are many parts and pieces that must be fitted together in the correct sequence for successful completion of the structure. The development of our Dyad partnership has been similar. The parts we needed to put together included an understanding of each other's professional perspectives, experience, approach, and personality. We were tasked to build a relationship between strangers (Sam and Ann) at the same time we were immersed in an enormous project and a larger multidisciplinary team. Even though we've been partners for 3 years, we continue to learn how to lead together, how to recognize each other's strengths and weaknesses, and how to achieve the synergy our complementary perspectives and skills should provide. Since each of us has experience as a spouse, we think that is not a failure to have not learned *everything* about each other in just 36 months. We especially think we should pat each other on the back to have bonded as well as we have in such a chaotic, stressful environment.

CHALLENGES TO BECOMING PARTNERS

Our arranged marriage has presented both challenges and opportunities for the organization and for both of us. We quickly discovered that there are specific skills we both need to hone. We both needed to learn to listen better and to understand how our dissimilar socializations affect our communication, as well as what we consider important to our clinical peers. Ann, the CNIO, tends to focus on the broader group of clinicians, from nurses to pharmacists, to lab technicians, and other ancillary staff. Typical of her profession, she is concerned holistically about all the activities of various healthcare providers who come in contact with patients and need to use electronic tools. Her focus is often on workflow, data entry, the recording of observations, treatments and assessments. Because she's been a bedside nurse, she emphasizes the need for IT systems to be useful in the evaluation of patient care and in capturing charges that result from that care. Like a typical nurse informaticist, she focuses on streamlining the effort and work to make it easier for clinicians to do the correct or right task.

Sam is more representative of his medical informatics counterparts. He is more focused on the physician perspective of care. His emphasis is on the processes for diagnosis and therapy as well as the orchestration of care between providers, clinicians, and healthcare teams. He is especially interested in systems that share information between settings and over time.

In our Dyad partnership, the CMIO tends to be more centered on technology and knowledge representation as well as the development of highly reliable systems. The CNIO focuses on operational processes. While the system benefits from two professionals who look at IT systems in a different way, we could easily fall into a dysfunctional marriage if one or both of us insisted that our limited resources be used to mainly support the development of the functions we see as most important. Part of our work together is to remind each other of this potential pitfall that could jeopardize the overall success of our mutual work. Our responsibility is to stay alert to our individual biases while learning about what our partner sees as important *and to understand why*.

Another challenge that we continually face is the scope and breadth of our shared accountabilities. We spend a majority of our time in separate places because of profession-specific activities. In addition, we usually find ourselves in different parts of the country because of the need to cover more ground. In other words, we can't go to everything together because most of the time we are both needed in multiple places, and we split up in order to have a presence in two locations at once. This creates a communication challenge. It's essential that we stay in touch so that both are aware of progress and problems that we need to either celebrate or work on with our team. We have learned that in an organization of our size, it is imperative that messages we give to our markets are in concert. Nothing upsets local teams more than perceptions that the national leadership is not in synch. We deliberately utilize frequent e-mails when we can't get together face to face, and work hard to remember to inform our partner about accomplishments and issues. Sometimes we forget to communicate when we should. We try to learn from those times and learn best when we have to invest time fixing issues that could have been avoided if we'd connected sooner.

THE DYAD AND THE FAMILY

As we were challenged to get to know each other and to colead, we have had the additional joy of a growing family to contend with. In a system as complex as CHI, it would be impossible for the two of us to provide the clinical informatics leadership needed in 19 states that stretch from the east to the west coast. Soon after our partnership was formed, we determined we would need regional CNIOs and CMIOs. We also decided that they, too, would be Dyad partners. We determined that whenever possible, we would allow marriages of choice. (This is not to denigrate our arranged partnership, but our hypothesis was that it might be easier for people to bond when they could select partners whom they personally interviewed for fit). As the national Dyad to whom these regional leaders would report (the CMIOs with a direct line to Sam and the CNIOs with a direct line to Ann, but with both groups reporting in a matrix position to the other national leader), we interviewed candidates together wherever possible, the second Dyad partner to be hired, was interviewed by the first. It is our perception that those individuals who had a say in hiring their Dyad partner bonded more quickly than those who did not. We don't know the reason for this. We are just reporting our observation!

As leaders of two different professions (nurses and physicians), we strive to communicate the same things to both groups. We have discovered that, even though we are one team, there are times when the nurses want to talk with the *nurse* leader and times when *only* the physician leader will do for a physician issue.

However Dyads come together, they face the same work of learning to lead together and to share accountabilities for the success of their shared goals. For us, the goal is the national implementation of a complex culture-changing IT system that clinicians can and will use for the betterment of patient care. Sharing the same objectives (as well as the same values that include improved service to our customers) is the underlying reason that we can work together even when we are very different. The physicians and nurses who have been paired to accomplish this work have formed a clinical IT family, with Ann and Sam as the matriarch and patriarch. That makes us responsible to role-model teamwork and to hold the nurse and physician Dyads who report to us to a standard of true partnership. In other words, we not only have to role model a functional relationship, we must insist upon it from others.

We have observed other Dyads who seem to think and act as one. That isn't us. Our personalities and leadership styles are very different. We have different approaches to get things done. We still have times when we need to confront each other over differences. We still spend time trying to understand the other partner's perspective. We don't always agree, but we keep our differences behind closed doors and present a united front once a decision has been made. We share a passion for the success of the OneCare Program. We both believe in the potential of informatics because it will make care, easier, better, safer, more satisfying to caregivers as well as patients, and more personalized. We know that we have complementary skills that will help all of this come to fruition. That's why even though our partnership started out as arranged rather than chosen, it isn't a dysfunctional marriage.

REFERENCES

1. Neville, A. (March 3, 2013). Why partnership is harder than marriage. Website: forbes.com, Retrieved from: www.forbes.com/sites/amandaneville/2013/03/01/why-partnership-is-harder-than-marriage
2. Kreitner, R., & Kinicki, A. (1995). *Organizational behavior* (p. 8). Chicago, IL: Richard D. Irwin Company.
3. Davis, R. C. (1951). *The fundamentals of top management*. New York, NY: Harper.
4. Adair, J. (1973). *The action-centered leader*. London, UK: McGraw-Hill.
5. Likert, R. (1967). *The human organization*. New York, NY: McGraw-Hill.
6. Gardner, J. W. (1990). *On leadership*. New York, NY: Free Press.
7. Mann, F. (1965). Toward an understanding of the leadership role in formal organization. In R. Dubin (Ed.), *Leadership and productivity*. San Francisco, CA: Chandler.
8. MacKenzie, R. A. (1969). The management process in 3-D. *Havard Business Review, 47*(6), 80–87.
9. Roby, T. B. (1961). The executive function in small groups. In L. Petrullo & B. Bass (Eds.), *Leadership and interpersonal behavior*. New York, NY: Holt, Reinhart and Winston.
10. Government Author. 21st century challenges: re-examining the base of the Federal government, Website: www.gao.gov, Retrieved from: www.gao.gov/challenges/healthcare.pdf. Accessed March 2, 2014.
11. Drexler, M. (Winter 2010). Can cost effective healthcare equal better healthcare? *Havard School of Public Health News*, Website: www.hsph.harvard.edu, Retrieved from: www.hsph.harvard.edu/news/magazine/winter10assessment
12. Corporate Authors (October 5, 2010). The future of nursing: Leading change. *Advancing Health*, Robert Wood Johnson and Institute of Medicine Report.
13. Maxwell, J. (2001). *The 17 indesputable laws of teamwork: Embrace them and empower your team*. Nashville, TN: Thomas Nelson, Inc.
14. Barge, J., & Hirokawa, R. (1989). Toward a communication competency model of leadership. *Small Group Behavior, 20*, 167–189.
15. Staff (2012). Five ways miscommunication led to disaster. myfivebest.com/five-ways-miscommunication-led-to-disaster
16. Barker, C. (October 5, 2012). 10 Deadliest air disasters caused by miscommunication. Website: bestcommunicationdegrees.com. Retrieved from http://www.bestcommunicationsdegrees.com/10-deadliest-air-disasters-caused-by-miscommunication

17. Staff writers (October 14, 2011). Miscommunications caused US drone deaths: report. *UAV News.* New York: Associated Armed Forces Press.
18. Staff (January 16, 2008). *Public health advisory: Edetate Disodium—Marketed as Endrate and generic products.* Silver Spring, Maryland. U.S. Food and Drug Administration.
19. US Army (1983). *Military Leadership, FM22-100.* Washington, DC: US Government Printing Office.
20. Wellins, R. S., Byham, W. C., Wilson, J. M. (1991). *Empowered teams: creating self-directed work groups that improve quality, productivity, and participation.* San Francisco, CA: Jossey-Bass.
21. Logan, D., King, J., & Fischer-Wright, H. (2008). *Tribal leadership.* New York, NY: Harper Collins Publishers.
22. Business Dictionary.com: *Generation X*
23. Klasko, S., & Shea, G. (1999). *The phantom stethoscope: a field manual for finding an optimistic future in medicine* (p. 124). Franklin, TN: Hillsboro Press.
24. Augsburger, D. (2009). *Caring enough to confront: how to understand and express your deepest feelings toward others.* Ventura, CA: Regal Books.
25. Thomas, K., & Schmidt, W. (1976). A survey of managerial interests with respect to conflict. *Academy of Management Journal, 19,* 315–318.
26. Dyer, W. G., Dyer, J., & Dyer, W. (2013). *Team building: proven strategies for improving team performance.* San Francisco, CA: Jossey-Bass.
27. www.merriam-webster.com /dictionary/trust
28. Covey, S. M. (2006). *The speed of trust.* New York, NY: Free Press.
29. Logan, D., King, J., & Fischer-Wright, H. (2008). *Tribal leadership.* New York, NY: Harper-Collins.
30. Sanford, K. (1998). *Leading with love.* Washington, DC: Vashon Publishing.
31. Graf, R. (May 2009). 10 Must do's for a successful happy marriage. Website: rgraf.hubpages.com, Retrieved from: http://rgraf.hubpages.com/hub/10-must-dos-for-a-successful-happy-marriage

Chapter 4

Power, Persuasion, Politics, and Perceptions

We refer to multiple studies and articles from the management and leadership literature in this book. To those who are cynical about the genuineness of leaders they may have experienced in the past, the conclusions drawn by experts and authors might sound a lot like methods for manipulation. For example, research that indicates that when a manager behaves in a certain way, team members will perform in a corresponding manner (such as the studies that equate manager relationship building behaviors to higher team member productivity) could be perceived as teaching managers how to manipulate those who work with them.

This is not what we want to impart with the inclusion of management research results throughout these chapters. Our purpose is to help those who select candidates for Dyad leadership roles, as well as potential and current Dyad partners, be deliberate in considering who should populate these important jobs, and what education and development we all need to implement a new model of leadership for healthcare system transformation.

Manipulation occurs when words or actions are used to control or sway others in a direction that is beneficial to the manipulator, and not necessarily in the best interest of those being swayed. The leaders we want in healthcare are those who deploy their influence for a greater good than themselves. They may need to learn new skills, and management research and theory can help here, but at their core, these leaders are authentic.

AUTHENTIC LEADERSHIP

Authentic leaders are those who are both true to themselves and honest with others about who they are. Because they are willing to admit to their own weaknesses, they make the best Dyad leaders. That's because they have a willingness to supplement their own (limited) skills with those of a partner.

As with every other aspect of leadership we can think of, there is research on leadership authenticity (and it supports the importance of this trait). As Ken Blanchard and Mark Miller point out in their book, *The Secret: What Great Leaders Know and Do*: "You must gain the trust of your people. If you don't have their trust, you'll never be a great leader" (1). Authentic leaders, because they do what they say, and say what they do, *are trusted by others*. Bernard Bass describes them as leaders who "align their interests with others and may sacrifice their own interests for the common good. Their communications can be trusted. ... They set examples to uplift the moral values of their followers ... they are concerned for their followers' development and well-being" (2). In addition, authentic leaders "do not *manipulate* followers or treat them as objects" (3). So, authentic leaders, as they learn more about leadership, will use management education and learning, not for manipulation but for self-development as leaders.

Among other areas of leadership development for Dyad leaders, we've identified what we call the four "Ps" of partnership that both leaders need to understand. These are Power, Persuasion, Politics, and Perception.

THE FIRST P: POWER

Power was mentioned in Chapter 1 as something that is multiplied when two Dyad leaders unite their skills and abilities to lead together. That's because two different leaders have combined their expert power (coming from two different areas of expertise) and referent power (power each receives from members of his or her own culture, who identify with him or her) to form a new entity, the Dyad, which has position power. The position of the Dyad in the organization grants the *partnership* power to influence those they lead in formal (straight line) relationships, those they have matrix or dotted line relationships with, and other colleagues who don't show up on any organizational chart as having formal or matrixed relationships. This position power of the *Dyad* empowers each individual partner in new ways. For example, a nurse leader or nonclinical administrator leader may have gained influence with some members of the medical staff because, added to her expert power as a nurse or administrator, and her personal power, based on her relationships, she may have been imbued with some of her physician partner's referent power by virtue of being his partner. In other words, physicians from his tribe may see her as representing him and be more receptive to what she has to say. The same can be said for the physician partner with members of the nurse or administrator's tribe. As we have mentioned elsewhere in this book, this sharing of power and influence allows the Dyad to "cover more ground" in places like meeting attendance, one-on-one discussions with others, and anywhere where representation of the Dyad is needed.

So, why all this discussion about power? It is important that those involved (from the executive who decides to implement Dyads, to the Dyad members themselves, to stakeholders of each partner) understands the power involved and that it is the new idea of *shared power*, which has implications for everyone involved. Both Dyad leaders should be comfortable with their power because it is an essential element if they are to influence others to take part in transforming the system. They also need to understand the current power dynamics of the healthcare environment.

Power in healthcare organizations has typically been imbalanced among the various professional cultures. While three groups—the board of trustees, the administration, and the medical staff—have been considered to be the power holders (in the past, some people described them as the three-legged stool of the hospital), most individuals within the system would not agree the three have actually had equal power. (In other words, some of the legs of the stool have not been perceived as equal.) Most of the people we have conversed with on this subject, regardless of the tribe they come from, have named physicians as the most powerful group. Their opinions appear to be based not so much on prestige (although medicine has been a high-prestige profession) as on the financial control this group has wielded. Physicians have long controlled where patients go for services, including hospital care. This has given them power over the hospitals because, as a group, they have literally controlled whether or not the hospital has any business (assuming there is a choice of hospitals). So, to others within the organization, it has appeared that individual doctors who bring the most business to the hospital have inordinate power over what capital equipment is purchased (even in cases where the hospital's ROI [return on investment] for a particular piece of equipment is poor to negative). In other cases, poor behaviors, including verbal and even physical abuse from some physicians toward hospital employees, appear to have been tolerated because of this "financial" power. Stories are told of CEOs and other executives who have lost their jobs because they did not keep physician "customers" happy or when medical staffs have pressured boards (often through votes of no confidence) to terminate their employment.

The minority opinion (from a few of our physician colleagues) is that the medical staff's power has not been big enough and that healthcare organizations would be run much more efficiently and better if the physicians had complete control. In addition, one medical colleague points out his perception that "Doctors are not in control. We often don't get the equipment we want. Furthermore, the board gives us our privileges, so if we need the hospital as our workshop, they have the power to take away our livelihood." (We did point out that the details of privileging have largely been delegated to formal medical staff bodies.)

Whatever the perceptions of power, or power imbalances, everyone we know seems acutely aware that power feels like it is shifting as we enter the next era of healthcare. Control over where patients get care appears to be moving to those who pay both hospitals and physicians, or, in some cases, the patients themselves. With the push toward clinically integrated networks, bundled payments, and more managed care, those who can partner well to reduce overall costs and increase quality outcomes will obtain the revenue to thrive. Within medicine, the power curve is shifting toward primary care providers, who can direct patients to specialists, when managed care systems reduce the opportunity for individuals to choose their own specialists.

During times of power shifts, there is considerable angst from those who perceive their power as decreasing. There is also a perception that, during chaotic times, "power is up for grabs." A very real dynamic today is the struggle over maintaining power (along with prestige and income) by those who see theirs decreasing and the grab for power by those who see an opportunity to take more. Dyad leaders need to understand the environment because some behavior of their stakeholders will be affected by this. They themselves may have emotions and biases about the shifts in the balance of power. This is a worthwhile discussion for the partners as they learn about each other, and how to work together to meet the organization's goals (Display 4-1).

Display 4-1 **The Shifting Balance of Power in Healthcare**

Dyad leaders must remember that those who have enjoyed or feel they benefit from the status quo will fight change. They also need to keep in mind that behavior is a function of what people value. Fighting a perceived loss of power might indicate that an individual values power for power's sake, or it could be indicative of a perception that power is needed to protect what the individual does value. (This could be as diverse as quality care for patients, income, status, or something else.) So, in helping the organization transform for the next era, Dyads need to discern what their team members really value and figure out a way to help them maintain or attain this (if it is in harmony with the organization's goals), help individuals change their prioritization of what they value, or assist the team member to depart the organization. (Sometimes that is the only answer, when individual, group, and organizational values cannot be aligned.)

Your reaction to the idea that leaders can help people change their values may be that this is not possible, because values are personal, and not controlled by others. We are not claiming that Dyad leaders can *change* people's values, but we believe that values that may have taken a "backseat" to others can be reengaged and brought to the forefront of people's motivations when they *are brought to mind*. For example, clinicians who value both professional status and the well-being of others may be willing to support change that improves quality of care or affordability of care (so that more people get care) even if their personal status may be threatened by changes in the healthcare system. One example is the physician who has resisted the idea of care delivered by advanced practice caregivers (in spite of growing evidence that they provide high-quality care at a lower cost) because he feels this will reduce the prestige of physicians. This physician may become a supporter of advanced practice when he realizes that, due to physician shortages, some people will not receive care without these new providers included on the healthcare team.

For many organizations, the rationale for implementing Dyad teams is about learning to share power in new ways. There is an underlying belief that, by becoming part of the formal leadership team, individuals will have more influence on what the organization does and on various individual team members and professionals within the system. While there is positional power that comes with the title and job (it can't be denied that those who supervise, evaluate, and determine the financial remuneration and work–life environment of others have control over them), researchers have repeatedly pointed out that power is not the same thing as influence. Power is the "potential to influence" (2), and it increases that potential. However, many a new manager has been shocked to learn that just becoming a formal leader does not enable her to make change happen. (She may even discover that the previous incumbent in the job she has wanted, so she could fix *everything* that she saw as wrong, wasn't as incompetent as she thought he was.) Physicians new to management may be especially shocked to find out that simply ordering a change (like ordering a prescription) does not make it happen.

Other influences can negate or reduce the manager's position power. These include the organization's traditions, systems in place, the power of other leaders who aren't in agreement, and the personal power of people who have no formal power at all. (These informal leaders can slow or even stop progress toward goals.) Of course, leaders can be autocratic and "order" some things to be done, but they cannot make change that fundamentally alters the organization without adding personal power to the power of the position.

Evidence from research "suggests that followers tend to consider the personal power of a highly esteemed expert more important than the legitimacy and power to reward and punish that may derive from appointment to a position of leadership" (2). The expertise may be derived from a profession, but it may also be established because of observed success of the leader in getting things done, ability to resolve conflict, perceived respect from his or her boss, or ability to inspire others. This last, closely associated with transformational leadership, includes the talent to "stimulate enthusiasm among subordinates for the work of the groups" by saying "things to build confidence in their ability to successfully perform assignments and attain group objectives" (4). In other words, people like people who make them feel good about themselves, so they grant these morale boosting managers the power to influence or *persuade* them.

THE SECOND P: PERSUASION

Persuasion (when used as another word for influence) adds to the power of leaders and groups to transform an organization *when it is not coercive.* This is the skill of helping others buy into the vision and understand not only how they will help the organization but also how they will help themselves. Persuasive leaders use facts and data when appropriate, but they must also have emotional intelligence and the ability to form relationship bonds. The most influential leaders are those who "walk the talk." An example of this is when colleagues are asked to behave as supportive team members, they are more likely to be persuaded that this is the right thing to do when they observe the two Dyad individuals acting as supportive partners. (So, if you did not already have enough reasons to become true partners, add the attainment of personal power to your list!)

Persuasive leaders do not see power as dominance over others. In fact, they are sometimes described as people who "multiply their power by sharing it." (Please note we did not say, as some people do, that they multiply their power by "giving it away.") That is simply foolish, not in accordance with accountable leadership, and a practice that has cause a control asymmetry problem between some professions, such as medicine and nursing. This has not served either the professions or the people they serve well. As an example, a qualitative and quantitative study of nurses in New Zealand showed that nursing leadership, attempting to improve patient care, were repressed and prevented from transformation by the political environment in which medical staff and managers had much greater power, status, and importance (5).

Those who share power don't see it as a limited asset. They actually gain more influence and achieve more power by working with other people. Those who seek to amass power by hoarding information (Kathy once worked with a leader who constantly said "knowledge is power" so he wouldn't share complete sets of data about the hospital's finances or other metrics with anyone) or by scheming to have more and more of the company's assets, including human assets, under their control (for personal gain) are not the leaders who will transform the company or the country. Consultant and writer, Catherine Robinson-Walker shares that people who participated in one of her leadership studies indicated that "the difference in working with those who share power with others, compared with those who exercise power unilaterally, is tremendous." They added that the latter model is "counterproductive" (6).

Sharing of power is called "empowerment" in much of today's literature. Empowered nurses and caregivers are called for in Magnet facilities and organizations trying to improve safety in the hospital. Empowered teams (self-directed work groups) are discussed along with their ability to help transform healthcare in Chapter 9. There are articles, seminars, and books about empowering patients to control their own care (7). Steven Shortell wrote, in 1996, that physicians need to be empowered to help change healthcare while controlling their own destinies (8). We agree with all of these ideas, because with empowered participants in transformation, we have increased the odds that we will get to our vision of better healthcare. *What Dyad leaders must do, if transformation is their goal, is ensure that empowering one group does not mean disempowering another.* They use their own power and persuasion to do this.

Persuasive leaders can influence others who have no reporting obligation to them. They do this through their relationships. They have influence because they are known to be authentic. And, they understand the organizational politics.

THE THIRD P: POLITICS

Politics are real in every human endeavor, as much as some of us would like to ignore them. We each have colleagues who have told us how much they hate organizational politics, claim they ignore politics and do quite well as leaders, or inform us they would never take a leadership position because they could not be political. We understand the first group's sentiments, do not believe the second group, and agree the third group just needs some education. (They are practicing politics in their everyday life but just don't realize it.)

Political behavior is a necessary part of life, unless you are a hermit who never interacts with another person. We know it can be negative in organizations and cause harm to individuals as well as the company. Some research results shared here have proven the ill effects caused by self-promoting organizational politicians:

▶ Organizational politics can cause job anxiety, stress, and dissatisfaction (9).
▶ Political leaders can cause cynical followers who doubt the organization's integrity (10).
▶ Politics can offset the usually positive effects of transformational leadership (5).

Despite the potential for negative outcomes when politics are wielded by some individuals, political skill is essential to Dyad leaders who want to persuade other leaders about organizational direction or decisions. Our definition of political skill is borrowed from the literature as "trying to show a genuine interest in other people, understanding people well, building relationships with influential people at work, and instinctively knowing the right things to say to influence others" (11). The difference between negative political maneuvering and positive political skill is the reason behind it: The first is for personal self-aggrandizement, while the second is to accomplish goals in support of the organization's mission.

The reason political skill is important to Dyad leaders is that transformation of an organization takes more than one group or project team. Many teams must come together and that requires cooperation of multiple leaders. At least one of the partners needs the abilities listed above in order to develop the social capital (trust from others in the organization with resulting give and take during negotiations) necessary to persuade others. Much of that capital comes from the *perceptions* others have of the persuader.

THE FOURTH P: PERCEPTIONS

Perceptions are what people believe about something or someone based on their observations or on other people's reported observations and opinions. Many of our colleagues often quip that "perception is reality." (Of course, this is not true. If a color-blind person perceives a stop sign is green instead of red, it does not mean that the stop sign is actually green.) What we believe our friends mean by this remark, is that, for the people who experience or discern something one way, it actually is that way. Our perceptions form our views and beliefs, including our stereotypes of others, as individuals or as groups.

Perceptions are important for Dyad leaders to consider in several arenas. Throughout this book we address the real and perceived differences between cultures, so we won't go into depth about these here. We've also noted that Dyad behavior is important so that others perceive the two leaders as true partners and that this adds to the power and influence of both. The other important realities for Dyad leaders, especially for those who are new to an organization or a formal leadership role, are that *early* perceptions about a leader can positively or negatively influence her effectiveness. The perception of authenticity, as we stated above, is one of the most important insights that others can have about anyone on their team, including Dyad partners, so it's important that new leaders do not project that they may *not* be authentic. This is a possibility with precipitous actions before thorough orientation and relationship development.

New leaders are often anxious to prove themselves, so they come into jobs ready to start making change immediately. Unfortunately, they may try to do this without establishing relationships or gaining political capital, without essential information or data to inform the changes, and without leadership skills or management tools (which they may not even be aware of). They may have blind spots based on cultural conditioning. They may believe that behaviors that seemed to make them successful in other roles will work just as well in their position as a leader or partner. They may think that the power they have gained through this new position negates the need to understand organizational politics. They may not understand the talents of others, including their new Dyad partners. As a result, they can start their new roles with actions and attitudes that can cause others to perceive them in a negative way.

We've observed that leaders who have rocky beginnings with an organization or group may have great difficulty overcoming negative perceptions, even when they (later) realize their early errors, get coaching, or change. Executives should caution their new leaders about this, and new leaders need to pay attention to:

1. *Learning about the organization, the culture, the people, the leaders, and the power distribution before suggesting, or trying to implement any changes.* Even if a new leader has been part of the organization for years (perhaps on the medical staff

or even in a medical staff leadership position), she probably does not have the big picture that others in management do. Trying to make changes before she learns that "she does not know what she does not know" is a misstep that could cause unnecessary animosity, anger, and long-lasting undermining of the leader. Current team members do not want to be told by a newcomer that what they have done in the past is useless and that the new leader is here to set everything right. Even if the leader is astute enough not to say these things out loud (although some are not that astute), actions can imply this to others. Other leaders will react with everything from mild aggravation to outright anger when their areas are affected by the new leader's early management blunders. In addition, errors made because of incomplete information can lead to the perception of incompetence on the part of the new manager, which *can stick to her for years*. Finally, new leaders may not understand that power is not always where they think it is, and they need to learn who has personal power as well as where informal leaders reside before attempting change.

2. *Realizing that everyone has blind spots, including themselves.* If the organization offers coaching from trained coaches, every new (and many experienced) leader should take advantage of this. If a formal program is not available, a leader can seek his or her own coach or counselor. The people who can best help them are colleagues who are different from them. In other words, a leader who really wants to avoid making errors due to blind spots should seek help from someone of the opposite gender, a different professional culture, or a different background. This is often the opposite of what professionals do. They seek advice from people like themselves, who have the same conditioning, and often the same biases and ways of thinking. In other words, they look for help from others who are most likely to have the same blind spots! This is more comfortable, but growth and learning comes with discomfort. It is essential that the person selected to help a leader grow is empowered by that leader to give him truthful feedback and advice, regardless of how painful it may be to hear. In the best of worlds, a Dyad partner can fill this role, or each partner can provide this invaluable service for the other.

3. *Understanding that the behavior that worked in another job or role may not be effective in this role.* This is especially true if the leader has come from a fairly homogeneous team to a diverse team. It's also true when the authority is different in a new job. For example, a physician used to writing orders for patient care is not used to having every order second-guessed or criticized. (Some physicians may disagree, citing new emphasis on evidence-based clinical practices as a way for their medical interventions to be criticized at every turn. In truth, a very small number of physician prescriptions, which in hospitals have been labeled with the military euphemism "orders," are actually questioned.) The doctor's authority is based on his medical education and experience.

This authority is not transferrable to management work. One of the things we usually tell new managers (those who have never managed any one) is "welcome to always being wrong." Our point is that managers make decisions, and there is almost always someone who thinks the decision isn't the right one! Leaders will need to have a thick skin about this reality. In addition, new managers who give orders, verbally or in writing, without explanations or involvement of others, are setting themselves up for difficulty establishing the relationships needed to transform an organization.

4. *Remembering that creating relationships and establishment of trust should be the first objective.* According to Stephen R. Covey, once trust is established, everything, including change, speeds up. Without confidence in the leader that comes from trust, the opposite occurs—hidden agendas, conflict, interdepartmental rivalries, and slowed decisions and communications all occur when it is missing. Stephen M. Covey (Stephen R.'s son) adds that character and competence must be demonstrated and *perceived* before trust can develop (12). Not paying attention to one through three above will harm the building of relationships. It may sound trite, but it is true: People want to think you care, before they care what you think.

This brings us back to authenticity. Pretending to care about people isn't what we are asking Dyad leaders to do. We need leaders who do care about people to transform healthcare. Authentic leaders have good self-esteem, but they also esteem others. Their own self-esteem comes from doing "esteem-able" things with honesty, integrity, and transparency.

Authenticity can be measured through instruments such as the Organizational Leader Authenticity Scale (13). However, most people feel they don't need to test their leaders with them. They can spot authenticity through actions. They perceive whether a person is really what her purports to be through his appropriate or inappropriate use of power, politics, and persuasion.

CHAPTER SUMMARY

Authenticity is an important trait for Dyad leaders who want to transform healthcare. It is key to their success that others perceive this attribute due to the partners' visible understanding of, and use of, power, politics, and persuasion. New leaders must be especially attentive to the first impressions of their teams and colleagues by learning about these "Ps" before they try to make change.

(When we shared our four "Ps" with a colleague, she said, "I see. You want us Dyad leaders to utilize four Ps for the good of the two Ps—our *people* and our *patients*." Even though we think patients will be replaced by "consumers" or "users" of healthcare" in the next era, when wellness care is more prevalent than illness care, we liked that.)

Dyads in Action

DYAD MANAGEMENT WITHIN THE CLINICAL TEAM

Stephen Moore

Dyad management, although gaining popularity, isn't an instant fix for organizational problems. Partnering doesn't work merely through putting leaders together and asking them to be accountable and responsible. Frequently, as discussed earlier, Dyad partners come from different educational and cultural backgrounds. They may have weaknesses in their interpersonal ability and skills, or management training. When backgrounds are disparate, it's to be expected that there is opportunity for conflict and disagreement. Elsewhere we discuss possible relationship challenges, but here I am sharing personal experience we have worked through for ourselves and those we supervise with conflict emanating from:

▶ Gender differences, including patriarchal and matriarchal management approaches to leadership
▶ Cultural differences including historical hierarchies established with physicians as "captain of the ship"
▶ Variation in "blind spots," those areas of one's understanding and personality that are clear to others yet hidden from the consciousness mind of an individual
▶ Competency and experience differences

In other chapters, we examine potential conflict areas more in depth. Our experience has taught us that (i) people tend to ignore or be aware of the effect their differences have on relationships and (ii) they seldom take the time to understand and address these. Failure to consistently recognize or deal with conflicts arising from differences in team members will minimize the opportunity to reap great outcomes from Dyad, Triad, or *any* management team structure. Sometimes, senior leadership can leave conflict resolution to the new partners. Sometimes, because of blind spots that everybody has, they must intervene to assist their Dyad, Triad, or other managers to grow in their team work skills.

GENDER DIFFERENCES

Some key gender differences that we have experienced, and learned from Dyads we supervise, threaten a Dyad team. These are as follows:

▶ *Verbalization versus nonverbalization of thought processes.* When two partners have varying expressive and reflective approaches, either can quickly come to the conclusion that the other is either not listening or making decisions without consulting the other.

▶ *Thoughtful consideration versus rapid decision making.* While these traits are not always gender specific, each can be a catalyst or serious barrier to programmatic success. Not recognizing the default decision process in one's partner, and in oneself, undermines programmatic timelines and deadlines, or results in unintended consequences when either approach is dominant.

▶ *Relationship-based versus program or duty-based interactions.* Men and women often vary in these interactions. Women are often concerned with the personal and developmental relationships within the team, while men assuming that relationships are based upon the job or program at hand and that the team and the partnership will naturally rally around this.

▶ *Body language.* Body language is perhaps one area where women are sensitive and observational, whereas (speaking in wide sweeping terms) men are blind most (if not all) the time. Underestimating this difference, and not asking for transparent feedback when posturing or body language is threatening to others on the team, can cause significant barriers to teamwork.

CULTURAL DIFFERENCES

We've experienced the need to examine culture as "the way we do our work," as we've grown our clinical Dyads. Clinical leaders from medicine and nursing, as well as from healthcare business specialties, have variable experiences that must be recognized and understood for the team to thrive. They include the following:

▶ *Physician educational process and training, with socialization that results in overreliance upon self.* This cultural background is the most difficult for physicians to recognize, understand, and incorporate a conscious questioning and consideration in day-to-day activities. What's worse, when deadlines or seriousness of tasks are imminent or heightened, their default behavior (self-reliance and tight hierarchical decision making) is enhanced.

The historical comparison to a captain's job is indeed mischaracterized by many physicians who take the role of sole leader to heart. They think this means the "skipper" must take on all responsibilities. In truth, the captain is dependent on her team to lead a ship or plane, especially in rough seas or during severe air turbulence. She empowers team members to make appropriate decisions for their roles. Physician education and culture has led to an "I must be the sole team member making decisions" thought process. We have seen clinical examples where this approach has been counterbalanced within a team-based rounding environment, to the benefit of patients. When physicians play *true* non–healthcare captain roles, the result has been dramatic improvements in outcomes reflecting safe practices, evidence-based interventions, and team-based patient care–related areas.

In addition, the educational process of a physician emphasizes competition and sole dependency in order to graduate, qualify for medical school, and find the best residency programs. "Team oriented" *it is not*. This is an area for growth that physicians must embrace in order to be successful as leadership partners.

▶ *Professional-level conflict*. Highly educated operational managers, nurses, and physicians bring competencies related to their professional training and learnings to the team. If the above team-oriented approach is not honed, these professional differences will often result in decisions made without the complete perspective of the team, thus jeopardizing consensus, joint understanding of the direction in which a project or program may go, or even failure of plans to be implemented.

▶ *Hierarchy*. Let's admit it upfront. Healthcare is one of the most hierarchical industries due to historical professional training, CEO business strategies to attract physician volume by fostering the independence of each physician in exchange for his or her business and by the sole reliance and captain of the ship philosophy at the foundation of the physician mindset. Breaking the mold in any of these areas means retraining, dealing with perceptions of diminished importance, and, for many physicians (if aggressively challenged), active resistance to change. Not breaking the mold leads to team dysfunction, passive resistance, and public recognition of the disconnects.

CONFLICT MANAGEMENT

Members of Dyads frequently report to different senior leaders. At the most senior levels of the organization, Dyad chief nursing officer (CNO) and chief medical officer (CMO) often report to the same leader, usually the chief operating officer or the chief executive officer. On the organizational chart, situated below these senior leadership positions are the direct reports from the nursing and physician areas. They are organized along clinical and professional lines. Thus, a chief medical informatics officer (CMIO), although teamed with a chief nursing informatics officer (CNIO), will report to the CMO while her or his Dyad reports to the CNO. Conflicts in any Dyad relationship usually are first surfaced in the direct reporting relationships and not through Dyad to Dyad meetings. Addressing conflict requires either a tight communication between the Dyad supervisors or a strategy of Dyad–Dyad ongoing meetings to ensure that conflicts are managed professionally and personally to the benefit of the organization.

The Dyad team structure brings physician leadership into a more formal operational relationship and has the potential to elevate and enhance nursing leadership into a stronger multidisciplinary clinical presence. It also presents the opportunity for conflict and failure. Recognizing the cultural, gender, and professional differences in Dyad partnerships are the first steps in building a management team for the future of healthcare.

THE CLINICAL SERVICES DYAD MODEL

Dyad management practice within the clinical services group (CSG) at Catholic Health Initiatives (CHI) developed initially with the CMO and CNO. Our national team consists of members competent in the specialties of nursing research, clinical informatics (including electronic health record implementation and optimization), clinician leadership development, nursing practice, supply chain, pharmacy clinical practice, quality, patient and employee safety, advanced practice nursing, nursing education and evaluation, evidence-based practice, and enterprise information (EI) and data warehousing. Through purposeful extension, Dyad management has become the default style of leadership within CSG, enabling our clinical leaders to approach their responsibilities through multiple perspectives and competencies, augmenting each other's skills while maximizing their contributions in support of the strategic progress of the organization.

CSG workflows contain complex and matrixed relationships with both national functional departments and local and regional care delivery centers. Although not assigned full accountability, many of the Dyad leaders in CSG hold important influential and advisory positions within strategic planning, finance, operations, mission, service line, and supply chain arenas. Therefore, in addition to our internal CSG Dyads, there are clinical leaders with Dyad accountabilities shared with other national functional departments. Shared here are some examples of both types of leadership pairings.

WITHIN CSG: OUR LEADERSHIP DEVELOPMENT DYAD

Over the past 3 years, CHI has pursued the establishment of structure and process in support of the need for clinical leadership development. As discussed in Chapter 2, many of our physician and nurse leaders, whether in a key clinical (e.g., CMO and CNO) role, or other leaders who support nursing care functions or clinical service lines, lack the comprehensive background, education, and skills to be holistic in their leadership competency. In recognition of this, the first Dyad formally established by the CMO and CNO was a partnership between the vice presidents (VPs) for leadership development (one MD and one RN), who work together to deliver clinical management education. As individuals, they have responsibilities for nursing education and policy, the hospitalist service lines, clinical operational excellence, and other clinical endeavors, but they are perceived as one by the organization within the context of leadership development. The VPs are supported by academic external partners who conduct research and teach at the graduate level. These experts supply core content material, while internal partners from the CHI human resources and mission departments assist in the creation of programs focused on transformational leadership. Content is tailored to include specific areas important to medical directors, hospitalist leaders, service line directors, as well as nursing leaders.

In the transformational leadership programs (TLDP), CNOs are invited along with their local or regional Dyad partner, as CMOs, to begin the process of self-reflection and growth both as individuals and as pairs. Indicative of the success of this program, our most recent group has had the addition of a CEO who requested and joined his CMO and CNO to form a Triad for mutual team development. The course interweaves the Dyad management theme, throughout the year long endeavor, specifically addressing the leadership skills and competencies necessary to be an effective leader. Over a calendar year, the course introduces three areas of foundational leadership. These are expressed as educational objectives.

The individual leadership objectives for TLDP participants are to

▶ Engage in committing to leadership formation, while also beginning the formation of a strong leadership cohort community

▶ Focus on developing leader self-awareness, self-focus, and self-regulation in the choices made for positively leading others to achieve higher levels of motivation and performance

▶ Learn core leadership framework and concepts, review personal multirater leadership/climate/culture feedback, and revise goals for leadership development based on this information

▶ Continually reinforce the improvement of leadership readiness for advancing a personal development plan, while practicing domains of leadership (*on the job* with emphasis on application)

▶ Prepare to continue self-development work with peer teams and coaches in the intervening months

The collective leadership objectives of TLDP include the following:

▶ To provide opportunities to link leadership development to the advancing of the organization's strategic focus

▶ To examine how to escalate positive leadership styles to others, at the team or unit level

▶ To explore how to promote an agile learning community that is transparent and innovative

▶ To work through leadership challenges, applying a framework and models that support positive forms of leadership style

The strategic thinking and leadership objectives of the program are as follows:

▶ To understand the importance of leading strategically as well as how strategic thinking and leadership build on the earlier framework, by focusing on change and cultural transformation

▶ To review feedback reports on strategic thinking styles and use this information to revise participant's leadership development plan

▶ To apply strategic leadership and thinking to addressing specific leadership challenges

▶ To develop a declaration of interdependence that outlines the way forward for supporting the cohort's continued interactions among members, as well as with other cohorts (past and future) to advance leadership development in CHI

▶ To celebrate participants' accomplishments throughout the year

The Dyad partners leading this work have synergistic personalities, professions, and experiences. Their backgrounds include nursing operations, hospital operations, physician practice management, and CMO work, as well as certification in mentoring. Their complementary personalities cap off an exquisite representation of Dyad clinical leadership in healthcare, interwoven with the development of others.

WITHIN CSG: OUR ENTERPRISE INTELLIGENCE DYAD

EI is another Dyad led responsibility within the CSG. The information enterprise consists of people and structures that lie behind the process of continuous performance management. Utilizing data warehousing, and external and internal sources for data management, EI facilitates the organization's capture and reporting of data, as well as its performance improvement responses (including change management workflows). This clinical area assumes the responsibility for reflection on the outcomes of such improvement efforts. As our commitment to the "Next Era of Healthy Communities" grows, the need to unite the technical capabilities of data warehousing and reporting with clinical interpretive expertise necessary across the continuum of care is growing as well. The depth of knowledge necessary to oversee operations of the data warehouse aspects is infrequently discovered within clinical specialists. We saw a Dyad opportunity to join these two areas of expertise.

CHI created two VP positions to reflect the growing complexity in information needs. One VP is a physician with clinical informatics training and primary care background, while the other holds the technical competency inherent to the successful operations of a data warehouse. There is an expectation that the two are seen as one unit, demonstrating for the organization the necessity not only for reliable and accessible data but also for the interpretive application of these data to support the efforts of performance improvement.

The EI Dyad management team has managed an external software information vendor change process, which has resulted in enhanced performance and turnaround of data and information, as well as clinical performance reporting at the end user level. Through the exercise of specific competencies and the vendor's commitment to new processes, the team has automated data exchanges (previously manual processes), coordinated the key data entry personnel for improvement and standardization of the data, and packaged opportunity analysis at the local level. They were careful to include clinical discussions pertinent to any adverse outlier outcomes.

The Dyad in this instance was a superior management structure because competence and skills required for this work were not present in any one background. By forming the partnership, we've been able to create an automated, standardized process for data on a monthly basis, *complete with* clinical interpretation. This facilitates the use of information by end users for improvement activities throughout the organization.

REACHING BEYOND THE DEPARTMENT: OUR PHARMACY DYAD

Pharmacy services in CHI reside in two national functional departments, in addition to the more traditional local leadership at the facility level. Clinical pharmacy and supply chain pharmacy share the mutual responsibility to maximize the supply chain distribution and utilization of drugs, as well as the clinical appropriateness of those drugs across the organization, its service lines, outpatient centers, and physician offices. Two pharmacists share this responsibility, one with skills in the procurement, 340b, and distribution worlds on the supply chain side. The other, a CSG member, is responsible for the clinical application of pharmacy, including generic substitutions, antibiotic deescalation, new drug evaluations, drug utilization evaluations, and technology (IT, smart pumps, etc.). Although job descriptions and responsibilities are quite different, the two work as a team with a united front to the organization in all of their assigned work. Procurement is not separate from use of medications!

REACHING BEYOND THE DEPARTMENT: OUR CLINICAL AND IT *TRIAD*

The effects of clinical IT on the future of care delivery and population health are staggering. Not only is healthcare tasked with the implementation of electronic health records but its optimization and upgrading for the clinical teams of pharmacists, nurses, and physicians that use it. The implementation of these records requires a team of personnel including those with clinical and technical IT expertise.

Clinical and IT professionals have a history of being at odds with each other due to varied experiential background. For example, to the IT department, a successful clinical IT implementation has sometimes simply meant putting in the hardware and software. Clinical leaders don't see an implementation as successful unless clinicians can use it! Such areas as medical and nursing workflow, juxtaposed with the technical needs to standardize and simplify, create conflict issues regardless of how well the team may understand their specific contributions to Dyad or Triad structures. (If men are from Mars and women from Venus, then clinical leaders are from Alpha Centauri and IT leaders are from Vega!) Often supervisory attempts to negate these dynamics have lead to frustration among team members. Relationships between these two groups must be managed actively, which requires hands on attention and time intensity that challenges even the most empathic of our senior leadership group.

Within this milieu are the CMIO, the CNIO, and the IT VP for clinical IT strategy. Rather than two partners, we have found that three are needed for clinical IT work. Triad model leadership is inherently more complicated than Dyad management, so relationship building must serve as a cornerstone for programmatic success. Three strong leaders from technical areas (IT and clinical IT), which are largely transactional in nature, must develop their relationship skills, both for themselves and their teams, in order to work together. *Their* leaders (the national CMO, CNO, and chief information officer), realizing this, have coached all three and provided team building opportunities.

LEADING THE CARDIOVASCULAR SERVICE LINE TOGETHER
Jerome E. Granato and Jennifer Bringardner

There is an old saying that "two heads are better than one." Is that what they meant when we were told that we were going to work as a "Dyad?" Or could it have meant that we were going to be more like Siamese twins, effectively joined together but ineffectively functioning as we were pulling in opposite directions? This Dyad leadership model was certainly going to be both new and challenging.

We were an "arranged marriage" brought together through the parental wisdom of the CHI corporate office. On the units, we were kindred spirits; a doctor and a nurse accustomed to working on behalf of the patients. In the C-suite, we were potential adversaries; an administrator and a clinician, each a passionate advocate on behalf of our constituents. How would this fit? What were we supposed to do? Only time would tell …..

Nearly 3 months later, the wisdom of this decision has become clear. Our sum is clearly greater that our parts and we have effectively moved forward, in lock step, toward the common goal of birthing a national cardiovascular service line. The design and oversight of an enterprise of this size and complexity requires a skill set that neither of us possessed. Collectively, however, we have been able to draw upon our relative strengths and advance the mission of the service line.

With a common vision of the future state, our disparate skills have come together to effectively paint a picture, without any gaps and colored in a way that neither could produce alone. Balancing goals and strategy, policy and guidelines, and wants and needs, we collectively move the enterprise forward. The success of the dyad model rests in the recognition that our job is like a see-saw. Sometimes one partner does the heavy lifting, at other times it's the other—but on average, our work load and contributions are equal and well balanced.

COMMUNICATION

Like any marriage, the key to the success of this one is effective communication. We meet every day and at multiple times. We travel together. We speak with one voice. In our interactions with staff and with our market-based organizations (MBOs), we are consistent and united in our approach and response. There are no back channels of communication that can subvert the role and effectiveness of our dyad model.

In projecting our unanimity, we have also created an internal structure that reinforces it. We have a weekly staff meeting with equal participation of both Dyad members. Our MBO meetings are similarly performed in unison and designed to project our solidarity. The success of our dyad, while based in effective communication, is secured by the mutual respect for each other.

DYAD ROLES: WHO DOES WHAT?

The day-to-day work falls into place based on our skill sets and strengths. As leadership partners, our areas of focus complement one another. Project management, the performance scorecard, business operations, budgeting, and human resource functions are typically managed by the administrative dyad leader. Matters pertaining to clinical practice, innovation and research, physician relationships, leadership, and mentoring are key areas managed by the physician dyad leader. Working with our team, we set the strategic direction for the service line. Together, we address matters of clinical quality, care process redesign, and efficiency. Working with the MBO leaders, we serve as a liaison with the various corporate departments to ensure our growth toward common goals.

OUR FIRST TEAM MEETING; THE DYAD TEAM IN ACTION

Prior to our first on-site meeting with one of our MBOs, we planned our approach. This was to be our first meeting with them as a dyad; our coming out as a complete team. Together, we developed an agenda that balanced our goals and objectives of the visit with the needs of the local team. While we were excited about our first meeting, our anxiety levels were high. We did not want to fail.

We began our day with a one-on-one session with the local cardiovascular dyad team. This initial meeting was to be more than a simple meet and greet—it was a time for us to begin developing the relationship that would carry us forward. That evening, we met with the larger physician team to learn more about their priorities and goals. We were counting on the amalgamation of our administrative and clinical skills to foster a sense of credibility and serve as the foundation for our work on behalf of MBO and the national enterprise. As the day unfolded, we had many opportunities to learn more about the local program, make introductions, and share experiences. Our mutual confidence and connection grew by the hour. It was rewarding to see the market physicians connect, on common ground, with the physician dyad leader. They readily shared their experiences and perspectives on a variety of topics. In a similar way, the administrative dyad leader addressed the business aspects of the service line, relating to the obvious challenges, potential rewards, and need to alter our approach to healthcare.

As our first meeting came to an end, it was apparent that the formation of a dyad team was a true asset—both for the national service line as well as for the local administrators and physicians.

With a foot in each world, we are bridging the needs of both groups. There is a sense of acceptance and common understanding and a sense of optimism that this novel model of management will not only succeed in advancing the mission, vision, and values of the service line, it will set the stage for the creation of new relationships and roles that will transcend the traditional operation of cardiovascular practice. The service line dyad is a well-thought-out marriage that will undoubtedly bear fruit for many years to come.

REFERENCES

1. Blanchard, K., & Miller, M. (2004). *The secret, what great leaders know and do.* San Francisco, CA: Berrett-Koehler.
2. Bass, B. (2008). *The Bass handbook of leadership, theory, research & managerial applications.* New York, NY: Free Press.
3. Henderson, J., & Hoy, W. (1982). Leadership authenticity: The development and test of an operational measure. *Educational and Psychological Research, 3*, 63–75.
4. Yukl, G., & Van fleet, D. (1982). Cross-situational, multimethod research on military leader effectiveness. *Organizational Behavior and Human Performance, 30*, 87–108.
5. Kan, M., & Parry, K. (2004). Identifying Paradox: A grounded theory of leadership: Overcoming resistance to change. *Leadership Quarterly, 15*, 467–491.
6. Robinson-Walker, C. (1999). *Women and leadership in health care.* San Francisco, CA: Jossey-Bass.
7. Cohen, E. (2010). *The empowered patient.* San Francisco, CA: Jossey-Bass.
8. Shortell, S., et al. (1996). *Remaking health care in America: Building organized delivery systems.* San Francisco, CA: Jossey-Bass.
9. Cropanzano, R., Hawes, J., Grandby, A., & Toth, P. (1997). The relationship of organizational politics and support to work behaviors, attitudes and stress. *Journal of Organizational Behavior, 18*, 159–180.
10. Davis, W., & Gardner, W. (2004). Perceptions of politics and organizational cynicism: An attributional and leader-member exchange perspective. *Leadership Quarterly, 15*, 439–465.
11. Treadway, D., Hochwarter, W., Ferris, G., et al. (2004). Leader political skill and employee reactions. *Leadership Quarterly, 15*, 493–513.
12. Covey, M. R. (2006). *The speed of trust: The one thing that changes everything.* New York, NY: Free Press.
13. Henderson, J., & Brookhart, S. (1996). Leader authenticity: Key to organizational climate, health, and perceived leadership effectiveness. *Journal of Leadership Studies, 3*(4), 87–103.

Chapter 5

Culture Shock: Dyads as Both Harbingers and Architects of Cultural Change

Some time ago, Steve and Kathy received a message. The e-mail was sent by a 20-something female consultant neither of us had ever met, although our healthcare system had been working with her consulting firm for 3 months. There had been a change in assignments in her firm due to turnover, and she wanted to introduce herself to the CMO and CNO who, as a Dyad, served as the two executive sponsors of the work she would be doing.

"Dear Dr. Moore and Kathleen," her salutation read. The rest of the e-mail was a pleasant note telling us that she would be working with us in place of Joe X, who was no longer with the company. She signed it with both her first and last name. Steve glanced at the note, replied in one sentence, copied his reply to Kathy, and deleted it. Kathy typed out a longer reply:

Dear Ms. X,

Thank you for letting us know about the change in your personnel. We look forward to meeting you and talking about how the project can best proceed. I'll have one of our assistants work with your assistant to set up a time ASAP because we would like to avoid any delays in the work.

On another subject, I feel compelled to mention something that I noticed about your message to us. I know it may seem insignificant to you, but I am concerned about your choice of forms of address in your salutation. You address my partner as Dr. Moore, while in the same line you greet me by my first name. I believe you will be more successful in your career if you demonstrate the same professional courtesy to two or more individuals *when you address them together*. In this case, that would require use of equivalent titles. If you are not comfortable calling both of us by our first names (Steve and Kathy), it would be appropriate to address us both in a more formal way. For me that could be Dr. (or Ms. since you can't be expected to know that I have a doctorate).

Thanks,
Kathy Sanford

You probably interpret this exchange of e-mails differently, depending on who you are. You might have groaned or gasped at the original e-mail salutation, as some female executive colleagues did when this story was shared. On the other hand, you might not have registered that anything was odd about the consultant's e-mail at all, like some physician colleagues. You might have considered Kathy's response as silly (who really cares enough about this to take the time to write about it). Or you might think, "Boy, that Kathy is sure defensive." You might think that the next e-mail Kathy got (from the consultant's supervisor) was "right on." Apparently, the young consultant had forwarded Kathy's e-mail to her, and the supervisor felt the need to defend her protégée. She wrote, "How was she to know what you wanted to be called? From now on she will address you as Doctor Sanford per your request. By the way, she only called Steve, 'Dr. Moore' *out of respect*."

Both the consultant and supervisor missed the point of Kathy's e-mail entirely. Kathy was not asking to be addressed by her academic credential. She was not asking that Steve *not* be addressed by his medical degree. She was asking that two individuals be addressed with the same level of formality when addressed together. The whole incident left her bemused and pondering two questions: (1) If Steve was addressed formally "out of respect," does that mean that the female nurse is less worthy of respect than is the male MD? and (2) Why did the young consultant feel the need to share this note with her boss, and why was it the supervisor who responded to Kathy's e-mail? Have we become so confrontation-averse that even pointing out an issue and/or giving advice is seen as an attack?

Whatever your thoughts are about this real-life e-mail exchange, it illustrates an issue for Dyad leaders. Your individual perception of this exchange is a product of your individual multiple cultures. In addition to each partner's professional culture, there are separate ethnic, generational, and gender cultures that affect how each views the world. "Little" things that may not seem important to one partner contribute to segmentation of people, which can make the development of partnerships more difficult. Each comes to the partnership with different biases.

Daniel Kahneman, the 2002 Nobel Prize winner in Economics, points out that human minds are both rational and irrational. His explanation of biases is that they are systematic errors that can interfere with accurate judgments and rational decision making. He points out that "awareness of your biases can contribute to peace in marriages and probably in other joint projects" (1).

Joint projects are the very essence of Dyad partnerships. While Dr. Kahneman mentioned peace as an outcome of understanding and dealing rationally with personal biases, we're substituting the word "harmony." Dyad partners will have disagreements to work through, but in the end, they need to work in harmony for the good of the organization. Co-management is a new way to lead. It is seen as a way to overcome a past lack of peace and harmony. For this model to fulfill its promise, we sometimes need to confront biases, stereotypes, and cultural differences that could undermine partnerships. We've already mentioned the physician versus hospital executive cultural gap, but there are three other areas that could interfere with strong partnership development if not understood: gender, ethnicity, and generation.

DYADS AND GENDER

Talking about gender and how it can cause challenges for Dyad partnerships could be a difficult subject for many. In fact, some people might stop reading this chapter right now, because they don't want to see (or hear) "more whiney words about how women have been discriminated against." Some might say that leaders are leaders and we need to stop pointing out that there are any differences between male and female managers. Others may be thinking, "Good! They are going to address what we all know is a problem in healthcare leadership."

If you are still reading, did you intuit that those we describe as likely to quit reading are male? Or did you discern that we are talking about females when we say some are glad this issue will be addressed? If so, you are falling victim to your own biases! We didn't say male readers are the former, and females are the latter, but you may have come to that conclusion, based on your intuition. (Kathy describes how intuition, even so-called "women's intuition" led her to a wrong conclusion in Display 5-1.)

Intuition is based on recognition of past experiences or perceptions. It is a fast way of thinking that, according to Kahneman, causes many errors, including overconfidence in our own beliefs. Slower thinking, or deliberate thought, is more rational, but harder, mental work (1).

As healthcare moves into the next era, we need to overcome generations of misunderstandings and communication problems between cultures so we can transform our systems. This *is* hard work. So, if you are still reading this chapter, we ask that you take the time to work harder. That is, take time to ponder what may or may not be true about gender in the healthcare leadership ranks, and how understanding personal biases can improve communication, trust, and respect between partners.

At the senior leader of management in healthcare organizations, there is one woman for every six men. However, there's a pretty good chance that Dyads will be

Display 5-1 **When Kathy's Intuition Was Wrong**

Fifteen years ago, I was invited to speak to an association holding its annual regional conference in Washington. The event planners had heard about a book I wrote and thought it might be of interest to their membership. They wanted my talk to match the book title: *Leading With Love*.

On the agreed upon day, I decided to attend other speakers' presentations to get a "feel" for the organization. To my chagrin, almost everyone in the audience was male. The speakers talked about things that were, to me, pretty "dry subjects," and although the engineers (that is who they turned out to be) were attentive, there wasn't much of a reaction to anything said, other than polite clapping at the end of each speech.

I knew I was in trouble. How was I going to talk about how to balance love for your organization, community, employees, leaders, and customers to this audience? Love? To men? To engineers? With multiple misgivings, I made the presentation. I figured I would make a quick getaway at the end and chalk this up to a learning, and that I should be more careful about knowing who I accepted speaking invitations from. Imagine my surprise when I could not leave the stage for 20 minutes after I finished!

The men who lined up to talk with me were eager to share tales of work lives where bosses treated them poorly, where there was no regard for the well-being of customers, and where they felt undervalued. These were males who wanted to be cared about at work. I was embarrassed by my bias about men and humbled to realize that my stereotype about anyone called an engineer was wrong. I've never forgotten that presentation, or the lesson it taught me. I know I still make snap judgments, and hold tight to beliefs that are probably flawed due to my cultural conditioning—but I do try to overcome these *when* I recognize them....

made up of partners from different genders. That's because most of these partnerships are in middle and frontline management, where 73% of the incumbents are female (2). An understanding of the opposite sex could be very helpful in learning how to work together effectively. At the very least, some misunderstanding may be avoided. (Our caveat is this: we are sharing what experts and research indicates about gender differences, but we also know that individuals from the same gender differ one from another and not every person matches what research says about the majority of people of his or her same gender!)

Research on women as leaders consists of studies about what people (both men and women) *think* about them, research on gender demographics and positions held, research on perceptions of what has caused (or appears to have caused) the proverbial "glass ceiling," and research on female managers' traits.

There was very little research done on women managers before the 1980s. Early books on the subject advanced theories that women would only succeed if they acted like men. This was because they were (without research) stereotyped as too "nurturing, cooperative, considerate of others, and participative" to be successful in the hierarchical model of leadership that was seen as appropriate for business success. Men were cast as the "natural" leaders for organizations based on a military command-and-control structure. That's because they were viewed as having "the right stuff" because they were the gender "known to be competitive, controlling, impersonal, and analytic" (2). (Today, those "female" characteristics are considered to correlate positively with leadership. Twenty-first century organizations and modern management theory indicate that we have a need for leaders to adopt democratic and team-oriented leadership styles that are supported by traits associated with women.) Display 5-2 points out that research done on only one gender cannot be automatically generalized to both men and women.

The earliest "theories" about females in leadership were opinions that echoed the thoughts of society at the time. Popular books on the subject started to appear in the 1970s, postulating that women and men are different but claiming that women can succeed in management if they behave like men. Male leaders are viewed as "ambitious, self-reliant, independent and assertive" (4). If women do not emulate these traits, their "feminine style of consideration and nurturance" causes them to lose the respect needed for effective supervision of others. Yet studies showed that women who *did* emulate men by becoming more "directive" were evaluated negatively, while men seen as directive received positive evaluations (5). Female leaders were supposed to be "indirect and nonconfrontational, while influencing others through hints" (6, 7). Nurses from that period remember being taught the same thing: "Never directly question the physician's orders or give an opinion on care. If you feel the patient is in danger or could be harmed by an incorrect order, ask nonchallenging or leading (suggestive) questions so that the doctor will 'come up with' the right answer *on his own*." One result of this style of communicating has been a view that women are

---

Display 5-2 **No Early Research on Women Leaders?**

The lack of early research on female leadership styles shouldn't come as a surprise to clinicians. In addition to the fact that there were few women leaders in business, research has been conducted with males as the "norm" for humans in other areas as well.

We now know that some clinical research, such as studies on myocardial infarctions, conducted with male subjects, led to a lack of knowledge about the very different physical symptoms for females experiencing heart attacks.

Even the widely believed theory that the human response to stress is either "fight" or "flight" has been shown to be based on male behavior. A 2000 study by B. Azar suggests that women do not respond to stressful situations by either becoming aggressive or fleeing. Instead, they become more nurturing and increase their affiliation with others (3).

There *have* been many studies on females as managers in the last three decades. A review of the literature shows that findings of various researches sometimes do not support other research conclusions. This is another reality that shouldn't surprise those of us who work in healthcare. Research results can be in conflict, so for our purpose, we're referencing "evidence" that is suggested by the preponderance of studies.

not leadership material. This bias persists in spite of research findings that male and female leaders are equally effective in leading organizations. The quality of female leader decisions matches those of male peers in effectiveness (8).

In Display 5-3, we've shared some of the differences between males and females that researchers have pointed out. What's most important about these studies is how they could affect males and females working *together* to lead. Research, in any field of study, can be used to enforce *or* dispel personal bias, which has the potential to decrease the effectiveness of mixed gender leadership teams. For example, if you believe that men will be more successful in these days of unprecedented change, the research saying they are self-reliant and assertive may reinforce that belief. If you believe that relationship building and communication skills will be essential for the future, the research on women could reinforce your bias that female leadership is superior. If your stereotypes aren't supported by studies, you might even choose to disregard the research as "obviously" poorly done. If your bias is strong enough, you could "pick and choose" only those research studies that support them!

There is good news for male and female leaders! As we move into the next era for healthcare leadership, more recent research indicates that *both* task (associated with males) and relationship (associated with females) management styles are important for transformation of our systems. Management theorists are now interested in "androgynous" leadership, in which "the more masculine task orientation and the more feminine relations orientation practiced by both men and women may make for the most effective leadership style" (23). As early as 1964, management theorists Blake and Mouton stated that "to be the best in their roles, managers must have both

---

Display 5-3 Differences Between Male and Female Leaders

Some studies have indicated that there *is* a difference between male and female leaders. For example, women have been shown to be less task oriented than are men. They also score higher on communication skills, according to a variety of studies:

▶ A 1999 study showed that women executives have better communication skills than do male colleagues (9).

▶ In groups, men compete to speak and interrupt each other, while women take turns speaking (10).

▶ Women are better at understanding the meaning of nonverbal cues (11).

▶ Women have been shown to score higher on tests measuring integrity (12).

▶ Men are more concerned with successfully completing tasks while female leaders seek "interpersonal success" (13).

▶ Women are more participative and democratic than are men, who are more directive and autocratic (14).

▶ A number of new studies (15–22) indicate that women tend to be more transformational than men while men score higher than do females on *all* transactional leadership scales.

a strong concern for performance and concern for people" (24). Current theorists state that stereotypical male styles are best for some leadership challenges, while stereotypical female traits are most effective in others.

Some leaders have already developed androgynous management methods. Those who have not, and find themselves in mixed gender dyads, have an opportunity to learn from each other, if they recognize the strengths of each, and appreciate each style.

LEARNING FROM AND ABOUT EACH OTHER

Catherine Robinson-Walker, who wrote *Women and Leadership in Healthcare*, says, "Deep personal change is difficult for men and women. Offering understanding as we strive for new relationships within ourselves and with others permits us to be compassionate rather than to place blame" (25). This is an important concept for Dyad partners to grasp. Personal and organizational change does not require figuring out who to blame for the current state of affairs (assuming that isn't a good state) for individuals or the nation. It does call for greater understanding of cultures and individuals so they can best learn together.

Learning to lead together, when we come from different cultures and histories, does involve personal change. It's easy (comparatively) to talk about the need for organizations to transform for the next era in healthcare, and not *too* much harder to describe how "they" must change so we can do this. "They" may be the doctors, the administrators, our employees, our bosses, men, women, or *whoever is not just like us.* Sometimes, even the most wise among us falls into a habit of focusing so much on the past, with its inequities and less-than-perfect record for solving societal (including healthcare) ills, that we put up our own barriers to moving together into the future. Sometimes, we react with anger, sadness, or incredulity at the current state of affairs. For example, when we (Steve and Kathy) learned *in 2014*, that 10 board members selected for a new board that was tasked with *transforming a healthcare organization* were men (9 of whom were white men), we were shocked. It seemed beyond belief that, as an industry that espouses, "evidence-based practices" for clinicians, a healthcare organization could ignore evidence that boards achieve more (and real transformation occurs), only when we increase leadership diversity. However, it is easier to understand how this evidence can be ignored when we pursue the hard work of learning to understand ourselves as well as *others.* For Dyad partners learning to lead together, this means strengthening each individual's *empathy* for those who come from a different history and world view. This practice of "putting ourselves in another's place" includes real sympathy for those facing monumental change in their lives, even while supporting and leading the change *because it is the right thing to do.*

While female leaders chafe at examples like an all-white, male leadership team in healthcare organizations where the large majority of employees are female, male leaders face their own challenges with getting ready for the next era. Judith Briles, among others, describes their modern experience as one of *privilege deprivation*. She says it's a psychological issue for white males, in particular, when women and minorities compete for positions of power that were previously only available to white men (26).

J. Rosener interviewed men from various industries and found that a common theme for many is that they feel under attack—but can't understand why. They know they are feeling a sense of "loss of power, loss of control, loss of male identity, loss of self-esteem, and increasing discomfort" (27). *In healthcare, that is similar to the message we're hearing from physicians of both genders.* Two dominant cultures in our organizations, male executives *and* the medical staff, are experiencing extreme discomfort based on what they *expected* or previously experienced in their careers. While other cultures within the organization may see the next era as a time of great opportunity for "making things *right* or better," this is a stressful time for those who view changes as a personal loss. Even when change is perceived as good, it's possible (and healthy) to have empathy for those experiencing perceived (or real) loss in status, income, or personal self-esteem.

It might appear to women that men are deliberately blocking their ascent to leadership. In some cases, this is probably true. In many, it may be subconscious thinking that gets in the way of male and female team work at the leadership level. Many of the "little things" listed in Table 5-1 are nonintentional. Forgetting this is to ignore the complexity of human motivations.

Judith Rosener describes discord caused when the two gender cultures don't work hard enough to understand each other. She calls it "sexual static," which causes discomfort for men and frustration for women. Because of this lack of comfort, men "unconsciously exclude women from the executive suite" (27).

Empathy for others who are either uncomfortable with change or actively resisting what they perceive to be a threat to their power (or financial privilege) does *not* mean accepting that "things could or should stay the way they are." We are on a fast track to the next era. We know we must transform. We know it takes both male (transactional) and female (transformational) styles of leadership to meet the organizations goals. So, when Dyads are formed to combine two cultures and two sets of skills, it's essential that we utilize both to the fullest. That requires conscious attention and communication: even if we are uncomfortable with certain topics. Harvard researchers Stone, Patton, and Heen acknowledge that "Gender is a difficult topic for most people to discuss, just as race, politics, and religion may be" (28). Their book title, *"Difficult Conversations, How to Discuss What Matters Most,"* indicates that it *is* most difficult to talk about the *most important things*. For Dyads of opposite genders to fulfill their promise of transformational leadership, they must engage in conversations one or both may be uncomfortable with. Not addressing issues related to gender is to avoid one of the most important topics for bonding. Without partnership bonding, we can't reach true leadership synergy.

Before the concept of two leaders combining skills as formal Dyads, many "twosomes" have worked together within healthcare to meet organizational goals. Often,

Table 5-1	**Little Things Make Up a Culture**	
Observations You Might See (If You Look)	**Implications**	**Changing the Culture**
All meetings between the male and female leaders occur in the male's office, regardless of who requested or scheduled the meeting.	The male is seen (maybe only by himself) or wants to be perceived, as the more powerful "peer."	Set up a corporate protocol: If no meeting room is available, the person who requests the meeting should travel to the other person's office.
Invitations to strategic meetings go only to the male (or physician) member of the Dyad.	He is really the "boss" or more important partner, at least in the eyes of others outside the Dyad.	Request that you are *both* invited to meetings. If only one has time to go, or you have decided to "split" meeting attendance, the Dyad partners will decide who will represent them.
Other leaders only say hello to the Dyad member of their own gender, even when the Dyad partners encounter them *together*.	"I only see or only respect the person of my own gender."	Rather than ignoring this behavior, politely mention it to the other leader. (This can be done with humor or a simple pointing out of fact.)
In lists of leaders, or minutes of meetings, only one type of professional has his or her name followed by his or her earned degree. Example: John Smith, Mary Jones, Jeff Cooper, MD, Linda Hoyle.	Physicians *are* more special and different from everyone else—and more deserving of respectful recognition. When one category of people is *more* special, others are, by implication, *less* special.	Set up a corporate culture protocol where all leaders are recognized by *either* their professional or educational designation. Example: John Smith, MHA, Mary Jones, PhD, Jeff Cooper, MD, Linda Hoyle, RN.
Physician leaders or in some cases, *all* male leaders are addressed by an honorific (Dr. or Mr.) while either nonphysicians or women are called by their first names.	See above.	Expect the same form of address when more than one individual is named in the same written or verbal communication.
Male colleagues frequently (or even occasionally) touch female colleagues (not inappropriate sexual touching) OR Sit in meetings, leaning back with hands clasped behind their heads, legs outstretched.	"I am your superior." (This type of touching sends this message) "I am the Alpha-Male in this room." Some people call this the "King Primate Position." (These are classic body language actions that send superiority messages)	Set up a course in body language for all team members to help everyone understand the importance of nonverbal messaging.

they were not positioned as equal leaders within the system. Today, some companies still appear to believe that one "Dyad" leader should report to the other. We have already pointed out why this is not a true co-leadership model. Co-leading does not mean superior–*subordinate* leadership. This is difficult for some hospital executives to "wrap their heads around" as clinically integrated networks evolve in which medical leaders "co-lead" with administrators. It's equally difficult when the male-dominated profession of medicine and the female-dominated profession of nursing lead departments or projects together.

Our gender and professional history makes it easy to understand why there are issues with equality in Dyad leadership. So does the fear of loss of power, as well as cultural conditioning that prevents some individuals from asking why we continue to maintain command and control models that have *no rational basis?*

For example, it is uncommon for individual hospital CNOs to report to hospital CMOs. Yet, it is not uncommon (although becoming less and less so) for system CNOs to report to system CMOs. (This reporting relationship may even be called a "Dyad," which is a misnomer.) Kathy has previously worked with male CMOs who actively campaigned to have the CNO (key associates), and the entire nursing enterprise report to them. Their rationale? Nurses work or *should* work for doctors. In addition, non-clinicians within systems have occasionally assumed that the CNO *does* report to the CMO. Their perception is that this is the "natural order of things" so they innocently believe that one profession, *and one gender*, automatically works for the other, even when introduced as Dyad partners. This is true even when it is apparent that *both* are executives who have not care for patients in years.

Root cause analysis (similar to those performed by clinicians when patient care errors occur) explains this phenomenon. Nurses in the majority of hospitals have traditionally reported to CNOs, who traditionally reported to hospital administrators (CEOs, or more recently, COOs), *not* physicians. However, at the patient care level, nurses (among other responsibilities) performed work prescribed by physicians for the patients. These prescriptions were called "orders." This word came from the military command-and-control style of leadership. Both the nursing staff and *the patients* were expected to do whatever the doctor *ordered*. (To the discomfort of some clinicians, patients are becoming empowered and educated so that they no longer always believe they must do what a physician tells them to do.) Nurses, who are licensed professionals, are governed by their own state boards and are responsible for implementing patient interventions that their medical colleagues have deemed medically essential but *only* when the nurse judges that the orders are appropriate. They are legally and ethically required to refuse to perform any procedure if they believe it is either beyond their scope of practice or harmful to the patient (or in today's parlance, the customer, or user of healthcare). Therefore, doctor's "*orders*" are really prescriptions, which can be questioned or not fulfilled by either patients or other healthcare team members.

Outside of hospitals, nurses have been employed by physicians within their private offices. But, the vast majority have not been employees of medical doctors. In spite of having worked side by side, there continues to be evidence that the two professions know less about each other than others (or they themselves) assume. Multiple articles and books mention how little the two professions know about each other. Most of these are about physicians not knowing what nurses do, what is involved in nursing care, or understanding the law and regulations that define this field as a separate profession. (Some have even voiced the belief that "nurses work under the physician's license, which is incorrect, as nurses can only provide care following the regulations provided by nursing licensure") According to a 2014 New York Times article, an eminent former medical educator, physician, and editor worked with nurses for decades before becoming a hospital patient. It was only at that time that he discovered he "had never before understood how much good nursing care contributes to patient's safety and comfort" (29).

Nurses have *not* traditionally reported to physicians. Nursing and medicine are separate professions, with what appears to be little understanding of the female (nursing) profession from the traditionally male-dominated (medical) profession. CNOs and CMOs are executives, not frontline clinicians. There is no rationale for CNOs to automatically report to CMOs. The *perception* of female nurse executives is that this only occurs because of (i) male executive and male CMO discomfort with a female culture, (ii) unconscious bias, (iii) conscious discrimination, or (iv) outdated command and control leadership models in which executives can't comprehend or don't understand the power in *new* leadership models where synergy of different skills used in partnership can transform organizations.

Leaders who are invested in or comfortable with current professional or gender relationships are able to rationalize *not* changing even while they preach change for everyone else. It's helpful to utilize a model called "generative" discussion to talk about *why current leadership models* exist, why they might not be effective for the next era, and what organizations should consider for their leadership teams of the future. (Display 5-4 explains generative conversations as well as the concept of root cause analysis.)

Display 5-4 **Tools for "Understanding"**

Root Cause Analysis is a method frequently used by clinicians to discover the *initial* reason for an error or poor outcome for patients. It can be utilized in any type of problem solving, both within and outside of the healthcare industry. (e.g., a wrong site surgery might be blamed on a nurse not speaking up when she/he believes an error is about to be made. However, the root cause might be an operating room culture where doing so is not acceptable, and thus the nurse fears reprisal from the surgeon.) Bias and stereotyping of others can be among root causes for poor communication in an organization.

There may be *more* than one root cause for a problem. The process can be used to help organizations transform and learn how to avoid problems before they happen.

Generative Discussions are frequently discussed in relationship to Boards of Directors or Boards of Trustees. However, they are also appropriate to reference as tools for communication for the exploration of factors and information around big issues, problems, or challenges. (There are emotional underpinnings to all of these, especially because solving them must involve change.) Generative conversations come *before* actions (supported by data). They are group interactions where ideas about a topic are candidly shared. Listening with an open mind is an important part of the experience in which participants share what they believe to be true, their ideas, and experiences. The goal of these planned discussions is to understand perspectives, connect and strengthen relationships.

Dyad leaders of different genders should have their *own* generative discussions, as part of learning about each other. If one actually does believe the other should report to him/her, it's important to acknowledge that, and *talk it through*. Hidden feelings and beliefs *will* surface in relationships as *problems* if there is not open discussion.

DISCUSSING THE UNDISCUSSABLES

Ryan and Oestreich have identified subjects that are widely considered as "undiscussables" at work. They've also noted that the "undiscussables" are being talked about, but in the wrong places, and not with those who *should* be discussing them, because their "underground" presence affects the morale and success of organizations (30). In other words, they are openly discussed by groups who feel discriminated against among themselves but not shared with those perceived as instigating the discrimination. Among these are "virtually all types of discrimination" that surfaces in their studies of workplaces. These researchers found that the most difficult thing for people to talk about is the issue of preferences given to one gender over the other within the organization.

We believe it is equally difficult to broach partner problems when they are based on gender, race, ethnic family of origin, or professional tribal bias. However, none of us have been promised an "easy" job when we choose to lead! Just as clinicians are not serving patients to the best of their ability when they don't consider the *reasons* for disease and address these, managers who are unwilling to consider reasons for leadership dysfunction (or even notice there *are* leadership dysfunctions) are not serving their organizations to the best of their ability. Functional, healthy organizations and functional healthy relationships require trust, respect, and communication. True communication between Dyad partners must include the difficult conversations. These lead to trust and respect. Display 5-5 lists reasons conversations can be difficult.

Joseph Luft and Harrington Ingham's model to help people understand themselves and others, referred to as Johari's window, pointed out that *one* of our four personality quadrants is what we know about ourselves, but others do not, and another is what others know about us, that we are blind to (31). When partners are able to share some of the former (not everything—we are *not* asking for complete disclosure. People deserve *some* discretionary privacy!), they bond better and learn ways to work better together. When the Dyad becomes close enough that both partners feel comfortable to point out areas in the latter, they are not only supporting the organization; they are supporting their partners' growth. Of course, this requires the maturity of the partner *receiving* input—defined as an openness to feedback and the potential that she would be a better or more successful leader (or person) if she made changes in behavior. (The other two quadrants of Johari's Window are what is known to both ourselves and others, and what is unknown by both ourselves and others).

Dyad leaders of different genders have not only an opportunity to enrich the skills and careers of their partners but also an accountability to their teams, customers, and

---

Display 5-5 **Why Conversations Can Be Difficult**

Every conversation is really three conversations:

1. What really happened?
2. What do we each feel?
3. What do each of us believe is our personal identity?

Most of us believe, deep down, that problems are because of the *other* person's selfishness, naiveté, controlling nature, or irrationality.

> The other person thinks we are the problem.
> We forget to disentangle intent from impact of other people's actions.
> Our assumptions about intentions are often wrong.
> Defensiveness is almost always inevitable and most of us assign blame.
> We forget that feelings matter in work discussions, or we claim that they don't.
>> —*Adapted from Stone, D., Patton, B., & Heen, S. (1999). Difficult conversations: How to discuss what matters most. New York, NY: Penguin Books.*

---

organizations for modeling leadership that will enrich the future of all. This modeling includes visible (i) support for leadership styles of both genders, (ii) willingness to question (and change) behaviors and beliefs based on cultural conditioning, and (iii) willingness to support a partner's attempts to grow and change. This includes forgiving *past* actions of the partner *or* of his or her profession *or gender*.

Before we address the first and second "modeling," we need to talk about number 3. Women and minorities have been subjected to discrimination in pay recognition and promotion into top leadership positions. People who deny this, remind us of those who deny that the Holocaust occurred in Germany. History is history. Horrific, horrible things have happened in this world. Prejudice and discrimination are real in society and organizations. Gender and racial bias, as well as social conditioning and culture have brought us to where we are today. However, as we've stated, some of these *are* conscious, and others are not.

When leaders of different genders are willing to grow by confronting their own biases (that includes *both* genders) and want to change, it cannot be taken for granted that their partners will "forgive and forget" personal past behaviors. Forgiveness is not always immediate, particularly when trust has been lost and needs to be regained. If an individual is additionally painted as "tainted" because of historical relationships between his gender or culture and hers, there is an additional challenge for Dyad leaders on the journey to true partnership!

A good discussion (difficult) between the two, early in the relationship, could be about their perceptions of the other's gender and culture preferences. This can set a foundation for (even more difficult) conversations about individual (real or perceived) actions, which divide Dyad partners rather than unite them.

Martin Luther King said that, "Forgiveness is not an occasional act. It is a permanent attitude." Without forgiveness (for real or perceived treatment, prejudice, or day-to-day "slights"), *no* relationship can thrive. (This is as true for Dyad leaders as it is for a marriage.) In his popular book, with the catchy title, *Men Are From Mars, Women Are From Venus*, psychologist John Gray make this point: "Gender insight helps us to be more tolerant and forgiving when someone doesn't respond the way we think he or she should" (32). That's why Dyad partners of different genders should take some time to gain knowledge about each other.

So what are some of the "insights" that might help Dyad partners understand their coleaders? Here are a few that psychologists, sociologists, and scientist–researchers point out:

‣ Men mistakenly expect women to think, communicate, and react the way men do. Women mistakenly expect men to feel, communicate, and respond the way women do.

‣ Men and women often don't mean the same thing even when they use the same words (32).

‣ Research suggests that men and women may speak different languages that they assume are the same language. They use similar words to encode disparate experiences of self and relationships. As a result, what is said may be systematically mistranslated. This created misunderstandings that impede communication and limits potential for cooperation in relationships.

‣ Men have difficulty in hearing what women say. Yet in the different voices of women lies the truth of an ethic of care, the tie between relationship and responsibility, and the origins of aggression because of a failure to connect (33).

‣ Generally, right-handed men act from *either* their left (brain) lobe, which is the teaching, verbalization, problem solving, solution giving side, *or* their right lobe, the artistic, nonverbal side. Rarely can they act from both the right and left lobes at the same time. On the other hand, women are capable of processing data from both the right and left lobes at once. This makes them capable of melding thinking *and* feeling (34).

‣ Men and women think differently, approach problems differently, emphasize the importance of things differently, and experience the world around them through different filters.

‣ Our brains differ in anatomy, chemical composition, blood flow, and metabolism. The systems we use to produce ideas and emotions, to create memories, to conceptualize and internalize our experiences, and to solve problems are different. Women have more connections between the two sides of their brains that may explain how they can process several streams of information at the same time, while men activate only one side of the brain while processing information (35).

‣ Women have learned that asking to be recognized for their abilities and accomplishments can be a mistake (because they may be "punished" by males in power).

▶ Men ask for things (like higher pay) two to three times more often as women do. They are expected to self-promote and, as a result, get more recognition and money.

▶ There are rigid gender-based standards of behavior at work. Women are supposed to be modest, unselfish, and not self-promoting. Their skills and contributions are undervalued so they are passed over for promotions, and they are often left out of the organization's information sharing grapevine (36).

▶ In meetings, a woman will come up with an idea, and a man gets credited for it when he mentions it later in the meeting (37).

▶ Even when women are successful, acceptance among male peers is not easy because men feel a loss of privilege or power (38).

▶ "For men, conversations are often negotiations in which people try to achieve and maintain the upper hand." For women, conversations are more often a way to connect or gain confirmation and support (39).

Legato (35), whose information on brain differences is referenced in the points above, has quite a bit more to say about communication between men and women. She shares that there is a body of evidence that men and women hear, listen, understand, and produce speech differently. While women are better at identifying and interpreting nonverbal cues like tone of voice and facial expression, men are sometimes better at identifying straight forward emotions like rage and aggression. Women find verbalization and listening easier. Men are more likely to stick to facts with greater efficiency in the words they use. Women use more facial expressions, tone changes, and physical gestures. Women more often answer questions with a story; men like to draw the shortest line between fact A and conclusion B. They also interrupt a lot—which makes women feel humiliated and disregarded.

STARTING THE JOURNEY TO BETTER PARTNERSHIP

Given these observed or researched difference in genders, where should Dyad partners *start* on their journey to a better partnership? We've already suggested a conversation (or multiple conversations) on experiences with perceptions of each other's cultures (or "tribes"), followed by dialogue (whenever appropriate) about specific perceptions of each other's actions. These don't always have to be about attempts to "correct" behavior, inform on blind spots, or ask for change. They should *also* include praise and appreciation for the partners sensitivity to differences, attempts to change herself for the good of a new next era culture, and personal skills/gifts he brings to the organization and the team. As Dale Carnegie pointed out years ago, "One of the most neglected virtues of our daily existence is the expression of appreciation" (40).

It's important for Dyad partners to look at their environment with newly sensitized eyes. This may happen initially as they work more closely together with a work partner than they have in the past. One regional system physician CMO who has a longtime reputation for being empathetic, inclusive, team oriented, and open (earned long before he became a Dyad partner) states he was unaware of the bias against having nursing leaders in the organization as part of the top strategic team. "I had always seen the CNO as a powerful person. It never occurred to me that she is not at every decision-making table. After all, she is responsible for the *largest* workforce in the company. She *always* gets things done and solves problems without placing blame on anyone. Until I took the job as her Dyad partner, I didn't realize that she accomplishes so much in spite of being handicapped by being excluded from important discussions. We're equals in the system, advertise our Dyad partnership, make rounds together on the units, and work together with the medical and nursing staff. Frontline nurses and docs get it—they see us as a pair and are happy about the collaboration we've sponsored between our two professions. But the male nonclinician executives? Not so much. I was appalled to discover that I'm invited to strategically important meetings while she's left off the guest list. The subjects we talk about aren't any deep dark secrets—and when they are confidential, it's not like she can't keep things quiet. She would add a lot to the conversation because, frankly, she knows more about hospital operations than I do. I've asked so many why she hasn't been invited that the other guys are getting annoyed. They just don't get it. So, my Dyad partner and I talked about it and decided we need to come up with other tactics besides me pushing—because we're a little fearful they'll stop inviting me, too … and we desperately need clinical input at the executive strategic level. I keep her informed of course—and we'll figure out how to get her to the table. But I still can't get over the resistance to including her—and I don't think the issue is her personally. It's their inability to see value in a female nurse voice at the table, even when we're planning future patient care."

Before his Dyad experience, this CMO hadn't been aware of the bias he's now seeing first hand. That's not unusual, as gender experts say that men (especially those from predominately white cultures) don't see what women (and minorities) see. They do not notice the invalidation experienced by women when they make statements in meetings or suggest solutions to problems only to have males repeat what they said later in the meeting, and then be given "credit" for what women brought up first (41). They may not notice that women are interrupted repeatedly by men, and sometimes can't seem to get a "word in edgewise" while they wait for "their turn" to talk. They might not notice when strategic meetings exclude women—either because they weren't invited or because the "meeting" occurs at an exclusive men's club or on the golf course. It may not be clear that two people with virtually identical ways of leading may be labeled hard, feisty, and unpleasant *or* courageous, no-nonsense and powerful just because of their gender.

Men might (and this isn't a sure thing) notice hostile sexism, when a woman is treated rudely (either in person or behind her back for "usurping" men's status and power in their traditional roles). It's less likely they observe (consciously) benevolent sexism in which women are offered protection and male chivalry for choosing to stay in traditional roles (42). They may be oblivious to the "little things" listed in Table 5-1. As stated in Robinson-Walker's book (25) men often just don't see what's happening to females in the organization around them.

If these realities don't naturally become clearer as Dyad partners work together, a female partner might become comfortable enough in the partnership to discuss these issues with the male partner. Together, they might brainstorm or strategize how to change the culture, *or* the male partner might go into a traditional "male hero" model. In that case, he'll immediately begin by advising (telling) his partner *what to do* to solve the problem. He might even take action himself, feeling *he* must solve the problem, and "fix things" for the sake of his Dyad, his team, and his company. He might believe this "action" on his part is the supportive thing to do. As multiple relationship authors (and wives) have pointed out, this isn't usually what the woman wants! She's looking for empathy and/or the problem solving that two equal partners could do *together*. If her male partner takes action on her behalf, she will be perceived as the "weak woman" who is only treated with respect because the strong male insisted on it. (And that isn't really respect.) She can't be a leader if her partner must "fight her battles" or solve her problems. In trying to help, he will reinforce stereotypes and disempower her. A much more effective plan to transform the culture begins with generative discussion (between partners) about gender issues. This is in keeping with discussions about *any* organizational challenge. Partners can then combine their knowledge and thinking to determine strategy and tactics.

One tactic could be an agreement to coach each other on better ways to talk to and understand the opposite gender. Women can learn from men how to best approach other men. Men can learn from women what would make them more effective when working with women. It's probable that men can teach women strategy and politics and women can teach men more about managing relationships.

Another tactic that works (when partners trust that they are looking out for each other's best interests) is to agree to observe each other during interactions with others and then offer feedback. When a partner observes behavior or communication that he or she perceives as disempowering or decreasing effectiveness, the each Dyad individual has agreed to share this with each other. This can be followed by peer coaching. In addition, *both* partners should hone their observation skills about the "little things" like the examples in Table 5-1. Both can point these out to others or request changes in the organization. In fact, it is much more effective for *each* member of the Dyad to do this. If it appears to *always* be the female requesting changes to organizational norms or customs, some might perceive this to be her "personal problem," or "self-esteem issue," or "push for power," with a resulting conscious or unconscious disregard or resistance to even small changes. (Some might claim these issues are ridiculously small to bring up—but paradoxically are not willing to change them, which would seem easy to do if they are truly inconsequential.)

Working together on gender issues for the organization has an additional benefit. Discussions about the overall culture have the potential to educate the Dyad leaders on their individual behaviors and opens up opportunities for candid conversation about the Dyad relationship.

OTHER CULTURAL DIFFERENCES FOR DYAD PARTNERSHIPS TO CONSIDER

A few years ago, Kathy took part in a discussion about diversity in healthcare leadership. The all-white, mostly male group of CEOs and COOs, were bemoaning the fact that they simply could not find minority candidates for executive positions. One, however, was very proud to announce that he was mentoring young black men who had recently graduated with MHAs. During a break, the CNO approached him. "That's great," she said, "So we'll soon be seeing diverse leaders from your organization at these meetings." Startled, he replied, "Oh, no, it will be at least 10 years before they'll even be ready for an administrative position."

Kathy knew that the CEO had an undergraduate degree in sociology and an MHA. She also knew that, after completing a 1-year administrative residency, he "started at the top" as a hospital COO (age 24) and was a CEO by 30. His COO, another white male, also boasted about his "first job" as an assistant administrator.

Her conclusion was (right or wrong): For this individual, an unconscious prejudice, means that minority leaders need more experience than do white males to prove themselves "worthy" of executive positions. She also perceived that, while proud to be mentoring black males, he seemed unaware of his blindness to this personal bias.

Professional backgrounds and gender aren't the only cultural differences that individuals in Dyads may need to consider and discuss in their journey to a trusted and trusting partnership. If there is a difference in racial and ethnic backgrounds between the two, it *is* conceivable there will be issues for the partners to talk about and resolve that would not be present if both were of the same cultural and ethnic background. It's also possible that peer coaching and specific support *may* be needed by one or both Dyad members.

Research on different leadership styles indicates that racial differences in management are *not* as prevalent as gender or professional cultural differences. A 1981 study found no significant differences in attitudes toward employees or preferred leadership styles among managers of different races (43). A 1998 study on job applicant's integrity, showed that race and ethnicity made little difference in scores, but women of all races scored higher that did men (12). Other studies have agreed that there are no significant differences between white and black leaders in values, motivation, or other personal attributes (44, 45). In spite of studies like these, minority leaders, like women, still experience interpersonal issues based on stereotypes and bias, both their *own* and *others*. These leaders (and those they lead) do not come from common cultures, either (even when different groups share in the diverse population known as "people of color") (46). In other words, individuals and individual cultures differ in both their socialization and experiences.

Because influence and comfort with coworkers is greatest among those who are "just like us," the increasing diversity among leaders and work teams means we should *not* ignore differences. We need to establish a comfort level with each other so that trust and mutual respect can thrive. A 1991 study by Cox and Blake showed that "well-managed teams with diversity in members can achieve greater performance and cohesion" (47). The same is true of Dyad partnerships. When Dyad partners come from different ethnic or racial cultures, and they can manage well together, they will help all members on diverse teams maximize the team's effectiveness. (This is discussed further in Chapter 9.) Addressing differences as partners is the first step in strengthening the partnership. For many people, this is one more of those "undiscussables." However, when differences remain undiscussed, intergroup bias can create discomfort due to "awkward social interactions, embarrassing slips of the tongue, assumptions, and stereotypical judgments." Sometimes, liking and respect are missing just because unintended slights or undefined bias decreases trust between the leaders.

Trust develops over time (48). It's based on perceived authenticity of others. An authentic Dyad partner doesn't have to be "just like me," but he does have to be willing to *learn* about me, admit she may not understand my background, challenges I've faced, my realities as a person and leader, or how I view the world. Building trust with a partner starts with a willingness to have conversations about how the two individuals might differ. A truthful conversation involves both individuals' willingness to share their beliefs about the other's culture, a nonjudgmental "ear" when listening to these (however inaccurate) perceptions, and a willingness of both to teach and learn from the other. Then, when trust in each person's authenticity is established, the two leaders can lead diverse groups together, comfortable in the knowledge that one will help the other avoid (as much as possible) those "awkward social moments" and slips of the tongue with multicultural team members. Table 5-2 lists some research findings on different minority races or groups and questions that would be "discussable." These could be a starting point for a conversation between Dyad leaders who are ready to get to know each other and understand each other—as long as it is remembered that people (including your partner) *are* individuals, so studies pointing to an entire group's experience or behaviors *might not* be reality for *your* Dyad partner.

Mainstreamers in particular may choose to avoid discussions about ethnic, social, or other differences. This can be because of discomfort or a "blindness" to their own biases or how their partners perceive the organization's hospitality and tolerance of diversity. Some partners may never have these conversations. However, choosing not to discuss the "undisscussable" may be undisclosed root cause analyses to a less than cohesive partnership and less than high functioning diverse team.

Table 5-2	Leadership and Workforce Research on Diversity and Culture	
Minority	**Research**	**Some Sample Relationship-Building Questions from the Dyad Partner**
African Americans	Some black managers feel research is dated and alienating. They perceive and are angry or hurt at subtle devaluation. Much of their experience is "invisible" to their white colleagues (49).	Have you had experiences and do you still have experiences where you feel devalued? What could I do to help the way the two of us change this attitude so *no one* feels this way?
	Black women executives are likely to suffer from interactive effects of racial *and* gender discrimination (50). However, they are likely to be androgynous leaders (which researchers say is *best* leadership style for this and next era) because they are *both* task and relationship oriented.	Do you perceive yourself as both task and relationship oriented? Can you help me become more androgynous in *my* style through peer coaching?
Hispanic/Latino Americans	Latinos are encouraged to express feelings and emotions, which can result in misunderstandings (51). They want time for socializing and sharing consistent with those from collectivistic cultures (a strong orientation to the cultural group good rather than individual good) (52). They describe themselves as more transformational than mainstream leaders do. They tend to "accept and favor social, gender, and power differentiation" (53).	Is this a description of how you perceive yourself? If so (assuming the partner is not as comfortable with lots of emotion at work and/or there is a differentiation between them or with their teams based on social, gender, or power), how can we work together to learn from each other what *our* partnership and team norms will be?
East Asian Americans (Chinese, Japanese, Koreans)	They are less able to move into management than African Americans and Whites (54). Along with women, Asian Americans in general have more intuitive ability than mainstreamers (55). They are stereotyped as passive and lacking in the assertiveness needed for leadership (56).	Have you had experiences when you've been undervalued as a leader? What can the two of us do to change our culture so no one feels this way?
South Asian Americans (Indians and Pakistanis)	They prefer to be benevolent autocrats who are nurturing and paternalistic *if* subordinates are obedient and respectful (57, 58).	Is this your preferred leadership style? How can we work together on what our partnership and team leadership norms will be?
Native Americans	Observed leadership tend to differ from one tribal culture to another. For example, most tribal cultures are patriarchal. Some are matriarchal. At least one group of studied Native Americans consciously avoid decisions made by a single leader (59).	What is your leadership style? How can we work best together, if our styles differ?

		Some Sample Relationship-Building Questions from
Minority	**Research**	**the Dyad Partner**
Arab Americans	Younger American Muslims are more religiously observant than their parents. They pursue Islamic traditions and practices with a social and political agenda (60). Accountability for one's actions is *only* to God (61).	Have you had experiences where you felt mainstream prejudice? What can we do together to develop a good work culture for our team?
"Mainstreamers" (not considered minorities, often White Caucasians)	They come from mixed cultures, based on such things as religion, sexual orientation, country of origin.	What is your leadership style? How do you think we can best work together to match the goals of our organization?

Table 5-2   Leadership and Workforce Research on Diversity and Culture (*Continued*)

GENERATIONAL DIFFERENCES

Because Dyad partners are at the same level of management in the organization, they tend to be from the same generation. They probably do not have generational, cultural challenges between each other, but they will (together) most likely be managing up to four (and some predict five by 2020) very different groups of people within their teams. We'll go into this likelihood in greater detail in Chapter 9 but mention it here in case a Dyad partnership *is* developed between leaders from different generational cultures.

Multiple books have been written about each other's generation's unique values, work ethics, work habits, and communication preferences and styles. *If* Dyad partners come from different generations, this is one more culture that they should explore together, as they determine the best way to communicate with *and* work together. Table 5-3 is a reminder of what these generations are with the caveat that some authors have slightly different beginning and ending birth dates for each group.

Kathy was recently a speaker on a panel discussing the intergenerational work force. As the panel members described the traits ascribed to baby boomers, generation Xers, and Millenials, she noticed a young woman becoming more and more agitated. She appeared to either disagree with what the panel was saying or disturbed by it. So, Kathy asked her what she thought about the presentation. "I am sick of hearing how baby boomers describe my generation," the young woman told her, "It's like you think we are all alike. We aren't. And, even if we are, it *always* sounds like *your* generation thinks my generation is causing the problems between us." Kathy's conclusion was (right or wrong): For this individual, it seems that baby boomers are biased against other generations—and are defining them

Table 5-3 Five Generations and Who They Are		
Generation	**Birth Years**	**Traits**
Traditionalists (or the greatest generation)	1922–1945	Adheres to rules and respects authority Hardworking Loyal to organization
Baby boomers	1946–1964	Values hard work Values education Requires high-quality work product Emphasize teamwork and face-to-face meetings
Generation X	1965–1980	Skeptical of authority Not respectful of hierarchy Not respectful of status Values self-reliance Demands high productivity Values personal time
Millennials or Generation Y	1981–?*	Diverse (1 in 3 is a minority) Optimistic Confident Civic minded Committed to moral and ethical principles Values full communication Wants speedy decision making
Generation 9/11 or Generation Z	?–?* There is considerable lack of agreement on when Y ends and Z begins (mid-1990s or mid-2000s)	Not schooled in social graces Sees community as virtual

Adapted from Benjamin, T. Demand media. *http://smallbusiness.chron.com/generational-characteristics-workplace*
Horovitz, B. (May 4, 2012). *After GenX, Milennials, What should the next generation be?* USA Today.
* *Different authors do not agree on when generation X ends and generation Z begins (or will end for whatever the next group is labeled).*

in a narrow, uniform way. It was a great reminder not to generalize information about any group to the point of believing the research is accurate about a particular individual.

CHAPTER SUMMARY

There are a number of different "cultures" each partner could bring to the Dyad. More important than the number is the conscious decision by both individuals to recognize that these exist and to learn about each other. This requires overcoming historic silos, conversations about the "undiscussables," and two partners who are willing to confront their own biases and stereotypes while they bond as a cohesive management team.

Dyads in Action

THE NURSE–PHYSICIAN DYAD AS TEACHERS AND COACHES
Pat Patton and Manoj Pawar

Successful organizations in healthcare will be those in which quality, safety, and patient experience can be optimized at an affordable cost. Achievement of this value proposition requires multidisciplinary teams to come together to reinvent how care is delivered. We believe that Dyadic leadership models are particularly well positioned to facilitate such a transformation.

As a Dyad in our organization, we share responsibility for the development and management of clinical leadership talent necessary for this emerging new era. At the same time, the task at hand has forced us to reflect upon our own Dyadic leadership relationship as a source of important learning.

DESIGNING A DYADIC LEADERSHIP RELATIONSHIP

We came to this large national system from somewhat different paths. Pat's journey brought him here from a prior role as the Chief Nursing Officer (CNO) and Chief Operating Officer (COO) of a regional system in one of the system's markets, and Manoj was the system Chief Medical Officer (CMO) for another system (external to our current organization).

Prior to coming to Catholic Health Initiatives (CHI), the *formal* Dyad leadership structure was unfamiliar to Pat. In his days as a CNO in Kentucky, he was actually functioning as part of a Dyad but didn't realize it! That informal relationship with another leader was very much like our formal Dyad structures today but was not intentionally established.

When Pat arrived at CHI in January of 2011, he had his first meeting with his boss, Kathy Sanford, CNO for the organization, shortly after locating his new office and getting settled. During this orientation and onboarding, it was explained that he belonged to the Clinical Service Group (CSG), one of the national groups that comprise the CHI structure at the corporate office. This group was led by a "Dyad" composed of Kathy Sanford and Steve Moore, the CNO and CMO of CHI, respectively. She explained that CSG operated through a number of Dyad relationships among its various leaders. She shared that the organization usually pairs a nurse and a physician in a formal partnership, so that they can accomplish CHI's goals in a more unified way. The Dyads communicate regularly, learn about the work each does, understands how their work is complementary, and consciously show a united front in all that they do. Pat learned that his Dyad partner would be Manoj. Their shared responsibility was to co-lead the organization's efforts to develop stronger leaders across a broad range of clinical and nonclinical areas.

Manoj, while never having experienced a formalized Dyadic leadership structure at the executive level (leadership Dyads were formalized for directors in his previous company), also functioned in a number of informal Dyads. These typically formed when key bodies of work required co-leadership. At times, these relationships consisted of partners at the same level in the organization but often involved hierarchical relationships.

Manoj came to CHI in 2010, a number of months prior to Pat. He, too, had been informed of the Dyad leadership structure that was intrinsic to the CSG. The organizational chart for CSG consisted of a number of Dyad relationships but not all of the roles had been filled. The role that Pat currently holds was at that time still just "a box on the organizational chart." During the months prior to Pat's arrival, Manoj started to get familiar with the organization and began to plan his work in anticipation of a partner that had not yet been hired.

Manoj recalls that he was struck from the beginning by how intentional and purposeful Steve and Kathy were in their efforts at co-leading, co-presenting, and co-managing the day-to-day affairs of CSG. Every detail, from visibility and presence to language, seemed to be part of a thoughtful approach to building the kind of culture that supported effective Dyad relationships. The purposeful modeling of these Dyad leadership behaviors had a significant impact on the two of us as we entered the organization and began to think about our own working norms.

Our relationship as a Dyad began smoothly and without bumps. One of the most important starting points for us as we started working together involved incorporating an important cultural element that we saw worked extremely well within CSG. This involved the cultural expectations that CSG would operate as a "flattened organization," without hierarchy. A subtle, yet important aspect of this desire for nonhierarchical relationships was that titles are not used when referring to one another. The implication *from the start* was that all leaders are partners on a level playing field, sharing in the responsibilities for the work ahead. Pat recalls that when he met Steve Moore for the first time, he addressed him as Dr. Moore, to which Steve responded, "We don't use titles here at the national office. Please call me by my first name." Steve continued to explain that "We drop titles so we can work together in a way that allows us to work as equals and without hierarchy getting in the way of full accomplishment of CHI's goals." This subtle point made a significant impression on us and everyone on the team. This was a palpable change from the way physicians wanted (and expected) to be addressed in Pat's previous organization. As we began working together as a new leadership Dyad, we were happy to adopt this norm.

Our initial focus in coming together was to treat the Dyadic relationship as something that we would design together, with purpose and intention. We wanted to build from what we observed was working well in the organization, as well as from our prior experiences with what worked well in less formally structured Dyads. An important starting point for this involved simply getting to know each other as people, making the fundamental human connections that are so important for effective relationships. Early on, we spent a great deal of time specifically for this purpose beyond our weekly meetings. Lunches together, coordination of travel for the market site visits that were part of our onboarding, and informal "drop in" conversations all provided time for us to better understand one another on a personal level. We shared our experiences and discoveries as we entered a complex, new organization. *This was very intentional to make sure that we not only solidified our Dyad relationship but to also visually demonstrate to the markets that we functioned as a Dyad team.*

Being conscientious about connecting our work routines when possible was an important part of our efforts to build a solid Dyad. Sharing an executive assistant made this easier, as did locating our offices adjacent to one another. These steps made it much easier to facilitate weekly huddles, to participate in conference calls together in one office (vs. isolated in separate spaces and on different phone lines), and to make it easy to have "drop-in," unplanned conversations.

We believe communication is the most important key to a strong Dyad relationship. Both ad hoc and scheduled meetings have been immensely valuable to our relationship and our work. Of course, many of our conversations may have nothing to do directly with a particular business objective. We find that these non–business-related conversations are just as important to our partnership. They set the stage for more effective work in goal- or project-oriented discussions. We get to know each other as people and develop our working relationship principally out of this informal communication. Inevitably, there are things we discover about each other that help us to communicate.

Without this background knowledge of who each of us is, our work-focused communication would not be nearly as effective. For example, if one of us is aware that the other is preoccupied, stressed, or frustrated with issues or challenges, we adapt our communication patterns and styles accordingly. Both of us experience times when other people dive into the tactical objectives and try to solve problems, without clearing up any issues that may affect another's ability to fully hear or understand. We are careful not to do that and have become trusted colleagues, as a result. We've learned that awareness of what's important to each of us as well as acknowledgement of our individual successes is a tremendous motivator.

Without first building the relationship, we would not be able to support each other and serve as confidential sounding boards (something individual leaders don't always have!). We are convinced that both regular formal and informal communications are essential for a successful Dyad relationship, and we've found that it's only possible through thoughtful and intentional effort.

We also spent some of our early time together in a more structured way, drawing on our experience in leadership development, to explore things that we knew would serve as a critical foundation for effective co-leadership. We shared our

▶ Personal mission, vision, and values
▶ Career aspirations
▶ Strengths and areas for growth
▶ Opportunities for complementarity
▶ Personality profiles and results of other developmental assessments (in our case, this included instruments such as Hogan and *Thomas-Killmann Instrument [TKI]*)

We felt that conversations around these topics would guide us toward more effective communication and shared understanding of how we view things (similarly or differently), and how we might use this knowledge to our advantage. By discovering and leveraging our potential synergies, we believed that we would be a more value-added leadership team.

SOLIDIFYING THE DYAD RELATIONSHIP THROUGH SHARED WORK

We built our Dyadic relationship quickly through these intentional communication efforts. We also felt that early projects and shared work were important for solidifying our working relationship. One particularly critical project that was formative for us and our working relationship was the co-development of a national program for clinical leaders.

We were tasked to build a leadership development program in cooperation with our mission and human resources (HR)/talent management groups. The focus on clinical leaders was based on the organization's executives' belief that much of the transformational work required for success in the future would be led by clinicians. Integration and coordination of care across the healthcare continuum, while also optimizing current operations, would require new ways of thinking, leading, and collaborating. It was felt that the CNOs and CMOs (as well as some clinical leaders in similar roles) would play a strategically critical role in leading these transformation efforts. For this reason, the CHI Board of Stewardship Trustees (BOST) asked that leadership development for CNOs and CMOs throughout the system be a key strategic priority. The trustees wanted a program that would make sure our leaders were prepared to lead effectively into the next era, and our Dyad was selected to lead this work.

In keeping with our established norms, we spent a lot of time discussing our experiences and perspectives on this challenge. We wanted to ensure that we developed a shared understanding of the issues and objectives. What ultimately emerged for us was a clear shared vision for the program, as well as shared values and principles in how we would bring this vision to fruition. We realized that we could serve as a catalyst for bringing together our colleagues from the HR and mission groups as key partners in this project. These internal groups, spanning historic company silos, would coordinate with an external partner from academia, adding another degree of complexity to the project. We understood that the relational components of this work—between us as a Dyad, between national groups, and between our project team and an external partner—would determine whether we would ultimately be successful.

As co-leaders of the initiative, we ultimately felt that the strength of our leadership as a Dyad would be perhaps the most critical leverage point. Our ability to remain in tight communication, and to constantly reevaluate our own perspectives, would be important prior to engaging other stakeholders. While there were certainly times when we found ourselves in disagreement, we were quickly able to shift to a mode of listening and understanding one another's perspectives, which allowed us to resolve any differences. We feel that this would not have been possible if it were not for the time we spent initially building shared vision and shared purpose—both of which were committed to fully serving the organization and the future participants in the program. While we did sometimes have differences in opinion on the tactics to achieve this goal, we trusted one another because we had learned we shared the same ultimate objectives. This level of trust, resulting from shared intentions and transparency, is what we feel makes our Dyad partnership strong. We did not have personal agendas for developing this program. We each wanted what was right for our organization and for the participants, and we had learned this about each other.

During our meetings with HR, mission, and our university partner, we were able to speak for each other if one of us was not able to attend. We could only do this because of our strong communication and through the trust we had built by focusing on ourselves and our Dyad relationship first.

COACHING TOGETHER

A second formative experience for our individual and shared development involved work we did internally as part of the CHI coaching community. The system had determined that part of the formation for leaders should be an opportunity to receive personal coaching from internally trained management coaches. Manoj had already been trained and had prior experience as an executive coach. However, the emerging coaching community within CHI provided a new context and a somewhat new model for coaching within the organization. So when Pat decided to be trained in the model, we chose to participate together. We would both learn new coaching skills and help develop the new leadership coaching program.

We started our coaching in CHI's program as a Dyad partnership. We went through the program together in May of 2011. After completing this program, we used our coaching techniques *on each other* (for practice more than anything). As we developed more and more skill in the art of coaching others, we discovered that our communication skills (which we already thought were pretty good) got better. We asked each other insightful questions. We questioned our own assumptions and biases and we helped each other learn more about ourselves. We developed a habit of coaching each other during decision making, not only for work we shared (such as the leadership development program we were building) but also for other unrelated areas where our work involved separate projects, in which we were involved individually.

Our work in coaching leaders at CHI has been particularly powerful for us, and we see it as a key component of our work in helping others in the organization. (We discuss this in greater detail in the next section, as part of our goal to be value-added leaders.)

SPREADING OUR IMPACT: MODELING DYAD BEHAVIORS AND COACHING FOR SUCCESS

When developing leaders, organizations tend to place a focus on individual and their development and growth, often in isolation from their larger teams. We see individual development as both important and essential. However, we also believe that there is tremendous value in developing Dyad partners together. For this reason, we have actively encouraged them to apply together to participate in a variety of leadership development programs that we have developed at CHI. In these programs, the development of individuals takes place at the same time as the development of the Dyad as a leadership unit. Action learning projects, supported by program faculty, can assist participating Dyads in the application of information learned and, more importantly, can support the deepening of the interpersonal relationship required for the Dyad to function effectively. Within the context of these programs, we also use the opportunity to model our own behavior as a Dyad, often co-presenting and co-facilitating, visibly demonstrating our collaboration in the work of coordinating the program.

Coaching is an important aspect of our approach for supporting developing individuals as well as Dyads. Each of us works with a number of internal coaching clients. These are typically executive level clinical (and some non-clinical) leaders. When we coach individuals, it is common that their roles emerge as a topic. Sometimes, this comes up when the leader is "stuck," in which case he or she may see himself or herself as alone in trying to meet a particular challenge. He may not have considered the potential role that the Dyad partner could play in solving the dilemma. For these scenarios, we help our CNOs, CMOs, and CEOs understand the full potential of Dyad partnerships through the coaching.

Coaching, at CHI, is a particular practice with a specific approach. While the term is used by other organizations to sometimes imply teaching, consulting, mentoring, or training, we use it differently. Consistent with the definition used by the International Coach Federation (ICF), we defining coaching as "partnering with clients in a thought-provoking and creative process that inspires them to maximize their potential" (ICF, 2013). We do this through a structured process and utilize a skill set that is honed through training, practice, and study. When we provide coaching for our leaders, we draw on a set of evidence-based practices as a part of our approach. Our goal is supporting individuals as they create and thrive in healthy Dyad partnerships. These coaching practices assist people, through insightful questions, to determine where they are "stuck" or where they want to go next. The questions serve as a springboard for individuals to help them gain deeper insight about their particular situations or concerns. This helps move individuals to engaged action.

The CHI coaching model utilizes powerful questions to catalyze insight (vs. giving advice, directing, or solving problems). The latter deprive the client from the learning that takes place through introspection and discovery. It is easy for us as human beings to be problem solvers. We tend to think we have all the answers and that it is just "easier" sometimes to provide these instead of helping the individual tap into his own creativity and resources to find answers for himself.

This coaching approach can also be used when dealing with a leader who is confused about the relationship with a Dyad partner. Questions such as "What have you done lately with your Dyad partner that has been successful?" or "Who can assist you with developing a stronger relationship with that person?" are examples of questions we have used to help individual clients plan for developing strong Dyad relationships.

Coaching clients to develop stronger Dyad relationships has been challenging as well as rewarding. Sometimes, we find that people are not aware of the importance of understanding one another as human beings, and the foundation this lays for effective partnerships. Pat has asked CNO clients that he coaches questions such as "When was the last time you actually sat down and had a cup of coffee with your Dyad partner?" or "When was the last time you asked your partner about his hobbies?"

In other situations, we find leaders who have functioned in long-standing silos. As a result, there are dynamics that are difficult for them to discuss. They are sometimes uncomfortable even talking to their coaches about these. They do not always have a good relationship (or any relationship at all) with a potential Dyad partner. Their silos have been created and fostered for many years and seem impenetrable. Since these perceptions deprive the Dyad partners from achieving the Dyad's fullest potential, helping clients break down silos is an important part of our work.

CNOs often perform their "nursing" leadership work in a silo that may not be self-apparent. For example, a CNO may, with the best intentions, be working on a project to improve aspects of nursing without involving his or her CMO partner. He or she may not realize that aspects of the nursing project could have relevance to physician issues and workflows. With busy schedules, it can sometimes seem easier to do the work alone than it is to engage a partner.

At the same time, the physician leader may be identifying problems and implementing solutions in isolation, without consulting the CNO. The unintended consequences of work done in isolation, without coordination between clinical leads, can create bigger problems in the long run. The ability to share perspectives on a problem in a healthy Dyad relationship can often lead to better, more sustainable solutions.

Physicians and nurses play roles that are particularly dependent on one another to create high-performing clinical organizations. Unfortunately, the importance of this relationship may be forgotten or not fully realized. Coaching clients as part of a "siloed" Dyad sometimes involves shining light on this with the client. A common "aha" moment for CMOs and CNOs is when we ask the question: "How is it you are doing your job the most effectively without your Dyad partner?" Leaders sometimes get defensive, when this is asked, they rationalize why they act the way that they do. It is part of the coaching process to help them come to the realization that through a strong Dyad relationship, they can help the organization and their team be even more successful.

CHALLENGES

We have experienced challenges as Dyad partners. The reality of working in a large, complex organization such as ours is that things are not necessarily black and white. For example, early on in our work as a Dyad, we began to realize that while there were a number of highly visible projects that we led together, there were also an increasing number of initiatives in which we did not share responsibility. There were times when it was not clear whether it was worth devoting time to sharing seemingly unrelated work with the other partner. What we found, however, is that there was considerable value in doing so. Manoj relied on the Dyad relationship as a place for generating ideas, as a sounding board, or as a place for thinking together. Pat often brought institutional knowledge and awareness from his prior role in a CHI market that was critical in providing guidance. Furthermore, the ability to share successes, challenges, and even frustrations was another way of checking-in with one another, providing a human context for what was happening for each of us.

Over time, we also discovered that we were part of multiple Dyadic relationships as it related to various work in the organization. The complexity of this is something we didn't necessarily foresee. Different Dyadic relationships bring with them different sets of shared expectations and norms, something that requires a great deal of flexibility.

CHI is a large organization with national scope. Because of its geographic reach, travel is a necessity. As one might imagine, travel has the potential to present a significant challenge for Dyad leaders. We've found that when traveling, it is important for us to connect virtually (by phone, e-mail, IM, or Internet) even when in separate locations. This commitment to checking-in has been important to the success of our Dyad.

Finally, time can be a challenge. With multiple, competing priorities, it can be tempting to delete the time needed for relational issues. We have found that, rather than leaving it to chance, we must schedule regularly occurring appointments to ensure that other commitments don't usurp the time needed for an effective leadership partnership. We viewed time committed to each other as a critical investment in the success of our Dyad.

OUR "BEST PRACTICES"

We pay a great deal of attention to intentionally and purposefully developing an effective Dyad relationship. We have leveraged what we have learned to spread our organizational impact, both through leadership development programs and through coaching. We also try to purposefully model some of the behaviors and activities that we feel have been critical to our success.

Both for ourselves and for those we coach, we try to take an approach that draws on the literature. These four principles have been particularly effective (62,63).

▶ *The Dyadic leadership relationship is acknowledged, supported, and expected by the other leaders of the organization.* Those supervising the individual leaders comprising the Dyad must acknowledge and fully support the partnership. To do so means honoring the individual roles as equal in status. Hierarchy differences between the roles would pose significant challenges for designing effective partnerships. Leaders must also take the time to meet with the Dyad together on a regular basis. While there may be job functions that are distinct, opportunities to spark collaboration must be thoughtfully designed and expected. As a result, major organizational issues must involve the Dyad as a unit, with both shared responsibility and accountability for outcomes. By seeking out opportunities that are complex enough to require extensive collaboration, leaders in the organization can create the conditions that accelerate the formation of an effective partnership.

▶ *While there are two leaders, CNO and CMO act as one in the context of the partnership and do so visibly for the organization.* This commitment brings with it a number of important implications for how the partnership performs. For example, healthy conflict and rich dialogue are essential for realizing the maximum potential of the relationship. At the same time, once the Dyad arrives at a decision, or comes to shared agreement on an issue, both leaders convey the same message to the organization. Neither member of the Dyad speaks ill of the other, nor do they dishonor a shared agreement after the fact. This particular point is critical, in that the risk for triangulation in most organizations is quite high, and wise partners take this into account.

▶ *The duality of the partnership is embraced, with attention toward eliciting complementary skills.* Early on in the partnership, it is critical to devote time in the development of a shared understanding of individual strengths and weaknesses. In the process, the Dyad comes to a collective understanding of how best to leverage complementary strengths for the success of the partnership and the organization overall. By spending dedicated time in exploring how they will best work together, CNO and CMO partners will most effectively create the synergy they seek. To embrace the duality of the partnership fully, humility is essential, with egos "checked at the door" by both.

▶ *Opportunities to foster the partnership are created geographically and temporally.* Close proximity is perhaps one of the most important predictors of a successful partnership. At CHI, attention has been paid to placing members of clinical leadership Dyads in adjacent offices whenever possible. The close proximity allows for a greater ease of informal collaboration. In addition, colocation makes it easier for partners to more rapidly evolve as sounding boards for one another. Finally, the geographic proximity facilitates regular meeting times for the coleaders to spend together. Regular "huddles" are a common occurrence for CNO–CMO Dyads at CHI (64).

CAUTIONS AND CONSIDERATIONS WHEN IMPLEMENTING A DYAD LEADERSHIP MODEL

Dyad partnerships may be implemented when an organization is trying to move a certain issue forward. Clinical Dyads are effective when patient care issues need to be addressed in a more concerted effort. Partners may be two nurses, a nurse and physician, a nurse and ancillary leader, or two physicians. However, Dyads are not necessarily the best leadership model for every situation. Many clinical leadership positions are appropriately filled by "single" individual leaders. Of course, those leaders still need to develop collaborative skills because there really are no clinical leadership jobs that don't require team work. All leaders have an accountability for this.

Accountability is another word for ownership. In a Dyad partnership model, the accountability or ownership belongs to both parties. Each person knows he or she will succeed or fail based largely on their Dyad partner's ownership. Manoj and Pat have developed an accountability buddy system. We check in on each other to find out how things are going whether they are our projects or not. When we know we are accountable to each other, it raises the stakes, even for individual projects.

We started our story talking about the importance of the relationship. We are ending it the same way. Leadership is about relationship building. This means not only with a Dyad partner but with other leaders as well. In some cases, it is not as easy as it was with us. It is hard to build a relationship when you are not fond of the other person. We have coached a few leaders who had designated Dyad partners they did not "like." As we worked through this, we spoke about how it isn't necessary to "like" another leader, but it is imperative to work with him or her. We developed techniques in order to build the relationship that would propel the partners forward into the future. This was not always easy, but it did work for most of our leaders. Building relationships sometimes needs to be done in ways that might not have been thought of in the past. Having a cup of coffee, taking someone to lunch, or getting to know him or her with a short 5-minute session may be all it takes to turn the corner on a relationship that has been struggling.

People want to connect on a personal level as well as on a professional level. It is possible to get to know them in ways that you haven't known them in the past. Ask about their children, their last vacation or events that are happening in their lives. One exercise we have some of our leaders do is to sit down with people they want a stronger relationship with. We suggest they talk about a time when they were happy, elated, overjoyed, or otherwise content. Tell them they have 5 minutes to tell their story. You will be amazed at what you can learn from that person in just 5 minutes.

Dyad partnership bonds are sometimes easy to forge and sometimes hard to make. Dyad partnerships that work well can be very rewarding. Our advice: Take time out of your day, or schedule time in your day to build or maintain your Dyad relationship. It will be rewarding for you, your partner, your team, and your organization!

REFERENCES

1. Kahneman, D. (2011). *Thinking fast and slow*. New York, NY: Farrar, Straus and Giroux.
2. Chase, D. (July 26, 2012). Women in healthcare report: 4% of CEOs, 73% of Managers, Forbes (Pharma and Healthcare), Website: Forbes.com, Retrieved from: http://www.forbes.com/sites/davechase/2012/07/26/women-in-healthcare-report-4-of-ceos-73-of-managers/
3. Azar, B. (2000). A new stress paradigm for women: Rather than fighting or fleeing, women may respond to stress by tending to themselves and their young and befriending others. *APA Monitor*, July–August, 42–43.
4. Moore, D. P. (1984). Evaluating in-role and out-of-role performers. *Academy of Management Journal*, *27*, 603–618.
5. Jago, A. G., & Vroom, V. H. (1982). Sex differences in the incident and evaluations of participative leader behavior. *Journal of Applied Psychology*, *67*, 776–783.
6. Rice, R. W., Instone, D., & Adams, J. (1984). Leader sex, leader success, and leadership process: Two field studies. *Journal of Applied Psychology*, *69*, 12–32.
7. Hall, J., & Donell, S. M. (1979). Managerial achievement: The personal side of behavioral theory. *Human Relations*, *32*(1), 77–101.
8. Muldrow, I. W., & Bayton, J. A. (1979). Men and women executives and processes related to decision accuracy. *Journal of Applied Psychology*, *64*, 99–106.
9. Menkes, J. (1999). *Gender differences in management styles*, Paper, Society for Industrial and Organizational Psychology, Atlanta, GA.
10. Grant, J. (1988). Woman as managers: What they can offer organizations. *Organizational Dynamics*, Winter, 56–63.
11. Hall, J. A., & Halberstadt, A. C. (1981). Sex roles and nonverbal communication skills. *Sex Roles, 7*, 273–287.
12. Ones, D. S., & Viswesvaran C. (1998). Gender, age, and race differences in overt integrity tests: Results across four large-scale job applicant data sets. *Journal of Applied Psychology*, *83*, 35–42.
13. Deaux, K. (1976). *The behavior of women and men*. Monterey, CA: Brooks/Cole.
14. Rosenfeld, L. B., & Fowler, C. D. (1976). Personality, sex, and leadership style. *Communications Monographs*, *43*, 320–324.
15. Bass, B. M., Avolio, B. J., & Atwater, L. E. (1996). The transformational and transactional leadership of men and women. *Applied Psychology: An International Review*, *45*, 5–34.
16. Murphy, E. F., Jr., Eckstat, A., & Parker, T. (1995). Sex and gender differences in leadership. *Journal of Leadership Studies*, *2*(1), 116–131.
17. Rosener, J. B. (1990). Ways women lead. *Harvard Business Review*, *68*(6), 119–125.
18. Daughtry, L. H., & Finch, C. R. (1997). Effective leadership of vocational administrators as a function of gender and leadership style. *Journal of Vocational Educational Research*, *22*(3), 173–186.
19. Van Engen, M. L., & Williamson, T. M. (2004). Sex and leadership styles: A meta-analysis of research published in the 1990s. *Psychological Reports*, *94*(1), 3–18.

20. Southwick, R. B. (1998). *Antecedents of transformational, transactional, and laissez-faire leadership.* Doctoral dissertation, University of Georgia, Athens, GA.

21. Carless, S. A. (1998). Gender differences in transformational leadership. An examination of superior, leader and subordinate perspectives. *Sex Roles, 39,* 887–902.

22. Eagly, A. H., Johannesen-Schmidt, M. C., & van Engen, M. L. (2002). *Transformational, transactional, and laissez-faire leadership styles.* Paper, Academy of Management, Denver, CO.

23. Park, D. (1996). Sex-role identity and leadership style: Looking for an androgynous leadership style. *Journal of Leadership Studies, 3*(3), 49–59.

24. Blake, R. R., & Mouton, J. S. (1964). *The managerial grid.* Houston, TX: Gulf.

25. Robinson-Walker, C. (1999). *Women and leadership in healthcare.* San Francisco, CA: Jossey-Bass.

26. Briles, J. (1996). *Gender traps.* New York, NY: McGraw-Hill.

27. Rosener, J. (1995). *America's competitive secret: Utilizing women as a management strategy* (pp. 84–100). New York, NY: Oxford University Press.

28. Stone, D., Patton, B., & Heen, S. (1999). *Difficult conversations, how to discuss what matters most.* New York, NY: Penguin Books.

29. Altman, L. (February 10, 2014). A patient's eye view of nurses. New York: *The New York Times Review of Books,* accessed @ well.blogs.nytimes.com/2014/02/10/a-patients-eye-view-of-nurses

30. Ryan, K., & Oestreich, D. (1991). *Driving fear out of the workplace.* San Francisco, CA: Jossey-Bass

31. Luft, J., & Ingham, H. (1955). The Johari window, a graphic model of interpersonal awareness. *Proceeding of the Western training laboratory in group development.* Los Angeles, CA: UCLA.

32. Gray, J. (1992). *Men are from Mars, women are from Venus.* New York, NY: Harper.

33. Gilligan, C. (1982). *In a different voice.* Cambridge, MA: Harvard Press.

34. Allen, P. (1994). *Getting to I do.* New York, NY: Harper-Collins.

35. Legato, M. (2005). *Why men never remember and women never forget.* UST: Holtzbrinck.

36. Babcock, L., & Lashever, S. (2003). *Women don't ask: Negotiation and the gender divide.* Princeton, NJ: Princeton University Press.

37. Robinson-Walker, C. (1999). *Women and leadership in healthcare.* San Francisco, CA: Jossey-Boss.

38. Koba, M. (October 31, 2011). Women in power: Yes, they are different from men. CNBC, 8:43 pm EDT.

39. Tannen, D. (1990). *You just don't understand: Women and men in conversation.* New York, NY: Morrow.

40. Carnegie, D. (1936). *How to win friends and influence people.* New York, NY: Simon and Schuster.

41. Marcus, L. J. (1995). *Renegotiating healthcare: Resolving conflict to build collaboration.* San Francisco, CA: Jossey-Bass.

42. Glick, P., & Fiske, S. T. (2001). An ambivalent alliance: Hostile and benevolent sexism as complementary justifications for gender inequality. *American Psychologist, 56*(2), 109–118.

43. Barati, M. E. (1981). Comparison of preferred leadership styles, potential leadership effectiveness, and managerial attitudes among black and white, female and male management students. *Dissertation Abstracts International, 43*(4A), 1271.

44. Watson, J. G., & Barone, S. (1976). The self-concept, personal values, and motivational orientations of black and white managers. *Academy of Management Journal, 19,* 36–48.

45. Allen, W. R. (1975). Black and white leaders and subordinates: Leader choice and ratings, aspirations and expectancy of success. In D. Frederick & J. Guittian (Eds.), *New challenges for the decision sciences.* Amherst, MA: Northeast Region of the American Institute for Decision Sciences.

46. Fine, M. G., Johnson, F. L., & Ryan, M. S. (1990). Cultural diversity in the workplace. *Public Personnel Management, 19,* 305–319.

47. Cox, T., & Blake, S. (1991). Managing cultural diversity: Implications for organizational competitiveness. *Academy of Management Executives, 5,* 45–56.

48. Lewicki, R. J., Stevenson, M. A., & Bunker, B. B. (1997). *The three components of interpersonal trust: Instrument development and differences across relationships.* Paper, Boston, MA: Academy of Management.

49. Livers, A. B., & Caver, K. A. (2002). Across the divide: Grasping the black experience in corporate America. *Leadership in Action, 22*(5), 7–11.

50. Parker, P. S., & Ogilvie, D. T. (1996). Gender, culture, and leadership: Toward a culturally distinct model of African-American women executives' leadership strategies. *Leadership Quarterly, 7,* 189–214.

51. Bordas, J. (1994). *Passion and power: Finding personal purpose: An essay on reflections on leadership.* New York, NY: John Wiley & Sons.

52. Zoppi, I. M. (2004). *The relation of self-perceived leadership and acculturation of Latinas in the U.S. Army.* Doctoral dissertation, College Park, MD: University of Maryland.

53. Triandis, H. C. (1984). *Selection and retention of minorities in organizations.* ONR Conference on Minorities Entering High Tech Careers, Pensacola, FL.

54. Bell, M. P., Harrison, D. A., & McLaughlin, M. E. (1997). *Diversity at the top: Effects of women and minority CEOs and directors on organizational diversity.* Paper, Boston, MA: Academy of Management.

55. Xin, K. R. (1997). Asian American managers: An impression gap? *Journal of Applied Behavioral Science, 33,* 335–355.

56. Yu, W. (1985). Asian-Americans charge prejudice slows climb to management ranks. *Wall Street Journal,* September 11, 35.

57. Sinha, J. B. P. (1980). *The nurturant task leader.* New Delhi, India: Concept.

58. Sinha, J. B. P. (1994). Cultural embeddedness and the development role of industrial organizations in India. In M. Dunnette (Ed.), *Handbook of industrial and organizational psychology* (2nd ed.). Chicago, IL: Rand McNally.

59. Bass, B. (2008). *The bass handbook of leadership.* New York, NY: Free Press.

60. Abdo, G. (2004). Alienated Muslims. In T. Halstead (Ed.), *The real state of the union.* New York, NY: Basic Books.

61. Scruton, R. (2002). The political problem of Islam. *The Intercollegiate Review, 38*(1), 3–16.

62. Sally, D. (2002). Co-leadership: Lessons from Republican Rome. *California Management Review, 44*(4), 84–99.

63. Heenan, D. B. (1999). *Co-leaders: The power of great partnerships.* New York, NY: John Wiley & Sons.

64. Patton, P. (2012). New clinical executive models: One system's approach to CNO-CMO co-leadership. *Nursing Administration Quarterly, 36*(4), 320–324.

Chapter 6

Dyads as Catalysts for Renewing the Strength of the Leadership Team

Not long ago, we were both invited to attend a 2-day meeting in another state. While it was billed as a retreat for clinicians, attendees included hospital executives and others, such as Human Resources and Finance leaders. There were a number of discussions about the future of healthcare, and the need for stronger partnerships in the future.

On the second day, one of the attendees brought up an issue that had apparently been bothering her for some time. "When I call a doctor at home or in his office, I am not doing it just to waste his time. I either need to get information about his patient or need to give him information. It's pretty insulting when he either hangs up on me, tells me not to bother him, or actually says very rude things—sometimes these guys don't call me back when I leave a message that it's really important for the care of the patient *right now*. This lack of respect is intolerable, and is not the right thing for quality patient care." The speaker's colleagues (from the same specialty) immediately chimed in, telling stories of times when care was compromised by this type of behavior, examples of when they were insulted by physicians, and about how they feel disrespected, and undervalued by members of the medical staff.

When they had completed their litany, three nursing leaders in the front row exclaimed, almost in unison, "You are describing what nurses have dealt with forever." The speakers looked chagrined, and even more upset. They weren't nurses. They were all MDs—hospitalists and emergency department physicians, attending this medical staff leadership retreat.

After this meeting, a nurse said, "Well at least they haven't had a scalpel thrown at them in the OR like I once did." The other nurses laughed, and some told stories of horrific verbal and physical abuse. Their laughter was the saddest part of the conversation because it indicated an acceptance of what would not be tolerated in any other American industry.

We share this story because it illustrates an issue that Dyad leaders will need to consider as they work toward a transformed healthcare future. While we've talked about the various professional cultures and differences that must be addressed as we come together as partners, there are other issues that Dyads cannot ignore as they become leaders for the organization. Behaviors and norms that have been tolerated, even treated with humor, will need to be addressed. Acceptance of a formal leadership position brings with it a responsibility to provide safe, respectful work environments for everyone.

You may be thinking that this is old news. Your organization may already be changing policies so that "poor citizenship" (a euphemism for abusive behavior) is part of the recredentialing process for your medical staff. You may have programs for physicians to help them handle their stress. Some might be labeled "anger management." If you are a physician, you may think we do not need to talk about this anymore. You may be tired of people always "blaming the doctors for all the dysfunction."

As the story above indicates, interpersonal issues are still causing problems in our organizations, even among groups many of us think of as one united tribe. (Of course, this is not true, as there are subtribes among a profession that result in perceived superiority or pecking orders. Medicine is no exception, with subtribes based on specialties, and even subspecialties.)

We use the story above as an example of civility problems in healthcare organizations, not as a condemnation of physicians as a whole. For one thing, not all surgeons throw scalpels at nurse, and not all doctors are rude or condescending to physicians of other specialties. In addition, physicians are not the only group with members (actually a minority of members) whose lack of civility makes the workplace unpleasant for others and, as a result, *endangers the quality and safety of patient care.*

CIVILITY AND WORKPLACE FEAR

Civility (courtesy, respect, and consideration of others) is not always present among those who work in healthcare. We've known experienced nurses who demean and mistreat new graduates (there's even a common saying among this profession that "nurses eat their young"), departments that denigrate other areas on a regular basis, members of one shift who verbally abuse (or disparage behind their backs) coworkers who work on another shift. We have also experienced rude and unkind managers.

An unspoken, and maybe unconscious, rationale for implementation of Dyad leadership is a hope that co-leaders will increase civility among their two tribes. As mentioned above, all leaders have a responsibility to provide safe, civil workplaces, and not just between their own professional cultures. New Dyads can't ignore the work environment. They need to actively address intergroup and interprofessional norms. They will have to intervene in relationship problems. In addition, if they do not have education and experience in management, they'll need to learn about human resources laws so that they do not make errors (while addressing relationship or personal problems) that would place the organization in a compromised legal or regulatory position. If they work in an organization where employees are represented by an organized labor entity, they will have to understand the rules and implications that go with this. (Labor Law and contractual agreements.) While "scientific" professions may think that this work is all "soft," individual co-leaders may discover that addressing relationship and personal issues is among the hardest things they have ever done.

Some interpersonal relationship issues may seem trivial and easy to solve with a simple "chat" or written policy; others may be obviously more complicated. Experienced leaders know that even some of the "easy stuff" isn't easy. A single conversation with a colleague or subordinate doesn't usually solve even straightforward issues. Policies, while important for documenting expected behaviors, don't guarantee that the behaviors will occur. For example, a physician colleague, new to his leadership role, learned from his Dyad partner that a female nurse had talked with the nursing leader about rude behavior from a male surgeon in which she felt both disempowered and disrespected. The two nurses had discussed their strategy for changing this dynamic. It included the nurse who felt disrespected solving the issue herself. With the nurse executive, she role-played a solution (the nurse had asked for coaching) in which the nurse would approach the surgeon and talk to him about how she perceived, and felt about, his words and actions.

The new physician leader decided he could take care of the problem for the nurse. He cornered his medical colleague in the hallway, told him the nurse was upset about his "boorish" behavior, and asked him to follow the hospital civility policy from now on. Satisfied that he had taken care of the problem, he reported this back to the nurse executive, and was perplexed when she was not happy.

The experienced nurse executive understood what Ryan and Oestreich describe as fear in the workplace (1). Workplace fear includes issues that might not come to mind to everyone, such as fear of being criticized, fear of not being seen as a team player, and fear of disagreements that might lead to damaged relationships. The nurse in this case, was also afraid of being "punished" by the surgeon.

She thought he might become even more imperious toward her, or refuse to talk to her, or speak badly about her to others on the team if a third party interfered in their relationship.

In this case, the nurse was right. The surgeon was furious that she had "run to Dad" (the physician leader), embarrassed him, and potentially affected his "citizenship" rating for recredentialing. Their relationship instantly became strained. When the surgeon came to her unit, he insisted on talking to other nurses about the care of his patients, even when those patients were assigned to her care. Now the nurse executive and nurse had a bigger problem. They needed to devise a way to repair the damage.

The medical leader had not wanted to make the problem bigger. Still playing the part of problem solver, he proposed that he would fix things by going back to the surgeon and telling him that "punishing" the nurse by refusing to work with her was not acceptable behavior! He still did not understand the ineffectiveness of this approach. (Over time, he learned, with coaching from his partner, the problem with his instinctual approach). Eventually, the nurse and surgeon worked out their issues, but hard feelings that could have been avoided persisted for some time. This didn't just affect the two professionals involved; it affected the efficiency of the unit (when the surgeon interrupted other nurses' work to talk with them about his patients). In addition to understanding the dynamics of interpersonal relationships, the nurse executive's strategy for helping nurses deal with interpersonal problems *themselves* was to empower them, by providing them with caring, confrontational skills they could practice with her.

The nurse leader knew that without the ability, skill, and organizational "permission" to talk with other team members *as equals* (human to human), interpersonal team issues would not be solved. As we move into the highly vaunted (and rightly so) team care of the future, organizations without this cultural norm will not succeed. (In Chapter 8, we delve further into specific challenges of the next era, including safety, and the importance of environments where every single team member must be able to talk directly to every other team member about anything that affects the work environment or care.)

Dyad leaders must manage the environment, understand relationship dynamics, and empower others. While one partner might take the lead in these type of "soft" skill situations, both must understand their importance. We do not mean to imply that only partners new to formal management would make the error attributed to the physician leader above. There are plenty of current leaders who practice paternalism, in which they "take care of everything" because they believe they know what is best for others, don't believe their team members could handle situations as well as they do, or don't take the time to coach and help team members develop their own skills.

If current healthcare leaders were all outstanding, we probably would not have the dysfunctional workplaces of today. As Marszaleck-Gaucher and Coffey pointed out *in 1990*, "for success in the future (healthcare) executives and managers must become more effective leaders" (2). They talked about the need to transform health-care *25 years ago*. So did V. Clayton Sherman, who said, in 1993, that "the denial of management problems by some in the healthcare industry will no longer stand" (3). Sherman's book was widely acclaimed and read by hospital leaders of that time. They touted his statement that "Passing the test of leadership means staying focused on the destination, not the difficulties and impossibilities of getting there, or the voices saying we shouldn't take the trip."

We are taking the trip right now, although it isn't exactly to the same destination as these leadership authors thought a few decades ago. Transformation is going to happen because of forces outside of the industry (government and private insurance payment reforms). Most know we are no longer an industry of hospitals, but one of healthcare systems. Still, Marszaleck-Gaucher and Coffey's assertion that management is responsible for the success or failure of the organization is true. So is Sherman's belief that we cannot deny our problems. We can't make management and leadership better if we don't look at *how* they can be better.

IMPLEMENTING EVIDENCE-BASED MANAGEMENT

During a healthcare model transition (at a time when we are implementing new leadership models, including Dyads,) is a good time to examine how to put better management and leadership in place. Rather than debate what "better" means, we should look to the growing mountain of management research. We should implement, along with Dyads, what Kovner, Fine, and D'Aquila (among others) call "Evidence-Based Management in Healthcare" (4).

The interesting thing about research is that it is often possible to find one or two that supports any argument we want to make. (Kathy jokes that she only chooses to believe clinical or health research that supports the way she wants to live. So, in her world, research that says salt is bad for you is faulty research. Studies that say salt doesn't have to be limited if you have a normal blood pressure and no health problems, is good research.) Executives can do the same thing with management research. For example, when nursing leaders bring up research that shows a direct link between staffing and patient quality results or mortality, some business leaders find other studies that show no correlation, to counter the nurse's assertion that more staff is needed.

As executives concerned with patient care outcomes, we are pressuring clinicians to decrease variance of care and utilize evidence-based protocols and practices, even if they can locate a random study that does not support the preponderance of evidence. So, although there may be differences of opinion, we believe leaders should pay attention to the broad findings of research that supports the selection of, education of, and practices of a particular type of leader, as we populate Dyads. We reference many throughout this book.

Findings indicate that to transform our organizations, we need transformational leaders. These are people who motivate others to excel, look to higher purposes, cope better with adversity, create vision, shape values, and help others deal with change. They raise the consciousness of others. They help followers understand their mutual interests in meeting organizational goals. They are optimists. They are able to get others to transcend their self-interest for the good of the group, organization, customers, or country. They are usually charismatic and inspirational. They question assumptions and, because of their own propensity to look at old problems in new ways, they encourage and aid others to innovate.

In addition, those who are able to transform organizations are interested in each of their team members as individual people. They recognize differences, serve as coaches and mentors, and help others to reach their individual potentials. They are superb communicators, and good listeners. They empower others, share power, and are able to put the organization's goals ahead of their own *or their profession's needs or desires*. They recognize their own areas for personal growth and development, are lifelong learners, and have high self-esteem, in spite of acknowledging their imperfections to themselves and others. As Bracey, Rosenbaum, and Sanford said in 1990, they demonstrate care by telling the truth with compassion; look for others' loving intentions; disagree with others without making them feel wrong; avoid suspiciousness; and recognize the qualities in each individual regardless of cultural differences (5). While both males and females can be transformational, females, as a group, possess a higher proportion of these traits than men do, which is why largely male leadership teams and organization boards should consider adding more females to their teams.

While emerging research is finding that there is more "nature" to what makes a great leader than previously believed, management and leadership skills can be learned, especially when individuals are willing to change beliefs and practices based on past socialization. Mentoring, coaching, and experience are all helpful to develop transformational leaders, but only when new (or experienced) leaders have the humility to know there are many things they don't know.

Many current leaders, for whatever reason, do not choose to empower others, and do not practice transformational leadership. One thought about why this is true in healthcare is because we have not given managers the education and coaching we are advocating be provided to Dyads. Executive leaders should consider this when evaluating the strengths and weaknesses of their leadership teams. The same techniques used to develop new Dyad leaders would help in the development of individual leaders. In fact, current managers who were originally placed in their positions based on clinical skills, but not given help to develop management abilities, might perceive the resources expended to develop physician leaders as a "fairness and justice" issue.

This is particularly true if they suspect that physicians are being educated to replace them in leadership jobs.

Executives preparing for the next era need strong, educated, committed leaders capable of transformation on their teams. While implementing Dyads or other new models of management, they should evaluate their current leadership team to understand the strengths, weaknesses, and any team gaps. If an honest evaluation of themselves and their organizations reveal a history of preference and promotion of transactional (task oriented) leaders over transformational (relationship oriented) individuals, it is time to balance the team. This can only happen if the executives understand that the value these leaders bring is as great (or even greater today) as that of transactional managers.

If individual growth opportunities are identified, single as well as Dyad leaders should be afforded these. However, as we have mentioned before, some people are simply not capable of learning the leadership or relationship skills needed to lead into the future, as either individual or Dyad leaders. After an assessment of the team, they may need to leave their positions.

LEADERS THAT MIGHT NOT BE A GOOD FIT FOR THE ORGANIZATION

In particular, we see the following types of leaders as more detrimental than value added to healthcare organizations in a time of transformation:

Authoritarian Leaders. These are managers who exercise position power rather than competence to lead as a way to enforce their will on others. They tend to have poor interpersonal relationships (6). They utilize punishment, or negative evaluations to induce performance (7). They do not do well in unstructured situations (which will be a problem in the chaotic days of change). They are often the same people as the power seekers listed next.

Power Seeking Leaders. These are leaders who seek power for its own sake, and not in order to do good for the organization or others. They are often forceful and argumentative, bossy or domineering. They like highly hierarchal organizations. They want high status, and insist on maintaining the trappings of high status, such as higher (or more prestigious) titles than others. According to research by Mowday (8), these leaders obtain emotional satisfaction from wielding power. In fact, they experience aggressive feelings and physiological reactions, such as the release of catecholamines (associated with emotional experiences), when they demonstrate they are more powerful than others.

Leaders with a great need for power prefer ingratiating followers (9). Ingratiating followers are not people who will point out problems in the leader's current organization! (This could be harmful to the company's future because transformation calls for an open culture where problems can be candidly identified and addressed.)

(We need to clarify that we are not against leadership power. All leaders seek and *need* power. The individuals we are describing here seek it solely for their own aggrandizement, and not for how it can be used in the service of others.)

Machiavellians. These are the leaders who believe that deceit and coercion are legitimate tools if used to meet goals. In other words, in their minds, ends always justify the means. Named for Niccolo Machiavelli, author of *The Prince* (10), their leadership style is based on being feared, rather than loved. However, recognizing the need to have others trust them, a Machiavellian individual can, and does, mask her character when she perceives it is important to appear moral, humane and sincere! There is actually a test called the Mach Scale to measure how Machiavellian a leader is (11) but we aren't advocating it be used as part of the leadership team assessment! Over time, Machiavellian personalities and tendencies will become apparent. Given the mission statements, visions, and values espoused by healthcare organizations, it is difficult to believe that any health executive would keep leaders with these propensities on their teams!

Self-Serving Leaders. These are the people in power positions who disregard the rights, values, and feelings of others. They view others are "instruments" to achieve their own goals (12). They tend to be narcissistic, and only want to hear advice that confirms their own opinions. They also tend to hold their subordinates in disdain (13).

Arrogant Leaders. These are the leaders who tend to think they are smarter than everyone else. Because of a self-image of superiority, sometimes honed in a profession that considers itself superior, they overestimate their own ability, and underestimate other people's ability. They often ignore advice from their team members, which leads to errors that could have been prevented (14,15).

Leaders Lacking Essential Traits. People who lack cognitive reasoning abilities, basic ethics, moral reasoning, integrity, or authenticity are not the right leaders for healthcare. Toxic leaders, who are abusive toward others, violate human rights, mislead others with lies, stifle criticism of themselves, cling to power, scapegoat others, or ignore or promote incompetence (16), should be removed from the management team. If education and support does not help those who lack the courage to lead in times of change, or need help with development of emotional intelligence, they, too, should not be kept in leadership roles.

Some leaders looking at this list of who is not appropriate to lead in an era of transformation might be offended that anyone would think that a healthcare executive would have kept leaders with these traits on his team. Or, they might think they are capable of choosing new (including Dyad) leaders without a list that points out who not to choose! Instead of being offended, we hope you will consider the possibility that there could be problem leaders within your organization, either due to innate traits or lack of education and support. Unless you have the good fortune (and the executive talent, because we know you deserve a large part of the credit) to lead in an organization with top employee engagement, physician engagement, quality, safety, and financial scores, there is a *possibility* the leadership team needs attention.

A few months ago, a healthcare consulting firm sent us a newsletter with the provocative lead-in, "There's an 80% chance that your manager isn't great." As managers ourselves, we laughed about it, and joked that we know lots of people who aren't in the "Great 20%" *with us*. It did get us thinking, though, about the need for greatness in our industry, as we move into the next era. It also reminded us that probably 90% of the people who got that letter believe they are among the top two deciles of great managers, too! Yet, multiple articles and books (and even movies that make the situation into comedies) continue to point out that organizations, including healthcare organizations, often suffer from a disconnect between those who do the work and those in positions to manage (or lead) it.

When we add the disconnection between leaders and frontline providers in healthcare to the divisions between physicians and hospitals, payers and providers, various clinical groups, and parts of the care continuum, it would be easy to say we just can't fix this. It's even easier to do what so many do so well: point fingers at everybody else for the problems in our industry. Responsible, mature leaders are not finger pointers. They tend to first look at themselves, and what they can control.

The Arbinger Institute published a book entitled *Leadership and Self-Deception* in 2002. In it, they point out that self-deception "blinds us to the true cause of problems, and once blind, all the solutions we can think of will actually make matters worse. That's why self-deception is so central to leadership—because leadership is about making matters better. To the extent we are self-deceived, our leadership is undermined at every turn" (17). We are cheerleaders for healthcare systems, and those who maintain the courage to lead them. That's why we wrote this book. We think there is some blindness about why and how systems are implementing Dyads and about the cultural and historical issues that will need to be addressed if we are to succeed as true partners in integrated systems. That's also why we think leaders need to look at the development needs of their current teams and choose wisely who will manage and lead in the next era. During this period, while we are forming new business models, or care models, the development of new management teams can and should spur the idea of assessing the entire leadership team. We will all need people with the right skills in the right jobs for the monumental work needed to change what many of us are able to admit is a dysfunctional environment.

CHAPTER SUMMARY

The selection of those who will lead healthcare transformation is vital to thriving in the next era. As systems designate and select Dyad partners, executives can consult management research as a guide to evidence-based leadership practice. In addition, implementation of new management models can facilitate assessment of current leader strengths and skill gaps that should be addressed to strengthen the organization's team.

Dyads in Action

EXPANDING ROLES OF DYAD LEADERSHIP IN HEALTHCARE

Stephen L. Moore

In March 2012, CEO Doug Hawthorne announced the creation of a Dyad leadership structure within Texas Health Resources (THR). The chief operating officer and a chief clinical officer would be responsible to Mr. Hawthorne for the entire clinical operations of the newly designed organization. "This Dyad leadership model has been adopted by other leading healthcare systems and has proven to be an effective structure for aligning operational and clinical sides of large, complex health organizations. So we are transforming our organization from being a hospital-centered system to become a well-connected and coordinated system of health service that strives to help people be healthy and well in addition to expertly treating disease" he said (18).

Texas Health Resources is not alone in adopting a Dyad configuration. Many health systems are migrating to this management model, either at the highest level of the organization or within the management structure of care coordination, service lines, vertical integrated delivery networks, or clinically integrated networks. Physician and clinical leadership roles are exponentially expanding in response to the organization's needs for clinical quality improvement, efficiencies of care, improved patient satisfaction, and enhanced performance across the continuum of care.

Before detailing Dyad management models in the above areas, it is important to characterize the actual qualities and operational responsibilities of Dyad managers. At THR, a physician manager and an operational leader are equal partners. An article in *Physician Executive Journal* of the American College of Physician Executives (ACPE) points out the importance of establishing clear accountabilities, qualities, and overlapping responsibilities in these new positions to bring clarity to the Dyad's roles.

According to the authors, Zismer and Brueggerman, physician and operational Dyad leaders share responsibility for

- the mission
- the vision
- the values
- the stated clinical, patient service and business goals
- the strategic plan and goals
- the performance scorecard or dashboard
- the culture.

The physician co-manager's role is primarily in

▶ quality of the clinical professionals and their work
▶ provider behaviors
▶ provider production
▶ clinical innovation
▶ compliance
▶ patient care standards
▶ clinical pathway and model management
▶ relations with referring physicians and provider "leverage"

The administrative co-manager has the responsibility for

▶ operations
▶ revenue cycle
▶ operations expense management
▶ capital planning
▶ staffing models
▶ performance reporting
▶ supply chain and support services (19)

Dyad management teams with clear and concise roles and shared responsibilities will perform the best across the new continuum of care business models. It is not important to share or divide the same responsibilities outlined above, but it is important to clarify specific expectations of all the distinct and shared roles.

The proliferation of Dyads in healthcare has occurred without a clear understanding of how to account for each role and its overall contribution to the outcomes of an organization. This lack of resolution in roles and responsibilities, within an environment of cultural and experiential diversity, is a recipe for the creation of conflict.

Let's examine a couple of idealized representations of Service Line and Care Management Dyad roles and responsibilities as well as opportunities for conflict these could engender.

NATIONAL SERVICE LINES: A CARDIOVASCULAR EXAMPLE

A national cardiovascular service line (CVSL) within a complex multifacility system is composed of Dyad leadership for the national structure as well as local operational and clinical Dyads at the local facilities. The national objective is to knit disparate and varied groups of local Dyad managers and physicians into a nationally focused, cohesive structure.

Skills necessary at the national leadership level include clinical knowledge, operational knowledge (including an understanding of supply chain, throughput, and Lean techniques), growth and development, and (perhaps most importantly) group and relational dynamics experience. There is a necessity for clear roles and processes, as well as an understanding of the cultural connections of each Dyad partner.

The clinical knowledge necessary to lead a CVSL is enormous, often overwhelming the physician leader's ability to manage competently across all aspects of diagnostic, chronic, interventional, electrical, and surgical cardiovascular care. A high degree of competency and training in interventional cardiology alone does not fully prepare a leader in the clinical realm. That's why the acquired skills of delegation, selection of local physician leaders to fill in competency gaps, and empowerment of other experts to make decisions is necessary to gain success. Relationship building with other physicians is required to create a team collaborative environment for the tackling of difficult tasks. Tasks may include widely variant activities such as pricing on single stent vendors, clinical outcome measurements, performance improvement in below median outcome measures, and the persuasion of one's colleagues to attempt a different care approach for the good of the patients and organization. Different physicians from among the service line leaders may exhibit skill (and interest) in specific areas or responsibilities.

Medical practitioners able to lead teams must be sought and developed through mentorship programs. This often necessitates the replacement of leaders with others who have the prerequisite skills and self-reflection ability necessary to manage with excellence. Leaders must understand their blind spots, including natural tendencies to over control and not delegate or share decision making.

Operational responsibilities within a service line may come in direct conflict with clinical imperatives. Examples of where operational and clinical objectives may collide include length of stay management initiatives, nurse staffing ratios, growth strategies, and supply or pharmaceutical utilization evaluation and improvements. Shared Dyad goals and vision for the Service Line provide a foundation upon which these natural conflicts may be adjudicated.

For example, a physician leader may insist there is a clinical need for utilizing a certain drug regimen for the benefit of patients. Her operational partner, looking at the variation in the usage of such a medication (in addition to the multimillion dollar spending on the drug), sees usage and cost as being the driving determinant of whether it should be allowed as part of the service line formulary. Both perspectives need to be considered by the leaders, who decide *together* on the inclusion or exclusion of this regimen. The physician brings clinical evidence to the discussion, while the operations partner provides a comprehensive business analysis approach.

Within the CHI Cardiovascular Service Line (CVSL), such a conflict arose over the use of the drug bivalirudin, used with an interventional stent procedure to prevent blockage of the stent. Bivalirudin reduces incidents of severe hemorrhage when compared to other (less safe) drugs. Even though Bivalirudin use is supported by the literature, national data revealed there was a sixfold difference in the usage of this drug across 12 cardiac programs within the organization.

A local physician leader was designated by the national physician leader to do a literature search and come up with the best recommendation for the drug's use. As a result, a three-tier approach to the drug was developed for the service line. It stratified low-, medium-, and high-risk patients with clear and concise recommendations for the use of the drug in each category, optimally steering the CVSL to a 50% or $4 million reduction in utilization. Management of variation and cost resided in the operational partner while the clinical solution lay within the expertise of local and national physician leadership. Building upon principles of mutual clinical respect, encouraged by frequent face-to-face meetings and relationships, "simple" operational variations were solved by the clinical representatives.

A cautionary note must be raised even with the success demonstrated above. In the creation of Dyad partnerships, and the incorporation of physicians into a greater clinical responsibility, there are tendencies to create an expectation that service lines be "physician led." This would literally imply the replacement of operational leaders with physicians. Physicians in most markets are woefully unprepared for this, not for a lack of clinical expertise, but because of a paucity of managerial skills as well as organizational perspectives important to balance the management model. Put rather simply, it is rare to find a "Renaissance" physician who has both the clinical and management experience to become an effective sole leader. This "physician-led" mantra may unfortunately lead physicians to an unrealistic conclusion that they already possess ability to fully lead alone. While "Renaissance" physician leaders are becoming more common, the number of positions requiring physician expertise as we prepare for the future outnumber these leaders. For the foreseeable future, an operational manager should round out the Dyad.

In response to gaps in physician capabilities, many clinical leaders including doctors, nurses, and pharmacists obtain higher management degrees such as MBA, MHA, or their equivalents. While helpful in navigating the operational and financial milieu of the complicated healthcare environment, these degrees do not automatically elevate clinicians to a level of operational competency to lead. (This is equally true for the newly graduated MBA entering healthcare for his first year of work.)

CARE MANAGEMENT DYAD PARTNERS

As the complexity of inpatient, outpatient, home, ambulatory, and skilled nursing environments becomes interwoven into the structures for managing population health, Dyad partnerships are surfacing in the areas of care management. Numerous professions are embarking into Dyad leadership relationships. They include the following:

▶ Physicians and nurses (home health and skilled nursing home management)
▶ Social workers and care managers in acute and postacute patient management settings
▶ Physicians and social workers in at-risk population management organizations
▶ Traditional inpatient and home/outpatient health coaches

Each of these professions brings an expertise and cultural competence to the Dyad partnership.

One of the emerging models is shared leadership between social workers and physicians. Many of these Dyads have been created because of the necessity to oversee the care of complex patient populations in either dual eligible or high-risk Medicare populations who require social work intervention. These populations certainly have complex medical problems, but their needs for solutions to access, compliance, and mental health require social work expertise. The social work role of coordinating community services, food and transportation, along with comorbid mental health treatment may play an even more influential role in establishing a stable medical scenario for individuals than the services of health coaches traditionally located within a medical home.

These Dyad relationships have yielded better patient care plans through personal interventions created by nonphysician professionals. In some of the more successful models (CareMore Medicare Advantage Plans, for example), physician medical models supplement a core of social and other needs met by a cadre of nonphysicians.

HOSPITAL LEADERSHIP MODELS

A physician as a chief executive officer in a hospital is no longer a rare occurrence. Physicians as chief medical officers paired in a Dyad model with either an operations or nursing leader is an emerging a predominant model. Physicians as chief medical officers paired in a Dyad model with either an operations or nursing leader is an emerging model. To declare this, a mature model, however, is a bit presumptuous. Historical and cultural influences make this pairing among the most challenging, for reasons well detailed in other chapters.

Dyad partnerships in healthcare within service lines, continuum of care models, full-risk care delivery models, and clinically integrated models are quietly joining other leadership models. Careful attention to the outcomes necessary for success, clear delineation of roles and accountability, and comprehensive understanding of the strengths of each Dyad partner's background and experience will make these new Dyad partnerships flourish well into the future.

DYAD CLINICAL LEADERSHIP IN THE AMBULATORY WORLD: MANAGING THE PHYSICIAN ENTERPRISE TOGETHER

James Slaggert and Richard Oken

In early 1999, Dr. Richard Oken was appointed as president and board chairperson for a large independent practice association (IPA) comprised of 600 physicians, > 90,000 covered lives in commercial and Medicare Advantage business lines in a capitated business model in Northern California. Later that year, Mr. James Slaggert was hired as the chief executive officer of the Company. This is the first person story of how these two, who had never previously met or worked together, formed a highly effective Dyad management team—the strength of which can be measured by their business success in this 12-year relationship.

THE EARLY DAYS: IN OUR OWN WORDS

When we began this journey, the IPA was facing several large problems including financial challenges, business defection by physicians, reimbursement pressures from health plans, and widespread physician dissatisfaction, primarily due to payment inequities among physicians. The company had a balance sheet showing negative $10M equity with impaired cash flow. Payor contracts required immediate renegotiation and member physician trust in leadership needed to be restored.

At the outset, we agreed to admit the serious nature of our economic condition, meet with our creditors and terminate inequitable contracts that were in place from the previous business model. We also released all consultants so that our Dyad would personally direct the company. We planned to build a reliable information system via partnership and explain to our physician shareholders the options of business as usual versus total restructuring of the company.

Fortunately, the physician board of directors and other key physician leaders of the IPA were fully supportive of embarking upon a turnaround to restore the company to financial stability. Without this underpinning of broader support, turnaround efforts would have failed.

ASSEMBLING THE TEAM

An executive leadership Dyad will not be successful without a talented management team and we were no exception. Key members of our team were the director of contracting, who could renegotiate payer contracts (subsequently this person was promoted to chief operating officer), the medical director who would promote quality of care linked to effective use of resources, and a director of Medicare services to coordinate all aspects of this critical line of business. With a small team, it was important to have trust and collaboration, values supported by both of us as Dyad leaders. We were fortunate to have a cohesive management team who stayed together loyally for several years.

In addition to the management team reporting to Mr. Slaggert, an executive committee of board officers was reestablished by Dr. Oken. This committee met monthly under delegated authority from the board of directors. Meetings were chaired by Dr. Oken and attended by the management team to promote collaboration between the governing board and management.

Key physicians were selected to chair subcommittees of Finance, Credentialing, Quality & Utilization Management, and Medicare Services that reported to the board. Dr. Oken, Mr. Slaggert, or a senior management executive was placed on each committee.

This ability to have governance and management on the same page strategically, while keeping a clear distinction of roles to avoid micromanagement of day-to-day operations by the board, was another critical support system to allow our Dyad to be successful.

VALUES, STYLES, AND PERSONALITIES

If we could point to two items that fueled our Dyad, it would be shared values and complementary personal styles. The values of honesty, integrity, open and forthright communication, and transparency served us well.

We communicated often with our physician members as well as hospital and health system strategic partners. Physician communication vehicles included frequent, written correspondence distributed across the physician membership, quarterly "Town Hall" meetings, quarterly primary care physician meetings, and regularly scheduled meetings with strategic partners. As a tightly connected Dyad leadership team, most written communications to our physicians were coauthored. We focused on one-page documents to be concise and gain maximum attention. We were also cognizant of the need to be honest and "tell it like it is," sharing both good news and bad. This open and transparent communication helped build trust and credibility with our board and member physicians, which was essential in resolving conflict.

We found that one-page communication vehicles were the most effective to correspond with our physicians, so we implemented this executive summary format widely. We also utilized face-to-face meetings with key constituents at their request or as needs emerged. These small group meetings, typically attended by both of us, were a key step in establishing trust between administration and our physicians.

Dr. Oken insisted that our performance was evaluated annually by the Board of Directors. Each year it was pointed out that a strength of our leadership Dyad was our complementary styles and personalities. Dr. Oken, a bit brash and fiery, was a very good match for Mr. Slaggert's more reserved and introverted style. These differences allowed us to function very well as a team when different situations benefitted from one, or a combination, of these styles. As we grew to know each other well (over 12 years of working together), we were able to recognize and use our contrasting styles to move our organization forward.

TRUST IN EACH OTHER

In short order, we developed a high level of trust and respect for each other. This was a critical element of successfully working together through a time of organizational uncertainty and turbulence. It was the basis for our ability to be on the same page strategically. It also allowed us to present a cohesive, unified position to both internal and external stakeholders and partners. Not that we were perfect (see "STUMBLES" in a few paragraphs), but we did focus on communicating clearly and often with each other. We wanted to ensure we were consistent in how we worked collaboratively with our Board of Directors, and how we viewed and implemented strategy, physician relationships, and operational direction.

As our mutual trust increased, and the Company's financial results improved, we shared the efforts and resulting progress through open and frank discussions with the Board on a monthly basis. Similarly, we presented financial and organizational results to our IPA member physicians on a quarterly basis. These forums, where we presented information as a team, helped continue to foster an environment of open communication. This helped tremendously in times of conflict.

Over time we learned each other's strengths and weaknesses. We were fortunate, especially not having worked together previously, to have balanced strengths and weaknesses that we were aware of, shared openly with each other and used to the benefit of our Dyad team leadership of the organization. For example, while Mr. Slaggert was building relationships with physicians in a new community, Dr. Oken was an established, credible physician with 30 years in the community. When Dr. Oken could be emotional, Mr. Slaggert could be calm and measured.

Even with these differences, we were both clearly focused on the success of the organization. This was evident to our physician partners as we worked together to dig out of our financial hole and stabilize the company for the benefit of our physicians and the patients we served.

FOSTERING DIVERSITY

Six years into our journey we were working well with our Board. With their direction, we began to actively recruit diverse physicians into positions of leadership for the IPA. Potential new physician leaders were identified by the then-current Board members based on exhibited leadership skills and potential age, gender, and ethnic diversity as well as business relationship strengths with the IPA.

Once potential physician leaders were ascertained, we each went out to meet individually with them in order to gauge their interest level in working with the IPA in a leadership capacity (either on the governing board or as a committee member). Due to the credibility we had earned with our member physicians and our reputation for being like-minded and presenting a consistent view for the direction of the company linked to strong support of the board of directors, we were able to individually communicate a consistent message that was viewed and heard by our physicians. They viewed us as two leaders in a partnership, speaking as one voice in support of the organization. This allowed us to efficiently and effectively gather feedback for our governing board, which used this information to add new energy and diversity to our physician leadership team.

Although we were not successful with all of our recommendations for new leaders, the end result was a board steeped in diversity in every regard: age, gender, race, ethnicity, and practice specialty.

STUMBLES

As in any relationship, we did make mistakes. The challenge with a Dyad is to jointly admit responsibility, not blame each other or hold grudges, but to appropriately fix the problem together and move on.

One striking example of a mistake we made was inconsistent messaging to our board of directors on a critical hiring recommendation of a medical director. We had two excellent final candidates, one internal and one external. The internal candidate was one of our highly regarded local physicians who had gradually moved from clinical practice to administrative roles. He was very well respected by our board and other leaders but lacked hands-on IPA medical director experience. The external candidate was an MD/MBA with a high level of progressive medical director experience, but unknown to our physician community beyond the interview process.

At the Board meeting where we were to make a final hiring recommendation, we were reminded that great communication must never be ignored or assumed. Unfortunately, we each assumed that we were in agreement on which candidate to jointly recommend to the board. This resulted in a split recommendation from the Dyad team on which candidate to hire. The board was confused, to put it mildly, as this was the first time we had not made a unified recommendation to them. We were asked to come back quickly with a joint hiring recommendation.

As we dissected this experience to learn, we realized that our mistake was simple and straightforward as well as fully avoidable. A critical communication step was missed, as we never confirmed our hiring choices with each other in advance of our board meeting. Rather, we each incorrectly assumed we were in agreement with the other.

This was a painful but valuable experience midway through our 12-year tenure. It caused us to redouble our communications with each other especially on recommendations to the board and committees. Lack of unified direction from Dyad partners is a sign of a dysfunctional team and we were not dysfunctional.

CONFLICT RESOLUTION AS A TEAM

As can be imagined, especially when faced with a $10M balance sheet deficit, our main conflicts with physicians in the IPA centered around finances and physician reimbursement. This was exacerbated by an inadequate financial support infrastructure, which led to conflicting data for negotiations between the IPA and member physicians. Added to this were real and perceived payment inequities among our physicians. This was a recipe for contentious and passionate negotiations.

As we approached physician compensation negotiations where we knew conflict was unavoidable, we took several steps as a leadership team. First, we presented our negotiation strategy and parameters to the board for their support. We also kept them fully apprised as negotiations proceeded. Then, as a Dyad team, we spoke with one voice of common purpose in negotiating sessions and jointly attended all critical meetings. This allowed us to work toward building relationships of trust, which we wanted to maintain when negotiations were concluded.

Of the several difficult negotiations with our member physicians, two were particularly contentious and required the use of an independent mediator. We are highlighting these here, as Case 1 and Case 2. Both of these negotiations were with single-specialty physician groups who were sole source providers of their clinical specialty in the community. In addition to working in partnership as a Dyad through the negotiations/mediation, we included individual board members on our team to promote balanced discussions and problem solving.

CASE 1

When our finance staff performed a comparative analysis of specialty physician compensation, one specialty was revealed to be paid higher than their peer group. This caused internal payment inequities in the IPA as well as dissatisfaction among the peer group due to lack of reimbursement parity. With the support of the board, we proposed to lower the compensation for these physicians to reach internal equity and fairness. As expected, the higher paid physicians were less than pleased and viewed this as a hostile action from the IPA board and leadership. Their initial reaction was to send their 90-day notice of contract termination to the IPA.

After a series of nonproductive and highly charged negotiation sessions, no common ground was established. A mediator was brought into assist, but still no solution was to be found. Ultimately, the physicians stopped treating our patients with 36-hour notice. This immediately escalated the situation from a contract negotiation to a patient care issue and caused the hospital's medical staff leadership body and ultimately, their governing board to become involved. We finally reached agreement on contractual terms, and patient care was restored without incident. The Dyad lesson we learned was that by working in tandem, both with our board and during negotiations and mediation, we were able to land at a reasonable conclusion and kept this valued group of clinicians in the IPA. Additionally, both we, as the Dyad leaders, and the board of directors gained additional trust and respect with the broader physician membership of the IPA for addressing this significant and divisive situation.

CASE 2

In a second situation, we also had tense negotiations with a sole-source, single-specialty physician group that proceeded to mediation. In this case, we experienced a much different and positive process and outcome.

This group of physicians was being paid less, on a relative basis, than their peer group. There was agreement between the Board and management to raise their compensation. The complicating factor was an assertion by the physicians that they had been systematically underpaid by the IPA for several years and therefore, demanded restitution. This negotiation occurred approximately 1 year into our Dyad partnership. Given the previously mentioned balance sheet deficit and cash flow issues, we were unable to provide the requested additional payment. As we proceeded through negotiations and mediation, hostilities lessened, cooperation improved, and a mutually acceptable solution was reached. As a bonus to concluding negotiations amicably and developing mutual trust among all involved, several of the formerly disaffected physicians assumed IPA committee leadership positions and one was elected to the board of directors.

This is one of our best practical demonstrations of working as a Dyad, so that $1 + 1 > 2$.

SUMMARY AND LESSONS LEARNED

During over 12 years of partnership, we lead a team effort to restore the IPA to financial strength and established trust as well as a cohesive culture among our physicians. The final chapter for us was when we successfully negotiated an affiliation with a larger IPA in the region. The Company had improved finances to reflect a multimillion dollar balance sheet surplus at the time of the affiliation, allowing a substantial distribution back to physician shareholders at the conclusion of the new partnership.

We want to share our major Dyad lessons learned. These include the following:

▶ *Trust in each other.* If there is disagreement on an issue, sort it out in private and provide a consistent and unified position to all stakeholders.
▶ *Establish and promote an environment of honesty, integrity, and transparency and be willing to accept constructive criticism.*
▶ *Communicate often and clearly with all stakeholders.* This is particularly important in times of change and potential conflict.
▶ *Expand the team.* A Dyad can be an essential leadership structure but management talent and governance support are critical.
▶ *1 + 1 = more than 2.* Bringing together our complementary styles, coupled with a physician/nonphysician partnership was very credible and powerful.

We would be remiss to overlook one intangible—friendship. Over the 12 years of respectfully working toward a common purpose and unified vision, a strong friendship emerged. This helped us to communicate openly, laugh frequently, and have work/life balance. Our friendship continues to this day.

THE QUALITY AND SAFETY LEADER AS NATURAL DYADS
Jeanie Mamula and Randy Wick

Successful Dyad relationships have to be closely aligned with an organization's core values and the attributes associated with each value. Often in the workplace, we are asked if, or we state, "I like this person." Sure, there are occasions when we work on projects and develop friendships with those team members who might have similar interests or hobbies. Although, we believe when we are asked whether we "like" a coworker or Dyad partner, the question is really "do we respect and trust him, is she sensitive to others, does he put forth his best effort, and does she do what she says she will do?" A successful Dyad relationship is predicated on these values and attributes.

In many organizations, quality and risk functions are operated in separate silos. Regardless of reporting relationships, we believe that quality and risk management working together will reduce the health risks of our employees and improve patient safety. We have experienced individual safety improvement projects that are conducted separately. These sometimes fail to address issues that are common to both disciplines, which squanders efforts and may not address all the risks. In our Dyad, as leaders from two different functional divisions at a national system level, we have come to focus and collaborate on developing a system wide culture of safety without regard to individual or favorite programs. These essential elements of the Dyad partnership include a commitment to safety, visibility, transparency, and continuous improvement. We know that is doesn't matter where or who we report to. It matters that we work hand in hand as a partnership sharing goals.

There is always work to do and that will never stop! We believe in monitoring and measuring outcomes of everything we do so that we can show progress toward meeting current goals and set new goals that will take us into a safer, higher quality next era of healthcare.

In September of 2009, First Initiatives' Insurance, Ltd. (FIIL) Board (a company owned by CHI) approved an update in the company's strategic plan to include a "Quality and Safety" strategy. The strategy included the following objectives:

▶ *To develop risk metrics:* Assist in the evaluation of clinical performance throughout the system through the development of risk metrics with CHI's operational groups.
▶ *To provide safety education:* Develop education modules for employees about patient, occupational and environmental safety.

▶ *To ensure data integration:* Strengthen relationships with the system's clinical services, business intelligence and Finance groups through integration of existing data sources.

▶ *To spread clinical best practices:* In collaboration with clinical services group, identify and disseminate evidence-based practices, as determined by our loss experience and clinical outcomes.

As a result of this strategic direction, the Risk and Insurance Management Group changed its focus from a claims- and insurance-driven company to a loss prevention and safety-focused organization. We were to establish a risk management operations team that would focus on (outcome based vs. process based) results, more collaboration with other CHI Groups, and a formal partnership with Clinical Services Group on one of CHI's Clinical Excellence Objectives known as "SafetyFirst."

Clinical Services and the Risk and Insurance Management Groups had worked together on a previously successful patient safety initiative entitled "CHI Perinatal Care Collaborative-Because One Is to Many." This was after the 2005, IHI release of the "Idealized Design of Perinatal Care" White Paper, which included characteristics of high reliability perinatal units. Our system's collaborative goal was structured as one of CHI's quality and patient safety strategic priorities. The intent was to eliminate preventable birth injuries by December of 2008 through empowerment of perinatal staff as we moved toward behaviors and processes designed to create a safe environment. The key theme was to create the safest environment possible by reducing avoidable complications.

The collaborative was sponsored by the Clinical Services Group and Risk and Insurance Management Group. It functioned through national web conferences, other formal communications, and resource sharing. These mechanisms offered several advantages to the hospitals throughout CHI, such as leveraging and spreading implementation of the work, access to peer expertise, creating accountability and commitment, and establishing a formal network and shared vision for reaching the objective.

We experienced success with the perinatal work as a result of the clinical division and the risk operation working hand-in-hand as Dyads. Both departments have credibility when it comes to information and resources around quality, loss prevention, and safety. CHI reduced the occurrence of birth injuries from a baseline of 4.85 per 1000 live births in FY05 to 2.06 per 1000 live births in FY08. Other groups became involved with the work, including knowledge transfer, nursing, and national clinical competency. The combined efforts created a successful team collaboration. We learned from this project that individuals from Clinical and Risk were good team leaders when they worked in a partnership that could reach many stakeholders within CHI to accomplish safety-related objectives.

As a result, when we embarked on our SafetyFirst program (CHI's Culture of Safety initiatives and movement to a high reliability organization [HRO]), we decided to formalize this model with a designated Dyad to lead the work. (One leader came from the Quality function of CHI's Clinical Services group. The other is a risk leader from the Risk and Insurance Management Group.)

SafetyFirst is a multiyear, system-wide implementation of highly reliable and safe practices that are monitored and measured by metrics focused on reducing serious harm to patients and reducing work-related injuries to our employees. Group Sponsors of this work are executives from clinical, legal, and risk management. The business partners designated to make up the leadership team responsible for planning and implementing change are the formal Dyad. The partners are Jeanie Mamula, VP, Quality Improvement, and Randy Wick, VP, Risk Management Operations.

How We *Were* Separate (Silos) and Then We *Weren't* (Dyad)

Jeanie: We had known each other for several years but weren't close, as our jobs did not totally interact and we met only occasionally at operations team meetings. We really began our partnership in 2009 when both of us were promoted from director to VP positions. Our jobs changed. We discovered that in some ways, they overlapped and we felt that we could help each other a great deal by working together. Some people think that risk and quality are separate functions. We believe that the two are synergistic and really are functioning ineffectively when not working together.

Randy: At the very beginning of the SafetyFirst program, we both recognized that neither of us had been involved in a body of work so large and significant for the organization. We were proposing a business plan that stated we were going to further develop and maintain a "culture of Safety" within CHI that would change perspectives and behaviors of all leaders and staff. That's pretty momentous stuff.

It quickly became apparent we had very similar beliefs and attitudes about the operational aspects of CHI. We had both been long-time employees working in different geographic locations and disciplines. I knew that Jeanie knew certain aspects of the company that I did not, and she felt the same about my knowledge. Because each of us was willing to share and be open and honest with the other, we were able to quickly agree on how we should approach things in order to get them done in the most efficient and effective manner.

As with many colleagues, Jeanie and I share common strengths in our respective areas of expertise, experience and skill sets. We recognized that one of us had certain skill sets and knowledge the other didn't, and vice versa. In order to be successful with the work, we acknowledged this and agreed to take turns the leading aspects of the work when individual skills would increase the chances of success. We also agreed to give unwavering support to each other. Our strengths are as different as our personalities, levels of patience, ability to use computers and software, organization and planning abilities, and technical or clinical expertise. As a result, we developed a style I think of as "pick up your partner/Dyad when you can." We also consider who has the time and resources and is best equipped to handle an issue or question. From the beginning, Jeanie and I have complemented each other and shared the work equally. That makes a great recipe for a successful Dyad relationship.

Historically, there has been shifting of focus and attention for the medical/legal, risk, quality, and regulatory arenas. This shift of priorities between one area and another has contributed to the creation of silos, whereby one discipline may be viewed as more important at any given time. In other words, people sometimes believe that, "my work is important than yours."

For example, the medical liability insurance crisis in the 1980s focused on needed tort reform, claims, and litigation in healthcare. This increased the perceived importance of risk functions. Rather than assigning status, we believe we have a common bond regardless of which area is getting the most attention at any one time. Our goal is to provide the best possible care to all of our patients without causing them harm. When we do this by working together, it will ultimately benefit everyone. As we say in risk management and legal, "the best loss prevention is high quality care." This mantra has enabled and facilitated the Dyad relationship between risk and quality.

Why We Knew We Had to Be Partners

Randy: To be successful in our SafetyFirst work, and to demonstrate shared objectives to all clinicians and staff working in clinical settings, we have a written goal that is everyone's number one priority:

> "Safety has to be the top priority at all levels of the organization. It has to be recognized as *doing the right thing* that is also good for our business. The message has to be delivered as one by various disciplines and groups, not just quality and safety. The more employees who 'get' this message, the better our opportunity for making positive changes in how we do things."

Jeanie: While we are very comfortable working together in our Dyad partnership, we recognize that much of what we do involves many other stakeholders and potential partners. In fact, the more we work together, the more we branch out to work with other groups. We currently work closely with no less than six groups on most of our projects. These include teams from evidence-based practice, physician enterprise, strategy, performance excellence, legal, communications/marketing, and leadership development departments. Depending on the project, we may work more closely with some groups, but all of those listed have some stake in our work. No matter who we're working with, we are the ones who are joined at the hip, and are the most knowledgeable about the entire scope of work, because we are the Dyad leaders for SafetyFirst.

Projects We Do Together

Jeanie: Initially, our biggest project together was the quality and risk conference that we hold annually. This was our first attempt to bring teams together. We had to come up with topics that were of interest and pertinent to both functions. For the first conference, we planned some breakout sessions and one half day session that was independent of each other's group. As we have continued to hold this annual meeting, we have improved at integrating the work that we do into mutual presentations. As a result, at our latest conference, all the breakout sessions were topically, not functionally, separated. That is, the self-selected attendees for each included both risk and quality team members.

As we have gotten to know one another better, we have discovered ways to leverage our complementary skills. We are able to leverage these in many areas. Randy sometimes calls me to discuss particular leadership issues he is wrestling with. Likewise, I frequently experience organizational issues (organization is not my strength) and I call on him for help to make sure that we are timely, concise, and consistent. Actually, one of the things that my team has struggled with the most is the rigor that Randy puts to all of his preparations for *everything*. It's all good, but it's just not my nature to be that strict on details. So, a change had to happen in my life, and in my team's, in order not to frustrate the folks on the risk side who were much more structured and prepared in everything they did.

To date, the biggest project we've done together is the high-reliability initiative, focused on patient and staff safety. The initiative takes the best of both the risk and quality worlds and uses knowledge and techniques from other industries to help us move to a standardized, safety-focused culture with the aim of zero preventable adverse events (or serious safety events). As this is a multimillion dollar initiative (as well as a strategic initiative for CHI), we started our work by building a business plan. This was a new experience for both of us. We really had to work closely to create a budget, using the best information we had from an outside vendor on how to put the initiative together. We had to do some guesswork on the amount of time it would take at each facility, the number of staff required to do the work, and the amount of money needed at each facility for staff education. We had already begun with pilot implementations at two facilities and thought we had a good handle on how to proceed. We did fairly well in the first year, but as we continued to implement our program throughout the organization, we realized that the scope was larger than we had imagined. We agreed that neither one of us was equipped to manage the initiative without coordinating assistance. With strong support from our sponsors, we requested a project manager from our internal project management office. Looking back, this experience brought us closer together, and we rapidly identified which of us had the expertise for various parts of the project. We continue to do much of our work together, but we hand certain things to the partner who can do the job quickest and best.

Randy: These are a few of the things we've been working on. They wouldn't be nearly as effective if we had not come together to lead as a Dyad:

▶ *Monday Quality and Safety Calls:* For many years, each of our respective groups held independent educational and training conference calls or webinars with our respective groups. Occasionally, there would be sharing of information or invitations to attend each other's call, although that was not the norm. As Dyad partners, we recognized the need to consolidate this work. This is more efficient and provides a forum for staff to learn about a variety of subjects. (Some of these are from their own disciplines, and some are from others.) By providing advance notice of the topic, staff can make informed decisions on their participation. Risk and Quality share the responsibility to provide topics each week. This is an example of coordinating our work and sending out the message that we need to learn, share, and grow together.

▶ *Quality and Risk Annual Conferences:* As Jeanie mentioned, these have brought us together to learn.

▶ *Clinical Risk management Incentive Plan:* This is the voluntary program for our markets where they can earn rebates on their insurance assessments if they implement or accomplish key safety initiatives. The Risk and Clinical Groups identify and support the connections between evidence-based practices, process improvement initiatives, as well as patient and employee safety to support CHI's quality and safety priorities. We avoid duplication and create synergy by doing this together.

▶ *SafetyFirst:* Jeanie is now involved with safe patient handling and movement, evidence-based practices, and development of CHI's Injury and illness prevention program. Her clinical expertise and operational experience is valuable and results in a better work product. Likewise, I participate in the development and review of evidence-based practices. I've been able to provide key data and metrics on falls and surgical adverse events.

How We Communicate

Jeanie: We think that deliberate communication about *everything* is probably the major key to developing a good Dyad partnership. We work independently and are geographically distant, so we depend on constant communication. No matter how well you get along, without that communication, misunderstandings of intent and content (even of e-mails) is a threat to good relationships. Probably the most valuable thing we did was to set up biweekly calls so that we could begin to feel comfortable with each other's thought processes and also kept each other up to date. (Did we mention we are physically located in different parts of the country?)

Even though we have standing phone meetings set up for every other week, we talk much more frequently. However, maintaining these standing appointments on the calendar ensures that even in our busiest times, we have scheduled time to get together for discussions about our respective worlds. Between those scheduled meetings and other calls, we are in constant e-mail contact. We spend a portion of our time getting to understand the perspectives of each other's discipline. While we're both focused on quality and safety, the perspective from the risk side is predominantly on error detection and prevention, while the clinical quality side is all about making improvements. I have learned a lot about the insurance and claims business, and how the learnings from the claims are used to try and prevent future events. Randy has learned how to utilize tools to not only find, but to fix, problems as we move forward.

Randy: I agree our relationship and communication are a combination of structure and free flow. Jeanie and I are aware of each other's responsibilities, and therefore respectful of each other's time and workload. We both make a special effort to return messages promptly or let the other know if we will be delayed in getting back to one another. The risks of not working together are the opposite of many of the items discussed previously. Today's healthcare environment is simply too complicated to "go it alone." Together, we've been able to improve safety and quality, including an overall reduction in the number of serious adverse events from FY10, as well as a reduction in major falls from FY12 to FY13.

How We Set Goals Together

Jeanie: We set our goals by challenging each other to push just a little bit further than what we thought might be possible. In particular, if a goal is more in one partner's purview, the other will challenge him or her to be sure we are setting a stretch (but achievable) goal. We consistently check in to be sure our personal goals are in alignment. We found that a good number of our discipline's definitions are not in sync, and we had to do a lot of collaborating to come up with definitions that were understandable and acceptable by both. An example of this was when we set our goal for patient fall prevention. We had separate ideas about what a near-fall is. We had to agree on how to describe levels of severity of injuries and how to work with our facilities to be sure they were collecting and reporting the data the same way. At the same time, we discovered that it wasn't just us who had a stake in this issue! (We discovered that many states also collect data using their own definitions, while entities like the ANA (American Nurses Association) have still another set. Without our willingness to collaborate and come to an agreement, we would have collected data that were not usable for our common goals.

Randy: A Dyad relationship creates increased accountability due to many factors. That's because we each want to hold up our end of the bargain. We want to make a difference. We want to do the best job possible. We don't want to disappoint our partner. As Dale Carnegie advises, "Give the other person a fine reputation to live up to." A productive Dyad relationship provides a perfect opportunity to do just that.

How We Ensure Other Members of the Team Understand the Importance and Functioning of the Dyad

Randy: I believe all of our respective team members understand the importance of working together in a Dyad relationship for the reasons we've mentioned. However, simply assigning a member of one team to work with another on a project does not guarantee success. Successful partnering starts with a shared vision and set of values for the work, on both team member's parts. As leaders and Dyad partners, we have made a special effort to bring team members together where feasible. We work to help them understand the importance of working together. However, there are many variables, and we have learned the need to pay attention to developing teamwork. It won't "just happen" for everyone.

The Dyad may also have some limitations. I invited Jeanie and her staff members to attend our risk management operations team meetings. I thought this would be another way to demonstrate our Dyad and the advantages of working together. While my staff members recognize the need for collaboration, they felt that our staff meetings should just involve our team. The combined group became a huge dissatisfaction for them. One of the team members brought this to my attention. I talked with Jeanie and she agreed to maintain separate functional meetings limited to our own staffs. The takeaway for me is that while there are certainly no secrets discussed in these meetings, there is still a need for specialty teams to work on their own issues in their own group meetings. We can still pull in other stakeholders (or your Dyad partners) before taking any organizational actions, but sometimes a smaller team just needs to meet with itself!

Jeanie: One of the things that we discovered about our Dyad partnership is that the partnership success did not automatically extend to all individuals on our teams. While we brought people together and asked them to work together, this didn't always go as smoothly as what we projected. We found that we were becoming the interceptors for problems. At first we allowed the problems to become ours to resolve. So, of course, team members would come to us with complaints about other team members and we would try to solve the problems. It took us a while, but we finally realized this was not our job and this was not helping our team. We had to come to an agreement between the two of us that we would no longer act when someone brought us an issue, but direct them back to the people with whom they were having problems (with some coaching on how to handle the issue.) We think this helped create a better atmosphere and collaboration within the team, although it hasn't completely healed all interpersonal relationship problems.

Fundamentally, it was the CHI core values we both hold dear to our hearts that helped us to become really good partners. We always had respect for each another, but after working together as a Dyad leadership team, this has become more than respect. It has evolved into reverence for the person that each of us is strengthened by a deep understanding of how we can carry out our values together. We think each of us demonstrates the organization's values in different ways, but we appreciate and understand this. That's what makes this type of leadership special and valuable to us, our team, and our organization.

REFERENCES

1. Ryan, K., & Oestreich, D. (1991). *Driving fear out of the workplace: How to overcome the invisible barriers to quality, productivity, and innovation.* San Francisco, CA: Jossey-Bass.
2. Marszaleck-Gaucher, E., & Coffey, R. (1990). *Transforming healthcare organizations.* San Francisco, CA: Jossey-Bass.
3. Sherman, V. (1993). *Creating the New American Hospital.* San Francisco, CA: Jossey-Bass.
4. Kovner, A., Fine, D., & D'Aquila, R. (2009). *Evidence-based management in healthcare.* Chicago, IL: Health Administration Press.
5. Bracy, H., Rosenblum, J., Sanford, A., & Trueblood, R. (1990). *Managing from the heart.* New York, NY: Delacorte Press.
6. Kalma, A. P., Visser, L., & Peters, A. (1993). Sociable and aggressive dominance: Personality differences in leadership style? *Leadership Quarterly, 4,* 56–64.
7. Smith, W. P. (1967a). Power structure and authoritarianism in the use of power in the triad. *Journal of Personality, 35,* 65–89.
8. Mowday, R. T. (1978). The exercise of upward influence in organizations. *Administrative Science Quarterly, 23,* 137–156.
9. Fodor, E. M., & Farrow, D. L. (1979). The power motive as an influence on the use of power in an industrial simulation. *Journal of Personality and Social Psychology, 37,* 2091–2097.
10. Machiavelli, N. (1513/1952/1961). *The prince.* (Rev. trans. E. R. P. Vincent). New York, NY: Mentor Press.
11. Christie, R., & Geis, F. (1970). *Studies in machiavellianism.* New York, NY: Academic Press.
12. O'Conner, J., Mumford, M. D., Clifton, T. C., et al. (1995). Charismatic leaders and destructiveness: An historiometric study. *The Leadership Quarterly, 6*(4), 529–555.
13. Hogan, J., & Hogan, R. (2002). Leadership and sociopolitical intelligence. In R. E. Riggio, S. E. Murphy, & F. J. Pirozzolo (Eds.), *Multiple intelligences and leadership.* Mahwah, NJ: Lawrence Erlbaum Associates.
14. Kroll, M. J., Toombs, L. A., & Wright, P. (2000). Napoleon's tragic march home from Moscow: Lessons in hubris. *Academy of Management Executive, 14*(1), 117–128.
15. Bass, B. (2008). *The bass handbook of leadership, theory, research & managerial applications.* New York, NY: Free Press.
16. Lipman-Blumen, J. (2005). *The connective edge: Leading in an interdependent world.* San Francisco, CA: Jossey-Bass.
17. The Arbinger Institute. (2002). *Leadership and self-deception.* San Francisco, CA: Berrett-Koehler.
18. Gamble, M. (2012). Texas health resources launches dyad leadership model. *Becker's Hospital Review,* March 8, 2012.
19. Zismer, D., & Brueggerman, J. (2010). Examining the "Dyad" as a management model in integrated health systems. *Physician Executive Journal of ACPE, 36*(1), 14–19.

Chapter 7

Learning Dyad Skills

Dyad leaders, and those who hire them, have a stake in making sure that appropriate individuals are chosen and then educated for the role of Dyad partner. The underlying reason we felt so passionately that this book needed to be written is that, recognizing the promise of better working relationships and improved coordination of both care and business models, healthcare systems are initiating co-management arrangements at every level. Our observation is that this is frequently done without thorough preparation before implementation. New models and systems should be designed purposefully. Individuals selected for these new roles should be selected and developed with special care. That begins with consideration of whether or not *any* individual who happens to be a member of one of the professions identified as needed in the Dyad can and should become a Dyad leader (or a single formal leader, for that matter).

One of the issues that has intrigued those who study management and leadership is whether there are natural born leaders or if anyone can be educated to lead. The answer is probably both/and. There are people who attract followers (something you must have if you are to be a leader!) whether or not they have been educated or trained in leadership. In Display 7-1, we share some of the new science around leadership.

Of course, we don't advocate, nor would it be feasible, for organizations to do genetic testing on applicants for Dyad roles. Nor should they be questioned on their parent's style of parenting! We included this research as a background for why some people could find it easier to become leaders while some *may* be more challenged.

We do advise careful comparison of the applicant with the job description and what needs to be done in the job. Those who have demonstrated a bent for transformation, who have great interpersonal skills, and who really want the job should go to

---

Display 7-1 **Destined to Lead? The Science of Leadership**

Recent studies indicate some individuals may have actually been predestined from birth to lead. As strange as this may sound, there is scientific evidence that biology influences who moves into *and is effective* in leadership roles! DeNeve et al. published results of one such study in 2013, which identified a specific genotype "associated with those who occupy leadership positions" (1). Preceding their study, other researchers found that approximately 30% of surfacing leadership traits, as well as differences that occur in leadership style, are explained by genetic factors (2–4). Current research is not just about what some earlier work looked at (correlations between being selected for leadership roles based on physical attractiveness, height, weight, energy levels, etc.) but about hormones, neurotransmitters, and neuroscience.

Other research looks for environmental determinants of leadership skill. Avolio et al., for example, discovered that authoritative parenting practices correlate positively with children becoming leaders in adulthood (5). This may be because children with commanding and firm (authoritative) parents score higher than do others in achievement orientation, self-confidence, reasoning ability, independence, care and concern for others, and industriousness (6–8).

So, leaders everywhere can give thanks to their strict parents!

---

the top of the list for hiring. We caution that this third point should not be assumed—just because an individual expresses interest in a management/leadership role does not mean *he or she really wants it.*

Why would a person apply for a job she doesn't really want? She may not understand the job, what it entails, what it would mean that she herself would need to change, or how difficult the role will be. Or, he may apply because he is trying to escape from a current position/job, and this one looks like a "way out." Or, he has been asked to do this and he is flattered by the assumption of his ability but does not do any self-examination of whether this is really what he wants. Or, she sees this as a step she needs to take in order to get the job she really wants. Executives and others putting Dyad teams together should consider all of these possible motives and consider whether they would affect the successful functioning of an applicant in the Dyad partnership.

NOT UNDERSTANDING THE JOB

Dyad leadership is new to many organizations, so it will be common that people don't have a comprehension of what it entails. While one Dyad applicant may see the advantages of two professionals working as partners, another, particularly if he is from a high-status profession, may assume he will always be the "prevailing partner." In other words, he may be conditioned to believe, as the evolving ruling class (the Pigs) in George Orwell's *Animal Farm* declared, "All animals are equal but some are more equal than others" (9). In his mind, the "partner" is actually subservient to him, and he, as the superior, will be the final decision maker *for everything*. We've observed that some executives have actually set their shared management models up this way. They label two leaders as "Dyad partners." On the organization chart, however, one person clearly reports to the other. This is *not* a Dyad partnership. It is simply a model where one person has been selected to report to another (like a CEO and COO). Usually the "superior" delegates operations to the other manager, but it is clear to all team members that there is a single top leader, even if he or she has no management experience and performs no management tasks. This can be a conscious choice that an organization makes, but should not be labeled as a Dyad leadership model. The top leader may have a shared leadership style (in which, regardless of the organization chart, he acts as a true partner to the subordinate leader), or he may not. He may be a figurehead placed to appease a group the hospital wants to "partner" with, while the real management work is performed by his "subordinate" partner.

In addition to not understanding leading as a partner, it might also be that some applicants new to formal healthcare leadership do not understand what it means to be in any management position. We've observed a few who struggle when they realize this is not the "easy" work they thought they observed from outside the formal leadership ranks. They approach the job like they approach clinical work ("I just give an order and it happens."), or they think managers have very little to do. It can be a shock to discover that healthcare leaders, if they are doing their jobs well, usually have more to do than they can get done in any day, week, month, or year. They are also shocked when they find out how very hard the "soft" stuff (relationship building, counseling, hiring and firing well, making decisions when neither is clearly the right one, listening, communicating clearly, balancing the needs of multiple stakeholders, balancing dollars and quality, etc.) really is.

It's important that applicants be educated about Dyad partnerships because there is a possibility that some may not want the job if the organization chart shows the leaders as equals. Applicants might also be less interested if they know what management really is, and that *even though they are experts in their nonformal leadership jobs*, they will not be experts in this new role. It can't be assumed that everyone who *thinks* they want this role *understands* the role, or that they would pursue it if they did understand.

SEEING MANAGEMENT AS AN ESCAPE

We've noted that occasionally, a clinician who wants a management job see moving into the formal leadership ranks as the "way out" from an increasingly difficult clinical practice environment. She complains that clinical work "isn't fun anymore" because of new technology (especially IT), new models of care (team vs. individual silo work), bureaucracy (increasing government, regulatory, or organizational red tape), decreasing income and/or increasing productivity demands, and decreasing status (at least perceived). Some may discover (even early in their careers) that they have made a career mistake. They've invested years and money into a profession and then find out they don't like it (or at least they don't like the type of work their profession actually does on a day-to-day basis). These professionals may see healthcare management as an escape from their problems or a place to bargain for an increased (or at least stable) salary, while their peers project decreasing income if they stay "in the trenches of direct care." Often the "escape" motive is combined with not understanding the job—and the escapee flees one job to accept another, where she may not be suited or fulfilled either! We do know some very successful managers who left clinician work because it was not a good fit for them. What differentiates them from colleagues is that they went into management/leadership positions because they wanted to transform healthcare. They wanted to lead and manage, in order to *improve healthcare or the organizational environment for others*, not *just* to escape from an unhappy experience, or for self-preservation reasons.

FEELING FLATTERED OR COERCED

Sometimes Dyad leaders don't even apply for the position. One may already be an employed manager who has previously functioned in a "single" role. He may take part in planning for a new Dyad model *or* be simply told that "this is the way we're going to lead your department from now on. You're getting a Dyad partner." Most often this occurs when organizations are trying to work more closely with independent or employed medical staff. The manager in place is usually a nonphysician clinician or business manager. The new Dyad partner is usually a physician. The organization perceives this model as the way to unite the two silos. Frequently, a doctor who is known to be influential with other physicians is the one selected.

In many of these new relationships, the physician is approached by healthcare executives and *asked* to take the role. This may involve negotiation if she does not want to leave clinical work ("OK, you can be a half-time clinician, and half-time manager"). It may be a "hard sell" if the physician has never thought about being a manager. ("You'll have 'a say' now in how this department is run. You can bring your clinical experiences and your knowledge of what physicians really need to a job where you can make decisions.") The physician may immediately see how she can be of value in the role. Or she may feel flattered that she's being asked to "lead" as a representative of her colleagues.

There are all kinds of potential pitfalls when leaders did *not* seek or choose to apply for these positions. These are amplified when team building is not planned and begun immediately as a formal process. The in-place (nonphysician) manager may lack education or skill in working as a partner and may undermine the new model. Or, he may fall into a cultural pattern in which he begins to take less accountability for decision making, acquiescing to whatever the physician leader wants, even if the manager is *the expert* in a particular situation. You may have heard these dysfunctional refrains from managers who feel disenfranchised:

▶ He gets paid twice what I get and *doesn't do anything*.
▶ She doesn't understand the complexities of what we're doing and just gets angry when she snaps her fingers and nothing changes.
▶ I don't get invited to meetings I used to go to. He does.

The physician who accepts the "nonposted" job (Human Resource talk for announcing a job opening that can't be applied for) has been invited into management. Like some who *do apply* for these roles, he may not understand the job. He may bring cultural entitlement with him. ("Sure we're both bosses, but I'm the **B**oss and you're the **b**oss right?") She may think this is really just a figurehead role, in which her only responsibility is to keep relationships "good" with the doctors while organizational leadership wants her involved in management tasks (or vice versa—she may want to be involved and leadership thinks they only want a figurehead!).

We believe that requiring physician leaders to apply for Dyad management (or *any* management) position is the best practice. Choosing an influential doctor just because he's influential (and may have no real interest in formal leadership) seems on the manipulative side, that is, hoping to utilize a doctor to get other doctors to do what the hospital administration wants, rather than a true partnership in which we figure out *together* the best course for all of us. Individual physicians can be *encouraged* to apply, just as any promising candidate for *any* job can be encouraged to apply when they might not recognize their own talent or potential. The very act of applying should prompt them to learn more about the work, and to at least *believe* it is work they want to do. The in-place manager will be more supportive if he has an opportunity to interview and take part in selecting his partner. Finally, while hospital leadership may firmly believe they know who would be best for the new role, they could be overlooking someone who would be even better. There may be another physician they haven't considered who has a passion for transformation, a desire to lead, unrecognized management skills, and an earnest thirst to learn whatever he can about formal leadership.

VIEWING DYAD MANAGEMENT AS A STEPPING STONE

Clinicians who want to get into healthcare management may jump at the chance to work in a Dyad model. Since these are usually implemented in middle or upper-middle leadership ranks, they are attractive entry points to a "new" career. Those who either understand they don't have developed management skills or don't want to do the work their complementary partners do, can view this model as a safe place to learn, supported by a partner who is usually seasoned in organizational life and knowledgeable about "how to get things done around here". They may consciously plan to take what they learn and move "up the ladder" to "higher" executive positions.

There is nothing wrong with planning a leadership pathway. Most managers do this. They are encouraged by educators and mentors who push them to develop their abilities with personal career goals in mind. For those who are just entering formal management, the Dyad model can be a natural place to start. It may not be (probably is not) the final leadership position desired by either partner. It may be accepted primarily as a stepping stone to the job someone really wants. That's okay, as long as Dyad leaders dedicate themselves to the work of the Dyad while they are in their Dyad roles. We've known managers who were so busy being "political" or trying to impress top executives with their individual leadership prowess that they've neglected some of the responsibilities of their current jobs. For Dyads, this can mean that one partner ends up doing the lion's share of the Dyad's work (while the other is building personal support for his or her ascension). It can mean that the hard transformational work is slower than it needs to be because the two do not share (as their primary goals) the development of an effective team which will support the organization's mission and vision. In other words, if only one partner is dedicated to the Dyad's success, the effectiveness of their shared leadership is diminished. So, when selecting Dyad leaders, personal long-term goals should be discussed with candidates, including what they want to do after their Dyad partnership jobs. Executives must stress that both partners will be held accountable for the Dyad's work.

A best practice that nurses and physicians have been taught for decades is that discharge planning (and discussion with patients and families) begins on admission to the hospital. This concept carries over to Dyad selection. Partners begin their education during the interview process. So while interviewers try to assess the interviewees, they can also educate on what will be expected of Dyad partners—such as the priority for Dyad and Dyad-led team success over individual glory. (Some applicants seeking star status may even deselect themselves for consideration in the partnership when they hear this expectation.)

Earlier in this chapter, we stated that a bent for transformation and great communication skills are important for Dyad leaders. Every organization will develop its own list of competencies expected from those selected for these roles. Typically, resumes, interviews, and reference checks are all used to select the candidates who are the best match. In Chapter 9, we share thoughts on interviewing. Superior interviewing skill can help prevent a placement error, but, there is no failsafe interview model.

Organizations are certainly looking for individuals who have demonstrated, or can learn, an ability to work in partnership. The Harvard Business Review's 1990 collection of "unique" perspectives on effective leadership includes thoughts about other traits today's healthcare organizations should consider in their selection process (and look for in their Dyad leaders).

▶ "Managers work at an unrelenting pace." Therefore, *we want Dyad leaders with high energy.* "The manager's effectiveness is significantly influenced by their insight into their own work." *We want leaders who know what their jobs are ... and have insight into their partnership role* (10).

▶ "Leadership inevitably requires using power to influence the thought and actions of other people." *We need leaders who are comfortable both with using power and sharing it with a partner so he or she is also able to influence people during this era of change.*

Leaders' "sense of who they are does not depend on memberships, work roles, or other social indicators of identify." While managers develop "through socialization which prepares individuals to guide institutions and maintain the existing balance of social relations," leaders develop "through personal mastery, which impels an individual to struggle in psychological and social change." *We need managers, but we must have leaders if we are to change and transform our healthcare system.* They cannot be rigidly frozen into professional roles and thoughts by their socialization (11).

▶ "What leaders really do is prepare organizations for change and help them cope as they struggle through it." *We need Dyad leaders who can help other cope with change.* "What executives need to do is not organize people, but to align them." *We need Dyads who are passionate about aligning people, and tearing down silos* (12).

▶ "Effective leaders are alike in one crucial way: they all have a high degree of emotional intelligence." It's not that the IQ and technical skills are irrelevant. They do matter, but mostly as threshold capabilities (entry-level requirements for executive positions). "Emotional intelligence is the sine qua non for leadership." It is twice as important as the others (IQ and technical ability). *We want intelligent leaders but we must have intelligent leaders who are high in emotional intelligence* (13). (See more about emotional intelligence in Display 7-2.)

▶ Inspirational leaders selectively show their weaknesses and rely heavily on intuition to gauge appropriate timing and course of their actions, manage with tough empathy (empathize with people but care deeply about the work itself), and reveal their differences (are willing and able to be seen as unique). *We need inspiration,* so should look for candidates who care for people and the organization's goals.

Display 7-2 Emotional Intelligence

Emotional Intelligence has been part of the popular management lexicon since the early 1980s. According to psychologist Daniel Goleman (among others), this type of intelligence is different from IQ (Intelligence Quotient), and has five components: self-awareness, self-regulation, motivation, empathy, and social skill.

▶ Self-awareness is "the ability to recognize and understand your moods, emotions, and drives, as well as their effect on others."
▶ Self-regulation is the ability to "think before acting."
▶ Motivation is "a passion to work that goes beyond money and status."
▶ Empathy is an ability to put yourself in another person's shoes or "understand his emotional makeup."
▶ Social skill is the ability to manage relationships and build rapport.

Goleman cites research suggesting "there is a strong genetic component to emotional intelligence," and that it increases with age. It can be developed by people lacking in some or all of the five components, but, "building one's emotional intelligence cannot—and will not—happen without sincere desire and concerted effort."

—Adapted from Goleman, D. (1990). What makes a leader? Harvard Business Review Article Collection (March–April), *pp. 35–44.*

"Many executives don't have the self-knowledge or the authenticity necessary for leadership." *We need Dyad partners who exhibit understanding of their own strengths and weaknesses and are "real" in their interpersonal relationships* (14).

▶ "Everyone wants some measure of control over his or her life. Yet some people's need for control is disproportionately high." In the long run, this can make leaders fail to deal with tough challenges because of a desire for a calm workplace. *We need leaders who understand that some chaos and conflict are inevitable.* They and their teams will need to function in an ever-changing environment where confrontations must occur.

"A grandiose sense of self-importance often leads to self-deception." "The absence of doubt guarantees serious missteps." "An inflated sense of self-importance encourages others to become dependent on you." *We want leaders with the humility to question their own perfection and develop other people's leadership skills* (15).

▶ A leader must be able "to articulate his vision in a compelling way." *We want Dyad leaders who can do this—communicate and get their teams excited about transformation.*

A leader must understand that "without implementation we'll be doomed from the start." *We want Dyad leaders who understand and can develop multidisciplinary teams who share enthusiasm for the team mission, vision, and goals* (16).

▶ "Proponents of all management styles will probably agree that to manage other people effectively, a person needs a battery of qualities that are not easily acquired. These include intelligence, energy, confidence, and responsibility … candor, sensitivity, and a certain willingness to suffer the painful consequences of unpopular decisions belong on this list." In short, we need, if not totally packaged in *one* of the Dyad partners, two leaders together who have *all* of these transformational skills (17).

Discovering these qualities, listed by various and well-known leadership scholars and experts, during the interview process and trying to ferret out their presence (or absence) isn't easy, but should be considered in situational interview questions (see Chapter 9, Display 9-2) and, if possible, in questions posed to the applicant's references, or people he's worked with in the past.

As we've stated, interviews are not infallible selection tools. We believe that many if not all Dyad partnerships selection errors could be prevented with a thorough assessment of the potential partners (see Display 7-3). Some organizations may balk

---

Display 7-3 **Executive Assessment**

Executive assessment for senior leaders is a best practice for large or complex organizations. This process combines online leadership assessments with simulations, problem solving measures, and interviews by a PhD in corporate psychology. Executive skill sets are broad, and there are many flavors of successful executive style. Assessment at this level is not a yes/no proposition so much as a prediction of behavior in a variety of executive performance domains. Triangulating data through multiple measures ensures depth and accuracy.

Executive assessment serves two primary purposes. The first is a "gut check" of the other data that the organization has gathered. Many times when a red flag is raised by an assessment, at least one individual in the interview process has spotted the potential challenge. Often, executives interview so well that potential challenges are fuzzy, and the interviewer does not have a way to corroborate their intuition. Behavioral science gives specificity and clear description to nuanced data about style, impact, and culture fit. The second purpose is to make strong use of data in developing a positive, productive relationship for the new Dyad team. Leaders who have the raw potential, but are not accustomed to the dance of shared power, benefit from using their results to have conversations that build effective collaboration early in the relationship. The assessment report, when shared in a feedback session, serves to build a development plan that includes engaging stakeholders, meshing with the culture, and working well with a new boss. Many organizations have a high rate of executive turnover. Catholic Health Initiative (CHI) has maintained a 95% retention rate of executives who have gone through executive assessment.

Getting started means ensuring that assessment components are tailored to the role and to the culture. Translating the strategic plan and cultural values to needed executive skill sets is an ideal place to start. These skills and competencies are then mapped to elements of the executive assessment. The length and complexity of assessments can be tailored by leadership level.

(Continued)

Characteristic/Competency	Measurement Element
Emotional skills	Online measure; follow-up interview
Strategic thinking	Critical thinking; pattern recognition in case study
Collaboration/shared power	Case study/role play presentation; online measure; leadership maturity interview
Learning agility	In Basket exercise; coaching exercise

Keys to Successful Use of Executive Assessment

1. Tailored process
2. Positive candidate experience
3. Dialogue with assessor about results during integration discussions
4. Delivery of feedback to the newly hired executive and boss
5. Development planning including relationship building and culture fit

—*Suzanne Miklos, PhD*

at the expense and time of these. We are assuming that the Dyad model is being initiated to meet strategic goals of the organization, and failure to select the right leaders or the right pair of partners can be costly when they are *never* able to become effective, or need extensive time to bond because of incompatibilities not identified early on. It's always less expensive to "fix problems" before they really are problems, and pre-hire or early post-hire assessments help executives do this. Results can be used to either decide not to hire an individual or to plan appropriate leadership formation activities early on. These can range from planned or even facilitated (by their shared "boss" or another third party) conversations and mutual exploration of each person's skills and management styles, to leadership development courses, to individual or team coaching.

CHAPTER SUMMARY

Management and leadership research is becoming what some might call "more scientific," as common biological traits are identified for those who lead. Healthcare organizations aren't planning to choose their leaders based on actual, physical DNA, but to make the best choices for their Dyad leaders they should interview and select partners carefully. There are a variety of traits listed by leadership experts that should be considered for each leader and explored through crafted interview questions. The strength of the Dyad model is that the two partners should have complementary skills, and *neither one must have "everything."* Both can grow in their individual skills, just as the Dyad is an entity can become stronger, with planned leadership formation.

Dyads in Action

COACHING FOR PARTNERSHIP SUCCESS
Diane Menendez

Above his doorway, the psychologist Carl Jung, an explorer of the unconscious, etched this quotation: "Bidden or unbidden, God is present" (18). Equally true in our experience is that when two leaders come together, bidden or unbidden, something else is called forth. The two create an invisible but felt third party, their *relationship system*. Napoleon Hill, an early pioneer in understanding mindset's powerful impact on results, articulated this third party presence when he wrote, "No two minds come together without thereby creating a third, invisible, intangible force which may be likened to a third mind" (19). With his characteristic optimism, Hill went on to describe the great energy that comes when the two join with a spirit of harmony to form an "affinity."[1] We can see this at work in various kinds of relationships: Ginger Rogers and Fred Astaire were individually great dancers, but their greatest fame came as a dancing pair. The Beatles had an impact on 20th century music far beyond the individual successes of John Lennon, Paul McCartney, George Harrison, and Ringo Starr. Closer to home, every family has a "third party" character created by the experiences, behaviors, and events shared by its members and their collective history.

Since this unseen but tangible relationships system profoundly impacts the results and relationships the Dyad partners create, it deserves attention from the moment leaders enter the Dyad. We believe that Dyadic leadership holds such power and promise for healthcare that it doesn't make good business sense to simply let this third party emerge through trial and error, as the two individuals come together. Instead, we recommend that Dyad partners contract with a seasoned coach to support them in *intentionally* creating the third party, their *relationship*. Through safe, confidential experiences, the coach facilitates the each partnership (i) to increase self-awareness, other-awareness, and awareness of the relationship as a *system* with its own independent uniqueness; (ii) to give voice to their individual and wants and to the needs of the relationship; and (iii) to establish pathways for continuing dialogue, celebration, and course correction. We know that a leader's first 90 days are critical to success. The same is true for the Dyad: the Dyad's first 3 to 6 months shape the collective view of its stakeholders and set in motion the dynamics the Dyad will need to harness and manage. Coaching works best when it begins early—as the Dyad joins up and meets its stakeholders, identifies desired results, and discovers obstacles to success.

---

[1] Unfortunately, great energy also emerges when individuals join and the third party relationship is dominated by conflict and disharmony. Neither individual intends to create discord. It's all too easy, however, for a conflictual relationship to result when leaders are seasoned in leading as individuals but novices at the challenges of leadership in a two-person system.

COACHING: A PROCESS, A PERSPECTIVE, A SKILLSET

If you are unfamiliar with professional coaching, you may be asking, "why consider coaching for a new Dyad?" At CHI, we have had an internal Coach Formation process since 2011, with the goal to develop a cadre of highly skilled internal coaches who can work with clients to develop top talent, launch leaders successfully into new or expanded roles, and support leaders without previous experience in faith-based healthcare to succeed within CHI. CHI models its coaching approach on the International Coach Federation's (www.coachfederation.org) expectations for professional coaches, which defines coaching as "partnering with clients in a thought-provoking and creative process that inspires them to maximize their potential." Coaches are not mentors, nor are they advice givers. Coaches draw on a set of evidence-based practices for creating insight, generating learning, and facilitating the coachee's movement from insight to right action. Coaching practices and competencies are based on creating strong relationships in service of excellent results. Coaches have expertise in building trust, acting with interest and curiosity (instead of making assumptions and judgments), acting in service of others, modeling vulnerability, summoning patience with their own and others' human fallibility, listening deeply, asking provocative questions, offering insightful observations, and challenging with respect, among others. Underneath coaching practice is an assumption that the coachee has the creativity and resources needed; the coach's role is to elicit ideas, insights, solutions, and strategies that enable the client to awaken a larger vision of possibility, to discover blind spots, resolve issues and move with committed action toward their goals. If a client is stuck, can't see options, has blind spots, then the coach's role is to catalyze insight and awareness of what was formerly not seen or acknowledged. Throughout the coaching conversation, coaches illuminate and validate the client's strengths and resources. Coaching invites us to move outside of our own perspectives and consider others' perspectives so as to motivate and inspire change.

At CHI, we take a holistic approach to coaching, incorporating as appropriate the Mind, Body, Emotions, and Spirit of the Leader. The CHI coaching model includes a three-level focus—*what* the leader does, *how the* leader does it, and *who* the leader is being and becoming as they enact their leadership. *Being* includes their values, means of connecting with others, and connecting with something greater than themselves.[2] Coaching a Dyad means that all three levels are present in any given coaching conversation, particularly the *who*, the *way of being* that the leaders choose. Alignment across the three levels is a leadership imperative, we believe.

---

[2] In our Catholic healthcare system, leaders often draw inspiration through connection with the legacy of our founding sisters' congregations—courageous, pioneering women who founded early US hospital systems in service of their missions to serve. Many leaders come to and stay at CHI because they connect deeply with CHIs' vision and values (Reverence for all life, Innovation, Compassion, and Excellence), and they want to serve in an organization that honors these values and supports Catholic social teaching to care for the poor and underserved. A coach works directly with the connections the leader makes that deeply touch the best within themselves and that lend them energy and courage to face obstacles and challenges.

An assumption Dyadic coaches make is that individuals *construct* their worlds—the world isn't simply outside waiting to be discovered. Instead, leaders bring the world into being through the lenses, the worldview, they inhabit. A leader's worldview reflects the experiences she has had, including her ability to see that her worldview is, well, just her worldview, not the truth. The coach helps the Dyad explore how each individual constructs the current reality as well as how they construct the truth of their system. From this perspective, truth is not fixed; we are all right and our truth is partial. Coaches also take a *developmental perspective* of human beings: they grow and change over time and enter qualitatively different stages of adult development, each of which supports a successively expanding perspective and repertoire of thinking and behaving. In essence, the perspective issue is critical to leadership. At more advanced levels of adult development, leaders are able to shift the subject–object relationships; said briefly, this complex concept means that a leader at the later stages can now see directly how they are seeing themselves; they see what mindsets they are incorporating as objects, not just as "what is." At earlier stages, leaders and others are unable to see their mindsets as something they choose and hold; rather they see them as "how it is in the world."

We believe that coaching Dyad leaders benefits from the coach's understanding of adult development stages: most coaching and leadership development aims at what adult development practitioners call *horizontal development*: leaders expand their skills, knowledge, methods, and processes for doing something, acquire new ways of organizing what they know, new repertoires of behaviors—but their developmental stage stays the same, just expanded. *Transformational development*, on the other hand, results in a vertical shift to a new "higher or later" developmental stage, containing new mental models and meaning making capabilities. A leading scholar in adult development, Suzanne Cook-Grueter, asserts that "Research shows that the level of personal maturity and self-awareness are positively correlated to the kind of life one creates with others at home, at work, and in the community."[3]

Successive stages we commonly see in organizations include the Diplomat Stage, the Expert Stage, the Achiever Stage, and sometimes the Pluralist Stage. Each stage includes the other stages and has a mindset, a relative ability to take a perspective on themselves, and growth edges. The Diplomat Stage, for example, highly values conformity, similarity of values and styles, and believes keeping harmony, is essential. At this stage, a leader will avoid conflict because it is "not me" and not see a way that conflict and differences can be surfaced without breaking harmony and creating disarray. Diplomats have a very short time horizon—planning 4 weeks in advance seems like sufficient strategic planning time. The next stage, the Expert Stage, has a

---

[3] CHI's Coach Formation includes developing their understanding of Adult Developmental Stages, how stages develop over the lifetime, and how to coach clients based on their developmental stage. A lengthy explanation is not possible here. Susanne R. Cook-Greuter "EGO DEVELOPMENT: NINE LEVELS OF INCREASING EMBRACE," downloadable at http://www.cookgreuter.com/9%20levels%20of%20increasing%20embrace%20update%201%2007.pdf.

mindset developed through mastering of a discipline, and prizes being right, creating perfection. Experts can often be argumentative team members: At the Expert Stage, a leader finds it difficult to admit he is wrong and gets into a potential myriad of conflicts over what is the right way—that is, his way, the way he has learned. Looking back at their earlier years as a practicing physician, many physician leaders I have coached and see the Expert Stage at work in their relationships with others outside of their specific expertise. They laugh when I introduce John Wooden's quote, "It's what you learn after you know it all that counts." For these physician leaders, growing into the Achiever Stage coincided with a new willingness to let go of the certainty of the Expert in order to join with others create greater chance in their world. At the Achiever Stage, the leader can be highly collaborative (vs. the independent style of the Expert), focused on getting results, and developing himself to be able to get them. Success is highly valued, not being right or creating harmony. When a Dyad pair consists of individuals who do not share the same stage, the partner at the earlier stage may find it difficult to see the world through the mindset of the other. Coaches can help communicate across this difference by acting as "stage translators."

In general, healthcare organization VP and higher leaders need to be able to operate at least at the Achiever stage to create partnerships in service of large projects, plans and change at the level the industry expects and needs (20,21). When a coach recognizes and understands the impact of development level, she can coach for insight into how the leader is making meaning of evens and into deficiencies and strengths that this meaning making brings with it. It is possible to expedite growth in developmental level through intentional experiential development using a variety of known practices: the use of Dialogue skills (suspending assumptions, perspective taking, and inquiry vs. advocacy skills); consistent reflective practices designed to help the leader see their behaviors much as a third party would see them and to reflect on their intentions; seeking consistent feedback and understanding that in every piece of feedback is a grain of truth to be mined for the leader's development. In healthcare, we also know that a time of service, delivering care in a country outside of one's own and immersing oneself in that culture, worldview, can—no guarantees!) create transformative developmental movement.

Development is shaped by experience. As a coach to a Dyad, my role is to illuminate the Dyad's perspectives and the behaviors and outcomes that result. Rather than "fixing" the Dyad, the coaching process pays attention to and evokes awareness of what is present and what wants to emerge from this two-person system.

To be successful, the Dyad partners will have to learn to use the mindset and skills that the coach uses with them. So while a coaching engagement has specific outcomes to achieve—in this case, the successful launch of the Dyad on a trajectory to achieve desired results—the coach models the power of the relationship skills the Dyad will learn to use with each other and those they lead (22).

A best practice for a Dyad in our CHI system is "create relationships first, then create results." Our President and COO, Michael Rowan, gives this advice to new leaders. He suggests that a new leader take time to get to know the organization and to build relationships with the stakeholders, before instituting major change. Stakeholders are more likely to want to align with the change when they feel understood by the Dyad. The coach works over a 3- to 6-month period to expedite the speed and intensity at which the Dyad relationship is built. Dyad coaching engages the two leaders in a confidential, intensive, and facilitated process that maximizes their ability to work effectively together to produce the expected results. The work takes into account strengths, style preferences, opportunities for development, worldview and cultural similarities, and differences—all in the context of the expectations and vision for the two together.

The rest of this chapter describes one path for coaching a Dyad and focuses on the new Dyad partners.[4] The process is based on several decades of experience using coaching to effectively launch partnerships, particularly where there is significant diversity between the partners. The coaching approach recognizes that the more diversity there is—in culture, thinking style, management style, gender, level of adult development—the more benefit the pair may receive from coaching as a means to capitalizing on differences rather than crashing under their weight. The coach brings an outsider's perspective and can help the Dyad initiate "crucial conversations" about the relationship they have created, so as to create more trust and find alternative ways to behave as they lead. Like any human system, Dyads are fertile grounds for "projection," assumptions a person makes about what motivates and guides another person. Projections emerge from the experience of the projector and are most often incorrect as they fail to account for the partner's unique experiences and mindset. Getting to the Dyad early creates an opportunity to address and eliminate projections through reflective dialogue.

The process we recommend for a new Dyad is to get underneath the polite façade of new relationships, to create a strong third party "*WE*" in their first several months together, before they must produce significant results (Fig. 7-1).

FIGURE 7-1 Process for creating a new dyad.

---

[4] A similar process can be effective in other relationships including established Dyads, strong or troubled Dyads. In the latter case, the Dyad may feel as if it is experiencing an organizational version of the Uncle Remus tale, "The Tar Baby." Despite knowing what to do—and what not to do—the pair collectively can't get unstuck from the current dynamics of their relationships.

CONTRACTING: ALIGNING ORGANIZATIONAL EXPECTATIONS

To succeed with Dyad coaching, expectations need to be aligned between the leader to whom the Dyad reports, the Dyad partners, and the coach. I initiate a meeting with whoever has initiated the coaching to discuss expectations and clarify issues of confidentiality—that is, what will be shared, with whom, and by whom. Often the HR business partner acts as an involved stakeholder in alignment meetings. HR may initiate a discussion when a new Dyad is to be launched, sometimes in advance of one or both partners assuming their roles in the organization. When the coach, HR business partner and the Dyad's leader meet to establish expectations and create alignment, the work agenda is as follows:

1. Clarify how success will be measured (i.e., the organizational measures of results as well as how the Dyad would be working and leading the organization). This includes specific discussion of behaviors—what the Dyad would be doing, what they wouldn't be doing as well as any organizational assessments commonly used of leaders, like CHIs *Leadership Effectiveness Review*, a yearly assessment based on CHIs values, and leadership competencies.

2. Identify a list of stakeholders critical to the Dyad's success, metrics to measure success at quarterly intervals, and other organizational realities at play. Surface any major opposition to the Dyad's work (i.e., local facilities may be resistant to a national service line leadership approach) that should be addressed early, as well as any "low hanging fruit," potential early wins.

3. Identify any "broken glass" that the coach or the Dyad might step on. "**Broken glass**" might include a culture's unspoken assumption that any person working with a coach has failed or is lacking in some way. In other cases, broken glass may include residue from a reputation that lingers from other roles or other systems. Healthcare is a close-knit industry and reputations, whether current or not, follow individuals throughout careers.

4. Prepare the HR business partner and leader to discuss the Dyad coaching engagement with the two leaders. In most cases, Dyads willingly engage in coaching to expedite onboarding. I suggest some talking points and clarify when I can take the next step to contact the partners.

5. Agree on how the HR business partner and the leader will support the Dyad during the coaching engagement. Common agreements include providing feedback, holding crucial conversations, avoiding triangulation, etc.[5] For example, I recommend that the Dyad meet with the coach and their leader (and perhaps the HR business partner) at specific intervals, commonly every 6 weeks, to discuss progress, share

---

[5] See K. Sanford's earlier commentary on triangulation in Chapter 9.

learning, gather feedback, and/or identify needed support. The meeting's agenda is set by the Dyad, with the help of the coach. Face-to-face meetings are preferred, and the coach should be present at the first meetings, to help facilitate dialogue among the three individuals. More important, the coach observes first-hand how the leader works with the Dyad. In essence, the three make a Fourth Party, which will have its own experiences and ways of engaging that can impact the Dyad. For example, if the leader tends to make eye contact with one partner more than the other, that behavior will have the impact of a "micro-inequity," unbalancing the Dyad's dynamics through the power of inattention to one partner.

6. I send a written communication to the two leaders that describes the Dyad coaching process: the initial self-awareness building phase, the frequency of sessions, the role of the Dyad as cocreators of the coaching, etc. A short meeting of the coach and Dyad partners follows to launch the coaching engagement through a preliminary discussion of their goals and desired outcomes for the coaching. This provides an opportunity for the coach to illustrate his/her ability to maintain focus on the two together (vs. on the individuals) and to create, without sugarcoating anything, an upbeat and positive context for the work to come. The coach also affirms that the real client is the Dyad, though some individual time will be spent with each of the partners. At the close of the meeting, we discuss the prework for Step II Self Awareness Building.

SELF-AWARENESS BUILDING

In this phase, the leaders complete prework activities, and after which they meet individually with the coach for debriefing.

In Chapter 1 of this book, Kathy Sanford wrote

> "The influence of the Dyad will not be effective if the two professionals do not come together as true partners, or do not agree on their vision or goals. The promise of this type of leadership will only be fulfilled when this occurs, when the partners learn to lead together by doing the right things … and to manage together by doing things right."

The prework activities focus on building awareness of their own mindset and perception of doing the right things, managing together, and doing things right. The first work with self-awareness is explored and debriefed at an *individual* 2-hour face-to-face meeting with the coach, preferably at a quiet space away from the leader's regular office. The preparation includes the following:

The Leadership and Partnership Timeline

This activity requires about 1 hour of preparation time. The leader is provided with a one-page timeline. The horizontal line representing "time" is drawn through the center of a large piece of paper; at the left edge of the paper is labeled "birth"; at the far end of the line and right edge is labeled "current." A vertical line extends at the left edge of the paper above and below the "time" line: above the line represents positive events, below the line negative events. The goal of the exercise is to identify the key events, both positive and negative, that have shaped the person's beliefs, experience, and behavior as a leader and as a partner. The instructions ask the leader to brainstorm 15 to 20 or more events in his/her life that s/he would label as *positive* and that have shaped his/her leadership (beliefs, practices, what I do, and what I don't do). Then, s/he brainstorms events that were *not positive* and which also have shaped his/her leadership. Next, s/he does the same for partnership, identifying 10 to 15 positive events that have shaped behavior and beliefs about partnership and 10 to 15 negative events that have impacted the view of partnership. The Timeline goes back to birth because we know that leaders who look backward and reflect become more capable of looking forward, as they must in strategic planning and intentional development. The Timeline becomes an anchor to the value of reflection.

Using the brainstormed list of positive and negative experiences, the leader labels and maps these on a timeline, using black or blue ink to connect the highs and lows on leadership, and red and green to connect the high and low events on partnership, adding dates and an event identifier. The end result is a unique graph with two lines running above and below the horizontal listing of years. This timeline will be reviewed first with the coach. The leader walks the coach through the timeline, sharing the stories of the events that have impacted him/her. The coach's role is simply to listen with empathy, to probe gently to heighten the leader's self-understanding of the significance and current impact of the events. The leader heightens his self-awareness through recounting the stories that have shaped him; when the current time is reached, the coach and leader work to identify what has been learned from this life review (both in creating the lifeline, telling his story to the coach). For example, one leader discovered that in the face of personal adversity, he tended to redouble his efforts toward professional success; this pattern resulted in extraordinary professional success but also created increasing isolation for him. He resolved to change this pattern as he entered into this Dyad. Another leader recognized that his deepest lows preceded his most profound highs, which increasingly involved happiness and satisfaction with children and family instead of work achievements. A theme in his individual coaching became how to maintain a healthy family focus despite a demanding role.

For the coach, this experience creates rapport with the leader and also illuminates the degree of comfort the leader has in personal disclosure, in exploring emotions and the impact of events. The coach can gauge the leader's challenges with authenticity or displaying vulnerability through this storytelling activity.

Preparing for Dialogue with the Dyad Partner

Each leader privately notes their responses to a set of prepared questions tailored by the coach for the particular Dyad. The leader will choose the responses to share first in the debriefing conversation with the coach and later with the coach and Dyad partner. In each conversation, the leader chooses to share what is comfortable from what s/he has written. The coach selects questions designed to prompt reflection, discovery, and a deep exploration. Sample questions might include the following:

▶ Who is a leader who is a role model for you? What makes them a role model for you?

▶ What partnerships have you seen that provide role models for a Dyadic partnership? What makes that pair a role model?[6]

▶ What is the best and most satisfying relationship you have had with a partnership, preferably in your work life or outside your family life? What key elements made that working relationship rewarding and satisfying to you?

▶ What is least satisfying relationship you have had of this kind? What elements made that relationship unrewarding and unsatisfying for you?

▶ What will be the behavioral "cues" that let you know the Dyad relationship has grown?

▶ What do you want others to say about your Dyad relationship? What do you NOT want others to say about your Dyad relationship?

▶ What is most important to you about succeeding in this Dyad? How will you measure the success of this Dyad?

▶ What hopes and fears do you have for your Dyad?

▶ What are the behaviors that give you a sense of being personally valued by a peer colleague? What are the behaviors that give you a sense of being personally devalued?

▶ If you could ask for just one thing from your partner, knowing that your request wouldn't be misunderstood, what would you ask for to help you in this partnership?

▶ Describe a specific leadership moment when you were at your best. When you are at your best, what are you doing, saying, etc.? What enables your best to emerge?

▶ How do you sometimes get in your own way?

LEADERSHIP SELF-ASSESSMENTS

Gallup Strengths Finder

While it is not essential to use standardized assessments with a Dyad, many healthcare leaders, particularly new physician leaders, have not had much opportunity for developing self-awareness through leadership self-assessments. I often use the Gallup Strengths Finder comprehensive assessment, which for $89 gives a rank ordering and

---

[6] The leader can draw on real-life experience or from other experiences—world figures, cinema, partnership in the business world, religious life, etc.

discussion of all 34 of the leader's strengths.[7] The advantages of this version over the less expensive top five strengths' report is that when comparing strengths reports, the Dyad partners may discover that they have some top strengths in common but that neither of them has other critical strengths, or they may have strengths that are the exact reverse of each other. In the early 1:1 with the coach, the review of the Strengths Finder is designed to help the leader acknowledge these strengths, to identify current examples of their use, and also to consider how these strengths might be positively used in the Dyadic relationship.

The Strengths Finder also educates the pair on one way to understand how to maximize effectiveness, identify strengths in others, and achieve success. The 34 Hogan Strengths are arranged in four categories critical to but not limited to leadership: *Executing, Influencing, Relationship Building*, and *Strategic Thinking*, each of which is important to leadership Dyads. At an early coaching session, the coach will array the partners' strengths (with their permission) under each of the categories to discover where they contrast and complement each other, and where the top strengths can be used effectively for the work to come. The Strengths Finder research distinguishes between *talents* and *strengths*, a distinction important to Dyad coaching. Talents are innate abilities that emerge early and that can be cultivated. Strengths, on the other hand, are talents that have been used and developed to quite a level of mastery, and which when used provide motivation, fulfillment, and a sense of flow. This distinction is important to the Dyad because a leader may need to use a talent but not find it fulfilling to use. At its best, the Dyad partners use their strengths frequently, which inspires ongoing energy and motivation.

Hogan Leadership Assessment[8]

At CHI, we use Hogan Leadership assessments in our Transformational Leadership Development Program (TLDP) for clinical leaders, as well as for prehire and other top-talent work. While other style and communication preference assessments also lend themselves to coaching, we recommend the coach choose assessments that will stretch the pair, help them experience a model or a mindset for looking at leadership, and also that are psychometrically valid. The Hogan assessment series are self-reports, psychometrically valid, and help leaders see their leadership styles as normed against other leaders. It includes three self-assessments: (i) the Hogan Potential Inventory (HPI) illustrates the ways the leader will act under "normal" conditions; (ii) the Hogan Development Survey (HDS) shows how the leader is likely to react under stress; and (iii) the Values Inventory is particularly helpful to support the

---

[7] The Strengths Finder Assessment was described earlier in the chapter by Kathy Sanford on Coaching Dyad Teams (https://www.gallupstrengthscenter.com/Purchase/en-US/Product?Path=Clifton%20StrengthsFinder).

[8] You can download sample Hogan reports from http://www.hoganassessments.com/content/hoganlead.

Dyad's discussion of motivating values. Interrelationships between the three reports are summarized in the Coaching Report.

Harrison Assessment

Another preferred self-report instrument for coaching Dyads is the Harrison Assessment, a tool which is useful in identifying challenges where the leader's behavior is not an ideal fit with their Dyad leadership role. The Harrison is taken on line, as are the other instruments discussed here. The coach works with the Harrison distributor to identify the "best fit" job description against which to report out the results. Harrison has developed a battery of role profiles for healthcare leaders and others, so that the individual leaders receive feedback on where they may find the Dyad role challenging, where it will be an idea fit for their strengths, etc. One of Harrison's great gifts to the coach is in its series of "Paradox Graphs," part of the individual profile. In 12 paradoxes related to leadership, the individual's scores are displayed in terms of whether they provide "balanced versatility" or are imbalanced. For example, one paradox related to how the leader communicates is "Frank versus Diplomatic." A tendency toward the more assertive pole (which Harrison describes as "dynamic") of "frankness" and at the same time a low score on the "gentle trait" of diplomacy could lead to a leader seeming very blunt; in the opposite vein, a leader tending toward high diplomacy and lower frankness could be seen as vague. In the Harrison paradox view, the best leaders have high capability in both traits; they show high versatility, able to be both frank and diplomatic at the same time and to choose the best approach for the situation.[9] Using Harrison's paradox graphs provides a rich environment for the discussion of how some traits we see as either-or, are really "both and" in the behaviors of mature and skillful leaders.

When selecting assessments, we recommend you choose either the Hogan battery or the Harrison Assessment, not both. Either can be complemented by the Strengths Finder, which is an easy tool to use in early Dyad meetings.

Debriefing Session

Once the leaders have completed the prework the coach schedules a 2-hour meeting with leader individually to debrief the prework. The coach treats the prework and assessments not as "truth" but as a worldview, a set of perspectives that have developed from the leader's experiences. The debriefing gives the coach an initial sense of how the leader prefers to work, what they do, how they do it, and who they are. This session helps "break up the soil" in preparation for the fertile work to come with the Dyad. We suggest that you not rush the debrief. The coach may need to hold several

---

[9] For more information on Harrison Assessments and sample reports, go to www.harrisonassessments.com.

debriefing sessions in order to complete the work. Not everything must be completely debriefed before the pair begins the coaching, however. Debrief the Timeline exercise and the Strengths Finder, examine the answers to the prepared questions, and that creates sufficient context to move into the Dyad meetings with the coach. Sometime during the session, the leader can ask the coach any questions that have arisen about the coaching approach, etc. I describe how I will be working with them at joint sessions: The coach's role is not to serve as a facilitator/trainer. Instead, the coach's role is to stand for the "third party"—the Dyadic system—and to focus on observations and insights about how this relationship system emerges in that moment.

From all the information exchanged, the leader needs to identify anything that she or he does *not* want to share with the Dyad partner at a session with the coach and the partners. I do not advise the coach to ask the Dyad partners to share the Hogan assessment reports directly with the partner. Instead, the expectation is that the coach will design the meetings so that they will share their perspective with sufficient depth (and safety) in order to ensure understanding of what is most critical, so that the Dyad can cocreate together.

THE FIRST DYAD COACHING SESSIONS

Within a week of the individual debriefing (or the first of the debriefing sessions), begin the regularly scheduled Dyad coaching sessions. Monthly meetings of the coach and Dyad, put on the calendar in advance, keep the momentum going (and the pressure on) to focus on the Dyad. Schedule the first two meetings to be slightly longer than subsequent sessions. I request that a first meeting begins with a meal, to set the value of hospitality that Catholic Healthcare embraces, and that we schedule 2½ to 3 hours, to allow time for sufficient energy and intensity to build. For each session, I distribute a short agenda in advance; sometimes there is specific pre- and postwork or a prereading. First meeting outcomes commonly include the following:

- To establish the Dyad manager's support for the coaching engagement
- To establish a safe and comfortable relationship with the coach and the Dyad
- To initiate a conversation about what energizes the Dyad about partnership and what challenges them about partnership
- To cocreate a draft vision for the partnership and some "rules of the road" or joint expectations that the Dyad can experiment with over the next period of time

Prework for the coach is to select an appropriate space to support the work to be done—simple, spacious both literally and emotionally, encouraging reflection, allowing for silence. Ideally the leaders will not be interrupted. I look for a room with a view that can call up a "larger than us" perspective just by looking out the window: a view of mountains, a wooded area, a place where birds might fly, etc. Do not hold sessions in rooms that feel confined or that lack windows, as we want a sense of the spaciousness of the designed alliance that the Dyad will create. I prefer comfortable armchairs, on wheels, that can be moved into a circle, with very small tables to hold coffee and materials. I want the Dyad to be able to face each other as they work. At times I will move out of their field of vision so as better to observe how the "third party" connects and uses its energy.

I invite the Dyad's leader to join us for the first 10 minutes of Session #1 to discuss his/her hopes for the work, expectations for success, and a celebration of the Dyad's energy and willingness to do this work. Frequently, I prepare the leader with a few talking points to enable a successful first session. At CHI, we begin meetings by having someone read a reflection that set a tone for the session. For a first session, I might choose a reflection on partnership, based on writing by Charles R. Swindoll (23):

> *Nobody is a Whole Chain.*
> *Each one is a link.*
> *But take away one link and the chain is broken.*
> *Nobody is a whole team.*
> *Each one is a player.*
> *But take away one player and the game is forfeited.*
> *Nobody is a whole orchestra.*
> *Each one is a musician.*
> *But take away one musician and the symphony is incomplete.*
> *You guessed it. We need each other.*
> *You need someone and someone needs you.*
> *Isolated islands we are not.*
> *Today let us be mindful that we need those who are our partners in this healing ministry.*
> *And, our growth is in our own hands.*

The coach suggests some basic and helpful ground rules for the meetings and invites the pair to add, amend, and comment. The practice of Dialogue as practiced by Bohm and others provides a good model for guidelines that will support the emergence of deeply connected Dyad (24). At CHI, we use Dialogue in our TLDP. Some Dyads may be familiar with these practices, which are *simple*—and not *easy*. I introduce this set of guidelines briefly by suggesting that here we are trying to use a way of being and talking with each other that will create something different than the usual discussions they experience. I post the guidelines in Display 7-4 on a flip chart and explain how they enable connection and relationship:

Two pieces of joint work occupy the balance of this session: (i) the Dyad is to create a joint vision of their partnership "at its best," over the next 6 months and (ii) to create a short set of guidelines that will enable them to begin to move toward that vision during the next 1 to 2 months.

Display 7-4 **Guidelines for a Deeply Connected Dyad**

LISTENING

> Listen deeply, without resistance.
> Listen to yourself as well as to others; notice and name thoughts, emotions, experiences, assumptions.

RESPECTING

> Look for what is highest and best in others.
> Be curious.

SUSPENDING (I.E., SUSPENDING JUDGMENT)

> Step back; see things with new eyes.
> Let go of certainty; ask "what am I missing?"

VOICING

> Speak from the "I"
> Share what is true for you now
> Overcome self-censorship

Stage setting for the joint vision asks the pair to discuss what they know about Dyads in their organization, successful ones in spite of the odds, and the challenges they have overcome.[10] I suggest they begin by sharing with each other their responses to earlier prework questions and then just talk with each other about what their vision for the Dyad might be and what part they would be playing in creating that vision. In the room, make sure the pair has lots of easel paper, markers, and room to post anything they want to use. I avoid overstructuring how they do their work. Instead, how they self-organize, speak to each other, who writes on the chart, how they sequence their interactions all are early ways I can observe the system creating itself. Unless something egregious happens, I don't intervene for the first 30 to 45 minutes of this activity. At an appropriate time, often after they create a first draft of vision flip charts, I will ask them to stop for a time and to debrief together how they are working together as a pair. My hope is that each of them speaks before I add anything, although sometimes I have to jump start the discussion, usually by celebrating something they are doing together. If they have a rich

---

[10] A 2011 set of interviews with CHI CNO/CMO Dyads identified these common challenges: (1) Time—the pull of daily activities that gets in the way of time together; (2) managing the political dynamics together without getting pulled apart; (3) finding early wins to celebrate. (4) In addition, the history of stereotypes that doctors have with nurses and nurses have with doctors, the power imbalance, can be challenging in order to show that this Dyad is different from the stereotype. (5) If goals set for the leaders are not sufficiently overlapping, this pulls the Dyad in different directions.

and juicy discussion about the Dyad, I add observations that provide dimension on the Third Party Perspective:

▶ Sometimes I ask questions that playfully draw on metaphor: "If you were a weather reporter, how would you describe the weather of your relationship?"[11] (Sunny, bright, rainy, clouds ahead.) "What's the forecast for the next month?"
▶ "I notice how easy it is for you to make eye contact and be in silence."
▶ "I'm enjoying the lightness you've brought to this last exercise as you playfully asked questions and toyed with cartoon characters. What would it be for you to sustain this lightness?"
▶ "I notice how easy it seemed for you to offer a light hug at the end of the vision. What a delightful way to build a relationship."

For this session, the way forward is to initiate creating a set of norms and expectations they will use to bring the vision into being in everyday work life. We brainstorm a typical set of dilemmas to address, usually including:

▶ What kinds of roles do you need to play? Who will do what, and how? (Draw on the Strengths Finder work).
▶ How will we communicate, how frequently? (Constant communication really helps Dyads in early stages, until they have built a relationship where they can speak with confidence about how the other will respond.)
▶ What common goals and metrics do you share? How will you stay focused, track progress, and celebrate wins together? How will you celebrate privately, and how publicly? How will you communicate goals to your teams?
▶ What will we need to decide? How will we make decisions?
▶ What will help you persist?
▶ How will we manage conflict and differences?
▶ How will we remain positive?
▶ How will we respond when someone criticizes our Dyad partner or their group and work?

I usually suggest that they just sit back, relax and talk, while I take notes. Since this is the last piece of this day, I want them to experience a natural conversation, where they can build off of each other and maintain the connection of eye contact, not worrying about who takes notes. I often just sit with them, taking notes on a notepad or iPad; I periodically repeat what they have said or show them the iPad screen to enable them to build upon ideas.

At the end of the day, I develop with them what coaches call "fieldwork"— actions to take between this session and the next that will create the way forward.

---

[11] I'm grateful to Phil Sandahl of the Team Coaching Institute for learning this question at a Team Coaching Workshop. www.teamcoachinginternational.com Phil's organization offers workshops to assist coaches in learning team coaching, though that is somewhat different from Dyad coaching.

The intention is to ground and deepen their learning together. Fieldwork examples might include the following:

▶ *Refining the vision.* Spend some time together refining your vision and speaking it to each other. When it sounds like you are satisfied, consider how you might best share the vision—with whom? How? How will you orchestrate your communication so that it subtly illustrates your relationship and connection? How will they both contribute? Who will speak first? How will they communicate their coequality?

▶ *Noticing opportunities for using strengths.* How can you build on what you have learned about each other and you distribute work, connect, delegate, work with stakeholders.

I close this session by asking them "What are you taking away from this session? What are your 'together' takeaways?" Notice that this isn't asking them to evaluate me or the session, as you might after a training program. The question puts their learning front and center.

Two weeks after this first session, I e-mail short readings or online clip assignments and ask the Dyad to review and talk together about them before the next session. This quotation from *Crucial Conversations* exemplifies the heart of issues they will face: what do people do that jeopardizes relationships?

"As people begin to feel unsafe, they start down one of two unhealthy paths. They move either to silence (withholding meaning from the pool) or to violence (trying to force meaning in the pool). Silence almost always is done as a means of avoiding potential problems, and it always restricts the flow of meaning. The three most common forms of silence are masking, avoiding, and withdrawing. Masking consists of understating or selectively showing our true opinion. Sarcasm, sugarcoating, and couching are some of the more popular forms. Avoiding involves steering completely away from sensitive subjects. We talk, but without addressing the real issues. Withdrawing means pulling out of a conversation altogether. We either exit the conversation or exit the room" (25).

A second excerpt is a set of notes from John Gottmann's research on what creates toxic relationships. Gottmann describes what he calls "The Four Horsemen that destroy relationships": the behaviors of *contempt, blaming, stonewalling*, and *defensiveness* (26). Gottman describes his research from couples who he describes as "masters" of relationships versus the "disasters" relationship in a 10-minute video on YouTube, another assignment on the Four Horsemen. I ask them to notice and note behaviors that they observe that exemplify the Four Horsemen and silence (usually appearing as Masking, Avoiding, or Withdrawing) and/or violence (usually appearing Controlling/Labeling/Attacking. Their noticing can be of each other and is also of any leader or person in the work or other environment. The list is anonymous—no names!—and I ask them to bring those notes to the next session.

SECOND DYAD SESSION (1.5 TO 2 HOURS)

Relationship Toxins

Whenever possible, hold the second and subsequent sessions in the same location as the first Dyad session; there is energy that carries over when a Dyad has a sense of "this is our place to work." Generally, the second coaching session has two objectives: (i) to dialogue together of what has gone well for them this past month and what challenges they have faced and (ii) to build their "conflict muscles" to reinforce alternatives to the Four Horsemen and silence and violence.

1. Begin with a quick review of suggestions for dialogue and also hang visibly a flipchart with their ground rules where they can easily see it.
2. Conduct a playful exploration of the Four Horsemen (contempt, blaming, stonewalling, and defensiveness) and of silence and violence. If the Dyad enjoys having fun, I might ask them to enact each of the six, that is, like an actor would play it. All three of us do this together, and I play too in this one.
3. Segue into a discussion of examples that they have observed this week, and the impact that each had on the conversation or relationship. As Dyad coach, I'm asking them to consider what could have taken place instead, and what they notice when someone is engaging in these behaviors, whether aware or unaware.

   Key points to make are that the six behaviors emerge when the person experiences what *Emotional Intelligence* author Daniel Goleman calls an Amygdala Hijack—that is, the person's emotional brain is in charge and they are captive of their primitive brain, in fight or flight mode instead of reasoning through the situation. The coach is "normalizing" the fact these behaviors occur in most human systems—and at the same time standing behind how negatively they impact relationships (particularly contempt according to Gottmann). For each of the toxic behaviors they observed, we talk about "antidotes," helping them forge an interpersonal "snakebite kit" that's available when needed. For example, rather than seeing a situation as "who is doing what to whom," we might ask a more system-oriented question: When this occurs in the system, what is trying to emerge? We will at some point make a segue to them as human beings, and ask: Which of the six toxic behaviors do you have to work to avoid doing? Which is hardest for you to experience? The intent behind this discussion is to build a path toward the Dyad understanding each other *before* they experience serious discord and use the six toxins to ramp up the head. As they notice, share, and claim what is their perspective, this creates steps toward recognizing when they may get caught up in toxic behavior and defusing the situation.

There are links between the toxic behaviors and the Hogan report HDS that illustrates how each Dyad partner behaves under stress. There are links between the toxic behaviors and the paradox graphs on the Harrison, where "flips" are noted if the person is under stress. If the Dyad is ready, we can make these links and describe personal patterns of behavior under stress. The coach goes first to provide an example, to normalize stress behavior, and to observe that it is helpful to know the first signs of a partner's stress behavior as the other member of the Dyad can step in to intervene when they are together.

4. The balance of the session is devoted to the Dyad reviewing what has gone well this past month, what were challenges they faced and how they met them, and any disappointments. I ask each of them to take 5 to 8 minutes alone to make some notes to themselves about answers to these questions. Then I lead them to discuss each question in turn. This is an opportunity to reinforce good listening skills and, if needed, to invite the Dyad to notice how they are responding to the examples and to each other.

5. We conclude the session with the brief use of a way of reflecting on a situation that was taught by the Gestalt Institute of Cleveland, where I did a great deal of my postdoctoral training. Each person is invited to make two statements as they consider the upcoming month: "I want … (fill in the blank) …." "We need … (fill in the blank) …." This can be challenging to a Dyad at first; however, as a practice, it provides an opportunity for the system to examine individual wants as well as what the system—the We—needs most at this time. The language of needs and wants reinforces that the system usually takes first priority in considering how to proceed. And the coach can expect that the two will have different perspectives on what the WE needs at this time. The point is not about being right: remember the coaching statement that "everyone is right, but only partially."

At the conclusion of this session, prepare fieldwork that will head this unique Dyad into the direction that it mostly needs.

COACHING SESSIONS 3 TO 6

As stated earlier, coaching Dyads requires uniquely tailoring a process to a particular Dyad and an organization. I recommend that the coach meet with the Dyad at least once monthly and in 1½- to 2-hour sessions. In some cases, the coach calls each individual once per month, too, to discover whether there are individual needs to address. I have also worked in cases where one or both of the Dyad partners had their own leadership coach. That works best when both the Dyad coach and the individual coach practice a systems view of relationships.

Either in between Sessions 2 and 3 or at the 3-month point, a meeting with the Dyad and their manager should occur. Essentially, it is an opportunity for the Dyad to share what they are learning and experiencing, to share victories, and to invite feedback. The coach should be present face-to-face or by phone to hear the feedback and then to examine what it may mean for subsequent work.

Between Sessions 2 and 3, I will ask each partner what they would most like to include in the next session or two. When Dyad coaching, some session elements recur:

▶ Beginning with Session 3, I will open each session with an "I Want/We Need" sharing. That lets us identify what is most important at that time for the Dyad.

▶ A debriefing, as in Session 2, of what has gone well, what have been challenges met, what are disappointments encountered. The coach's role is to help the Dyad practice outstanding listening and to be able to engage in Dialogue work as a twosome. Periodically, the coach can intervene to reinforce what is occurring that is enhancing the relationship, or to make a process observation about the Dyad as it does its work. I stay very sensitive and aware of nonverbal behavior and take opportunities to explore what is occurring by one or both parties. Sometimes I include a "just in time teaching" or promise to send something based on what happens in a session. I like to ensure that at least one of the sessions has focused on "repairing" a difficult conversation or a time when one of the relationship toxins was surfacing; this ensure that the Dyad has the experience of understanding that repair is possible and that it can even make a relationship more solid.

▶ We close with statements of "takeaways" for the individuals and the Dyad.

▶ Each session needs to include some celebrating and exploring what is working—it gives the Dyad heart for the work ahead and balances tendencies to focus only on what is missing. We return to the vision and the "rules of the road" as context for each session.

OVERSERVING THE DYAD

At some point, the coach and the Dyad will benefit from observing the Dyad leading a meeting or giving a presentation. This enables the coach to observe the Dyad in another context and to hold a dialogue about anything that tripped them up. The coach can serve as witness in this way, as the partners are "in it," so to speak. It is fairly common for the Dyad to experience breakthroughs of insight and collaborative behavior after the coach observes and debriefs a meeting. The greater the coach's skill at process observation, the more beneficial observation becomes.

Other sessions include whatever tools or learning could best support the Dyad. We might take some time in a session to use the process from Crucial Conversations, for example, to work through a difference between the partners. If conflict becomes an important theme, the Thomas Killmann Conflict Inventory (https://www.cpp.com/products/tki/index.aspx) provides a self-assessment and a report that is simple and that gets to each of the Six Toxic behaviors, though it uses different language. Social Styles (http://www.tracomcorp.com/solutions/by-element/social-style/model/) is a simple but valid tool that can create insights if the partners have very different thinking and communication styles. Social styles identify four primary styles: Driver, Analytical, Expressive, and Amiable. Each style has a core desire as well as a typical orientation toward results and relationships. Any tool that describes differences positively—and a tool that the coach is comfortable with using—can have a positive impact.

At some point, we will talk about key signs that the Dyad is maturing: partners can speak with some confidence about decisions and issues, knowing that they can speak for the other partner. They hear positive feedback about their reputation from others in the organization. They ask for feedback about their Dyad from stakeholders, and they may ask the coach to conduct interviews to gather that feedback.

CONCLUDING THE ENGAGEMENT

At the 6-month point, conduct a check in. At that point (or even earlier), the engagement may be concluded if the original goals have been met. Dyad work provides a rich and compelling experience for the coach and the Dyad—and sometimes participants want to prolong the engagement because it provides connection to someone who has witnessed their journey. My preference is to close at the 6- to 7-month period and to hold a concluding session where coach and the Dyad share their learning and appreciation. Another concluding piece of work is for the Dyad to craft a brief development plan to maintain their success. At the last formal session, I give each partner a small token that represents something about their partnership and about the work we did. One Dyad was so taken with the metaphor of "what's the weather like in here," that I gave them each a small temperature device (get the name …) that sat on their desks as a reminder of our work together.

SELECTING A COACH

Not every skilled executive coach is up to the task of coaching Dyads. We suggest you interview coaches and look for experience in working in partnership as well as in coaching more than one person in relationship. Coaches with training in systems and relationship work—in either organization or family systems training—are most likely to be successful in this work. If you plan to use internal coaches for Dyad coaching, you may want to have them work as pairs in their first several engagements. This can ensure success in two ways. First, the pairing will ensure that nothing gets missed. Second, a skilled pair of coaches can model partnership for the participants.

REFERENCES

1. DeNeve, J., Mikhaylov, S., Dawes, C., et al. (2013). Born to lead? A twin design and genetic association study of leadership role occupancy. *The Leadership Quarterly, 24,* 45–60.
2. Arvey, R., Rotundo, M., Johnson, W., et al. (2006). The determinants of leadership role occupancy: Genetic and personality factors. *The Leadership Quarterly, 17,* 1–20.

3. Arvey, R., Zhang, Z., Avolio, B., et al. (2007). Understanding the development and genetic determinants of leadership among females. *Journal of Applied Psychology, 92*, 693–706.

4. Ilies, R., Gehrardt, M., & Le, H. (2004). Individual differences in leadership emergence: Integrating meta-analysis findings and behavioral genetics estimates. *International Journal of Selection and Assessment, 12*, 207–219.

5. Avolio, B., Rotundo, M., & Walumbwa, F. (2009). Early life experiences as determinants of leadership role occupancy: The importance of parental influence and rule breaking behavior. *The Leadership Quarterly, 20*, 329–342.

6. Baumrind, D. (1991). The influence of parenting style in adolescent competence and substance abuse. *Journal of Early Adolescence, 11*, 56–95.

7. Darling, N., & Steinberg, L. (1993). Parenting style as context: An integrative model. *Psychological Bulletin, 113*, 487–496.

8. Parker, G., & Gladstone, L. (1996). Parental characteristics as influences on adjustment in adulthood. In G. R. Pierce, B. R. Sarason & I. G. Sarason (Eds.), *Handbook of social support and the family* (pp. 193–318). New York, NY: Plenum Press.

9. Orwell, G. (1946). *Animal Farm*. Mass Market Paperback, 50th Anniversary Edition. New York, NY: Signet Books.

10. Mintzberg, H. (1990). The manager's job: Folklore and fact. *Harvard Business Review Article Collection* (March–April), pp. 1–13.

11. Zaleznik, A. (1990). Managers and leaders; are they different. *Harvard Business Review Article Collection* (March–April), pp. 15–24.

12. Kotter, J. (1990). What leaders really do. *Harvard Business Review Article Collection* (March–April), pp. 25–33.

13. Goleman, D. (1990). What makes a leader? *Harvard Business Review Article Collection* (March-April), pp. 35–44.

14. Goffee, R., & Jones, G. (1990). Why should anyone be led by you? *Harvard Business Review Article Collection* (March–April), pp. 45–52.

15. Heifetz, R., & Linsky, M. (1990). A survival guide for leaders. *Harvard Business Review Article Collection* (March–April), pp. 73–80.

16. Peters, T. (1990). Leadership: Sad facts and silver linings. *Harvard Business Review Article Collection* (March–April), pp. 87–94.

17. Peace, W. (1990). The hard work of being a soft manager. *Harvard Business Review Article Collection* (March–April), pp. 103–108.

18. *Attributed to the philosopher, Desiderius Erasmus*. Retrieved from http://www.goodreads.com/quotes/323449-bidden-or-unbidden-god-is-present.

19. Hill, N. (1937). *Think and grow rich*. Cleveland, OH: The Ralston Society, p. 252.

20. Torbert, W. (2009). *Action inquiry: The secret of timely and transforming leadership*. San Francisco, CA: Berrett-Koehler Publishers.

21. Torbert, W. (June 2013). Listening in the dark. *Integral Review, 9*(2), 264–299.

22. Patton, P., & Menendez, D. (2013). Coaching on the run: Building capacity and capability for the future. *Nurse Leader, 11*(3), 30–31, 39.

23. Swindol, C. R. (2003). *We need each other [today's insight]*. Retrieved from http://www.crosswalk.com/devotionals/todays-insight-chuck-swindoll/today-s-insight-june-8-9-2013.html

24. Bohm, D. (1992). *Changing consciousness*. Retrieved from http://usineaprojet.wikispaces.com/file/view/aaa%20read-practice-of-dialogue.pdf/34572363/aaa%20read-practice-of-dialogue.pdf

25. Patterson, K., Grenny, J., McMillian, R., et al. (2011). *Crucial conversations: Tools for talking when the stakes are high*. New York, NY: McGraw-Hill.

26. Gottman, J. (January 2, 2010) *The four horsemen of the apocalypse*. Retrieved from https://www.youtube.com/watch?v=CbJPaQY_1dc

Chapter 8

What Do You Believe?

Do you believe? That was the question posed by Catholic Health Initiatives' chief operating officer (COO) at the system's 2012 market leader's meeting. The COO, Michael Rowan, MHA, challenged his audience of operations and functional leaders to examine what they think will be necessary in the next era of healthcare. He emphasized that before the group of operations and clinical leaders could begin to strategize and plan for the future, individuals needed to consider their convictions about what needs to change. He did this by asking, "Do you believe …

▶ That the future is about population health management?
▶ That the industry will move away from a focus on volume of procedures?
▶ That it's not just about hospital administration anymore?
▶ That your comfortable role that you have been successful at will need to change?
▶ That home care is going to be as important as hospital care?
▶ That, as a physician executive, you can stand in front of your professional colleagues and hold them accountable to a higher standard of clinical care and a lower cost to provide that care?
▶ That honest, uncomfortable conversations with physicians about the required standard of care and about their incomes are a prelude to partnership and not career-limiting conversations or a prelude to a vote of "no confidence"?
▶ That you can bring your local board to a larger, big picture conversation, away from just talking about the monthly and financial and operating statements?
▶ In the value of capital investments in risk and insurance versus a new da Vinci Robot?
▶ That you can effectively manage in your market without full, direct control of all functions (finance, billing and collection, supply chain, information technology, etc.)?

231

▶ That you can go home to your local market and stand in front of your board, your executive team, your middle managers, your frontline staff, and your medical staff and tell them the world has changed and that they will need to make changes to be successful in this new world?"

At the time (2 years is not that long ago in linear time, but ages past based on thought progression and spread of ideas), these were provocative queries, even though the healthcare field was collectively discussing the changes implied by every one of these questions. Some, such as the issues about population health and home health, were based on macro healthcare trends. Others, like the one about locus of control for some support functions, relate to the evolution of large systems from holding company prototypes to operational models. Still others involve shifting relationships, particularly with physicians.

All of us can ask similar questions in our organizations. When we pose questions like these to our leadership teams, boards, and staff, we help everyone think. When we discuss our thoughts in generative conversations, we are better able to come to shared answers. Otherwise, some of us may have very different ideas about what the organization's vision really means or about how much change must actually occur if we are to fulfill that vision. Without a collective answer to where we believe we are going, we cannot begin the journey to go there. So, for our purposes, we would add these questions to the ones our COO posed. Do you believe ...

▶ That quality and safety must improve in your organization?
▶ That providing value for patients should be our number one goal?
▶ That patient and family (or users of healthcare) experience and satisfaction must be a major focus for your system?
▶ That employee and physician engagement is important to your organization's success?
▶ That cultural differences of all kinds can and should be addressed and mitigated in the interest of both patients and the workforce?
▶ That transformation requires breaking (disrupting) the present reality and implementing much more change than simply tinkering with current systems?

QUALITY AND SAFETY

The most quoted reports about quality and safety failures in hospitals have come from the Institute of Medicine (IOM). Authors and speakers still seem to quote two aging papers more than any other when this subject comes up. The first is the 1999 *To Err is Human: Building a Safer Health System* (1), and the second is the 2001 *Crossing the Quality Chasm: A New Health System for the 21st Century* (2). The IOM has published many other calls for action since these, including their 2004 *Keeping Patients Safe: Transforming the Work*

Environment for Nursing (3), but none seem to have caught the attention of people like the first two. This might be because we were so shocked when they presented statistics about the tens of thousands of Americans who die from medical errors.

There is plenty of additional evidence that quality and safety are problems in our organizations. Some of these are reports from regulatory bodies, some are research studies, some are safety alerts that come to providers after someone has been harmed, and some are each organization's own internal reports on mortality, core measures, hospital-acquired conditions, and others. Until recently, most of the focus on quality has been on the inpatient side of care, but there is more emphasis recently on outpatient sites, especially since hospitals have acquired a larger number of physician practices. Quality data are beginning to be gathered from physician offices through the Physician Quality Reporting System (PQRS) of the Center for Medicare and Medicaid Services (CMS). However, as physician researchers at the Weill Cornell Medical College report, PQRS measures do not include all the suggestions from the IOM on safety, effectiveness, patient centeredness, timeliness, efficiency, and equity (4). Their lead researcher has suggested that true quality in clinics and physician practices could be measured through never events (things that should never happen, like a procedure done on the wrong limb), prescription errors (including prescriptions for antibiotics that are not indicated), failure to report critical test results to patients, office-acquired infections, failure to monitor for adverse effects after a prescribed treatment, and diagnosis errors. We expect that, over time, there will be more scrutiny on quality at every site of care.

Safety continues to be a priority for organizations, too. Most hospitals have some sort of program to increase patient safety. Our chief medical officer (CMO)/chief nursing officer (CNO) Dyad, in partnership with our safety and risk executives, has initiated a system-wide program based on safety wisdom from the aviation and nuclear power industries. The major concept is to ensure care team members focus on the right thing to do before errors happen. We've changed systems, procedures, and work flows to help staff focus on the potential for harm. We have also found that the power gradient between staff members can be the root cause for medical errors. In other words, patients are being harmed because people who feel less powerful than others are not speaking up when they could prevent errors.

We know we are not facing this cultural problem alone. According to a 2013 survey by the Institute for Safe Medication Practices (ISMP), almost half of the 4884 respondents (of whom 68% were nurses, 14% were pharmacists, 4% were physicians, and 2% were quality or risk management staff) stated they did not question orders they felt were wrong because of their past experiences with intimidation. In some cases, as reported in the survey, patients were harmed as a result of this fear. Both nurses and physicians encountered disrespectful behavior from other physicians. Nurses reported intimidation from faultfinding, shaming, thrown objects, and insults due to race, religion, gender, and appearance. Pharmacists reported disrespect from physicians and nonphysicians, more often in the form of reluctance to work collaboratively or follow safety practices. As the ISMP relayed, "Surveys expose healthcare's continued tolerance and indifference to disrespectful behavior. These behaviors are clearly learned, tolerated, and reinforced in the healthcare culture, and little improvement has been made in the last decade" (5).

Dyad leaders share a responsibility for quality and safety in areas they co-lead. They have expert, position, and personal power to influence different team members to make the changes needed for improvement in quality and safety. They are also able to address environment or cultural problems together. The Dyads we have initiated with a concentration on quality and safety include (i) a leader from risk and insurance with a leader from quality, (ii) CMOs and CNOs at the national, regional, and local level, (iii) quality leaders from the clinical services group and the physician enterprise group.

Our experience has been that strongly bonded Dyad leaders are addressing these cultural issues in places where single leaders did not. You will see some examples in our Dyads-In-Action stories. It appears (and we plan to study this) that there is a perceived safety in numbers. Two leaders seem to be more likely to empower staff to stand up to bullying behavior, or to address this behavior together, than a single leader is. This may be true even when the single leader is from the same professional culture as the disrespectful or intimidating person.

VALUE FOR PATIENTS

In the October 2013 Harvard Business Review, Michael Porter and Thomas Lee state that the number one strategy for healthcare organizations should be to provide value to patients, which is defined as achieving the best outcomes at the lowest costs (6). Their assertion is that only physicians and provider organizations can do this, because "ultimately, value is determined by how medicine is practiced." Their care model is to organize patient care around specific medical conditions with care provided by multidisciplinary teams who work together regularly with the goal of maximizing the patients' overall outcomes as efficiently as possible. They suggest the teams be led by a physician, clinical care manager, or both (in other words, a Dyad.)

Porter and Lee aren't the only authors talking about the need to provide value or the idea that multidisciplinary teams are the caregivers of the future. In hospitals, and in physician practices, teams with shared goals are becoming the norm. Leaders endeavor to optimize the skill mix of team members to increase both the team and organizational value to patients. A growing number of these members are advanced practitioners (nurse practitioners and physician assistants). Their inclusion on teams has been growing because of the looming shortage of primary care physicians, but also as part of the movement to have each caregiver operate at the top of his license. In other words, value is provided when less-expensive team members are able to perform duties that don't require the skill and education of another team member.

The CMO of the Institute of Healthcare Improvement (IHI) is quoted in an advisory board update as saying, "In many primary care practices today, physicians are doing a great deal of work that could be done by others on the team" (7). Others, including us, believe that there are tasks being performed by nurses and other professionals that could also be done by less costly team members. Part of improving value is changing the responsibilities of team members to appropriately utilize skills. Once teams are formed, leaders should plan a methodology to measure and improve their efficacy. In Display 8-1, we share *one* tool that has been developed to do that, while evaluating co-leadership effectiveness.

Of course, this changing of roles is not easy. Some caregivers enjoy duties that don't require their education or skill. When professionals have an emotional attachment to what the job has been in the past, they will actively resist changing any part of their roles. Unfortunately, as Porter and Lee state, "Providers who cling to today's broken system will become dinosaurs." Leaders who believe this, especially leaders from the physician ranks, will also need to believe what the COO posed in the first set of questions above. They will perceive that they have a responsibility, both to

---

Display 8-1 **Clinic Contour™**

Patient outcomes and patient safety are tied directly to the effectiveness of the healthcare team delivering those services. High-performing teams, however, don't just happen. It takes intentional effort, structure, and leadership to establish and sustain teamwork. It is even more challenging to perform as a team when co-leaders are involved. A co-leadership environment is one where leadership is shared jointly between a clinical lead and an administrative lead; this environment is generally found in most medical clinics and other healthcare delivery sites where there are multiple physicians.

Clinic Contour™ is an online assessment tool developed by the Trispective Group to diagnose the challenges specifically encountered by co-leadership teams working in healthcare. Clinic Contour™ diagnoses both team and co-leadership effectiveness across four areas:

1. Team mindset
2. Clinic structure and activities
3. Team relationships
4. Co-leadership effectiveness

The resulting output provides co-leaders and their teams a detailed view for how they can improve their effectiveness and create better patient outcomes. Participation in Clinic Contour™ always includes a detailed assessment and results debrief with the option of adding additional coaching and development to improve team performance.

From Linda Adams, Partner, The Trispective Group.

the organization and to their professional colleagues, to hold them accountable to a higher standard of clinical care at lower cost so that both will survive.

Executives who believe that value is the number one goal for organizations can't ignore the need to implement multidisciplinary teams, while ensuring that professionals are being utilized in the most efficient way. They should consider the benefits of enlisting empathetic, but realistic, Dyad partners, who may have more influence with their change resistant colleagues.

PATIENT AND FAMILY SATISFACTION

Customer service in healthcare has been getting more attention lately. This is partly because the Hospital Consumer Assessment of Healthcare Providers and Systems (HCAHPS) is now among the measures used in the formula to calculate how hospitals will be paid through the government's hospital value-based purchasing program. The newer Consumer Assessment of Health Providers and Systems (CAHPS), also developed by the CMS, has been implemented to evaluate patient experiences in provider offices, so that CMS can publically report how patients perceive key aspects of their care. Sometimes, organizations use these surveys as a proxy for customer satisfaction, even though CMS is careful to point out that patient experience is how patients perceive key aspects of their care, while customer satisfaction, and the tools that attempt to measure this, are about how satisfied they were with their care (8).

The new focus on patients as customers is not just about payment formulas, though. As the consumerism movement is growing, and as more users of healthcare have opportunity to select which clinically integrated networks or accountable care organizations they want to be part of, there is increasing emphasis on development of customer loyalty. Even when individuals receive their insurance through their employers, they often have a choice of plans and the providers associated with these. In addition, employee satisfaction with care influences their employer's choice of insurance and providers included in the plans. Patient–consumers are becoming better educated about value (cost and quality) as well as less satisfied with what they perceive as poor care—which is often more about customer service than actual quality!

Unfortunately, customer service has not been a strong point for healthcare providers. Long waits in physician offices or emergency departments have been the norm for users of healthcare. Lack of responsiveness to patient or family requests as well as rude behavior has not been rare. Sharing of patient information still occurs, in spite of widespread education on the Health Insurance Portability and Accountability Act (HIPAA), which requires providers of healthcare to ensure the privacy of patient health information.

Organizations are attempting to improve their customer service through a variety of policies or procedures. Emergency departments institute "no wait" policies, in which the goal is for all patients to be taken to examination rooms when they arrive, rather than having them take a seat in the aptly named "waiting room." When people must wait, staff members are assigned to speak to them at defined increments of time so that they do not feel ignored or forgotten. Individual television sets are placed in exam rooms, where more waiting may occur. Staff members are educated to use "scripts" when answering the phone or talking to customers. Standards are set on how fast call lights must answered.

Many hospitals have improved their food service departments, implementing menu choices, and on-demand food delivery. Others give roses to patients when they are discharged. Some upgrade television choices and offer Internet availability in patient rooms. There is a long list of amenities being tried to gain customer loyalty.

All of these may improve how people view their site or environment but might not get to the root cause of poor patient perceptions of the care they receive. That's because the *care* doesn't come across as *caring*. Kathy realized this when she spoke, years ago, to a room full of emergency department staff members, including physicians. She was sharing the poor results from their patient satisfaction survey, as part of a conversation intended to get input on how the group could improve their scores. The response from the staff was neither embarrassment nor concern. Instead, the sentiment they echoed was this: "We are busy saving lives. Patients should be grateful for our skill, and not expect us to be nice, too."

All of the amenities, scripting, and education that healthcare organizations implement will not improve the user of healthcare's experience if there is an underlying attitude that the providers of care are more important than the receivers of care. Unfortunately, a culture of self-importance exists among at least some members of the healthcare team, and that can't be changed with scripted words or good food. If you are in denial that this could be an issue in our industry, please stop and think about this: why is there so much emphasis about our need to *become* patient-centered? Shouldn't those who come to us for care be able to expect that we have always put them in the center of what we do? Could it be that our hierarchal history has placed our ultimate customers lower on the pecking order than clinicians, even if subconsciously? Has that resulted in some lack of concern for treating them with respect, kindness, and service? Or, is an environment where lack of civility between clinicians, managers, and employees is tolerated affecting how customers are treated, too?

We must consider the possibility that our culture is less than truly patient centered. To turn around, a culture will require a leadership team that makes it a standard operating procedure to vet every policy, procedure, and decision by asking, "How will this affect our customers and how will they perceive this?" A best practice for getting patient input to help answer this question (for selected actions) would be to establish and seek input from a patient and family advisory committee (see the "Dyads-In-Action" story at the end of Chapter 9).

Another best practice is to consider any evidence that establishes a link between patient satisfaction and other aspects of the organization's culture. For example, there is some research that where nurses perceive they have a more favorable practice environment, there is a significant and positive correlation with HCAHPS scores (9). The message is this: a customer service culture is about the *entire* culture of the healthcare organization. Addressing customer service without addressing how the team, including managers, treat each other is not adequate for organizations that want to become truly excellent at customer service.

Because healthcare leaders have multiple goals and responsibilities, we've seen some organizations assign responsibility for important areas like customer service or quality, to one functional leader or area. As a result, there are departments and managers with titles like vice president of quality and director of customer service. These can be, and are, important and useful roles but not when it is assumed that *they* have the accountability for quality and customer service.

Quality leaders do not *provide* the care that needs to be of high quality. Customer Service Departments cannot ensure that patients and families receive respect and kindness at the point of care! They can gather statistics, compare metrics, offer education, and inform operations leaders of problems. They can devise and administer programs to apologize, explain, or attempt to mollify upset customers through gifts that range from a box of candy to reduced bills. However, it is better for everyone (the organization and the customers) when there is nothing to apologize for! That responsibility—to develop, monitor, and nurture cultures where employees and nonemployed physicians believe and act with civility and concern, so that customers perceive these—falls to operations leaders.

Most of the Dyad managers in hospitals and clinics are operational leaders. They can't delegate responsibility for customer service or quality to centralized functional departments. They are accountable for leading their teams in the development of a culture of service and quality. As with all cultural changes, this will require use of their confrontational skills (outlined further in Chapter 9, Box 9-3), communication skills, education skills, and coaching skills. It will also require courage, including the courage to terminate (through firing or loss of hospital privileges) team members who cannot change. Willingness, or the motivation to do this, comes back to the question: Do you believe that patient and family experience and satisfaction must be a major focus for your organization?

EMPLOYEE AND PHYSICIAN ENGAGEMENT

It's increasingly common to hear leaders preparing for the next era speak of their need to have "engaged" employees and medical staff. "Engaged" means more than "satisfied"—it means that those who work for an entity profess an attachment to it. Engaged employees are enthusiastic about where they work, agree with the company's mission and goals, and are concerned about its reputation. As a result, they have the institution's best interests at heart.

The level of both employee and physician engagement is often measured by one of the commercially available engagement surveys. The vendors who provide these instruments also compare individual organization's "engagement" to others in their database (survey results from all who subscribe to the same engagement measuring tool) so that healthcare management teams can not only graph their own engagement scores over time, they can compare themselves to peers. It is likely that you already know your engagement scores. If not, you can contract with one of the national companies who can survey both your employees and medical staff so you *will* know.

Knowing the scores is important, but believing they make a difference to your organization's ability to thrive is more important. Most important of all is taking action to increase them if they are not high. Engaged employees understand how their role supports the organization's success. They feel valued in workplaces where they know their opinions count, where they are supported, and where they have resources needed to do their jobs. The people most likely to influence engagement of healthcare team members are the people who have position power, which means they are usually the organization's management team. So, if either group (or both employees and medical staff) is not engaged with an organization, it is the collective behavior of leaders that is most responsible.

We sometimes point to all kinds of reasons for low engagement scores: the amount of change, a less than civil environment, communication problems, and our poor financial performance (leading to lack of job stability and security). Some may blame employees themselves for their lack of education and training, their decade of birth (as in labeling the younger generations as not interested in engagement), or poor attitudes. All of these can be transformed, managed, or mitigated by leaders.

People with position power have an accountability for engagement scores. There is a leadership "chain" from the CEO to the frontline leader that can be broken at any level. In other words, the CEO may have engaged senior VPs, who may have engaged VPs, who may have engaged directors, who may have engaged direct reports, and so on—but at any level, this engagement might not continue. This can be because of poor selection of leaders for that level or lack of training, education, and coaching of people placed in supervisory positions. An interesting analysis would be to study the engagement of each "level" and determine where the engagement drops. In other words, at what level in the company does engagement drop off, with marked less loyalty and enthusiasm for the work and the company? That would be the place to put the preponderance of resources toward leadership selection and development! It is probably the level where the most problem employees accumulate (those who have unacceptable performance or are interpersonally toxic but are allowed to stay on the job or keep hospital privileges); where rudeness and incivility continues without intervention; where team members do not feel like a team because they do not have a say in how their work is done; where communication is poor; and where hierarchy and status is more important than doing the right thing, such as speaking up when others are disrespected or when quality and safety are at risk.

Engaged employees and physicians are empowered. Research shows that the most important factors in successful empowerment are sharing information about the organization, promoting understanding about it, building trust through divulging sensitive information, and replacing hierarchies with teams (10). In concert with our assertion that engagement can, and does, fall off at certain levels of management, management writer R. Forrester says that empowerment needs to come from the top, cascading from higher to lower levels in the organization, as each level becomes knowledgeable, familiar, and comfortable with sharing it (11). Wherever this willingness to share information and power stops is where the disengagement begins!

Dyad leaders are often put in place to unite different cultures. To do that requires an engaged group of people from different tribes. Paradoxically, the Dyad model may be put in place to solve engagement problems at the level where this has historically dropped in the organization! If you believe that employee and physician engagement is important, the selection, resocialization, education, and coaching of appropriate Dyad partners are essential for the success of the organization. Leaders who are willing to tear down hierarchy, build teams, and share power are what is needed.

CULTURAL DIFFERENCES AND TRANSFORMATION

A major tenet of this book is that Dyads are mostly put in place where two different professional cultures need to work more closely together in order for the organization to meet its goals. If you do not believe that there are cultural differences based on profession, there is a less compelling rationale for implementing Dyads, although a case could still be made for combining two sets of skills when the leadership tasks are simply too much or too varied for one person to master. If you do believe there are professional cultural differences, as well as other cultural differences that can both enhance and challenge the partnership, it is important not to ignore these but to help or encourage new leaders to hold crucial and difficult conversations as part of getting to know each other, determine roles, and develop a partnership that really works.

If you believe that tinkering with the current structure and system will change the organization enough to thrive in the next era of healthcare, or you don't think there will be a need for change, implementing new management models is probably not worth the effort. It will cost twice as much (or more) to put two leaders where once there was only one. The time and effort that they will need to build their partnership can be avoided if there is no need for a major cultural overhaul. However, if you believe transformation is a must, we advocate for the Dyad model, when it is implemented well, as a strategy for developing and strengthening the bonds between previously siloed professions or functions.

What you believe as a leader will inform the strategies you choose for the future. You may or may not agree with the beliefs our COO asked about a few years ago. You may not believe in what we listed as our beliefs. In addition, you may not think it takes a Dyad to address any or all of these issues. We do urge all healthcare leaders to determine what you believe about the next era of healthcare, so you can strategize for your preferred future and implement the leadership model that could best help you get there.

CHAPTER SUMMARY

Before planning strategy, organizations need to define what leaders and their teams believe about the future and what elements of the company will need to change in order for it to thrive there. This will require dialogue to ensure that the team agrees, or shares an understanding of the vision, and what it will take to get there. Implementing Dyads or any new model of leadership should only occur after that occurs, to ensure the model supports what will need to be done to attain the vision.

Dyads in Action

DYAD LEADERSHIP: UNTANGLING OPERATING ROOM LATE STARTS

Michael S. Hein and Francine Sparby

THE RATIONALE FOR DYAD LEADERSHIP

Leadership models are structured approaches to providing effective facilitation, communication, collaboration, and decision making within an organization. From the adopted model flow the behaviors and structures of the organization as a whole. Organizational success is determined by the intentional decisions leaders make about the relationships and the structures they will build.

Healthcare organizations are complex entities where customers rightly demand the highest quality, safest, and lowest cost care that meets their needs and expectations. As medical knowledge and technology have proliferated, medical care has become highly specialized and fragmented. Patients seeking care are increasingly older, sicker, and the medical care they need requires highly effective clinical partnerships between multiple providers of care. It is increasingly apparent that within this milieu effective, efficient, patient-centered care requires a team-based approach (12).

Health systems in the United States are historically physician centric. In the 20th century, American society elevated physician professionalism to an elite status. Most health systems today live in the shadow of this legacy (13). Developed over decades, discipline-specific organizational structures, regulatory and local policies, bylaws, and procedures collaborate to promulgate this traditional deference to the physician. As a result, discipline-specific silos and institutional obstacles to collaborative practice models have been hardwired into the hospital organization.

Nurses and physicians have distinctly different professional cultures that at times are at odds with each other (14). At the interface of the patient, however, these two professions are united by three common values. These are quality, safety, and efficiency. Both professions hold at the very center of their professional credo an unrelenting focus on delivering the very best, evidence-based clinical care. Closely attendant to the core value of quality is safety. Efficiency is essential during times of financial challenge, which seems to be the steady state for healthcare. More than ever before, both professions are harried, and the need to deliver high-quality, safe care in a timely and *efficient* manner is paramount.

These three values draw nursing and physicians into a tightly entangled professional relationship. The patient is wholly dependent upon this partnership being, at a minimum, effective, and ideally superlative. The best performing healthcare systems demonstrate a culture where there is a mutually reinforcing acknowledgment and respect for different professional roles, where disciplines are jointly hyperfocused on the patient and where there is a relentless joint pursuit of measurable performance (15). The pivotal relationship within this clinical care team is between nurses and physicians. If this dyad relationship falters, the entire care team unravels and the patient suffers the consequence (16).

The CMO and CNO must model this pivotal clinical relationship (17). They must create the structures that facilitate the replication of this dyad relationship throughout their organizations, and they must nurture and reward the cultural transformation that they are intentionally constructing. This transformation will result in high-quality, safe, efficient care that meets the needs of the rightful recipient of our collective efforts—the patient.

This story shares our development of a dyad CMO–CNO leadership model in a traditional community-based, nonacademic medical center along with some of our lessons learned. While there are many positive fruits of our labor, we will highlight one of our challenges: the surgery division and late operating start times.

STRUCTURAL AND POLICY CHANGES

We acknowledge up-front that our hospital is on a journey that has no end. We have not arrived, and we have many lessons yet to be learned. But every great journey begins with the right first choice. In our case, we were intentional about selecting CNO and CMO partners who had demonstrated a commitment to effective dyad relationships in previous roles. Both valued the partnership and had the personal and professional maturity to build an effective working relationship. The CNO was already in place. The onboarding of the CMO occurred at a time when the national organization was implementing a new dyad leadership model.

Once we were both on board, our initial steps included a review of our current leadership model. We looked at existing bylaws, patient care policies, procedures, and safety initiatives to identify and change the structural and policy underpinnings that were reinforcing a separation of our two silos. A prime example was a complete revision of physician peer review.

Previously the initiation and adjudication of peer-reviewed cases rolled to the CMO rather than the medical staff. Nursing staff had a completely independent review process. Often, identical cases were reviewed separately and in isolation. This resulted in redundant or disparate adjudication, remedies, or identified process deficiencies. This practice eliminated opportunities for dyad interactions at the division or department levels in oversight of clinical quality.

The changes we made included implementing case reporting and review flow from physician case review to nursing case review and vice versa, and a restructuring of the medical staff into divisions led by physician–nurse dyads where process deficiencies were presented, and solution finding initiated. This more distributed leadership structure transferred physician peer review to the medical staff and transferred nursing–physician conflict and solution finding from the C-suite dyad to the department and division level. This was a much more effective forum for change.

A review of the nursing professional practice leadership model revealed a top–down nursing organization, which lacked bedside nurse participation in shared decision-making councils and a supporting professional practice model. Parallel work began with a commitment to redesign the nursing organization practice model consistent with the American Nurses Association Credentialing Centers Magnet standards. Nursing peer review continued to meet to review nursing standards of practice with a reporting structure back to the medical staff and quality committee.

Other mission-critical committees and work, especially those considered "physician" or "nursing" meetings, were restructured. Nursing department leaders were partnered with departmental and divisional physician chairs to cochair historically physician-only meetings. Key performance committees, for example, those focused on CMS Core Measures, matched nurse leaders and physician leaders. All clinically focused performance improvement teams (Lean/Six Sigma in our organization) were required to have nurse leaders and physician champions/leaders paired together. The Medical Executive Committee membership, with support of the physician leadership, was modified to include the CNO. The standing nursing quality committees were altered to require physician membership. Every nursing committee and physician committee was reviewed, and membership was altered to include dyad relationships where appropriate.

The administrative supportive departments of quality, safety, risk, infection prevention, abstraction, medical staff office, and physician recruitment and retention were redesigned, restructured, repurposed, and colocated into a combined department designated the Center for Clinical Care Excellence (CCCE). This department was co-led by the CNO–CMO dyad. The department vision was focused on serving all clinical staff (physicians, nurses, and others) as data-driven knowledge-crafters catalyzing continuous clinical improvement. The CCCE has become a power-plant driver of clinical LEAN process improvement spread and implementation, standardization of performance improvement reporting, organizational learning, data infrastructure deployment, and subsequent rapid acceleration of striking improvements in mission-critical clinical quality.

THE DYAD PROFESSIONAL RELATIONSHIP

While these structural and policy changes were facilitative, they were the result of the CMO–CNO dyad leading by example. Without a transparent and personal commitment to the dyad relationship, these successful structural changes would have resulted in nothing more than disruption and a forum for discord.

The CNO met with the CMO weekly to review key issues, initiative progress, tackle common problems, formulate common strategy, and work through disagreements and conflict between themselves or their respective arms of the clinical team. There were frequent "huddles" to address emerging challenges that served to craft a joint response and key talking points. Key strategic initiatives were developed, initiated, and communicated jointly. For example, they served as executive sponsors in the creation of a patient and family advisory council, in which both were active participant members. Each advocated for the other's key initiatives. For example, the CMO advocated and participated in the magnet journey. The CNO advocated and advanced the development of a formal physician leadership development program. Likewise, the CNO and CMO were evaluated by and held accountable to the same performance metrics.

Effective modeling of dyad leadership is generated from mutual respect and admiration for each other; and appreciation of each other's roles and responsibilities. It's difficult to determine whether the work itself created the close professional dyad relationship or whether the effective work was the result of the relationship. Either way, both the work and the relationship must exist in order for the outcome to be authentic and replicated throughout the organization.

PHYSICIAN LEADERSHIP: A GAP THAT IMPAIRS

In our traditional community-based hospital, which we believe mirrors most similar settings, there are significant differences between the nursing and physician leadership structures. Nursing is usually well established with emerging leaders (managers), more mature leaders (department leaders), and a number that serve as informal leaders (i.e., clinical nurse specialists). This provides a remarkably rich suprastructure for responding to organizational challenges. Even so, additional modification focused on the development of an effective clinical practice model and shared leadership councils increased nursing autonomy and involvement in Councils. Nursing leadership development was enhanced under their shared governance council participation. Therefore, the CNO has a relative wealth of individuals and leaders to partner in leading the organization.

In contrast, the physician leadership structure had been weakened by years of inattention. The medicine division and surgery division were defunct, without designated physician leaders. The CMO position had been defined by the organization to serve as a "policeman"; hence, all medical staff issues were referred to the CMO. With no underpinning team of emerging physician leaders, division leaders, and effective informal leaders to help adjudicate issues, this "super-policeman" of the medical staff was quickly inundated to the point of paralysis. Long-standing issues remained entrenched and unresolved. The medical staff perceived the hospital administration as ineffective, and since they were not empowered or positioned to identify and address their own physician-specific issues, they criticized the hospital for issues that arose from the medical staff themselves.

Dyad leadership is built upon equity. This is as true for the relationship between the CMO and CNO as it is for the organization. We recognized the inherent inequity described above, especially in regard to operational responsibilities and access to leadership and management support for the CMO. Unaddressed, we knew this reality inhibited the organization from moving forward on major change initiatives. It also created an environment that made effective leadership for the CMO impossible.

This spurred the CNO and CMO to advocate vigorously for formal physician leadership development (which was implemented). They worked closely together to establish dyad leadership within the reconstituted medicine and surgery divisions. Additionally, the CNO encouraged closer collaboration between the CMO and nursing department leaders and paved the way for transforming frontline nurse to physician communication practices. We revised our chain-of-command policy to create bridges from nursing management to equivalent physician leadership levels nearer the frontline. The CNO strongly advocated for, as a first step, direct nursing-to-physician resolution of conflicts at the point of care rather than the filing of incident reports and/or escalations to the CNO or the CMO for resolution.

The CMO worked with the medical staff to change their practice of asking nursing to communicate with other doctors. Instead, they were encouraged to speak directly with their peers (improved MD-to-MD communication). These and other changes resulted in an environment where nursing leaders felt comfortable sharing information with physicians on core measures, standardized order-sets, improvement projects, and other change initiatives. Physician confidence in nursing skill was increased as a result of the widespread use of the structured communication tool SBAR (*Situation Background Assessment Recommendation*).

The recognition of the inequity between physician leadership resources in comparison to nursing leadership resources was a pivotal point in our organizations experience with dyad leadership. The collaboration to reinforce, establish, and support each other's "arm" of the clinical leadership realm was the main impetus toward removing barriers to interprofessional communication and collaboration at all levels. The dissolution of these barriers positioned the organization for remarkable acceleration of clinical performance improvement.

CULTURAL TRANSFORMATION ACCELERATORS

Our work around Dyad leadership did not occur in a vacuum. There were several enabling organizational change efforts that served to reinforce the type of culture we were striving for. It was the conviction of our senior leadership team that exceptional care for patients requires an organization that is patient-centered, team-based, data-driven, and continuously improving.

Three major initiatives were deployed to accomplish this vision for the organization. We found that they all reinforced the organizational changes wrought by the Dyad leadership we embraced and implemented. These three initiatives were high reliability organization science, LEAN/Six Sigma performance improvement, and just culture.

High reliability organization science, branded "Safety First" in our organization, is moving us from a blame-based culture to a learning-based culture. We found that in order to reduce harm to patients, an organization has to cultivate widespread psychological safety. Within that environment, team members freely report and/or act to prevent errors from happening. An organization that gives undue deference to the physician may hamper nursing from feeling safe to speak up. When this happens, harm can come to patients. The lessons learned, and changes resulting from Safety First, especially in reference to the nursing–physician relationship, underpinned our efforts to create dyad relationships throughout the medical staff and nursing leadership corps.

LEAN/Six Sigma performance improvement science in our organization emphasizes data-driven, team-based solution-finding to improve quality, safety, and efficiency. This methodology has been highly effective for structuring our improvement work and reinforcing our efforts to be data driven in our improvement efforts at the frontline. Each clinical improvement project is team based and frequently dyad led. Because LEAN brings physicians and nurses together to work on their shared core values of quality, safety, and efficiency, we have found this to be a highly effective catalyst for dyad partnerships.

Just culture methodology was introduced to the management team prior to implementation of Safety First, just after onboarding of the CMO. These methods establish a standard approach to errors that reduces blame in the culture, facilitating open and transparent conversations about harm and safety. This feeds into transparent quality and safety conversations between nursing and physicians, reinforcing dyad relationships.

AN OUTCOME: IMPROVING OPERATING ROOM LATE START TIME

Our operating rooms are like many others. For years, late starts were common. This inefficiency is self-perpetuating, notoriously chronic, and difficult to change. Past efforts had failed to create even minimal temporary resolution. Because the processes effecting start times are complex and interdependent, change is difficult and requires the cooperation and collaboration of multiple disciplines. Most notably, as is the case with most clinical inefficiencies, it is highly dependent upon physician action.

Successfully addressing this chronic patient and physician dissatisfier required (i) a multidisciplinary team that was physician led; (ii) structured performance improvement methods; (iii) clear, actionable, reasonably accurate data; (iv) division-level nursing–physician dyad leadership, and dyad–executive leadership sponsors, with participatory removal of existing barriers; (v) transparent, safe communication within the context of a multidisciplinary surgery division; (vi) shared core values for improving quality, safety, and improving efficiencies; and (vii) results.

All the organizational changes described previously from the deployment of the dyad leadership model were required to achieve success in this project. The structures created to facilitate divisional level physician–nursing dyad leadership provided a trust-based relationship between the two leaders who had the most influence over the operating room—the surgery department nursing director and the physician chief of the surgery division. The newly created surgery division meeting, led by the dyad, provided a forum for open discussion and debate about the problem. The newly created Center for Clinical Care Excellence and the LEAN/ Six Sigma–based performance improvement team provided reasonably accurate, actionable data that created knowledge about the actual state of affairs regarding late starts. The Lean/Six Sigma team had provided standardized Green Belt education to the nursing director of surgery, so she had the knowledge and skills to lead a structured improvement process. Two emerging physician leaders provided peer-based leadership and commanded adherence to the identified interventions. The cultural changes from Safety First and Just Culture had minimized a blame-based

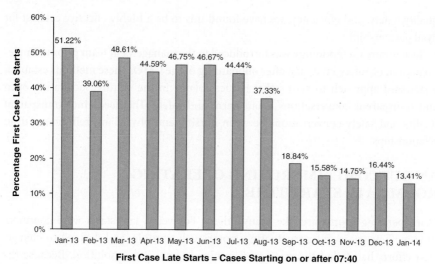

First Case Late Starts = Cases Starting on or after 07:40

© Center for Clinical Care Excellence, Saint Francis Medical Center, Grand Island, NE   January, 2014

FIGURE 8-1   Operating room first case late starts. Start time is 07:30. Late starts are those surgeries starting on or after 07:40. Start time is considered time to incision. The intervention began in September 2013.

culture in the OR, creating an environment of collaboration and respect, focused on finding and fixing problems.

While early, the results are impressive and representative of the outcomes we've seen replicated in multiple venues and projects (Fig. 8-1). One of the emerging physician leaders who served as a cochampion for this project stated, "I've never seen a project like this actually work!"

SUMMARY

Healthcare of the future demands team-based care. At the center of the most effective clinical-based teams are strong, collaborative nursing–physician leaders in a dyad relationship. In order to create healthy nursing–physician partnerships, physician and nursing leaders must join together in a mutually reinforcing professional relationship. They must also create structures that cascade and replicate this relationship and operationalize the model in key management, administrative, departmental, divisional committees, and work teams.

ACKNOWLEDGMENTS

We thank Rebecca Shuman, RN, Steve Schneider, MD, Bruce Koefoot, MD, and Donald Kropf, MD, for their leadership in the Operating Room late start time project.

INTERVIEW WITH A DYAD: THE CMO AND CNO
Cary Ward and Libby Raetz

Cary Ward, MD, has been the CMO for Catholic Health Initiatives St. Elizabeth Regional Medical Center in Lincoln, Nebraska, since 2002. When his first CNO Dyad partner accepted the hospital president role, he interviewed and helped select his new partner. They were hardly strangers. Libby Raetz, RN, was the nursing director for the hospital's emergency department. Both had previously served on the board of a federally qualified health center. Both had been front-line clinicians in the community, Cary as a primary care physician and then as a hospitalist and Libby as certified emergency nurse. Both were active in their church. Their sons had been in school sports together, and both boys became certified as nursing assistants before college. Cary and Libby were professional and personal acquaintances who never expected to become halves of an official clinical executive leadership team. When Kathy Sanford interviewed them about how they experienced this change in their relationship, they were 3 years into their Dyad roles.

Kathy: Cary and Libby, thanks for taking time out of your busy lives to talk about life as a dyad. Cary, you have more experience at this type of management than Libby. She's your second CNO partner. You willingly entered into this model for a second time. So, there must have been a positive outcome from your first Dyad relationship. How would you describe that experience?

Cary: It was great. The CNO and CMO roles overlap in so many areas, and by working closely together, we were able to accomplish more than if we'd operated separately.

Kathy: Can you give me an example of what you accomplished together?

Cary: Well, one thing I'm proud of is the Leadership and Safety Rounds we initiated together. When the CMO and CNO go unit to unit, emphasizing ways to keep patients safe while providing high-quality care, it's obvious to all of the frontline teams that theirs is important work. I think it's an effective way to model clinical teamwork for the good of those we care for. And, it showed staff that both of us have a sincere interest in their well-being. We kept lists of issues staff members brought up, followed through on addressing those issues, and then reported back to staff about that follow through the next time we were on the unit. By doing this together, physicians, nurses, and other team members saw us as a united front.

Kathy: Was presenting as a united front important?

Cary: Yes, it was—and is, with Libby, too. We're going through so much change, and there are more challenges than other clinical leaders can cover in a day—or a week, sometimes! When others know we're working together and when they actually see us together, they're more comfortable going to either one of us for advice, assistance, or with issues. Because there are two of us available, it's easier for people to find one of us and things get addressed in a more timely way. That's better for the organization, the patients, the caregivers—and for us, too.

Kathy: So, with your first dyad partner, and with Libby, you're comfortable having the CNO address issues for from the medical staff?

Cary: Of course! What's important is getting the job done. It's about mutual respect, with no personal professional ego getting the way. We have to work together, include each other in all the clinical components and do what's right, regardless of whether we're working with doctors or nurses. In fact, in some cases, Kim (*his first dyad partner*) was more effective with certain physicians than I was. One surgeon always liked taking his problems to Kim for solutions, if he had a choice.

Libby: And the same holds true for nurses. They see Cary as their leader, too. Sometimes, they take clinical operation problems to him because they see him before they see me, but sometimes some personalities just "click" even if they aren't in the traditional nurse-to-nurse or doctor-to-doctor chain of command. We're a team, and either of us can solve problems.

Kathy: So, it sounds like both of Cary's dyads—Kim and, you, Libby—have been good with Cary!

Cary: Yes, Libby picked up the torch from Kim, and we've continued to grow as partners.

Kathy: Libby, what is it that makes Cary such a good dyad partner?

Libby: I believe that a successful dyad partnership is one where you learn from each other. Cary is an incredibly good listener. He is diligent about thanking people for what they do. People can tell that he really cares about them. I've watched him and learned from him. Being his dyad partner has made me a better leader.

Cary: Well, that goes both ways. Libby is one of the most positive people I know. She lifts spirits when times are tough. And she tackles tough issues head-on, no matter how unpleasant that can be. She's creative and has good, novel ideas. I've learned from her.

Kathy: It sounds like what is said about another partnership, a good marriage: The best are those in which each partner becomes a better person individually and when the two combine different skills to make a stronger whole. In your case, I hear you both saying each dyad partner becomes a better leader and that your individual personalities and skills complement each other to make a stronger team.

Libby: That's exactly right.

Kathy: I do have to ask, because you are different individuals, and you come from different professional cultures: Have you had major disagreements or friction over leadership styles or decisions? And, if so, how did you work them out?

Libby: We haven't really had any major clashes ….

Cary: But, if we ever did, we'd talk it out privately, behind closed doors. Then, once we'd agreed or settled an issue between the two of us, we'd present a united front in public.

Kathy: Back to that united front again!

Libby: It serves us well—there's none of this triangulation that can cause so much dysfunction in teams—none of that, go to Dad to complain about Mom or vice versa.

We once had to counsel and then remove a disruptive colleague from his leadership role. We did it together, and that's worked out well. Of course, he won't speak to either of us!

Kathy: The two of you certainly embody partnership. Not everybody has an official partner. How do others, those who aren't in a formal management role like yours, react to the two of you when you're both part of a larger team?

Cary: We've actually been part of a larger team where there was friction and fairly serious disagreements. We've been able to stand together on clinical issues that are important to patients, physicians, and other staff members. We believe we've been better able to bring balance to the value equation—where both cost and quality are essential to a successful organization. Clinicians have a stronger voice when physician and nurse leaders stand together.

Libby: I think the additional value we bring to larger teams is our obvious partnership. Just as Cary and I learn from each other, our other team members learn about teamwork by observing us.

Cary: We actually are deliberate about things we do to demonstrate teamwork. We make presentations together the way you and Steve (Kathy's dyad partner) do. People notice that, just like we noticed the seamless way you present every other power point slide when you present together. It's a powerful way to point out the effectiveness that can be achieved when nurses and doctors or nurse leaders and physician leaders are united in their passion for outstanding clinical care.

Kathy: Are people besides nurses and physicians noticing this partnership?

Libby: Yes! We present together at our board quality committee. As a result, board members see us as competent clinicians who have our leadership act together. Because we work for a Catholic organization, we've met together with the Diocese to discuss clinical issues of interest to the Church, and the clergy see us as a Dyad. Community members call on both of us when ethical issues come up.

Kathy: What are the things you think you've accomplished better as a Dyad than you would have as individual clinical leaders?

Libby: We're especially effective when there are personnel problems in one of both of your areas of responsibility. It's not easy for leaders to solve interpersonal team issues alone. I think both of us were pretty good at that sort of thing, but we're even better together. I mentioned how we worked together, first trying to help a clinician change his abusive ways and then removing him from his leadership role when he just couldn't change. We've also tackled the issue of a provider with a substance abuse problem. We've worked together to confront issues directly. We've referred two medical colleagues to the PULSE program for disruptive physicians. One doctor left our organizations when we intervened.

Cary: It's too bad that we can't help everyone change or become better team players, but we can't have a hospital where bullying is excused or ignored. The staff are appreciative and talk openly about how much better the working environment is because everyone knows that Libby and I stand together to make teamwork collaborative and communication civil.

Libby: We orient new staff together, and one of the points they all appreciate is that we have zero tolerance for disruptive behavior from anyone, regardless of how talented or smart they are—or how much income they generate for the hospital.

Cary: The value in our Dyad isn't just about personnel issues, though. We are proud of the work we did together on putting together a bundled payment as part of the hospital's orthopedic initiative. Having both of us at the table ensured that we knew the costs and clinical resources needed to make what some people see as just a financial model work well. Together, we brought knowledge of how to make the operation work.

Libby: We make our safety rounds together, too, so we're seen as both concerned about quality and safety. All of our team members want to stay focused on doing what's right for patients, knowing that both their clinical leaders do, too. Well, that helps everyone feel better about continuing the really difficult work of frontline care and still maintain the true caring they all started with.

Cary: Our Safety First Program, based on safety programs from the aviation and nuclear energy industries, is a new way of thinking. No matter how intuitively correct new things are they involve change. Change is tough for everyone—so it's important that we demonstrate, together, how important this particular program is.

Kathy: Can you give an example of how you made the hospital environment safer?

Cary: Sure. We had an issue with Bariatric patients refusing to allow staff to use the Bariatric lift to move them.

Libby: And some nurses who weren't using the lifts …

Cary: Patients even said they wouldn't come to our facilities if we insisted on using them, but we changed the hospital policy to require lift use on every patient over a certain weight. Libby and I stood firm on enforcing this policy.

Libby: Staff injuries were reduced …

Cary: And we haven't lost any patients!

Kathy: Have you had any surprises in this new style of leading? Or big learnings?

Cary: We've discovered it's a good idea to have a meeting before the meeting! Before any major meetings with our team members, we get together and make sure we're in agreement from the clinical side of things.

Libby: It's actually come pretty easy to us. We were friends and colleagues before we were Dyad partners, so it may have been easier for us. I really appreciate the leadership classes our organization offers. Dyads are encouraged to attend and learn management skills together. It's not equally easy for everyone, but we've mentored dyad teams who will work with or report to us—and it's rewarding to see them grow in leadership together.

Cary: It's been so natural and productive for us that I've been shocked when we've been part of larger state-wide groups. As a Dyad, Libby and I come together to big clinical tables—and she's the only nurse there! These groups are trying to tackle big challenges for the future. They're solving operational problems, and they don't include important hospital operations experts—the nurse leaders! It's mind boggling, but they don't know what they don't know—we're working together to help these business and finance leaders *see* and understand the value of a united nursing and physician leadership. We're a lot alike, but we're different, and we bring different skills and knowledge, which makes us a strong leadership team. Hospitals leave nurses out of so many things—I've heard leaders say, "Well, we would include them, but they're intimidated when we bring them to the table. They don't speak up, so we don't include them" … Hmm, we don't have that problem!

Kathy: You are a wonderful example of Dyad leadership! What would you say, individually, is the biggest benefit for you personally, to be part of this pair?

Cary: The best thing about being part of a Dyad is realizing you can't come up with all the ideas. Hospital management is so complicated. There are so many moving parts. Being a dyad leader with a partner who is bright, someone you respect and can trust to do what's best for patients and to share new possibilities—well, that's a blessing.

Libby: Senior leadership can be lonely sometimes. So much has to be kept confidential. It's wonderful to have a partner you can admire for clinical and leadership skills and who has your back. We can talk openly about anything, bounce ideas back and forth while knowing nothing we say to each other will be repeated outside our private conversation. We can give and get advice, and debate things in private. Plus having a great Dyad partner makes work fun.

Kathy: It seems you two were made to be Dyad partners even though you were brought together by chance.[1] Thanks for sharing your story and for choosing to lead.

A CONVERSATION WITH LEADERS: HOW DOES DYAD LEADERSHIP OR SHARED LEADERSHIP APPLY IN HOSPITAL MEDICINE?

Thomas Frederickson, Joe Mangiameli, and Amanda Trask

The idea of working in leadership pairs, and in working in teams to care for patients is growing. The following is a discussion on how teamwork works well in hospital medicine (often referred to as the "Hospital Medicine Service Line").

In hospital medicine, hospitalists have the opportunity to work in Dyads and teams every day. Depending on the role of the hospitalist, partnerships, and relationships can vary. "Everything we do as hospitalists depends on our ability to function well in teams, to organize teams, to bring people together in teams," says Thomas Frederickson, MD, SFHM, FACP, MBA, Medical Director, Hospital Medicine, Alegent Creighton Health. He, his Dyad partner, Joe Mangiameli, RN, MSN, and Amanda Trask, MBA, MHA, FACHE, CMPE, one of the national leaders of the

---

[1] Interviewer's note: Cary and Libby continue to serve as clinical Dyad partners in Nebraska. They've often marveled at the coincidences that brought both of them to their leadership positions and their formal partnership. They are both active in the community; both sat on the Board of a Federally Qualified Health Center that has been recognized for its outstanding provision of care to vulnerable populations. In Cary's office, he is proud to display the John F. Finegan Award for Outstanding Practice as a Family Physician. It was named for the Lincoln, MD who started the Lincoln Family Practice Program. It was awarded to him in 2006. Libby knows a bit about the honor that was Cary's to receive. John Finegan was her father.

Hospital Medicine Service Line, recently took part in a conversation about Dyads and teams. Together they addressed several questions.

HOW DOES THE MODEL OF DYAD LEADERSHIP APPLY DAY-TO-DAY IN HOSPITAL MEDICINE?

In a typical workday, a hospitalist is a potential co-leader of multiple teams. Traditionally, hospitalists have been thought of as "just another physician rounding on patients in the hospital." Until the recognition of the Dyadic (and larger team) leadership opportunity at the point of care is realized, the physician–clinician team has not been leveraged. While we aren't talking about formal, organizational chart Dyad partnerships, we believe even temporary, multiple teams benefit from co-leadership. Sometimes this is *more* than two leaders.

One example of co-leadership in the day-to-day routine of the hospitalists is when a hospitalist, nurse leader, and care management leader meet regularly with the patient and/or family to evaluate the patient's care plan. When this relationship is formalized into a care team, with the patient as the center of focus and member of the team, the patient's plan of care can be realized in a more timely manner. There is more complete information, input, and feedback from various clinicians. This relationship is often referred to as multidisciplinary rounds. In our case, we see it as sharing leadership.

Every team member has a voice in planning and delivering care. Reliance on the specific expertise of each care provider leads to better collaboration and allows all aspects of the patient's care plan to be considered.

HOW DOES THIS APPLY IN HOSPITAL MEDICINE MEDICAL PRACTICE MANAGEMENT?

As the industry of hospital medicine continues to mature, more and more value is placed on the team relationship between a hospital medicine physician leader and an administrative operational partner. The recognition of hospital medicine as a formalized medical practice has led to a strengthening of the physician leader and operational leader relationship.

By pairing a hospitalist leader with an operational leader, while matching the right personalities and unique talents, the leadership team is able to influence positive change and ensure success of the collective. It is not that any one person has more or less knowledge to offer, rather it's the power of the team that makes for greater strength and knowledge. One real-life example of this Dyad relationship is our leadership partnership at Alegent Creighton Health in Omaha, NE.

Joe Mangiameli, RN, MSN, is the Director for Hospital Medicine Services at Alegent Creighton Health. He is the administrative leader of the Hospital Medicine Service Line Dyad. He says, "As a Dyad, we try to leverage our expertise and relationships in the organization. We each bring different experiences to the table that complement the other's skills."

Tom Frederickson, MD (the physician leader of the Dyad), says, "First, it *has* to be a relationship. We have to understand each other. In everything we do in the program, we try to think strategically. It helps to have different backgrounds, expertise, relationships, experiences, and points of view."

Dr. Frederickson also indicated that "another real, practical aspect of our effectiveness is the ability to divide and conquer. We strategize about what needs to be done, appraise each other on our progress, and advise on directional changes to be made. One example of this is around process improvement. We had an opportunity to improve the revenue cycle by changing how we captured the physician charges. As a physician, I was able to explain to our physicians why it was important to do this and then provide education for the change. My administrative partner, Joe Mangiameli, was able to focus on other administrative aspects and work with other departments to ensure implementation of the changes. Our different strengths and responsibilities meshed together to get the job done. We helped each other out and moved more quickly through the project than if one of us had to lead it alone."

Both partners agree that their leadership Dyad, which is similar to a strong ambulatory practice management leadership design, encourages practice strategic planning, analytics, clinical collaboration, and application of practice leadership principles in a hospitalist practice environment.

HOW DO DYAD LEADERSHIP PRINCIPLES APPLY IN THE HOSPITAL ADMINISTRATOR RELATIONSHIP WITH HOSPITALISTS?

Hospital medicine leaders also have team relationships with the hospital C-suite. Since all hospitalist efforts and decisions affect the quality outcomes of patient care, there is a need to create dyad relationships with hospital medicine leaders and hospital leaders. We must bring the clinical and business side together for the success of the organization. And, of course, since hospitalists work closely with nursing, there is a natural partnership that needs to be nurtured and cemented with the CNO.

In both small and large complex healthcare organizations, creating formalized Dyadic relationships and ensuring frequent communication leads to a higher degree of collaboration, cooperation, respect, and trust. Both parties, hospital executive leaders and hospital medicine leaders, need to recognize the opportunity to cultivate a partnership relationship to ensure a full understanding of shared goals and pathways for the achievement better outcomes for our patients and organizations.

HOW DOES THIS EMPOWER HOSPITALISTS TO INFLUENCE THE INDUSTRY?

Hospitals are some of the highest cost venues in healthcare. And, since hospitalists fully focus on hospital care, this group of providers has the opportunity to significantly impact the cost of care for a population. In the next era of healthcare, ensuring the most appropriate use of acute care is a key to managing the costs. By enlisting the interests and input of hospitalists, healthcare organizations can achieve improved care in a population management scenario. Leveraging the dyad relationships enables hospitalists and organizations to shape the future of healthcare.

Working with multiple subject matter experts with complementary strengths on a common platform enhances not only the quality of the outcome but the timeliness as well. Patient care can improve, implementable plans for change can be stronger, the timeline for completion of a project can be improved, and more cost-effective operations can result. In addition, we can transform the hospital culture to be focused on quality, safety, and service to our patients. The results of leading together will be beneficial to them, their families, our caregivers, and our organizations.

REFERENCES

1. Staff. (November 1, 1999). *To err is human: Building a safer health system*. The Institute of Medicine of the National Academies.
2. Staff. (March 1, 2001) *Crossing the quality chasm: A new health system for the 21st century*. The Institute of Medicine of the National Academies.
3. Page, A. (Ed.) (2004). *Keeping patients safe: Transforming the work environment for nurses and patient safety*. Washington, DC: The National Academic Press.
4. Bishop, T. (March 21, 2013). Health care quality measurement for doctor's offices needs improvement. *Journal of American Medical Association (JAMA) Online*.
5. Corporate Author. (October 3, 2013). *ISMP medication safety alert*. The Institute for Safe Medication Practices.
6. Porter, M., & Lee, T. (October 2013). *Providers must lead the way in making value the overarching goal* (p. 19). Harvard Business Review.
7. Corporate Author. (December 4, 2013). *Quote of the day*. Advisory Board Daily Briefing.
8. Staff. (May 6, 2014). Consumer assessment of health providers and system (CAHPS). www.cms.gov, Center for Medicare and Medicaid Services, (http://www.cms.gov/Research-Statistics-Data-and-Systems/Research/CAHPS/index.html)
9. Kutney-Lee, A., McHugh, M., Sloane, D., et al. (2009). Nursing: A key to patient satisfaction. *Health Affairs, 28*(4), 669–677.
10. Randolph, W. (1995). Navigating the journey to empowerment. *Organizational Dynamics, 23*(4), 19–32.
11. Forrester, R. (2000). Empowerment: Rejuvenating a potent idea. *Academy of Management Executive, 14*(3), 67–80.
12. Doherty, R. B., & Crowley R. A. (2013). Principles supporting dynamic clinical care teams: An American College of Physicians Position Paper. *Annals of Internal Medicine, 159*, 620–626.
13. Krause, E. A. (1996). *Death of the guilds: Professions, states, and the advance of capitalism, 1930 to the present*. New Haven and London: Yale University Press, 36, 38–44.
14. Thomas E. J., Sexton, J. B., & Helmreich, R. L. (2003). Discrepant attitudes about teamwork among critical care nurses and physicians. *Critical Care Medicine, 31*(3), 956–959.
15. McCarthy, D., Mueller, K., Wren, J. (2009). Mayo Clinic: Multidisciplinary Teamwork, Physician-Led Governance, and Patient-Centered Culture Drive World-Class Health Care. A Case Study: Organized Health Care Delivery System. New York: The Commonwealth Fund Publication No. 1306, 27, p. 2.
16. Baldwin, K. S., Dimunation, N., Alexander, J. (2011). Health care leadership and the dyad model. *Physician Executive Journal of Medical Management, 37*(4), 66–69.
17. Patton, P., & Pawar, M. (2012). New clinical executive models: One system's approach to chief nursing officer-chief medical officer co-leadership. *Nursing Administration Quarterly, 36*(4), 320–324.

Chapter 9

Forming Dyad-Led Teams and Multiple Partnerships

W hen Kathy's book, *Leading With Love* (1), was published in 1999, she got a lot of feedback, both from people she knew and from others who found ways to contact her. Some people liked the concepts in general or expressed interest in a particular idea. Others gave advice about how she could have sold more books if she had changed a couple of words. For example, a management consultant suggested that "love" might be too strong a word for the title—he thought "caring" would go over better with male readers. Another felt that concepts related to a female leadership style would be more acceptable if it was giving an androgynous label instead of "maternalism."

All in all, the people who took time to contact the author offered their opinions with thoughtful and polite words. However, one e-mail from Germany, after a European publisher produced a German language version of the book, was less courteous, which makes it the most memorable.

The writer was not a fan. "It is women like you," he wrote, "who have destroyed the American economy. Stop spreading this pap about loving your employees. We've babied workers and given them everything ever since women have wormed their way into management. Work is not a place for all this touchy feely junk. Industry will not survive anywhere in the world if people don't start doing their jobs and stop questioning their leaders. Productivity in America is dismally low because of what you are preaching. All this attention focused on the happiness of workers instead of concern for the success of the corporation is going to put those workers you say you love right out of work. You and your kind make me sick because you are destroying the world." (These are not his exact words. We have changed a few because this is not an R-rated book.)

It was obvious that this man had not read the book. If he had, he would have known it was not about "making employees happy," but about conscious leadership attention to balancing the needs of organizations, communities, customers, leaders, and employees, for the good of all. The e-mail implied a few other things, too. It could be inferred that the writer was not happy with women in management and that he was angry about something, most likely something that had happened in his working life, *probably something very personal.*

Work *is* personal for all of us. Many, if not most, of us spend more of our waking time at work than we do at home. Our careers, our jobs, our teams are all important, if only because we depend on them to support us in meeting our own financial needs. Our experiences, good and bad, influence how we feel about the company, team-mates, and ourselves. Regardless of how the e-mail writer above feels, there is a grow-ing body of research that caring for those we work with is not only good for them but also a good leadership practice.

Recent longitudinal research by management professors Sigal Barsade (Wharton) and Olivia O'Neill (George Mason) shows that employee work connections that are warm and affectionate lead to a positive emotional culture among work groups. Where this occurs, employees express more job satisfaction, and greater commit-ment to their organizations. One result of this is lower job turnover and reduced absenteeism (2). Barsade and O'Neill call this kind of affection for team members "companionate love," to differentiate it from romantic love. (Sanford used the word "maternalistic love" for the same reason.)

Barsade and O'Neill's studies were first conducted in healthcare settings, but then expanded to a broad range of industries where they found that "Regardless of the industry baseline, to the extent that there's a greater culture of companionate love, that culture is associated with greater satisfaction, commitment, and account-ability" (2).

Of course, we would have been attentive to their first research studies even before they were extended beyond healthcare. As an industry entering a new era, complete with a slightly murky future (none of us has an exact crystal ball of what healthcare will look like 10, 20, or 30 years from now), we need committed, engaged employ-ees more than ever. It is difficult to undergo massive change in any case, and with unhappy team members, the size of the challenge is multiplied at least 10-fold. Healthcare organizations survey their employees and medical staffs about their sat-isfaction, and leaders talk about the importance of engaged employees almost as much as we discuss the satisfaction of our patients/customers. We also believe that employee satisfaction directly effects that customer satisfaction. The information in Display 9-1 gives credence to that belief.

Prior chapters have talked about how each person comes to work with a background that includes socialization from a variety of cultures (professional, gender, family of origin, religion, race, ethnicity, etc.). In this chapter, we are concerned with a culture

---

Display 9-1 **A Correlation Between Healthcare Employee Satisfaction, Quality, and Customer Satisfaction**

RESEARCH FINDINGS

Disengaged employees negatively affect quality of care and patient satisfaction (3).

Happier employees lead to patient loyalty (4).

Employee morale is strongly correlated with patient satisfaction scores (5).

Employee satisfaction, quality, and patient satisfaction are all interrelated (6).

Satisfied nurses make less medication errors (7).

Hospital departments with higher levels of employee satisfaction provide better experiences for patients (8).

RN job satisfaction has significant effect on patient satisfaction with nursing care and overall patient satisfaction (9).

Nursing work environment is significantly correlated with all Hospital Consumer Assessment of Healthcare Providers and Systems (HCAHPS) measures (10).

---

that is a conglomeration of all these cultures—the culture of a workplace, or more specifically, the culture of teams who work with Dyad leaders.

TEAMS AND CULTURE

Both of us, separately and together, have been hearing the word "culture" a lot lately. Sometimes, it is used to describe the good things about an organization, or at least what someone aspires to or wants to believe (or wants others to believe about it). We see Google proclaiming that "we strive to have an open culture—in which everyone is a hands on contributor and feels comfortable sharing ideas and opinions" (11). TRX Training Centers claims that their company culture "blurs the lines between work and play" (12). BAE Systems, whose products include military, defense, security, and cyber intelligence services, says "we have a culture of total performance—a commitment to the highest standards in every aspect of the way we do business. This is guided through four embodying elements: customer focus, financial performance, program execution, and responsible behavior" (13).

Do these descriptions paint a picture of how it would be to work for these very different organizations? How about these comments about corporate culture from two healthcare systems:

> "Among other tenets, the Mayo Model of Care is a big part of our distinctive culture, which is rooted in the ideals of our founders: teamwork, collegiality, professionalism, mutual respect, and commitment to progress for the organization and individuals. We foster a culture committed to teamwork and we put team success ahead of individual success" (14).

"In order to encourage transformation, a capacity for innovation and change must be forged into an organization' culture … this type of culture expects innovation and change of its leaders, and encourages, supports, and rewards them accordingly. We know not every attempt to innovate change is successful, but we want our leaders to know it is safe to try."

—Kevin Lofton, CEO, Catholic Health Initiatives (15)

"Culture" is also used to describe big concepts that an organization is either pursuing or trying to eradicate. On the pursuance side, for example, the American Hospital Association speaks of a *culture of quality* on its home page (16). Many of our hospital colleagues talk about a *culture of safety*. Others speak of their cultures of innovation or teamwork, or fun.

What healthcare leaders want to eradicate (at least we hope we all want to get rid of these if/where they exist) are *a culture of fear* (17), *a culture of nonsupport for innovation* (18), and *a culture of rigid silo work* (19).

To reiterate, we are focusing here on the culture of the teams that work with Dyads. However, in order to do that we must remember that specific teams do have cultures. They are part of the larger organizational culture, and they are influenced by the multiple cultures of every single individual team member.

ABOUT TEAMS

Throughout this book we have sometimes referred to teams managed by Dyad leaders as either teams or work groups or groups. (We did this to make the words we use more interesting by avoiding the monotony of repeating the same word in close proximity.) This would earn us a scolding from a number of management leaders, who point out that groups and teams are not the same thing. Groups are a "collection of people with common boundaries and who sometimes share broad objectives." Teams are "groups focused on tasks with narrow objectives" (20). In comparison with groups, teams have a stronger sense of belonging by members of a team, and members have more specialized and differentiated roles (21). An example might be that a cardiovascular surgeon belongs to a *group* of all of the organization's cardiovascular surgeons, and is also a member of an interdisciplinary *team* whose objective is to standardize clinical practices as part of the goal to improve quality of care provided to all of the system's cardiovascular patients.

The popularity of teams and teamwork as a subject for research has grown over time, as has the use of them as work models. It's been estimated that 85% of large companies utilize teams to accomplish their work (22). Research supports the efficacy of this, as team decision making has been shown to "be more effective than the decisions of individual members" (23). The higher productivity in the United States, where we actually use less employees to accomplish the same work (in spite of Kathy's e-mail detractor's claim to the contrary), is probably partially due to "the switch from assembly line work to teamwork" (24).

Dyad leadership is most frequently established in healthcare organizations when teams are diverse. That's because one of the driving rationales for appointing leaders from different professional cultures is to co-manage multidisciplinary teams. The good news for Dyad leaders is that research supports the superiority of diverse teams in decision making. The challenge is that while they make "better, more informed decisions," they "have a harder time reaching consensus" (24). That makes intuitive sense, of course, because of the variety of professional and other cultures from which individual team members come. People often identify with their jobs (or professions) more than their organizations, so as a result, they become less supportive of other departments in the organization. However, on the plus side, multiprofessional teams can "help leaders interpret environmental ambiguities" (25). This is a strength in these days of less than well-defined futures for healthcare systems! Diversified groups contribute to "surveillance of the environment outside of the organization and provide boundary spanning" (26). We know we need this as we break down silos to become true healthcare systems rather than a collection of silos providing separate, and sometimes duplicative, services to our communities.

The move from more homogeneous silos to multidisciplinary teams will require deliberate attention from Dyad leaders. As we've explained, influence is strongest when people are similar, and *by definition*, similarity is less in a more diverse group. There may be inequities in influence when it is *not* appropriate (as when it's based on cultural conditioning rather than expert knowledge of a particular subject). Of course, higher level of influence *is* appropriate when a project or decision has specific needs for the expertise of an expert team member. For example, it is appropriate for the pharmacist on a team to have relatively more influence than other team members when discussing drugs, but not when discussing the best procedure for preventing patient care falls, even though drugs may be involved in these. Individuals from groups that have considered themselves to be superior to other groups may have trouble accepting equality of team members when working together on projects. Some team members, because of tradition or culture, may have more trouble being heard by other team members—and that defeats the purpose of them being on the team. Each person is in place to bring his or her unique skills and talents to the table. The table has to be prepared (by the Dyad leaders of the team) so he or she can serve these up!

Researchers on what makes multidisciplinary teams most effective in meeting organizational goals agree that every team member's input to decision making should be treated as important and every member's response to decisions already made should be important, too. Each team member must be able to air issues, seek clarifications, and engage in "constructive conflict." However, constructive conflict is only constructive if it concerns opinions on what is the best way forward to meet the *team's* goals, which must be in support of the organization's goals. As Bernard Bass and other management experts emphasize, "members should be replaced if they are unable to overcome protecting their own turf or show mistrust of others or lack of commitment to collective intentions" (24).

The protection of turf that could interfere with teamwork might be on behalf of an individual's personal job territory, or, as we pointed out earlier, on behalf of an entire group such as the individual team member's profession. Because cultures have such strong influence on people, Dyad leaders should expect that some of the behaviors Bass says should call for removal from a team will occur. We believe that putting a clinical (or other) multidisciplinary team together without anticipating some of this behavior is naive. One individual's professional culture has taught him that the profession is more important than the organization and makes him the most important member of the team. Another person's gender experiences has taught her that she cannot trust the motives of males to do what is right for all unless it furthers his career. A third might mistrust every team member of another race because of personal experiences with prejudice or inequities.

We also think that immediate expulsion from the team for any sign of these tendencies is counterproductive. If members cannot overcome cultural conditioning or forgive past perceived injustice and lack of trust, they will eventually need to be removed from the team for the sake of the organization. After all is said and done, the team must be able to function effectively, and it won't be able to do that if individual members can't learn to be good team players. The important words in the preceding sentence are the first four—*after all is said and done*. It is up to the Dyad leaders to *do the "all"* before banishing the errant team member! Many initially poor team members can become productive with education, coaching, and leadership.

A competent Dyad leadership team will know who their team members are, consider what cultural biases they *may* be bringing to the group, and anticipate what issues these may cause. They will plan together how to avoid issues by taking action before they happen and then to act, if, despite best efforts, the problems listed by Bass do occur. (The partners are preventing problems before they occur, but preparing an action plan in case, despite best efforts, they do occur. They aren't, in other words, "waiting for the burglar to break in before they buy the burglar alarm.")

As with almost everything about management, there is research and management expertise in the literature on what good leaders do when they are aware of potential issues. For example, leaders of effective teams facilitate their members' discussions about teamwork and encourage members to give honest, open feedback to each other about their team skills (27). The leaders are responsible for pointing out and appropriately managing "boundary spanning" conflicts (28). This is a term applied whenever historical silos are bridged. For clinicians (and others), it is when traditional boundaries between individual professions and jobs are no longer "sacred" and other people or professions begin to perform work or take on responsibilities once believed to belong only to one group. As we intuitively surmised, "leaders are more effective when they are proactive and assess potential problems before they occur" (29).

Of course, the most proactive thing managers can do is to hire people who have team mindsets. In their book, *Empowered Teams*, Wellins, Byham, and Wilson point out that, "Many teams have discovered that good selection of (team members) is a critical and often irreversible part of the process (of forming functional teams). If the team is inadvertently stacked with dysfunctional members, it will be difficult to change their behaviors or remove them from the team without disrupting the cohesiveness of the team" (30). In a perfect world, all potential employees would be tested for their teamwork skills before being hired, if the work they need to accomplish requires teamwork. (There are a *few* jobs that can be done all alone in isolation, so teamwork might not be needed there!) In Chapter 7, we talked about preselection testing that can be done for leaders, including Dyad partners, which will give employers a psychological profile that can guide hiring decisions. However, the world is not perfect. In times of limited budgets, the expense of this type of testing for every potential team member might be something that organizations choose to forgo, since the number of people who will need to work in teams is so high.

In the place of preemployment personality testing, good interviewing skills can be used to help with selecting team members. While interviews and reference checks are not perfect, they do help interviewers get a better perception of job fit, when the interviewers are skilled, and know what personal qualities they are screening for. Interview questions need to be crafted to "get at" these specific traits. Human Resources professional Tracie Grant shares sample questions that can be used to explore the interviewees' team skills in Display 9-2.

Even with exquisite interviewing, however, sometimes the people who are interviewed and hired are not the same people who show up for work! In other words, what some people say they have done (or will do in a new position) when *applying* for a job doesn't match actual performance when they *start* the job. This can be because of their blind spots (as in Johari window) or their conscious choice to say what they think the interviewer wants to hear. In addition, as Dyad leaders put together teams of people from separate silos in order to thrive in the next era of healthcare, they may have no choice but to add team members who they either know or strongly suspect will have problems with teamwork, based on their professional cultures. Finally, it will be a rare opportunity when a Dyad partnership gets to choose all members of their teams. Most of the time, many of the team members are already in place or have been selected when the Dyad becomes their leaders.

Whether the leaders get to choose their team members or "inherit" them, one of the first proactive actions of Dyad partners is to begin the steps of team building. Multiple

---

Display 9-2 Interview Questions for Selection of Multidisciplinary Team Members

▶ Tell me about a time when you had to work closely with peers as a team in order to be successful.
▶ Describe a situation where you were not successful participating in a multidisciplinary team.
▶ Tell me about a time when you had to put your ambitions after the needs of the team.
▶ Tell me about a time when you had to build consensus with many stakeholders before moving forward with an initiative or project.
▶ Tell me about your experience with a highly matrixed organization. What did you find satisfying? Challenging?
▶ Describe a politically sensitive situation that you were in and how you handled it.
▶ How do you hold others accountable to achieve results? Give me an example.
▶ Tell me about your work with team member engagement and alignment.
▶ Tell me about a time when you had a part in building a new team, department, or initiative from the ground up.

The key to making these questions into a great interview is the in-depth probing questions that follow. Ask questions to understand the whole story, the individual's part in it, and the outcome.

From Tracie Grant, Director, Human Resources, Catholic
Health Initiatives, Denver, Colorado

---

researchers have noted that teams develop in a consistent set of phases. It has been pointed out that groups must work together for a period of time before they can behave as a team, so to expect teamwork just because a group has been brought together to accomplish particular objectives is unrealistic. High-performing teams start off well (with leadership that understands the steps of team building) while low-performing teams fumble and stumble when just getting started, and *often never recover* from this (31), so it's imperative that early work is done to turn a group into a team.

The stages that teams progress through are commonly termed forming, storm- ing, norming, and performing. Early researchers thought these phases were always in order and separate from each other, but later studies show they can overlap and sometimes alternate (32). So, if you want to sigh with relief or "high-five" your Dyad partner when a storming period seems to be over, that is okay, but don't believe that team conflict is over for good.

Dyad leaders will probably be in a hurry to get to the performing stage (where team members begin to make progress toward the team goals) because of the per- ceived need to respond to a changing environment as quickly as possible. The part- ners need to understand the need to *manage* each stage and not try to "gloss over" or ignore the experiences of the group members. If this isn't done, the group may *never* perform at a high functioning level, as pointed out in the research referenced above.

In the forming stage, team members get oriented to other team members, the Dyad leaders, and the stated purpose for the team's existence. At this point, members are described as being polite. In the storming phase, conflict becomes evident, as members jockey for position, try to exert status differentiation, and respond to both with emotion. During norming, group cohesion develops, members begin to communicate and develop norms. When they finally get to performing, team member functional roles have been established, relationships are clear, and tasks are effectively performed (33).

Teams are fully developed only when they attain a high degree of "shared purpose, commitment, trust, and drive" (34). Given the professional cultures of members and deeply ingrained status differentiation in healthcare (as described earlier in this book), the storming period has the potential of crippling future team accomplishments if Dyad leaders do not take active steps to develop teamwork. This is not the time for normally laissez-faire managers to leave the team to its own devices and imagine they will "figure it out on their own." It may not be the best time for totally democratic leadership (even though this style, in which leaders share decision making with others, *is* desirable once a team of experts is educated to solve problems together). This period of team formation probably calls for a mix of *reinforcement* leadership, in which the Dyad leaders consistently approve the correct performance of members and make suggestions for improvement (35), or a bit of authoritarian leadership directed at individuals who are immature in teamwork skills and inexperienced in treating others as equals (36).

TEAM BUILDING FOR THE DYAD'S WORK GROUP

People who have been in organizations for any period of time probably have opinions, and sometimes deep emotional reactions, to anything labeled as *team building*. These can range from the positive ("it was the best thing we ever did to change our group into a functional working team") to negative. ("It is a horrible waste of time as well as money.") We've been around long enough to know that at least some of the people reading this book are already rolling their eyes. We can almost hear your thoughts or verbal groan: "Oh, no, they're not going to suggest another ridiculous exercise. Not another event where we have to describe our personalities as musical notes, or tell two truths and a lie to each other so they can guess which is untrue, or list our good and bad traits, or give each other step by step instructions on how to do things like bake a cake, or fall straight back into each other's arms so we can learn to trust we'll be caught before we get hurt."

That's not the kind of team building we want to talk about here, although we are not discounting these exercises as ways to get to know each other as people *and* to have fun together. (One of our own regular exercises at weekly team meetings is to have a few members draw seemingly mundane questions out of a "story jar," which they answer. Last week's question was "What did you eat for lunch in school? Did you take lunch or buy it? Describe your lunchbox, if you had one." Usually the answers elicit comparisons to other team member's experiences and lots of laughter. This was certainly true when one of our very professional, seemingly straightlaced, health conscious team members revealed that rather than spend the lunch money his parents gave him for food in high school, he bought cigarettes and went to the high school smoking lounge!)

Since we think knowing each other, laughing together, and having fun makes the environment less stressful even during times when work pressures can cause high anxiety and tension, we utilize and enjoy these exercises. These types of group activities do contribute to the team culture, and having fun at work can become an important group norm. However, what we want to talk about now is the work involved for Dyad leaders and their teams to build a team infrastructure that will support the evolution of a high-functioning multidisciplinary team. We want to help Dyad leaders avoid what Patrick Lencioni labels the five dysfunctions of teams—absence of trust, fear of conflict, lack of commitment, avoidance of accountability, and inattention to results (37).

William Dyer, of Brigham Young University, wrote his book on team building based on 25 years of working with a variety of organizations. He describes the characteristics of effective teams as: possessing clear goals that are understood and accepted by all team members; existing in a climate of trust and support; identifying and working through differences between people rather than ignoring, suppressing, or allowing them to build into open conflict; and populating with members who understand and "accept their roles in the work unit and how they fit into the overall framework of both the team and the organization" (38). His list of tasks for new teams (which he says are basically the same as those of established teams that are not as functional as they could be) are to build relationships, establish climate, and "work out methods for setting goals, solving problems, making decisions, ensuring follow-through and completion of tasks, developing collaboration of effort, establishing lines of open communication, and ensuring an appropriate support system that will let people feel accepted and yet keep issues open for discussion and disagreement."

How can Dyad leaders plan to address each of Dyer's tasks during the stages of their team's formation? We have suggestions, gleaned from both the literature and our own experiences. A good time for beginning to build relationships is from the very beginning, during the "polite" days of forming. Dyad leaders need to model respectful partnership behaviors, in which they deliberately present concepts together, co-chair meetings, support each other's ideas, and avoid any of the "little things" (like title inequality) that indicate they are anything other than equal leaders of the group. They need to pay particular attention to avoidance of "triangulation."

Triangulation is a psychological term first used extensively to explain issues in families, which is also now commonly used in organizations. The word describes behavior of three group members (family or work team) we'll label as members A, B, and C. In triangulation, member A, rather than speak directly to member B about an issue, disagreement, or problem, communicates with member C about member B. We have seen this commonly play out when members A and C are from the same cultural professional, gender, or other "tribe," of which member B is not. So, for example, a female nurse member of the team, upset by behavior of a physician member, complains to the female nurse Dyad leader, rather than confronting the male physician she is upset with. This behavior is common and occurs because of fear (when it is believed that confronting person B will cause us discomfort or retaliation), bias (a belief that "person B is incapable of changing anyway because he comes from that self-centered, narcissistic profession"), a desire to be rescued (person A hopes that person C will take care of the problem for her), or lack of skill or comfort in relationship preserving confrontation (person A fears that the relationship will be impaired beyond repair). When the team is co-led, triangulation can also be a conscious tactic to "split" the leaders, play one against the other, and therefore (maybe) not have to behave or perform according to group norms or organizational expectations.

Dyad leaders are susceptible to triangulation because we are members of different cultures and (like all people) most easily influenced by people who are like us. We may even have long-standing friendships with team members from our own culture. It's essential to acknowledge this and actively work to avoid allowing it to happen. The partners need to agree up front that when a team member attempts this tactic, the Dyad leader in the "C" position will cut off the conversation, not listen to the complaint about his partner, and insist that person A speak directly to person B. (There is an exception to this "not listening" to person B part of the agreement. If person A is seeking coaching on how best to communicate with person B, person C can listen to the issue, give advice on how he has best learned to communicate with person B or members of her culture, and then insist that person A will not only approach person B directly but will report back on having done so. In that case, person C must hold person A accountable for caring enough about team cohesion and interpersonal relationships to do this.)

Establishing the climate must begin in the forming stage, and will be very important during storming. Dyad leaders should, early on, work with the group to establish norms, knowing that is very likely people will forget some of these when conflicts arise. Norms and team rules should be discussed, agreed on, and *documented*. (That documentation is going to be important when the storm breaks!) Among the norms should be team rules that address Dyer's list: how the team will set goals, solve problems, make decisions, ensure follow through and completion of tasks, collaborate, communicate, and ensure that every voice is heard in discussions. The expectation of civility should also be discussed as a group norm. Civility describes what courtesy, consideration and respect will look like, even when people disagree. It's surprising how often team members, in the heat of discussion, are simply rude to each other.

It's also not uncommon for individuals not to recognize that others *perceive* them as rude.

Kathy once convened a meeting of obstetrical (OB) medical staff and nursing staff to discuss how they could communicate better with each other. During the meeting, nurses stated that one physician in particular was short-tempered when nurses asked questions and was rude to them on the telephone. The chairman of the OB department was solicitous. "That's terrible," he said, "give me his name and I will speak to him." Three nurses answered in chorus, "It's *you*." The physician was genuinely shocked, and to his credit, sought further input on why he was perceived as rude and *changed the way he communicated* to become among the *most* civil medical team members.

Dialogue and documentation of group agreement on these norms will be more effective if actual potential issues are talked about and written down. For example, it may be very easy for a member who comes from a high-status profession to honestly and earnestly agree during the forming stage that he believes every member is equal, has the right to be treated with the same respect as other members, and will be encouraged to voice disagreement. Yet, when the storming phase begins, he may interrupt others, openly scoff at their inputs, and even get annoyed if he is addressed by his first name in a meeting. Having written examples that he agreed to, along with the rest of the team, will be immeasurably helpful in addressing unacceptable behaviors (defined as behaviors that the groups has already agreed are not part of their norms or which will impede growth of team cohesiveness). If team members are unable, or unwilling, to discuss examples of what will be acceptable, Dyad leaders will need to bring up potential scenarios, and document, with the group, how these will be addressed.

If you think that talking about and documenting specific examples of how team norms will be acted out is "overkill" for documenting norms, please remember that different cultures, and different individuals, don't always perceive spoken or written words the same way. The entire group make agree on the generic rule that "all members of the group will be treated respectfully" without actually understanding what other members think is the behavior that exhibits respect. It takes time to have these discussion early in team development, and extra time and effort to document them, but in the long run, the team will be stronger and have an easier time getting through storming.

In 1963, Clovis Shepherd wrote in his book on the sociology of small groups that "a small group does not become successful by ignoring differences, and demanding that members love one another and spend much time together" (39). While recent studies seem to indicate that the latter part of his statement might not be as true today as his research indicated then, we agree that the first part is still true. Groups do not become successful by ignoring differences. Part of Dyad-led team conversations should be an acknowledgement that members do come from different cultures. It should be recognized that their cultural differences and experiences will enrich the group. This should be followed by the reasons for the team's existence and the individual member's inclusion: the organization's mission, vision, goals, and the team's part in meeting those goals through specific objectives and responsibilities. All team members should agree (out loud and for the rest of the team to hear) that they support all of these and that they understand the culture of the group cannot be subverted by individual cultures. One norm that will help this new culture to develop will be an agreement that members will care enough to tell each other when they perceive less than full allegiance to this agreement. The principles of caring confrontation should be reviewed *more* than once, as they apply to various examples of when they *should* occur (Display 9-3).

Display 9-3 A Review of Caring Confrontation

Most of us have worked in organizations (at some time in our careers) where we've been among colleagues who marvel at what seems to be management's lack of attention to when leaders *or* team members appear to be less than competent, out of step with the organization's professed values, or openly working to block the company's progress toward stated goals. When a perception that nothing will be done about problem behaviors becomes widespread, employees can become disheartened, less engaged, and more likely to become enactors of problem behaviors themselves. They begin to believe that leaders are also not competent *or* don't care enough about the organization and employees to take action. This is *one* reason it's essential for leaders to hold team members accountable for their conduct as well as their progress toward goals and objectives.

Leaders are *not* the only ones who should hold others accountable. All team members have a stake in what other team members do when their deeds influence the work environment. Everyone can learn and use caring confrontation in their team relationship.

Confrontation is not easy for many of us, but it can be learned. Caring confrontation skills should be discussed and described when teams set up norms. Individuals who have difficulty with this may need individual coaching.

It's important to understand the why, what, and how when choosing to confront another team member. It is caring when we *respectfully* communicate our own thoughts and observations because we care enough about *something* to risk the discomfort this might cause. In other words, we care about *something* (the organization, team goals, relationships, or another person), which is the "why" for confrontation. We communicate our needs, wants, or perceptions. This is the "what" we do in confrontation. We do this in a respectful manner. This is the "how" of confrontation. Caring confrontation is *not* harsh criticism. It is not simple accusations of wrong doing. Done well, it provides information that the other person can choose to use.

In David Augsberger's book on caring confrontation, he reminds us to

- ▶ Confront only with real and genuine concern
- ▶ Confront tactfully (gently)
- ▶ Confront constructively (without blaming, shaming, or attempting to punish)
- ▶ Confront with acceptance and trust (assuming a positive intent on the other person's part even if behavior has been less than civil or acceptable)
- ▶ Confront clearly (state what you personally observe, how you feel or sense others feel, and what you suggest could be done better in the future) (40)

Dyad leaders building their teams and establishing a team culture must pay attention to each of these tasks. This will take transparent, open communication with the entire group and, in some cases, candid discussions with subsets or individual team members. Some members may have a more difficult time adhering to group norms, and part of the Dyad leadership responsibility is to appropriately coach, educate, or counsel (as in corrective counseling), and/or remove those members who are disruptive to team cohesion and development of a group that cares about each other as well as the organization.

THE EMOTIONAL CULTURE OF THE TEAM

Barsade and O'Neill's study on companionate love in organizations and its positive correlation to job satisfaction and decreased turnover (referenced above) is something Dyad leaders should pay attention to. It certainly appears to correlate with an annual survey (done by the recruitment and staffing firm NSI) of literature on the largest group of professionals in healthcare. That survey invariably includes relationships with other team members and managers as a top reason for nurses leaving or *staying* with a healthcare system.

Sanford postulated in 1998 (41) that theoretical management techniques come to naught when they are missing balanced and loving concern for customers, communities, employees, and organizations. She compared great leadership to great parenting, and work groups to families. Some very successful organizations are making this same work–family correlation and subscribing to the idea that employee teams do want to be cared about by those they work with. Lowe's, the home improvement store chain, for example, put out a 2012 report that sounds like it was adapted straight from *Leading with Love*. They believe that they must balance responsibility to employees and shareholders with commitment to customers and communities (42).

The *Men's Wearhouse*, another chain store group, shares on line that its "core set of values include nurturing, growing together, admitting mistakes, promoting happy and healthy lifestyles, enhancing a sense of community, and striving to become self-actualized people" (43). That certainly sounds like an environment where employees are cared for.

In a Harvard Business Review Blog about Barsade and O'Neill's research, they share that other large organizations are interested in creating or maintaining caring cultures. They reference Pepsi-Cola's management principle of "Caring" and Whole Foods' management value of "Love." They share that Zappos (the online shoe company) openly describes itself this way: "we are more than a team—we are a family. We watch out for each other, care for each other, and go above and beyond for each other" (44). In our own industry, we have indicators that caring and love are not felt by team members. According to Paul Spiegelman and Brett Berrett, authors of *Patients Come Second*, the healthcare industry (which is supposed to be a business about caring for others), is woefully poor about caring for each other. Speigelman and Berrett point to the silo problem we've identified in this book. They describe physicians as highly trained technicians, hospital administrators as highly educated executives, and nurses as extremely compassionate and competent caregivers who have not learned to work together as a team or how to treat each other well.

As healthcare insiders, these authors assert that poor patient care experiences in healthcare organizations will not improve until hospital cultures are changed by whatever it takes to get these different groups to learn to care about each other (45). Dyad leadership is one of the tools to accomplish this. We believe that organizations who thoughtfully and carefully plan, install, and utilize the Dyad model of leadership will lead healthcare to what Malcolm Gladwell describes as a tipping point (46). When enough Dyad partners learn to respect and care for each other, and then spread this culture to their multidisciplinary teams, we will be on the road to changing the entire healthcare culture so that we can transform the system for our employees, communities, and customers.

If this sounds impossible, consider that Gladwell's well-argued assertion is that minor alterations, when they are carefully conceived and put into practice, can result in transformational consequences for individuals, organizations, and industries. This new model of leadership is not minor but will only change relationships among the major players in healthcare if it is, indeed, carefully *conceived and implemented*. That means just what it says: organizations that are interested in Dyad leadership cannot just *tell* two leaders they are now co-leaders. They need to develop their Dyad model so that individuals become true partners who can then develop *their* teams to not only work together to accomplish goals but to establish a culture of caring.

It is likely that at least some of the members of the Dyad-led team have become disillusioned with healthcare in general and their organizations in particular over time. Some may come to the multidisciplinary team as cynics who have lost faith that we can ever change the system or age-old relationships. They may find it hard to believe that they will be treated as equals in the group, that the leaders are true partners, or that they are cared for as individuals. Others may be apathetic. Still others might think the current system has worked well for them and are angry that the world is changing. Team building could be seen as manipulation by management, or just another fad that will soon pass, leaving the organization and those who work there no better off than before.

Seth Kahn, in his book on change, says of his management consulting experience, "In 75% of the cases I have encountered, apathetic, cynical, and antagonistic people can be overcome with personal handling. This is an extraordinary percentage. This means the issue is how they are perceived and treated rather than insurmountable opposition" (47). His suggestion, based on experience, is to tell disaffected team members that you want to understand their points of view; then listen carefully, with empathy to what they have to say; ask them for advice as to how you can work together; give them your opinion on this; and be honest about where you disagree. These are steps to diffuse any emotional antagonism.

V. Clayton Sherman claims in his book, *Creating the New American Hospital* (written before the emphasis on healthcare systems but still valid for its emphasis on the need for change), that employee disengagement is because "job security has not been provided, abuse of staff is tacitly allowed, dissatisfaction and turnover is high, and employees are undertrained and underutilized, illustrating a belief that people can't do more or better than they do now" (48). Since he wrote this, in 1993, job security has become even more tenuous, as the work of providing care is moving to new sites. This, along with the other issues he lists is still a problem for the "traditional" healthcare employees (nurses and others). They are now also a problem for their physician colleagues.

The idiom, "What you focus on determines what you miss" can be applied to Sherman's concern that the emphasis hospitals place on finance has come at a cost to employee satisfaction and engagement. He, and others, believe that a healthcare organization's first priority should be to its people, which will then lead to better care of customers and the work that will make the organization successful. Many current systems continue to focus on finance. Dyad leaders can widen the organization's lens to include its people, starting with a caring culture for their own multidisciplinary teams.

One way to begin is to take the time to help group members remember why they came into healthcare in the first place. Members can be encouraged to share the most joyful times they've experienced as healthcare professionals. Doing this, in team meetings, reminds individuals that they have made a positive difference in other's lives (we're betting, based on our experiences, that the most joyful times will almost all be about this!) The sharing also helps team members know each other better and begins to change perceptions of who each of them *really* is—once the trappings of different professions and educations are stripped away. Knowing each other can be the beginning of trust.

Another method that can be used to help teams learn to care about each other is to utilize personality tests that all members of the team take, and then have the results shared, and explained, to the group. (Some of these tools were shared in Chapter 7.) It is easier to work together when members understand the strengths and weaknesses of each team member. It is also easier to forgive perceived "slights" when differences are understood and when Dyad leaders consistently emphasize that the diversity of personalities and skills is a strength for the team, with no set of personality attributes described as being better or more important than others. One popular tool for sorting individuals is the Kiersey Temperament Sorter. It's used to describe individuals as being among 16 different types plus 32 "mixed" types of temperaments. Many people are familiar with this tool, from which they learned whether they are extroverted or introverted, guided by sensation or intuition, most comfortable with thinking or feeling, and strongest in perceiving or judging (49). Display 9-4 describes one tool that can be used to help team members understand their strengths, which we think is especially important to team members.

Display 9-4 One Useful Tool in Team Development*

The Gallup StrengthsFinder (SF) is a tool that can be used to help work teams better understand each member's strengths. While most of Gallup's books seem to orient toward formal, officially named leaders, the strengths this instrument helps identify are as relevant to frontline leaders (which can be any member of the team, especially as Dyads lead to shared leadership) as they are to the executive suite.

SF makes a distinction between talent and strength. This is helpful, because a team member may have a lot of talent, but it is a focus on developing that talent, ongoing use of it, and the zest from using it that makes it a strength. This distinction helps teams look carefully at how they assign work.

The SF divides the leadership strengths into four domains: executing, influencing, relationship building, and strategic thinking. Team members who complete the tool discover which of 34 leadership themes are their greatest strengths. Because the themes correlate with the domains, they also learn which domain is strongest for them.

Gallup's research shows that no one leader must be balanced in all four domains, but the team needs a balance of talents and strengths. If a team finds its members don't have strengths in one or more of the domains, there needs to be a discussion on how to compensate for the missing elements.

Adapted from Rath, T., & Conchie, B. (2008). Strength based leadership: Great leaders, teams, and why people follow. *New York, NY: Gallup Press.*

---

*Communication style tools can also be helpful in team development. We believe use of tools like these can be important early on in team building. We also believe that the diversity of multidisciplinary teams that consist of members of both genders and a variety of ethnicities will have more opportunity for balance among talents and strengths, even if communication among members may require extra effort.

Almost any book or author who talks about team building mentions the need for team members to understand and support the organization's mission, vision, and goals. We agree with this, and understand that many leaders think they have fulfilled this "step" in building supportive teams of employees by simply providing the written versions of these three things to every new employee. Others, considering themselves to be more competent in leadership, may verbally "share" them in a meeting—and then promptly check that "task" off their team building "to do list." We believe that great leaders talk about all three continually, and remind team members as well as individuals, how their work is contributing to them. They make the mission and vision "come alive" as something that will make a difference—to the organization, to its customers, to the community, or even to the world. In other words, they help team members see their work for what it is—part of a legacy. At our organization, for example, we talk about the mission and vision as part of what we want to do as *our* legacy: transforming healthcare in America.

The mission and vision are part of the "why" we do what we do. Part of caring about team members is ensuring that all are involved in "complete" communication. Complete communication is not just sharing data or informing people what has occurred or will happen. It also includes consciously remembering to share the *why, the what, the how, and the who.* The "why" is an explanation of reasons for each and every decision that needs to be made. The mission and vision, as we stated, are part of this, but there are often other reasons for specific changes or plans. The "what" is the decision itself. The "how" includes specific actions that will occur to implement the decision, and the "who" includes those who will do the work involved and/or are accountable for successful implementation. Every team members should know all of these for team decisions and actions, so that they can support the team members involved.

Supporting each other is what Barsade and O'Neill's companionate love is about. They describe their vision of a workplace where team members are free to express warmth like this: "Imagine a pair of coworkers collaborating side by side, expressing care for each other, safeguarding each other's feelings, and showing compassion when things don't go well" (2). For leaders, there needs to be a realization that "Workers are not just hired hands. Employees have a lot of stuff attached to those hands, and they bring that 'stuff' to work. Their personal goals, needs, fears, talents, problems, and abilities come with them. People want to be cared about. They want to be esteemed by others. They want some control over their lives, and they want to accomplish something that has meaning. Since so much of life is spent in the workplace, it makes perfect sense that these wants should be part of what people hope to receive in exchange for the work they do. Along with the need to be cared about comes a desire to have those who are in power positions—their managers—demonstrate caring" (41). That caring includes a sensitivity to work–life balance as well as attention to work team dynamics.

Dyad leaders on a quest for a caring team environment will notice and reward caring behaviors and teamwork, as well as accomplishment of individual and team goals through evaluations, letters for personnel files, public recognition, or even material rewards (like raises!). Conversely, individual actions that are perceived to indicate a lack of concern for others need to be pointed out to the individuals and *not rewarded.* In other words, Dyad leaders need to intervene when team members are disrupting the cohesiveness of the team. This is practicing the reinforcement type of leadership mentioned above. Display 9-5 contains a questionnaire for leaders to consider when self-evaluating their caring behaviors.

Multidisciplinary teams of the future may not have the same challenges as those being formed among seasoned professionals today. There is a growing movement to begin educating clinicians together and to teach teamwork to future practitioners, and not just in the United States. At the University of Toronto, for example, a project known as Interprofessional Education and Care (IPE/C) is under way. Based on

Display 9-5 **Leadership Questionnaire #2: Do You Love the Employee Team?**

1. Do you actively think about your associates and take actions to help them stretch and grow?
2. Do you know your associates' career goals? Do you look for opportunities to help them meet these goals?
3. Are you a cheerleader for associates whether they are winning or losing?
4. Do you champion your associates' causes with other departments or higher management?
5. Do you really listen to your associates with your mind and heart?
6. Do you counsel associates on appropriate behavior, confront inappropriate behavior, give honest feedback, and discipline when necessary?
7. Do you treat all associates equitably, without prejudice or discrimination?
8. Do you share information, good or bad?
9. Do you consider the organization and its people's future when making decisions?
10. Do you accept and maintain accountability for leadership?

From Sanford, K. (1998). Leading with love. *Olalla, WA: Vashon Publishing.*
Used with permission.

multiple studies and reports, the leaders of this project state that patient care will only improve in quality and safety when:

1. Practitioners understand they are part of a diverse team
2. Practitioners communicate effectively with patients, families, and other members of the team
3. Practitioners know what other team members do
4. Practitioners know how to work together to optimize care throughout the continuum of care (50).

The universities that are beginning to change their models of education so that clinicians are not educated in silos, and will learn team skills before they graduate, understand that care will be transformed only when clinicians learn to work in teams. While this is good news for the future, Dyad leaders are more likely to be leading teams of seasoned clinicians, who do not have the benefit of that education. Dyad-led teams probably do not have teamwork education. That is why we advise that early management of the newly forming team be a combination of reinforcement, autocratic interventions, and democracy. Over time, and after appropriate education, when the team moves to performing, democratic or shared leadership will become more effective.

Helpful team building education for members of a Dyad-led team includes the following:

▶ The history of healthcare organizations and the separate professions
▶ The current healthcare state of affairs and what is prognosticated for the next era

▶ Research on cultures—professional and others
▶ The Dyad model (why, how, what, who)
▶ What the professions of various team members studied as well as what their jobs entail
▶ Teamwork 101

TEAMWORK 101

Dyad-led teams in healthcare will include clinicians, who are used to education that is based on research. There are numerous studies on teams and teamwork that could be shared with them. Because teams are made up of people, there is additional literature on the psychological and sociological theories that formed the underpinning for much of that research. For the purpose of learning to work together, we think only limited reference needs to be made to these. The team doesn't really need all of the science behind teamwork practices in order to learn them—and if individuals truly want to become management and leadership scholars, they can do that at their leisure! We include some of the research in this book—but only as a way to help new Dyad leaders understand our rationale (and because one of us is a management research geek!)

We want to help you avoid a mistake we have made in educating teams: Do not assume that any team members, even those who have been formal managers for years, know the vocabulary of *teamwork* or are experts in making a *team work*. If some members are offended by the "basic" nature of education, so be it. It's important that the group is educated together so they can practice good teamwork together!

Teamwork 101 includes the following: (i) the characteristics of high functioning teams (Display 9-6); (ii) the problem-solving (Display 9-7) or decision-making process (Display 9-8); (iii) communication techniques, including conversations around conflict, negotiations, and *caring* confrontation (how to openly address disagreements or conflict because the issue is important enough to be addressed, while maintaining concern/regard for the person being confronted, as described in Display 9-3); (iv) what it means to be accountable to the team and for individual assignments; and (v) the definition of words the team will use as it builds cohesion: mission, vision, goals, strategy, norms, team rules, participative, and shared leadership.

SHARED LEADERSHIP

We believe that the Dyad partners' goal should be to guide their team to a point where the team can practice shared leadership. As mentioned above, this will probably not be appropriate until the assembly of individuals from different professional cultures has become a team rather than a group. However, early education on shared leadership will help the team develop skills to attain that status. This education is important

Display 9-6 Douglas McGregor's Characteristics of an Effective Work Team

- The "atmosphere" tends to be informal, comfortable, relaxed. There are no obvious tensions. It is a working atmosphere in which people are involved and interested. There are no signs of boredom.

- There is a lot of discussion in which virtually everyone participates, but it remains pertinent to the task of the group. If the discussion gets off the subject, someone will bring it back in short order.

- The task or the objective of the group is well understood and accepted by the members. There will have been free discussion of the objective at some point, until it was formulated in such a way that the members of the group could commit themselves to it.

- The members listen to each other! The discussion does not have the quality of jumping from one idea to another unrelated one. Every idea is given a hearing. People do not appear to be afraid of being foolish by putting forth a creative thought even if it seems fairly extreme.

- There is disagreement. The group is comfortable with this and shows no signs of having to avoid conflict or to keep everything on the plane of sweetness and light. Disagreements are not suppressed or overridden by premature group action. The reasons are carefully examined, and the group seeks to resolve them rather than to dominate the dissenter.

  On the other hand, there is no "tyranny of the minority." Individuals who disagree do not appear to be trying to dominate the group or to express hostility. Their disagreement is an expression of a genuine difference of opinion, and they expect a hearing in order that a solution may be found.

  Sometimes there are basic disagreements that cannot be resolved. The group finds it possible to live with them, accepting them but not permitting them to block its efforts. Under some conditions, action will be deferred to permit further study of an issue between the members. On other occasions, where the disagreement cannot be resolved and actions is necessary, it will be taken but with open caution and recognition that the action may be subject to later reconsideration.

- Most decisions are reached by a kind of consensus in which it is clear that everybody is in general agreement and willing to go along. However, there is little tendency for individuals who oppose the action to keep their opposition private and thus let an apparent consensus mask real disagreement. Formal voting is at a minimum, the group does not accept a simple majority as proper basis for action.

- Criticism is frequent, frank, and relatively comfortable. There is little evidence of personal attack, either openly or in a hidden fashion. The criticism has a constructive flavor in that it is oriented toward removing an obstacle that faces the group and prevents it from getting the job done.

- People are free in expressing their feelings as well as their ideas both on the problem and on the group's operation. There is little pussyfooting; there are few "hidden agendas." Everybody appears to know quite well how everybody else feels about any matter under discussion.

- When action is taken, clear assignments are made and accepted.

- The chair of the group does not dominate it, nor on the contrary, does the group defer unduly to him or her. In fact, as one observes the activity, it is clear that the leadership shifts from time to time, depending on the circumstances. Different members, because of their knowledge or experience, are in a position at various times to act as "resources" for the group. The members utilize them in this fashion, and they occupy leadership roles while they are being used. There

(Continued)

is little evidence of a struggle for power as the group operates. The issue is not who controls, but how to get the job done.

▶ The group is self-conscious about its own operations. Frequently, it will stop to examine how well it is doing or what may be interfering with its operation. The problem may be a matter or procedure, or it may be an individual whose behavior is interfering with the accomplishment of the group's objectives. Whatever it is, it gets open discussion until a solution is found.

From McGregor, D. (1960). The human side of enterprise. New York: McGraw-Hill Book Company. (pp. 232–235). Used with permission.

Display 9-7 Problem-Solving Templates

The Five Whys	Used to	Get to root cause by repeatedly asking Why?
The Deming Cycle	Used to	Systematically solve problems by using an iterative process of Plan-Do-Act-Check
8D Report	Used to	Emphasize team synergy for product and process improvement
A3 Report	Used to	Address root causes on one sheet of paper
Fishbone Diagram	Used to	Focus on causes of problems rather than symptoms
Practical Problem Report (PPS)	Used to	Do straightforward problem solving
Pareto Analysis	Used to	Focus on efforts with greatest improvement potential
Brainstorming	Used to	Generate large numbers of ideas from the group
Affinity Grouping	Used to	Gather large ideas and organize them
Quality Control Incident Investigation	Used to	Identify nonconformance to quality processes and generate action plan
Cause and Effect Matrix	Used to	Generate possible causes of problems
Preventative Action Request (PAR)	Used to	Eliminate potential root causes before problem occurs
Corrective Action Request (CAR)	Used to	Request root cause remedy of contractual noncompliance
Supplier Corrective Action Request (SCAR)	Used to	Systematically solve a supplier quality concern
5 Principles for Problem Solving	Used to	Problem solve and plan corrective action for nonconformance
Deep Drill Analysis	Used to	Understand why the quality system failed

From the Chart it Now Web site: http://www.chartitnow.com/Problem_Solving_Templates.html. Used with permission.

Display 9-8 **Decision Making**

In their 2009 book, *Evidence-Based Management in Healthcare*, authors Anthony Kouner, David Fine, and Richard D'Aquila stressed the importance of using research evidence when making decisions. They stressed the importance of ensuring that information gathered for decision making is assessed for its accuracy (credibility), applicability to the decision at hand, and accessibility.

Their template for decision making includes framing the question behind the decision, finding sources of information, assessing accuracy of information, assessing applicability and actionability of the information, and determining if there is adequate information to make a decision.

This concept is important for multidisciplinary teams when contributing to or making decisions. Our healthcare culture might lead us to be influenced by members of high-status professions who offer opinion or conjecture or members whose contributions are based on emotion. We are beginning to insist on evidence for clinical interventions. We need to do the same thing for operational actions.

Adapted from Kovner, A., Fine, D., & Aquila, R. (2009). Evidence based management in healthcare. *Chicago, IL: Health Administration Press.*

---

because we have found a great variety in what people *think* shared leadership is. It's also important that team members understand that, regardless of education, status, or position power, this type of team leadership involves informal, plural leadership (where different members lead at different times). In most of the work where Dyads are appropriate for team leadership, the shared leadership model does not replace the need for formal positions, that is, the two individuals who make up the Dyad leadership partnership.

Shared leadership is "a group process." It is "distributed among the team members and derives from them" (51). It occurs in organizational structures where hierarchy has been flattened (or at least reduced in height). Mature (having established a functional, democratic, respectful, mission-driven, healthy norm–following culture) teams are the only ones that can practice well in this type of model. Shared leadership is a cooperative endeavor—it is not a model of "leaderless groups." It *is* an endeavor where different team members lead when they are the best prepared to do so for a specific project—and where individuals take the initiative to do work that they observe is needed for the team's success (52). Because multidisciplinary healthcare teams consist of highly educated professionals (some of whom have a professional history of autonomy), the team autonomy that comes with shared leadership should appeal to them and enhance their job satisfaction.

The road to shared leadership in our model begins with educated Dyad leaders who understand the stages of team development and are alert to *when* their own leadership styles should evolve. As teams mature, the leaders can move from more autocratic styles (necessary only when strong professional cultures interfere with the development of teams of "equals") to more participative styles to shared leadership. (We make it sound like this always occurs, or always occurs in a progressive line. It doesn't. New team members, changing environments, and other disruptions in team development will call for Dyad leaders, as the formal leaders, to audit team culture and utilize leadership styles depending on situations.)

Even early in team development, leaders will most appropriately act more as facilitators than dictators. They will facilitate the team's discussion on norms, teamwork, and communication. They may need to step in to discourage monopolization of discussions by stronger personalities and ensure that the quieter people are heard. They give feedback to the group and individuals on their team effectiveness. This is important early on to make sure everyone understand the importance of their own and others' contributions. Dyad leader use of an autocratic style should be measured and used only when professional cultures over power the group's intention to build its own culture.

Multiple studies show that leaders who are democratic, participative, and relations oriented are more successful in accelerating the development of a cohesive team. Dyad leaders who can practice this with their teams will speed individual member's self-confidence, which will help with team bonding. Even when the leaders make final decisions, if their decisions reflect the team's recommendations, the team performs better (53). When teams evolve into shared leadership, Dyad leaders should not have to intervene (at least not very often) in team politics. Members will enforce their own group norms, by confronting lack of adherence. (That alone should encourage Dyad leaders to pursue shared leadership!)

Even at the performing stage of team development (and even if teams are practicing shared leadership), Dyad leaders cannot slip into laissez-faire leadership. (This is also called inactive leadership because it is descriptive of leaders who avoid their supervisory or management duties.) Dyad leaders have *formal organizational leadership positions* and the accountabilities that accompany that designation. Leadership roles can be shared, but accountability cannot be delegated. Dyad leaders must pay close attention to the results, or outcomes of what their teams accomplish (even if team members are doing this, too, as we want them to), and take corrective action. They also need to keep in mind that no team is ever permanently fully formed for peak performance forever. The "change out" of even one member can change team dynamics and put the team back into "earlier" stages like forming or storming.

Performing is all about pursuing and accomplishing goals. In Chapter 10, we address the work of Dyad-led teams, which involves change, transformation, and innovation of healthcare organizations.

THE LARGER TEAMS

Most of what we have been talking about involves small or co-located teams. These are groups with specific jobs (such as running a clinic or managing a service line) or projects (building a new hospital, implementing a clinical IT system). Members are typically located in the same community. We (Steve and Kathy) have such a team that reports to us at the corporate level of the system (in Denver). While some members of the national clinical services team have solid reporting lines to Steve, and others have solid lines to Kathy, everyone in our clinical services group reports to both through a matrix to one or the other. This isn't the model everyone will use, but it works well for us.

This small team has been formalized and has bonded. It has goals and norms, and we have intentionally worked on team building over time with all of the members. Even though travel is extensive for most team members (the company's geographical spread is from coast to coast in 18 states), we hold weekly team meetings (with some members on the phone). It's challenging, but doable, to maintain a team culture.

Our larger teams are another story. Steve, as chief medical officer (CMO), has responsibility for the practice of medicine across the system. Kathy, as chief nursing officer (CNO), has accountability for the practice of nursing across the system. Of course, with over 100 facilities (in 18 states), including hospitals, long-term care, outpatient clinics, home health, and a variety of other healthcare facilities, neither can have intimate firsthand knowledge of day to practices by either profession. We are part of a clinical leadership infrastructure that includes our national clinical team, regional nursing and medical executives, and local market clinical leaders. Many of the leaders are paired as Dyads already, and we are planning for more two-people leadership partnerships.

We bring this up because other System Dyad leaders will find themselves in this same situation. What is our responsibility for partnering our two areas of accountability and for team building with teams we do not see regularly (and in many cases, do not even know personally)? Does a Dyad relationship even make sense in such a large arena?

We believe that not only does it make sense to have a formal partnership over the practice of these two professions, but also it is essential to system success in the next era of healthcare. While care is local, national systems are beginning to centralize some functions and standardize others. Because of new technologies, improving data collection (which informs new metrics), and growing evidence about best practices, it is becoming more common for clinical practice to become standardized across a system as well. Nursing and medicine, as well as the other clinical and *nonclinical* professions, must plan these centralizations and standardizations together. Standardizing clinical practice in national silos is *as negligent* as managing in silos at a more local level. The dysfunction of silos at the national level will be repeated and duplicated throughout the system, from national, to regional, to local, to clinical working unit level.

For team management to work for system-wide initiatives, the infrastructure of Dyads or other multidisciplinary models must be established at *every* level of the organization. This can seem mind-boggling, creating more complexity in management. While Dyad partnerships add to leadership executive effectiveness, they can also result in new and different relationships that some Dyad partners aren't familiar with. One of these is matrix management.

MATRIX MANAGEMENT

Matrix management is a leadership model in which individuals (and sometimes teams) have more than one reporting line. Seasoned healthcare managers have probably experienced this type of organized structure, but for Dyad medical staff partners who are just learning about organizational hierarchies, this is another complexity to working in an already complex system. Dyad partners, *as individuals*, may have matrix reporting relationships with others that their partners do not. In other cases, the Dyad as an entity has a matrix relationship with other groups. (There is no way to simplify healthcare organizational matrix structures as they are lived, but we'll try to simplify the explanation.)

Matrix leadership in healthcare is based on the need to bring different disciplines together for projects, or ongoing interdependent work. Earlier in this chapter, to simplify the discussion of teams and team building, we allowed readers to assume that the multidisciplinary team reports solely to the Dyad in a "straight line." Straight line on the organizational chart (also called solid line reporting) is what most of us think of as a traditional hierarchical reporting structure. Managers in this relationship often are the persons employees consider their "main boss" because this manager usually has the final word on hiring, evaluating, and firing employees. Organizations determine what management position has the straight line based on different criteria. These may be function, location, *or* team.

For example, all nurses in a system might have a straight line (albeit through levels of managers) to the CNO. This is a solid line reporting based on *function*.

In other cases, in a large system, with multiple work sites, nurses might report straight line to an individual market or facility executive. This is based on *geography* or a local (or regional) operating model. Finally, at least some nurses may report on a solid line to a leader based on a structure of multidisciplinary *teams, not* function, *or* geography. Organizations need to determine what works best for their strategies, and what works best *today* may not work well *next year* as strategies evolve. (More on this in Chapter 10.) We expect that reporting structures will be in a state of flux for the foreseeable future (and probably forever).

Managers involved in matrix management, who do not have solid line responsibility to employees, are described as having dotted line relationships. In the examples described above, if the functional leader has the solid line to nurses, geographical leaders (like local CEOs) or team leaders have dotted lines. If the solid line goes to a multidisciplinary team leader, functional *and* geographical leaders have dotted line relationships with appropriate team members. When large organizations do not select one model (and most do not, for a variety of strategic and tactical reasons), the various reporting relationships can become extremely confusing!

One big positive to matrix management is that it is a way to cross over or span boundaries between classic silos and interdisciplinary misunderstandings. It *should* be more flexible, make teamwork easier, and help individuals gain larger views and perspectives when they have accountabilities to more than one "tribe" (such as their professional tribe and their team tribe). However, it is difficult to put into practice. People who have "more than one boss" can get confused, feel pulled in different directions, and become frustrated with too many priorities. The two supervisors can also become frustrated when they feel they've "lost control" over human assets that they can no longer deploy 100% for *their* goals. Those who have the "dotted line" may need to get work done through influence built on relationships. If they are more comfortable as transactional leaders who feel they need "command and control" power to "get things done," they will chafe under this model and may actively campaign to get the solid line switched to them!

The result of poorly implemented and defined matrix management can be strife between the managers, confused and overtaxed employees (including middle managers), and conflicting loyalties of team members. Matrix management can also be used to avoid change by professionals who don't want to "team" with other professionals. Even if the straight line is to a manager outside of the professional silo, those professionals will choose to treat their functional leaders as *the Boss*. It's a recipe for triangulation, mentioned earlier in this chapter.

CUTTING THROUGH THE COMPLEXITY TO MANAGE IN THE MATRIX

Dyad partners need to take time to understand what the matrix relationships are in their organization as a whole, and what they are for them as individuals, a Dyad, and team leaders. They need to be able to explain them to team members and to support the leaders with whom they share matrices.

The place to begin is with the Dyad itself. It is likely that some of the shared team has a solid line to one partner, and others have a solid line to the other. In that case, the Dyad team members are automatically part of a matrix, or the Dyad can't function as co-leaders. During the "norming" stage of team development, this Dyad–as–Matrix needs to be openly discussed with the team. It must be clear to the members that this partnership does not support triangulation and that there are or may be certain specialties that each partner provides for the entire team, regardless of solid line or straight line reporting. In our Dyad, any member who needs leadership help with data or statistics goes first to Steve, because he is a master of business intelligence. Others, regardless of specialty, might approach Kathy on coaching about a particular thorny relationship matter. Of course, any member can seek out either leader, but we don't take offense (we appreciate it!) when individual leadership skills are utilized by every team member. (In fact, most of the time, team members seek leadership help from each other, not us!)

FOR MATRIX RELATIONS OUTSIDE OF THE DYAD

There is a likelihood that some of the Dyad's primary team members will have matrix relationships outside of the team. Whether a solid or dotted line, these relationships and *all matrix relationships* should be defined and documented. Transforming companies are messy, and both leaders and team members must learn "to live in the grey" (where everything is not clearly delineated in black or white), but when it is possible to define solid roles, it should be done. Reducing some of the chaos and confusion makes it easier to deal with the slush that can't be solidified.

Leaders should *not* simply tell people they report in a matrix model. The roles of *everyone* in that matrix should be clearly identified. Job descriptions or policies and procedures can be utilized, but the important things that *must* be clarified include the following:

▶ Which leader has the solid line? (and conversely, the "dotted" line)
▶ What do the two lines mean in general?
▶ What do the two lines mean specifically?
▶ How are priorities for the Matrixed employee determined?

Even when roles have been documented, there will probably be conflicts (often over priorities) from time to time. The *three* (or more) people involved in the Matrix should meet *together* to talk about the challenges of multiple priorities and *together* determine the variety of projects in place as well as their order of priority. That's the best way to avoid triangulation or misunderstandings.

BEYOND DYADS

The Dyad as a term, concept, and management model has become part of our organization's common vocabulary. We use it to describe two leaders in formal, permanent (or as permanent as possible in these days of perpetual change) management roles. We also have begun to refer to temporary partnerships of two colleagues as a Dyad. These are often planned by executives or managers, but sometimes two colleagues will spontaneously become short-term partners in order to accomplish specific objectives or projects. They refer to themselves as Dyads.

A new term has begun circulating in our corporate office: *triads*. Small teams of three have also begun to work together. Most commonly these trios have consisted of two clinicians (from different professions) and a finance colleague. In addition, some of our system's hospitals refer to their hospital president, CMO, and CNO as a Triad. (It gets really confusing when these three add their CFO to the mix. Then, they call themselves a Triad Plus One—probably because "Quadrad" is just too strange on the tongue.) We think that more than two leaders is a leadership team (and doesn't need another designation). Our major concern at Catholic Health Initiatives (CHI) (and for this book) is with the two *formal* leaders who are hired to work together to transform our organizations through shared management and the reduction of silos. We think this model is what is needed *right now* for the next era of healthcare. We also know that management and leadership will continue to evolve, and models not yet conceived may be best for the next era +1! Shared leadership is rich with possibility, and we're looking forward to seeing what comes next.

CHAPTER SUMMARY

Dyads don't work alone as a twosome. They have larger work families, or teams. Teams with two formal managers have the same team formation challenges as other groups brought together to meet organizational goals. They have an additional complication *because* there are two leaders, but being led by a Dyad is advantageous as well. When individual managers have learned to share leadership with each other, they can more easily transfer the skills of that partnership to support the evolution of shared leadership among the entire team. Team building is important for the development of both teamwork and team member leadership skills.

Dyads in Action

ONE COMMUNITY ORGANIZATION'S APPLICATIONS OF THE DYAD MODEL

Good Samaritan Hospital (GSH) opened in Kearney, Nebraska, in 1924, sponsored by the Sisters of St. Francis. In 1996, GSH became part of CHI, a system originally formed by consolidation and transfer of sponsorship from three Catholic healthcare organizations. GSH currently has 256 staffed beds on two campuses. These include the main acute care hospital and the behavioral health program located at the northwest campus. As an American College of Surgeons verified level 2 trauma center, comprehensive services are provided to support the regional healthcare needs of a large referral area (350,000 people in the primary, secondary, and tertiary services areas of Nebraska and Kansas). Services provided include acute care services: neurosurgery, cardiovascular (including open heart), neonatal intensive care services, critical care, cancer care, rehabilitation, and behavioral health services, as well as air and ground transportation services, 911 services for the city, and skilled nursing care. Kearney has been a single hospital community since 1951, with GSH providing the only acute care hospital services to the area.

In 2009, this situation was changing. As a result, GSH was facing hospital competition for the first time in decades. There were problems between local medical staff members and the organization. Hospital administration needed to take a hard look at what was needed for the community, Kearney's clinicians, and our patients. Among other actions, it was determined that learning to manage *together* could help us prepare for the next era of healthcare and improve partnerships. The following four stories explain how we started on the journey to Dyad (and Triad!) leadership as a methodology for learning to lead together.

DYAD PARTNERSHIP TO SUPPORT A PHYSICIAN AND HOSPITAL BUSINESS RELATIONSHIP
Larry E. Bragg and Carol Wahl

The concept of "parallel play" comes from the discipline of developmental psychology. We think it's applicable in healthcare because of historical relationships between hospitals, physicians, and other clinical providers. The concept refers (in psychology) to the developmental stage in children where they are "absorbed in their own activity, and usually play *beside* rather than *with* one another" (54). This is a stage that precedes the more complex stage called cooperative play. When we were writing this manuscript, this idea was loosely applied to how we have evolved from historical silos to a physician and hospital administration partnership. We believe Dyad partnerships will lead us to the cooperative collaborations needed in the future.

GSH began exploring new ways to work with physicians as true partners in the operations and delivery of care in 2009. As a result, we developed a co-management business relationship in which key physicians and hospital leaders aligned to partner in the leadership of surgical services. A physician and hospital administrator Dyad relationship was formed between the two of us—Larry Bragg, MD, and Carol Wahl, RN, Vice President of Patient Care Services.

At that time, there were approximately 126 physicians on staff. Local physicians had traditionally embraced the independent medical practitioner model. There were employed physicians in a few surgical specialties (neurosurgery, cardiovascular, and endoscopy), behavioral, and the emergency department. However, the majority of physicians in the community were associated with one of three large private physician multispecialty practices.

During the summer of 2009, rumors surfaced about a plan to build a second hospital in Kearney, which would be physician owned. As more information became available, it appeared that the rumors were true and that areas of physician concern had prompted this intention. These were

▶ A perception by physicians that their decision-making impact had deteriorated to responsibilities for credentialing and peer review. Physicians perceived that they had little say about hospital operations that impacted their practices, including capital equipment purchases. They voiced frustration that strategic decisions that impacted their work environment were made at higher levels of the organization, without physician input.

▶ The trend toward employment of non–hospital-based physicians alarmed medical staff members because of the potential that their practices would be impacted. Physician recruitment decisions were being made without local practitioner input regarding community need for various specialties. There was concern that physician revenues would be affected.

▶ Healthcare trends that focused on reducing costs were causing reduced revenues along with increased expenses in physician offices. Some doctors felt that by owning their own hospital, they could gain a new personal source of revenue.

GSH was experiencing similar areas of concern. Decreasing reimbursement made it clear we needed to maintain market share, reduce costs, and improve quality outcomes. It was also apparent that in order to thrive in the new healthcare environment, we needed to consider new approaches. CHI, as a large healthcare system, was aware of these increasing challenges and provided leadership in the quest to improve quality and reduce costs.

Clearly, we were all (the national company, the hospital, and the medical staff) headed on a journey where a common vision and goals, aligned incentives, trust, and collaboration are essential for moving forward. GSH began looking for potential opportunities to work with physicians in a different way. We wanted a new model to increase physician and hospital engagement.

Assisted by experienced facilitators, key hospital administrators met with specialty groups of physicians: surgery, cardiology, primary care, and family practice. Various concepts of co-management were presented and explored by the different groups. The sole group of physicians, who decided they wanted to examine the potential of these concepts further, was the multispecialty surgical group. They agreed with the hospital that alternative models of management should be investigated.

The surgical group expressed that a new hospital could result in a significant impact to the broader community of central Nebraska by actually causing reduced availability of services. They believed that the programs and services needed to support a comprehensive trauma program could be at risk when some specialty surgeons no longer practiced at GSH. In addition, they feared that access to capital for purchase of technology required to care for complex patients could be reduced when two hospitals shared the care of patients in such a small market.

Previously, surgeons, anesthesiologists, and the hospital had successfully collaborated on the establishment of a free standing outpatient surgery center. Because of this history, the group felt there was potential for a partnership where all had aligned vision and goals. The group was committed to improve surgery services, thereby improving access and care outcomes and reducing inefficiencies that contributed to higher costs of surgical care.

After careful consideration of the advantages and disadvantages of various partnership models, the physicians and hospital administrators decided to pursue a clinical service line co-management agreement (CMA). Both groups saw this as a proven model, a path with a predictable implementation plan, and a compatibility of integration with current operations. However, they also knew there was a high level of complexity in this relationship because the partnership involved the services of an entire surgical department instead of a narrow specialty service line. There was some physician skepticism about the sincerity of the hospital to fundamentally change how surgical services were managed. These feelings were mitigated when the physician and hospital team, facilitated by the physician and administrator team of Larry Bragg and Carol Wahl, openly discussed specific responsibilities of physicians and the hospital. There was dialogue about decision-making authority, which was committed to a binding agreement. A summary of the key components of our CMA is listed in Display 9-9. Our work plan for implementing this agreement is identified in Display 9-10.

A Joint Operation Committee (JOC) was formed to perform the activities defined in our agreement. The JOC is composed of six physicians, one nurse anesthetist, and seven hospital leaders, including the CEO. Every month, the team meets to set priorities, review activities, approve recommendations of subcommittees, monitor performance metrics, and receive reports. Subcommittees are formed to complete work based on the annual strategic plan. These are led by a specific Dyad partnership of a physician and hospital leader assigned responsibility for specific goals. An ann ual report is developed to summarize accomplishments and achievement of performance metrics. Examples of Dyad-led partnership accomplishments (to date) include the following:

▶ Development of a charter that defines responsibilities, ground rules, and meeting requirements of the team
▶ Improvement in Surgical Care Improvement Project (SCIP) measures through process changes
▶ Improvement of employee and physician satisfaction (per survey results)
▶ Reduction in turnover times through implementation of LEAN processes
▶ Reassignment of block times based on utilization

Display 9-9 **Summary of the Clinical Service Line Co-management Agreement (CMA) Components**

▶ Purpose of CMA: improve the quality of the service line and reduce overall cost of healthcare to the community.
▶ Physician specialists provide the hospital with a high level of management services in a specific clinical service line.
▶ Payment to physicians include: base fee calculated on fair market valuation of time spent in providing management services, which included a performance bonus based on achievement of specific performance objectives
▶ Primarily a service agreement

Display 9-10 **Summary of CMA Implementation Work Plan**

1. Complete CMA letter of intent (LOI) and term sheet with interested physicians
2. Select physicians who will be offered opportunity to participate in LOI
3. Engage valuator acceptable to hospital
4. Determine base fee under CMA and performance parameters (before and after LOI)
5. Determine performance bonus methodology
6. Physicians form Limited Liability Company (LLC) with members (owners) who intend to sign binding CMA
7. Draft CMA
8. Obtain written valuation
9. Obtain signatures of all parties
10. Identify initial members of the joint operating committee (JOC)

▶ Design of a new surgical services suite, including sterile processing (120,000 square feet), with a well-planned move, redesign of processes, community tours, and equipment demonstrations
▶ Reorganization of the department to meet subspecialty needs
▶ Improvement in organization, function, and outcomes of sterile processing
▶ Recommendations from team members for capital equipment and lease expenditures
▶ Recommendations for specialty physician recruitment needs
▶ Prioritization of surgical needs and changes during a year in which we experienced interim surgical director leadership
▶ Reduced implant pricing as a result of negotiation with vendors.

We (Larry and Carol) were selected as the formal Dyad leaders of the JOC by the team. From our perspectives, a critical reason for our Dyad formation was the belief that a new partnership model was both needed and possible to move surgical services forward toward optimal performance. With our shared willingness to continually work together for the good of the organization, we serve as liaisons with physicians, nurses, department employees, other departments, administration, the physician limited liability corporation (LLC), and CHI. Our achievements have often occurred through a leadership influence model versus direct authority over team members.

Both of us recognize that our co-management is part of a legal agreement with identified roles and responsibilities. A major responsibility for us as partners is to assure that key terms of the agreement are being met. We know that communication of priorities, issues, and accomplishments are essential. Opportunities to do this occur at the board level, administrative meetings, physician meetings (including the integrated leadership team [ILT] meetings), and through various groups within CHI. As Dyad leaders, we check in regularly with each other to share information and assure we speak with one voice. An additional focus we share is to consistently be alert for signs that decisions are being considered through the traditional hierarchal administrative approach versus bringing them to us as co-managers for discussion and decisions. As a way to counteract this potential slippage, we utilize "just in time" meetings and e-mail conversations when timely decisions are needed.

Each of us had previous leadership experiences that helped prepare us to work as partners. Doctor Bragg had served as medical staff president, chairman of the surgery department, medical director for trauma, and on various physician/administrative committees over his years of practice. Ms. Wahl came to the Dyad with both nursing and MBA education, a healthcare leadership and clinical background, and a strong commitment to partnerships and shared decision making through her experience and support of a nursing shared governance organization.

We've learned that the benefits of a Dyad partnership are similar to the benefits of any CMA. However, the working relationship is different from what either of us had experienced in traditional medical staff or administrative committee work, because there is an *experienced* balance of power. While we did not specifically articulate this core value to each other in the beginning, our commitment to a new way of seeing the world has led us to rely heavily on each other's opinions and expertise. Somehow, in this formal relationship, it seems easier to seek advice and input from each other on critical issues. Perhaps, this is because we are searching for answers to common goals or because each success and goal achievement increases our comfort working together. We have developed a deep trust and believe this is based on careful adherence to honesty and transparency in all issues.

An additional benefit of our hospital/physician group co-management model is that physicians are compensated, based on fair market valuation for time they spend on complex initiatives. In the past, time spent away from the office or surgery suite to work on hospital goals could result in reduced income for physicians. In order to maintain income and efficient schedules, doctors devoted less time on nonclinical activities, such as meetings and problem resolution sessions. Because of how we've implemented co-management and compensation, hospital leaders are less hesitant to request physician time for the discussion and resolution of issues. Physicians have actively engaged in important meetings that they previously chose not to attend. For example, during our sterile processing improvement project, physicians attended frequent interdisciplinary meetings to identify and support solutions for the improvement of services. This was a new level of involvement from them, and as one physician who participated said, "I never knew there were so many kinds of steam!" In other words, by working together on problems, everyone had the opportunity to learn about the complexities of solving these problems and to contribute their wisdom in order to do this.

In the past, a number of hospital problems seemed to become chronic. It was difficult to resolve them due to differing impacts of various solutions on individual physicians. With co-management, which included the ability for physicians to spend time meeting together, the physician group was able to discuss these impacts, negotiate, and speak with one voice about how to solve age-old problems. Rather than advocating for individual capital equipment requests, physicians in the hospital can now work together to prioritize equipment needs based on the strategic goals of the organization. (There is also the potential for a performance bonus when goals are achieved. This incentive helps to provide focus on accomplishing the priorities of the surgery service line.)

We've seen some additional benefits to working together. Physicians, through their LLC, recognize the effort and support of perioperative and perianesthesia staff through donations to our foundation to support a surgical services education fund. In addition, the physicians are more active in dealing with disruptive behavior issues. They are willing and able to discuss behavior expectations with peers, although authority for formal action still resides in the formal medical staff processes.

During the first years of our partnership, we have had an unrelenting focus on improving operations and the work environment for both physicians and staff. We've embarked on difficult conversations regarding physician recruitment, strategic positioning, market services, and new delivery models. We're concerned with both day-to-day operations and strategic issues. Clearly, our Dyad partnership and our co-management team have moved from parallel play to cooperative play. We believe we have built a strong foundation for our Dyad partnership that can, and will, evolve to even greater levels of collaboration. The issues we need to address will increase in complexity during the next era of healthcare, and we'll be able to build on current success and relationships to propel us toward a transformational future.

BEYOND THE DYAD: WORKING WITH THE BIGGER TEAM
Michael Schnieders

I arrived at Good Samaritan Hospital in June 2010, knowing that I was entering the organization at a time of crisis. A large number of physicians on the medical staff had lost confidence in hospital administration and had begun the process of building their own hospital. Kearney, Nebraska, has a population of about 33,000 people. This is not a large metropolitan community by any measure. It's certainly not a place that needs a second hospital!

During the interview process, I noted that a majority of the questions concerned whether or not I, as a potential hospital president, would be supportive of a team culture versus a "me" culture. That informed me right away that GSH was on the right track for a successful future. I had no problem with a team culture. My management style is definitely that of a team leader, not as an autocrat at the top of a pyramid. The hiring team liked that, because I got the job.

I had just settled into my office, when I was introduced to Dr. Mark Wenneker of the Navigant Consulting firm. Mark arrived at Good Samaritan for his first visit within a week of my arrival. Catholic Health Initiatives (CHI) had contracted with his company to assist in identifying the underlying hospital/physician issues in the Kearney market and to propose a path to a better partnership. Our goal was to assess physician leadership, hospital leadership, our current management model, and the ability of hospital stakeholders to collaborate. Navigant's assignment was to recommend a model that was to be designed around a physician–hospital relationship to improve patient safety and quality, as well as enhance physician and hospital adaptation to healthcare reform.

The consultants reviewed our documents, meeting minutes, strategic plans, financial statements, clinical quality data, consumer and physician satisfaction data, medical director agreements, medical staff and organization articles and bylaws, and organizational reporting relationships. They really got to know who Good Samaritan Hospital is at the same time I was learning about my new organizational "family." During their engagement, they interviewed multiple physicians and administrative leaders as well as CHI regional and national executives.

While the document review and interviews were being completed, we formed a steering committee of interested physicians and GSH senior leaders. Our consultants met periodically with this group to keep us informed and receive timely feedback and input. They recommended that a more collaborative leadership structure that would bring physicians and the hospital together as a force for improving care in our community. During our discussions, the steering committee agreed on the following guiding principles:

▶ Our focus must always be the patient.
▶ We are all committed to improving quality.
▶ We will be a transparent group, but keep confidentiality when necessary.
▶ We will create links between the new forum and the medical staff structure.
▶ We will seek participation of CHI leadership when appropriate.
▶ We will commit to improving communication between physicians, hospital administration, and board.

The steering committee recommended that we institute a permanent, integrated leadership team (ILT), and as the hospital president, I fully endorsed this recommendation as an important step to cementing a new shared leadership model. It was planned that the ILT would have a close working relationship with both the medical staff and the hospital president. Members of the ILT would include physicians, members of senior leadership, the vice president of medical affairs, and the medical staff president. Early questions that the steering committee addressed included the following:

▶ How many physicians should be a part of the ILT?
▶ How will the members of the ILT be identified?
▶ Who is the final decision maker if the group cannot come to consensus?

▸ What are the decision rights of the ILT? (In other words, which decisions could ILT members make and which decisions should be made by someone else such as leadership of the physician limited liability corporation, the hospital president, or CHI?)

The steering committee recommended that I meet with the current chief of staff and the past chief of staff to finalize the operational details of the ILT. Although I didn't think of this team as a triad, and didn't refer to the group as a triad, I realized later that a temporary triad leadership team was completing the details and formation of our ILT! While I was familiar with Dyad leadership from previous experience with academic health centers, I was not familiar with triad decision making.

As a small team of three, we accepted the steering committee recommendations. We determined the size of the group, how the members would be determined, criteria for membership, meeting frequency, and then documented the purpose of the ILT. The three of us were able to accomplish these things because we had a shared vision and common values. We clarified that the ILT was not a decision-making body but a provider of input and advice to the president. We realized that the ILT would need to use the influence model. In other words, they could make change through influencing others. (Once the ILT was assembled, the group itself further defined their vision and ground rules.)

The ILT has been meeting monthly since December 2010. Following our guiding principles of focusing on the patient and improving clinical quality, we determined that this new team would charter clinical operational councils that would be organized around strategically important clinical areas with facilitation of physician engagement. One of the overarching goals was to form a new partnership between physicians and administrators, so these councils would be led by a physician and an administrator Dyad leadership team. We see this as a visible commitment to Dyad leadership at Good Samaritan Hospital. We had experience with co-management already because of our establishment of the surgery co-management agreement just prior to my arrival. Therefore, we knew it could work here.

The ILT viewed the surgery co-management group as a clinical council. In addition to the surgery co-management council, the ILT has now formed seven additional clinical councils: Hospital Inpatient Medicine, Cancer Care, Cardiology, Maternal Child Health, Emergency-Trauma, Behavioral Health, and Innovation councils. The Innovation Council, as the name implies, is to focus on clinical care in a new world of healthcare delivery. Each of the councils has Dyad leadership in place. Our Dyad partnerships currently consist of a physician and an administrator. Each council reports approximately twice a year at one of our monthly ILT meetings. This keeps physicians, administrators, and the hospital president aware of the issues and strengths of various clinical programs in the hospital.

The Dyad leadership experience at GSH has been outstanding. It has brought physicians and administrators together in a formal relationship with shared expectations and accountabilities. Clinical problems have been avoided and other issues have been brought to resolution much earlier and easier than the past relationship would have allowed. Hospital administrators have a better understanding of day-to-day issues that physicians face, and physicians have a better understanding of the challenges in the administrative world. Both groups are learning to walk in the other's shoes.

Some issues we have had to face are how our organization interfaces with other organizations that do not have Dyad leadership in place. Organizations that do not have Dyad leadership sometimes question how decisions are made here, who makes decisions, and our timeline for making decisions. I understand how some of my peers question the wisdom of historical hospital management relinquishing or sharing some decision-making responsibility. I believe that this type of thinking will no longer serve the healthcare industry in a future where we need to tear down silos. The future requires that we all become better able to collaborate and share decision making, especially with physicians, if we are to transform healthcare for the betterment of our communities.

Co-management or Dyad leadership is not new to everyone. As I stated earlier, I was familiar with this model from past working experiences. However, it is new to many people and requires careful planning to ensure it is implemented well. Like everything in our industry, leadership by two leaders may evolve. We could have organizational leadership by multiple leaders. Through various recent serendipitous events, I have read about and heard of others employing a triad leadership model. After some reflection, I realized that triad leadership was key in how we formed the ILT as well as the ongoing partnership work at GSH. The ILT was refined by a triad of the hospital president, the current president of the medical staff, and the past president of the medical staff. The ongoing ILT is a triad of previously siloed cultures, with the three components being physicians, administration, and the hospital president. Successful triad leadership, like Dyad leadership or *any team endeavor*, requires that partners share and understand their common values and goals. Only when this is true can the partners align to accomplish transformation.

As with any change, it's important that progress toward objectives be measured. At the time we began our triad approach (combined with Dyad leadership teams), our goal was to improve partnerships. The need to do this became a burning platform because of a crisis with physician satisfaction at GSH. When we began our new co-management, our health stream physician satisfaction score was at the 2nd percentile for "communication between the medical staff and the administrative team." We were at the 3rd percentile for the "administrative team's involvement of the medical staff in hospital-related decisions." In the past 2 years, we have seen GSH move to the 38th percentile for communication with physicians and to the 58th percentile for physician involvement in decision making. Of course, our goal is to be close to the very top, and we are not content with these scores. However, changing perceptions and cultures takes time and is very difficult, so we are encouraged that we have made this progress and continue on an upward trend of improved physician and hospital relationships. We strongly believe we have done the right thing in these partnerships, and although we have obstacles and challenges ahead, we have a new organizational base to help us work these through *together*.

DYAD LEADERSHIP AT THE UNIT LEVEL
Dennis Edwards and Kimber Bonner

Nineteen years ago, an informal partnership between medicine and nursing started in our ICU at Good Samaritan Hospital. We didn't call it a Dyad because we had never heard that term or thought about this relationship as being something new or different. It just made sense that the two professions come together to make decisions for the betterment of our critical care unit.

Dyad leadership provides the support our unit needs in such complex areas as staff–physician relations, quality, and clinical outcomes. By collaborating, we have been able to manage and lead a busy inpatient area with strong clinical leadership.

Our 16-bed ICU serves a population that has to travel great distances to access care, from the northern tier of counties in Kansas to the northern Nebraska border. We offer a level 2 trauma center, neurosurgery, cardiac, and vascular surgery, as well as most medical specialties. The nurses and physicians care for patients ranging in age from 1 to 100 with all the expected variations in acuity.

Dr. Dennis Edwards has been the medical director of the ICU since 1995. Initially, his responsibilities were confined to those issues that physicians traditionally have responsibility to oversee, such as peer-reviewed treatment guidelines. The ICU nursing director was responsible to the organization for staffing, ICU budget, implementing organizational protocols, policies, and procedures, as well as the clinical competence of the nursing staff. It soon became evident to both leaders that the majority of challenges in a unit don't fall into discreet categories of a medical staff issue versus a nursing staff concern. As a result, medicine and nursing embarked on a path to create shared responsibility for all unit issues, from staffing levels to treatment guidelines.

Early problems in the critical care unit included low morale among the nursing staff. The turnover rate among the ICU nurses was approximately 50%, with an extensive use of travelers to meet minimum staffing requirements. Because of this, there were frequent diversions of critical patients to other hospitals, which resulted in frustrated providers. While the ICU nurses were known as experts who provided exceptional care, they were also known as strong intimidating individuals. The unit was a difficult place to work as a new employee because of the experienced nurses less than nurturing behaviors, as well as the complexity of multiple patient types. In addition, the physical unit was in need of upgrading.

When the medical director and nursing director began working together, they knew they would need to address both the physical environment needs and a new culture if the unit was to thrive and serve the community. They campaigned for a new unit and worked together to change the culture. While their separate constituents applauded the idea of an upgraded space, they were less supportive of a leadership team that worked together across two different clinical cultures. The two leaders were surprised by significant push back from both physicians and nurses when they worked *together* to solve problems that would have historically fallen under either nursing or physician peer review. They began to realize that there are natural tendencies for groups to form as separate "tribes" and that by working together they weren't merging physician and nursing tribes but linking them to accomplish common goals. They needed to help their constituents understand this.

GROWING PAINS

The ICU director/medical director Dyad became more of a formal relationship when the two leaders worked together to design and develop a new ICU. Both partners, as well as the whole team, contributed to the physical design. For example, the physician leader envisioned a physical space where caregivers could walk around the patient bed providing care without having to move equipment. It was his idea that double doors and wider hallways should be built to accommodate beds without having to worry about damaging door frames or struggling to turn beds at sharp angles when moving them. The nurse leader weighed in on other equipment locations that would enhance direct patient care. Multiple clinicians made a group decision to install special flooring. The wood-looking laminate flooring was designed to extend up the lower part of walls in order to prevent seams that could potentially harbor contaminants. It was input from the interdisciplinary team supporting the Dyad that led to patient- and staff-centered decisions about the physical unit. The result was a beautiful, state-of-the-art, intensive care unit with a spacious room design. Because the leaders of this project communicated with and shared concerns of their different stakeholder groups, the physical design of the unit works for the entire healthcare team. Team members from various professions could see a visible proof that working together led to a positive result.

Of course, a well-designed, future-oriented unit does not provide a perfect patient care environment when behaviors within the walls are not healthy. The Dyad leadership partners had a common vision for an ICU culture where teamwork would improve patient care as well as job satisfaction for team members. In 2007, GSH decided to adopt TeamSTEPPS (Team Strategies and Tools to Enhance Performance and Patient Safety). TeamSTEPPS is a systematic approach developed by the Department of Defense and the Agency for Healthcare Research and Quality (AHRQ) to integrate teamwork into practice (55). The process is designed to improve quality, safety, and efficiency. Through conversations between leadership and the Dyad leadership of the intensive care unit, it was decided that the ICU would be in the first phase of a hospital wide rollout.

As part of CHI, GSH utilizes a change management process. In accordance with this, key staff were identified to be master trainers within the ICU. These individuals were enrolled in a 2-day training program where they learned the tools and techniques of team steps so that they could help educate the rest of the staff in the ICU. All staff was required to attend an 8-hour education session where tools and techniques were taught. The implementation of this team methodology was a key pillar to the changes that would occur in the ICU. Physicians, nurses, and other team members learned to coordinate their activities to make patient care safe and efficient. This was a definite change from what had happened in the past! The program could not have been implemented successfully without the shared passion and accountability of the two Dyad leaders to implement a teamwork culture in the ICU.

Following the implementation of this team model, GSH addressed the need to increase accountability among team members. The organization decided to adopt the Just Culture program to help develop an open, fair, and just culture supportive of safety (56). This process, associated with David Marx, supports a culture of open communication to encourage accountability and support safe behavioral choices by staff members.

GSH trained all leaders and supervisors within the organization on the concepts of Just Culture. An algorithm that is easy to follow was shared throughout the company. This helps people decide whether coaching, counseling, or disciplining is appropriate when an error is made. Previously, there was a wide spread perception that any mistake would result in discipline for those involved. With this new algorithm, the organization was educated to understand the need for an open environment where employees are held accountable for their actions but not blamed or shamed for making mistakes.

Even though education and training was provided throughout the hospital, it was understood that leadership teams needed to hold people accountable for implementing any new program. The director of ICU and the ICU medical director, supported by the vice president of patient care services, set and communicated Just Culture standards for a high-performing ICU. Expectations of staff included that they would discuss their concerns with each other, rather than coming to the Dyad leaders to "fix" every problem. When staff identified issues, they were expected to bring suggested solutions to the leadership team. Because both Dyad leaders agreed with this approach, processes and standards began to change, with a resulting improvement in the ICU environment.

After GSH's adoption of TeamSTEPPS, CHI adopted a system wide program called SafetyFirst. This program encourages staff to speak up whenever they see a safety concern. It encourages and promotes the reporting of all safety incidents or "near misses" (where a safety event almost occurs but is prevented) through the national safety reporting program. SafetyFirst is compatible with, and supported by, our ICU

TeamSTEPPS program. That made it easy for staff to adopt the new requirements for more reporting, as well as the processes for resolving safety issues. They were able to observe the Dyad leadership in the ICU increasing their interprofessional communication and resolving problems that had been caused by a culture where there had previously been fear of speaking up when team members of perceived higher status engaged in unsafe practices.

INVOLVEMENT IN OWNERSHIP

When GSH incorporated shared governance for the hospital employees throughout the organization, the ICU Dyad leaders assisted with professional growth of a new unit-based council (UBC) within the unit. It is through this council, that the majority of clinical decisions are made for the unit. The council provides a forum for staff to communicate both to the medical director and the nursing management team of the ICU. As a result, staff members feel empowered and realize they need to *own* their practice as well as the success of the entire unit. Interviews previously completed by the management team are now peer interviews with an innovative part of the application being a shadowing program where all applicants spend time on the shift they are applying for. This allows staff to get to know applicants, explain expectations of working on the ICU team, and give feedback into the hiring process.

The ICU unit based council also provides a forum for the discussion of quality and practice issues. The unit selects representatives who serve on house-wide practice, quality, professional development, and research councils. These representatives bring information back to the unit based council so that staff has the opportunity to provide input into overall organizational change. Depending on the topic or issue at hand, physicians and other disciplines attend UBC meetings. This allows a multidisciplinary team response to topics, which makes the team stronger and more cohesive.

The UBC has grown and matured over the years. Every new applicant, employee, or medical staff member is informed that this is the decision-making body of the unit. Through this shared governance innovation, the ICU has improved patient care, quality, safety, and overall patient and staff satisfaction. As a result, our ICU unit, which was dysfunctional before the implementation of Dyad leadership, was awarded the Beacon Award of the American Association of Critical-Care Nurses in September 2013. Display 9-11 describes the Beacon Award.

It was evident through the application (written by staff nurses) for this award that nurses not only feel an ownership for their practice but also realize that Dyad leadership has led to the success of the unit. Good Samaritan ICU was the first intensive care unit in Nebraska to be designated as a Beacon unit. The award and recognition is something that staff, medical staff, and leadership of GSH can point to with pride.

Display 9-11 **American Association of Critical-Care Nurses (AACN) Beacon Award for Excellence**

AACN's Beacon Award for Excellence provides a road map and tools to assist hospital units on their path to excellence, honoring individual units that distinguish themselves by improving every facet of patient care. The Beacon Award's three levels of designation recognize significant milestones along a unit's journey.

▶ For patients and families, the Beacon Award signifies exceptional care through improved outcomes and greater overall satisfaction.
▶ For nurses, a Beacon Award signals a positive and supportive work environment with greater collaboration between colleagues and leaders, higher morale and lower turnover.

From the AACN Web site: http://www.aacn.org/WD/BeaconApps/content/mainpage.
pcms?menu=BeaconApps.

CONTINUING EVOLUTION OF ICU AND DYAD LEADERSHIP

In August 2013, GSH was awarded the Planetree Gold Designation. (Please see Display 9-12 on Planetree.) The ICU, along with the rest of the hospital, met comprehensive standards that demonstrate a strong patient, family, and staff culture. Many of the standards could be a challenge to accomplish in a traditional ICU because of the focus on increased patient and family involvement in care decisions, as well as increased access of families to the ICU. However, in the GSH ICU, touch base (care planning) rounds, bedside shift reports, and interprofessional rounding have been implemented to improve communications and patient care handoffs. Families are now able to be present during codes and have unrestricted access when the patients prefer this. They also take part in care planning with the patient's permission. The Dyad leaders were instrumental in supporting nursing staff and physicians as new protocols and processes were put into place to engage patients and families as *full members of the patient care team.*

In 2013, the medical director and Kimber Bonner, the ICU nursing director, took another step toward formalization of their Dyad partnership with the development of the critical care council (CCC). Members include the unit's intensivists, hospitalists, and nursing staff and other disciplines. The ICU Dyad leaders co-lead the meetings. Development of our 24/7 eICU and the need to develop protocols for evidence-based practice guidelines prompted the initiation of this group. One council recommendation was that physicians attend daily multidisciplinary rounds. Since intensivists have begun doing this, the clinical partnership among the team has grown even stronger.

Through the CCC, we receive recommendations for equipment needs for the unit, such as the new bedside ultrasound machine. The council has also initiated and approved protocols for mobility, delirium, and sedation in the ICU.

Display 9-12 **Planetree**

The Planetree Organization was founded in 1978. For nearly 40 years, the company has partnered with providers to transform their cultures in order to organize all care around the needs of patients.*

Planetree is populated with leaders who are advocates for patients and families to have a voice in their care. They believe

- ▶ "That we are human beings, caring for other human beings
- ▶ We are all caregivers
- ▶ Caregiving is best achieved through kindness and compassion
- ▶ Safe, accessible high-quality care is fundamental to patient-centered care
- ▶ In a holistic approach to meeting people's needs to body, mind, and spirit
- ▶ Families, friends, and loved ones are vital to the healing process
- ▶ Access to understandable health information can empower individuals to participate in their health
- ▶ The opportunity for individuals to make person choices related to their care is essential
- ▶ Physical environments can enhance healing, health, and well-being
- ▶ Illness can be a transformational experience for patients, families, and caregivers."

From the Planetree Web site: http://planetree.org.

---

*To become a Planetree-designated site requires blinded selection by an independent committee, "based on review of policies, practices, and written documentation verified by patients, residents, family, and staff focus groups" that 11 dimensions of patient-centered care are in place.

Interprofessional discussions regarding management of bi-pap (a bi-level positive airway pressure machine used to help get more air into a patient's lungs) in the ICU and other clinical areas has led to organization recommendations for the provision of more effective care.

SUMMARY

Dyad leadership has led to stronger teamwork between physicians and others on the interdisciplinary care team. The ability of leaders from two different tribes to work so closely together inspired and encouraged the rest of the team to do the same. The unit, once considered among the most dysfunctional in the organization, is now recognized as being a highly reliable patient care area, which continues to set high goals for improvement. The shared vision between the Dyad leaders has evolved into a shared vision for the unit, as well as professional, action-oriented teamwork between physicians, nurses, and other providers of care. This has resulted in reduced lengths of stay, improved quality outcomes, and implementation of high standards through evidence-based practice. Employee satisfaction has increased. Staff turnover has decreased. There is currently no usage of temporary travelers to fill positions, and there have not been diversions due to staffing for a long time!

Having a committed team is vital to success. That begins with committed leadership, and in the GSH ICU, that leadership is a Dyad. The task for these two partners and their teams is to continue to sustain their commitment and develop leaders of the future who also are able to work together *as a team*.

DYAD LEADERSHIP: CO-LEADING THE PATIENT AND FAMILY ADVISORY COUNCIL
Ellen Gitt and Judith Sims Billings

Good Samaritan Hospital's first Patient and Family Advisory Council (PFAC) was formed in 2004 and has been an active part of our hospital's patient-centered care initiative since that time. In 2004, as we were developing initiatives and actions based on patient's input, we felt we needed to have the patient's voice represented in decisions. While we had individual input on specific issues, we did not have the collective voice to give us confidence that the actions would be the most appropriate over time and in differing settings.

Our first PFAC meeting was held on January 2004. The purpose of the council was to

- Provide a patient-centered view of the hospital
- Actively dialogue with the community
- Establish person-centered priorities
- Extend patient experience initiatives
- Increase consumer awareness in patient experience and hospital/community issues.

The membership of the PFAC consisted of former patients or their family members, along with several hospital representatives. Twenty community members, randomly selected, participated in the monthly meetings. In the beginning, the chair of the PFAC was the Director of Service Quality at the hospital while the Vice President, Patient Care Services served as the executive sponsor. Topics were determined based on recommendations from hospital leadership and staff and included such issues as wayfinding, marketing preferences, advance directives, and Internet availability to patients. During discussions, PFAC members expressed interest in knowing more about various topics, so continuing education was provided. (The flight and ambulance program were always popular.) Over time, a mystery shopper program was implemented to give the hospital feedback on "are we doing what we say we do?" and also to give the PFAC members a chance to view the hospital from a different lens.

Minutes were documented from each meeting and distributed to the directors and administrative team. A spreadsheet was kept of ideas and shared widely in the hospital. A key principle was to provide follow-up to every idea proposed. We responded that either we would implement, place on the priority list to implement over time, or not implement due to a specific reason. An annual report was shared with the PFAC each December, detailing the accomplishments of the council. Council members also shared feedback on how the council could be improved. Each year, more than 90% of the members stated that the council was a valuable use of their time. Some of the members wanted to extend their term, but our goal was to start with a new group of members each calendar year. Several members continued on in a hospital volunteer capacity.

Examples of accomplishments were numerous and far-reaching into the hospital. The PFAC suggested a "One-Stop-Shop" for outpatient services, which became Good Samaritan's Ambulatory Care Center, and featured a private entrance and admissions desk. They helped develop personal health information cards, which have been distributed to nearly 60,000 people. They selected the employee name badges we use today with contrasting colors, larger letters, and an "RN" designation for nurses. They contributed to the formation of patient orders, entitled "Patient Rx." The pediatrics unit was renovated based on the forthright information from a recent family member. A healing garden was established, based on an experience of a family member needing a quiet and peaceful environment to handle grief.

The PFAC continued to evolve, with members attending various hospital committee meetings. A member of the PFAC actively participates on our Planetree (patient-centered) Steering Committee. When "lean" process improvement teams form, members are queried whether they would like to participate. One member was an essential member of the admissions lean team, which redesigned how we admit patients to our facility.

Clearly, the PFAC was an integral team to our organization. Many improvements were made because the patient's voice was heard and valued. Yet the role of the former patients and family members was primarily participative, with hospital management providing direction and leadership. The focus of the agendas was on patient satisfaction and patient experience. A true partnership had not yet developed.

In 2010, CHI developed a priority evidence-based practice of PFAC implementation in each of its (then) 76 healthcare facilities. CHI had previously declared "person-centered care" as a core value of care, and service development and the implementation of local PFACs would extend this priority.

A group consisting of national and ministry leaders was formed to develop the components of implementation. A comprehensive toolkit to assist CHI facilities was developed and included resources such as: a charter template with key expectations/standards for implementation, metrics to measure success, training resources, best practice references, and marketing templates.

The new CHI definition of the PFAC was as follows. "The Patient and Family Advisory Council is a formal structure for collaborating with patients and families (as defined by the patient) in policy and program decision making in healthcare settings to improve safety, quality, and the patient experience."

The standards developed for this national implementation of local PFACs included that following:

▶ A Dyad partnership relationship with the designated hospital leader and a patient/family member co-leading the Council
▶ Meetings held at least quarterly
▶ Agendas that included hospital data/information on quality, safety, and patient experience
▶ Selection of a shared priority project that had a support of the hospital's administrative team
▶ Reporting of outcome, process, structure, and person-centered metrics
▶ An annual report to the hospital board of directors with the Dyad partners presenting the information

The new PFAC format was implemented in July 2010 and continues today.

Good Samaritan Hospital's PFAC evolved into a widely welcomed phase II. Judith Sims Billings, an engaged PFAC member, was selected as the Dyad partner of Ellen Gitt, Director of Service Excellence. Judy had been a well-known community leader (Associate Dean of the UNMC-Kearney College of Nursing) prior to her retirement and had remained active in many community activities. Judy's knowledge of team, structure, and healthcare was a plus from the beginning.

Ellen and Judy develop agendas together that are of interest and importance to the community, not just topics that are of interest to the hospital. As an example, the chief financial officer spoke at a recent meeting on finances of a healthcare system and financial assistance provided to uninsured or underinsured patients. This was very eye opening to our PFAC members and created a dialogue on the provision of community services. The PFAC members also want to know who is leading healthcare in our community, and our hospital president (Michael Schnieders) is a popular council guest.

Quality and safety information is shared openly. While HCAHPS patient satisfaction information had been a common agenda item, we moved into new territory with quality and safety transparency data. Discussion of national resources for quality information is also shared and discussed (i.e., the presence and comparison of HealthGrades data).

The first priority project selected was "quiet at night." The project was approved by the administrative team and the board. The council decided that a hospital team should be developed to move on this initiative in a timely manner with the team leader routinely attending the monthly PFAC meeting to get input and guidance as needed. The end result was a significant increase in the HCAHPS ratings for this question.

There are many positive outcomes of having a Dyad leadership team. Having one nonemployed Dyad leader helps bring a strong community perspective to the group. A consumer can be a source of "rumors" in the community and help identify hot topics that are of importance to community members. Sometimes, the consumer leader is comfortable enough to bring up tough questions that other PFAC members are not comfortable bringing up. PFAC members are also excellent ambassadors for the hospital in the community.

Patient and family engagement in quality and safety issues is essential to achieving improved, cost-effective outcomes. Transparency is important to achieving these results. The PFAC has a vested interest in the quality of care delivered and can champion changes.

Since implementing our Dyad leadership model, our consumer co-leader has presented PFAC priorities to the administrative team, as well as to the board of directors for their approval. We have found that by having PFAC priorities presented to the administrative team and board by a consumer, the priorities presented seem to have increased visibility and credibility. This level of visibility also supports goal accomplishment and achievement of results.

This feeling of accountability is bidirectional, with the PFAC expressing increased engagement and responsibility for the success of initiatives. Just having a consumer as part of the PFAC Dyad leadership makes the PFAC members feel more strongly that the council is integral to the community and that their opinions are valued and their voices are heard.

Some challenges we have found in implementing a Dyad leadership model for our PFAC was in initially determining the role each leader will play in the meetings. At first, it seemed that we relied on our consumer co-leader to only be responsible for providing the opening reflection at each meeting. We were somewhat hesitant to request increased time and involvement from a person who was already generously volunteering her time. We learned that volunteer co-leaders do want to *lead*. Now the meeting leadership is shared.

Hospital staff and leaders will always want to get "in front" of PFAC members as a way to get consumer opinions on a service or project before proceeding. Our PFAC groups over the years have shown they are deliberate in their discussions and insightful about their experiences and perspectives of healthcare. Some recent examples of PFAC support include that following:

▶ Hands-on experience with the hospital's Web site to determine the ease of navigation for our consumer population
▶ Testing reaction to marketing campaigns
▶ Evaluating the patient room service menu and process prior to implementation
▶ Participating on the dismissal process improvement and falls LEAN teams
▶ Advising physician clinic leadership on patient-/family-centered functions (such as limited wait time, timely communication of tests, documentation of test results)
▶ Trying out meals in the new cafeteria
▶ Understanding the roles of the hospitalists and community physicians

We continue to evolve in our discussions of quality and safety issues. We struggle with the potential HIPAA and management risk issues of discussing specific events and the balance of transparency.

Dyads are used throughout our national and local organization as a model for building teams and cohesion. As we continue with our safety and quality culture, the patient voice has become integral in our forward movement, and the council serves as a credible, reflective voice on our journey. It is a logical evolution to share leadership with patients and their families. We have found that having a Dyad leadership model for our PFAC has strengthened our team and brought us closer to having a true patient partnership.

REFERENCES

1. Sanford, K. (1999). *Leading with love*. Olalla, WA: Vashon Publishing.
2. Barsade, S., & O'Neill, O. (April 2, 2014). Wharton School of Business. *Why fostering a culture of "companionate love" in the workplace matters*. Retrieved from https://knowledge.wharton.upenn.edu/article/fostering-culture-compassion-workplace-matters/
3. Al-MailQu, F. (2005). The effort of nursing care on overall patient satisfaction and its predictive value on return-to-provider behavior: A survey study. *Quality Management in Health care, 14*(2), 116–120.
4. Atkins, P. (1996). Happy employees lead to loyal patients. *Journal of Health care Marketing, 16*(4), 14–23.
5. JCAHO. (2005). *Health care at the crossroads: Strategies for addressing the evolving nursing crisis*. Chicago, IL: JCAHO.
6. Newman, K., et al. (2001). The nurse retention, quality of care, and patient satisfaction chain. *International Journal of Health care Quality Assurance, 14*(2), 57–64.
7. Rathert, D., & May, D. R. (2007). Health care work environments, employee satisfaction, and patient safety: Care provider perspectives. *Health care Management Review, 32*(1), 2–11.
8. Pettier, J., Dahl, A., & Mulhern, F. (April 2009). The relationship between employee satisfaction and hospital patient experience. *Forum for People Performance Management and Measurement*. Retrieved from http://www.marketing.org/files/NYHQ_HR_Final.pdf
9. Sengin, K. (January 1, 2001). The relationship between job satisfaction of registered nurses and patient satisfaction with nursing care in acute care hospitals. *Scholarly Commons*, University of Pennsylvania (Unpublished Dissertation).
10. Lee, K., Ann, et al. (July/August 2009). Nursing: A key to patient satisfaction. *Health Affairs, 28*(4), 669–677.
11. Google Company. *www.google.com*. Retrieved from http://www.google.com/about/company/facts/culture. Accessed May 20, 2014.
12. TRX Training. *www.Trxtraining.com*. Retrieved from http://www.Trxtraining.com/discover/who-we-are/culture. Accessed May 20, 2014.
13. BAE Systems. *www.baesystems.com*. Retrieved from http://www.baesystems.com/our-company-rus/about-us/our-culture?_afrLoop=1840298051332000. Accessed May 20, 2014.
14. Mayo Clinic. *www.mayoclinic.org*. Retrieved from http://www.mayoclinic.org/jobs/physicians-scientists/mayo-culture. Accessed May 20, 2014.
15. Corporate Author. (Sept/Nov 2006). Transforming health care: Vision and culture. Denver, CO: *CHI Initatives*, p. 1.
16. American Hospital Association. *www.aha.org*. Retrieved from: http://www.aha.org/advocacy-issues/healthforlife/culture.html
17. Ryan, K., & Oestreich, D. (1998). *Driving fear out of the workplace*. San Francisco, CA: Jossey-Bass.
18. Clayton Sherman, V. (1993). *Creating the New American Hospital*. San Francisco, CA: Jossey-Bass.
19. Willcock, D. (2013). *Collaborating for results: Silo working and relationships that work*. Farnham, England: Gower Publishing.
20. Hackman, M., & Johnson, C. (2013). *Leadership: A communication perspective* (6th ed.). Long Grove, IL: Waveland Press.
21. Hughes, R. L., Ginnett, R. C., & Curphy, G. J. (1993). *Leadership: Enhancing the lessons of experience*. Homewood, IL: Irwin.

22. Lawler, E. E. III, Mohrman, S. A., & Ledford, G. E. (1995). *Creating high performance organizations, practices, and results of employee involvement in Total Quality Management in Fortune 1000 companies.* San Francisco, CA: Jossey-Bass.

23. Michaelson, L. K., Watson, W. E., & Black, R. H. (1989). A realistic rest of individual versus group consensus decision making, *Journal of Applied Psychology, 74,* 837–839.

24. Bass, B. M. (2008). *The Bass handbook of leadership, theory, research, & managerial applications* (4th ed.). New York, NY: Free Press.

25. Zaccaro, S. J., Rittman, A. L., & Marks, M. A. (2001). Team leadership. *Leadership Quarterly, 12,* 451–483.

26. Ancona, D. G., & Caldwell, D. F. (1988). Beyond task and maintenance: Defining external functions. *Group and Organization Studies, 13,* 468–494.

27. Tannenbaum, S. L., Smith-Jentsch, K. A., & Behson, S. J. (1998). Training team leaders to facilitate team learning and performance. In J. A. Cannon-Bowers, & E. Salas (Eds.), *Making decisions under stress: Implications for individual and team training.* Washington, DC: American Psychological Association.

28. Giles, H., & Mann, L. (2003). A model of R&D leadership and team communication: The relationship with project performance. *R&D Management, 34*(2), 147–160.

29. Morgeson, F. P., & DeRue, D. S. (2006). Event criticality, urgency, and duration: Understanding how events disrupt teams and influence team leader intervention. *Leadership Quarterly, 17,* 272–287.

30. Wellins, R. S., Byham, W. C., & Wilson, J. M. (1991). *Empowerment teams.* San Francisco, CA: Jossey-Bass.

31. Erikson, J. (2003). *Exploring variations in team development across high and low performing project teams.* Paper. Seattle, WA: Academy of Management.

32. Heinen, J. S., & Jacobsen, E. (1976). A model of task group development in complex organizations and a strategy of implementation. *Academy of Management Review, 1,* 98–111.

33. Tuckman, B. W. (1965). Developmental sequence in small groups. *Psychological Bulletin, 63,* 384–399.

34. Avolio, B. J., & Bass, B. M. (1994). *Evaluate the impact of transformational leadership training at individual, group, organizational, and community levels.* Binghamton, NY: Binghamton University, Center for Leadership Studies.

35. Spector, P., & Suttell, B. J. (1956–1957). *Research on the specific behavior patterns most effective in influencing group performance.* Washington, DC: American Institute for Research.

36. Taylor, H. (1980). Effective leadership styles. *Canadian Manager, 5*(5), 12–13.

37. Lencioni, P. (2002). *The five dysfunctions of a team.* San Francisco, CA: Jossey-Bass.

38. Dyer, W. (1987). *Team building: Issues and alternatives.* Reading, MA: Addison-Wesley.

39. Shepherd, C. (1963). *Small groups: Some sociological perspectives.* New York, NY: Chandler Publishing Company.

40. Augusberger, D. (2009). *Caring enough to confront.* Ventura, CA: Regal.

41. Sanford, K. (1998). *Leading with love.* Olalla, WA: Vashon Publishing.

42. Corporate Author. *2012 Annual Report.* Lowe's Corporation.

43. Corporate Author. *Men's wearhouse.* Retrieved from http://employment.menswearhouse.com/ats/advantageSelector.action;jsessionid=F64A7CDF7E883D595B9229093443FC9B?type=culture

44. Harvard Business Review. (January 13, 2014). Retrieved from http://blogs.hbr.org/2014/01/employees-who-feel-love-perform-better

45. Spiegelman, P., & Berrett, B. (2013). *Patients Come Second.* New York, NY: An Inc. Original, distributed by Greenleaf Book Group.

46. Gladwell, M. (2002). *The tipping point: How little things can make a big difference.* New York, NY: Little, Brown and Company.

47. Kahan, S. (2010). *Getting change right: How leaders transform organizations from the inside out.* San Francisco, CA: Jossey-Bass.

48. Sherman, V. (1993). *Creating the New American Hospital: A time for greatness.* San Francisco, CA: Jossey-Bass.

49. Kiersey, D., & Bates, M. (1978). *Please understand me: Character and temperament types.* Del Mar, CA: Gnosology Books/Distributed by Prometheus Nemesis Book Co.

50. Nelson, S., Tassone, M., Hodges, B. (2014). *Creating the health care team of the future.* Ithaca/London: ILR Press/Cornell University Press.

51. Pearce, C. L., & Sims, H. P., Jr. (2002). Virtual versus shared leadership as predictors of the effectiveness of change management teams: An examination of aversive, directive, transactional, transformational, and empowering leader's behaviors. *Group Dynamics: Theory, Research and Practice, 6,* 172–197.

52. Ray, D., & Bronstein, H. (1995). *Teaming up: Making the transition to a self-directed team-based organization.* New York, NY: McGraw-Hill.
53. Phillips, J. M. (2001). The role of decision influence and team performance in member self-efficacy, withdrawal, satisfaction with the leader, and willingness to return. *Organizational Behavior and Human Decision Processes, 84,* 122–142.
54. Bakeman, R., & Brownlee, J. R. (1980). The strategic use of parallel play: A sequential analysis. *Child Development, 51,* 873–878.
55. Agency for Health care Research and Quality (AHRQ). http://www.ahrq.gov/
56. Just Culture. http://www.justculture.org

Chapter 10

What We Say Today May Not Be True Tomorrow

We have named this chapter after a saying often heard at our team meetings. In fact, those words are frequently part of presentations we make to both internal and external audiences, as well as to individuals in private conversations. Actually, the title above is only the first sentence of our probably-monotonous-to-others two-sentence recitation. The second is, "That does not mean we're not telling the truth today."

What we say today might not be true tomorrow. That does not mean we're not telling the truth today. This has become our mantra because so many things are changing rapidly. Not only are industry macro-changes occurring due to shifting sites of care, new technology, new competitors, and new partnerships (and, of course, new payment systems), there are various fluctuations in markets that leaders and organizations must nimbly respond to if they are to survive and thrive. Responding means changing tactics, altering goals, or even considering total business transformation. (This means adding new products and services and discontinuing other, traditional work.) We've heard so many of our colleagues express sadness, bewilderment, and anger, with the same underlying theme—they did not foresee this much disruption in their careers. This is clear from the associate degree nurse (ADN) who told Kathy, "But I was promised by my high school counselor there would *always* be jobs for me in the hospital." It's evident from the psychiatrist who said, "When I gave up my private practice to join this place, the CEO told me the hospital would *never* close down the mental health unit. I was lied to!"

When the high school counselor advised the student who was considering an associate degree, she probably had every reason to believe (in the middle of a nursing shortage, and at a time when most hospital nursing jobs were open to ADNs) that she was giving good and accurate advice. Her "crystal ball" didn't tell her that the number of acute care beds needed might shrink someday, or that healthcare systems might change educational requirements for their registered nurses.

When the CEO made his statement to the psychiatrist considering employment, he probably believed the hospital *would never* close its busy mental health unit (the only one in the community). Unfortunately, implied or perceived "promises" made in one era can't be kept when the environment changes, *as it always will*. We remind our teams and audiences of this, not because we're trying to lessen our accountability to work with our teams toward a *preferred future*, but because we understand the importance of helping the entire team learn resilience and flexibility.

RESILIENCE AS A SKILL FOR THE FUTURE

Resilience is the ability to cope with challenges, setbacks, or change without becoming overwhelmed with distress. Resilient people are aware of their changing environment, accept that part of life is change and challenge, and believe that their own actions and choices will affect outcomes and the future. Psychologists state that some people are naturally resilient, but others can learn to increase their resilience if it is not an innate trait. In Display 10-1, we share ways that leaders can help their team members become more resilient. We also try to be transparent, sharing what we know today, aware we may have more (or different) information tomorrow.

We know that environmental change takes its toll on people. One of our physician colleagues confided a few weeks ago that he had decided to retire even though this is much earlier than he had planned. When we asked why, his response was direct. "I didn't sign on for this," he said.

What he didn't "sign on" for was the new world of healthcare. He told us he has no interest in world of computers and telehealth. He had not imagined, for most of his career, that his partners would someday seek hospital employment, leaving him either as a sole provider or forced to become an employee himself. He's not in favor of "team care" and doesn't like just about every change he sees coming. He was resigned and a little sad. One of our colleagues says he's struck by how many clinicians, particularly physicians, are coming to grips with the fact that they aren't passionate about the work they do. They confide that when prestige, money, and job autonomy are threatened, they realize that the *work* of being a medical doctor (MD) or (DO) isn't really what they love.

We have empathy for our colleagues who "didn't see it coming." We also have empathy for others who are facing change. But we know that change is inevitable, and that as leaders, we have responsibility to foster and nurture both change and transformation *for the good of all*.

Display 10-1 **Helping Employees Stay Resilient during Change**

According to Katherine Klein and Edward Bowman of The Wharton School of Business, leaders can help their teams become more resilient when they focus on relationships, efficacy, a positive affect, and learning (1).

RELATIONSHIPS

Employees who feel engaged with the organization will be less overwhelmed when stressful events occur. Engagement comes with feeling part of a bigger whole. Dyad leaders who ensure every team member is supported, encouraged to contribute to problem solving, and treated with civility, respect, and kindness will improve the work experience for everyone. Hopefully, this doesn't come as a surprise, but research shows that most people want to be cared about at work. They want friends there and are happiest when they know their leaders care about and appreciate them (2).

EFFICACY

Team members who know they make a difference will be more likely to cope when the environment is challenging. Dyad leaders help them know how important they are when they take time to recognize their contributions, give them "stretch" assignments, and point out how their jobs support the mission and goals of the organization (3). As Brockner points out in his book on Self-Esteem, "The ways in which goals are set, performance is appraised and feedback, rewards are administered … are predictive of how people think, feel, and act at work" (4).

A POSITIVE AFFECT

Leaders who find reasons for joy at work through celebration of successes improve the potential that change won't cause distress for the team. There is research that happiness at work is contagious. Optimistic managers who have a sense of humor and express gratitude for their team members are an asset to the organization (5–7).

LEARNING

There is the potential for growth, in times of change, even when change is imposed and not welcomed. This is also true when errors are made or decisions turn out to be less than optimal. Leaders can point out what individuals and the team have learned and provide an environment where it is safe to report mistakes so that everyone can learn how to prevent similar occurrences in the future. People are more resilient when fear has been replaced by confidence that it is safe to try new things, even if they might fail, and where "blame and shame" are not part of the culture (8).

The ability to create an environment where these four factors are practiced are closely correlated to the traits of transformational leaders discussed in Chapter 2.

We separate "change" from "transformation" because they aren't exactly the same thing. To differentiate them, we like Karen Buckley's and Dani Perkin's definitions. They define change as "the modification of beliefs, behaviors, and attitudes." On the other hand they say, "transformation is profound, fundamental change in thought and action creates irreversible discontinuity in the experience of the system" (9).

Dyad leadership is a beginning step in transforming an organization. Management theory, even when hierarchies are flattened, is almost always around the *individual* as leader or manager. The body of knowledge about managers comes mostly from research about single formal leaders in single formal positions, even though team-work, both *between* single leaders or among their teams, has evolved as a popular area to study.

In healthcare, when two leaders from different silos become formal leaders together, the system is definitely experiencing something new. Organizational leaders and team members may view this as a positive change, as we describe in Display 10-2. On the other hand, it could be disruptive to individuals and teams. Whether viewed negatively or positively, Dyads result in irreversible discontinuity *if* executive leadership selects, educates, coaches, provides infrastructure, and holds the new partners accountable for co-leading in a new way.

Display 10-2 How Dyads Are Perceived by Non-Dyad Leaders

What do leadership dyads mean to leaders who may not be part of a dyad, but observe them at work? We asked some of our system's senior leaders their thoughts on this model of management. The leaders:

   Steve Kehrberg, Senior Vice President, Supply Chain
   Peggy Martin, OP, JCL, Senior Vice President, Sponsorship and Governance
   Colleen Scanlon, RN, JD, Senior Vice President, Advocacy
   Bob Strickland, Senior Vice President, Performance Management

WHAT ARE YOUR PERCEPTIONS OF DYAD LEADERSHIP IN THIS ORGANIZATION?

Steve Kehrberg: Because a Dyad consists of two leaders from different professions, I get a more holistic view when I talk to them about a supply chain issue. Dyad leadership brings a broader understanding of work streams and how multiple stakeholders will be affected. Having the clinical members of our leadership dyads engaged in supply chain issues is a huge advantage. It gives us a focus on the bigger picture, which always includes financial matters but also matters of quality, utilization, and clinical outcomes. That bigger picture also helps us align our systemwide supply chain initiatives with the work done in our markets.

Bob Strickland: Dyad leadership helps remove barriers between administrative leadership and clinical leadership. Because they work as a team, Dyad partners can constantly assure that both administrative and clinical areas are fully aligned. I believe this enhances our organization's ability to move toward excellence within the framework of the Institute for Healthcare Improvement's "Triple Aim," maximizing the quality of clinical outcomes, the cost of care, and the patient experience.

   Of course, not all Dyads are an administrative leader paired with a clinical leader. For example, our chief medical officer and our chief nursing officer share leadership of our Clinical Services

Group. Their dyad pairs the physician perspective and the nursing perspective. In all cases, the nature of a dyad prevents myopia in leadership.

Peggy Martin: Our clinical Dyads are a wonderful model. Because of shared leadership, our organization's Clinical Services Group has become a community of collaboration. I see and experience this collaboration in those who report to Dyad leaders too.

Colleen Scanlon: The Dyad relationship between leaders models highly effective collaboration that can lead to positive results. It allows for the open sharing of ideas and can lead to creative solutions to problems and general innovation.

DO YOU BELIEVE THE DYAD LEADERSHIP MODEL IS IMPORTANT IN THE NEXT ERA OF HEALTHCARE?

Colleen Scanlon: Effective Dyad leadership has been, and will continue to be, important as healthcare transforms and new models of delivery and financing are implemented.

Bob Strickland: Absolutely. I believe that healthcare organization decisions have to be framed in terms of the goals for the next era of healthcare. In order to excel, we must be able to manage clinical and financial risk in a way that will lead to consumer trust. Quality of care, cost of care, and patient experience will all be critically important: no one element can be ignored without risking success in the others. I believe that Dyad leadership is the best way to lead within that tripartite framework.

Peggy Martin: In my opinion, the Dyad concept complements the very founding of our system: the sisters who put Catholic Health Initiatives together did so, wanting to show how important collaboration is for the future of faith-based healthcare. The women religious who participate in this organization believed then, and still believe, that the future of the Catholic ministries depends on collaboration between the sisters and the laity. Leadership Dyads are an even more contemporary example of this collaboration for the good of healthcare.

HOW DOES DYAD LEADERSHIP ADVANCE OR PROMOTE THE ACHIEVEMENT OF STRATEGIC GOALS?

Bob Strickland: Our strategic goals all point toward success in the next era of healthcare. Without Dyad leadership, we would run the risk of emphasizing one "corner" of the Triple Aim at the expense of the other two.

Colleen Scanlon: Dyad leadership fosters open communication and mutual respect not just between the Dyad leaders but other leaders working with them. It can create engagement and the participation of other leaders in achieving strategic goals. An effective Dyad partnership helps create a positive work culture.

Steve Kehrberg: Dyad leadership helps accomplish transformational change, not just incremental change. For example, the purchasing of clinical equipment and supplies used to be about making sure a physician or clinician had everything he or she wanted for a case or procedure. Now, we're focused on systemwide standards that are aligned with the organization's goals. Often, implementing these systemwide standards requires us to change from an all-source or multisource situation to a reduced sourcing model, which can be challenging. Our move to a sole-source standard for drug eluting stents, for example, would never have been the success that it is without the strong Dyad leadership of our cardiac service line.

(Continued)

WHEN IT COMES TO CLINICAL/QUALITY INITIATIVES, WHAT'S THE VALUE OF PARTNERING A BUSINESS/ADMINISTRATIVE LEADER WITH A PHYSICIAN LEADER?

Steve Kehrberg: For me, it's moving from providing physicians and clinicians with their individual product preferences to making collaborative choices based on evidence-based product selection. The transformational component of this comes in working with dyad leaders in clinical areas to move from a focus on getting the best prices for individual preference products to a much broader focus that includes price, but also quality, utilization, and outcomes.

Colleen Scanlon: There's a clear interface between clinical initiatives and operations, so having effective partnerships between those leaders is important. The content expertise of each leader can inform and influence the other.

Bob Strickland: It's entirely possible to push for initiatives that will improve quality without being mindful of cost management; or, to push for cost management without being mindful of quality. Dyad leadership is the ideal model for keeping both quality and cost in mind at all times, as well as thinking in terms of overall value. An organization that manages either cost or quality effectively but allows the other to slip will not viable in the long term. Both perspectives are critical.

HOW MIGHT ADMINISTRATOR/PHYSICIAN LEADERSHIP DYADS BE IMPORTANT FOR FUTURE PARTNERSHIPS WITH PHYSICIANS?

Colleen Scanlon: Historically, physicians have operated as solo practitioners, and even team engagement was challenging. Due to the status of physicians in clinical settings and in healthcare organizations overall, physician leader support of and engagement in Dyad relationships is essential.

Bob Strickland: Physicians trust other physicians. They know that physician leaders understand their daily struggles in the current healthcare environment. Our physician leaders can frame the realities of managing a complex organization in terms that other physicians understand and relate to.

Steve Kehrberg: When physicians see value and incentive for their participation, it becomes easier to achieve physician engagement, and the engaged physicians become part of a bigger solution that provides value for all. It may be important to figure out how to reward physicians who get involved in our projects. The reward wouldn't need to be in the form of compensation; it could be recognition, additional capital access, etc.

WHAT EFFECT HAS DYAD LEADERSHIP (WORKING WITH TWO LEADERS) HAD ON YOUR WORK, OR ON HOW YOU DO YOUR WORK?

Steve Kehrberg: It makes my work much, much easier when sourcing physician preference items. I am able to get an opinion that two leaders have vetted well with their individual professions and stakeholders from one source—the Dyad. In our purchasing of drug-eluting stents, cardiac rhythm management devices, and orthopedic and spine products, we've been able to make changes that have yielded cost improvements of $45 million.

Bob Strickland: One of my areas of responsibility is to provide executive leadership for clinical and performance excellence (CPE) initiatives. We realized early that this would require strong clinical leadership and strong administrative leadership. Following the lead of our Clinical Services Group, we recruited a physician to work in a Dyad with an administrative leader to provide day-to-day leadership for all CPE initiatives. This is just one example of how we consider the dyad leadership model to be critically important to our future.

WHAT ADVICE WOULD YOU GIVE AN ORGANIZATION THAT IS PLANNING TO IMPLEMENT THE DYAD LEADERSHIP MODEL?

Steve Kehrberg: It is very important that you get two leaders with complementary skills who are able to make decisions based on what is best for the total organization. We'll make the type of dramatic transformation needed to succeed in the next era of healthcare only with significant changes in our utilization practices, which will require behavior change. Leadership Dyads help us make fact-based decisions about clinically effective products for systemwide use. When we in supply chain work with the Dyads that lead our clinical areas, we can change products and behaviors.

Colleen Scanlon: There needs to be clear organizational support for Dyad leadership among the most senior leaders. It would probably be helpful to create some commentary about dyad partnerships, the benefits and goals, their role in achieving organizational goals, etc., and to share that across the organization, so there is a shared understanding of what Dyads can do.

Peggy Martin: It's important for Dyads to show collaboration between female leaders and male leaders, to show the equality of women and men in the healing environment. It makes everything well rounded and real.

— *Donnell Martinez, RN, MSN, Director, Marketing and Clinical Communications, CHI.*

In their 2000 book, *Healthcare Teamwork*, Theresa Drinka and Phillip Clark note that "organizations seem to be reluctant to accept and support interdisciplinary leadership. Healthcare organizations are no exception" (10). They go on to say that, "organizations seem to be returning to earlier theories where leadership is focused on *a* leader. Leadership as an interdisciplinary phenomenon is still in its infancy."

Dyads are an interdisciplinary model that should lead to more shared leadership practices among disciplines. (We're already seeing formal triads emerge, both in our organization and others.) We believe this because in order to be effective as a Dyad, two leaders must learn to *share* management and leadership. Once this occurs, it becomes easier and more natural for them to educate others about "taking turns leading," or leading together.

Sometimes team members without formal training in partnering as leaders emulate the model because they see its benefits. In Display 10-3, two of our team members describe their Dyad and how it evolved *without* a formal designation. They observed their leaders' partnership and realized that their own effectiveness and job satisfaction would be enhanced by forming a Dyad. Their use of Dyad leadership evolved into shared leadership for their group that hadn't planned or considered this evolution!

Of course, shared interdisciplinary leadership among other team members is less likely if the Dyad does not develop as a true partnership. One of our colleagues, from the CFO world, tells about his early experience (before the term Dyad was used).

Display 10-3 **Dyad Leader Support**

At first, Linda and Karen joked about being Dyad partners. We are senior executive assistants: Linda Pickett supports Kathy Sanford and Karen Moses supports Stephen Moore. Steve and Kathy are Dyad leaders and so, by extension, we figured we were as well. We have come to realize the advantage of this trickle-down thinking.

We are more valuable to our leaders as a *partnership* of support. It is critical that we work closely together to understand the many facets of their responsibilities and be able prioritize the demands that are made of them. We are not clinicians, but we have caught their passion for doing what is right for the patient.

Because we attend many of their meetings, we understand the issues at hand and the resources employed to address these issues. Kathy typically works with Linda and Steve with Karen. However, either can call on us to communicate a sensitive message, find someone in a hurry, or make a last minute travel change. With similar electronic access, either one of us can answer their questions from the road.

We sometimes hear from someone outside Clinical Services that he or she is not sure of who supports who. We consider this a compliment! We work hard to be available to everyone and represent our execs and each other. There is a delineation, however. We have a tremendous respect for each other and know when to defer to the other.

We also feel very fortunate to rely on each other as partners. Like our Dyad leaders, we aren't joined at the hip. We learn things individually. We don't always attend the same meetings. So together we understand more of the whole picture; we are able to fill in the gaps for each other, understand the nuance of important decisions and huddle about how to handle whatever crops up.

Together we serve as formal Dyad leaders of a team of executive assistants who support the vice presidents who report directly to Kathy and Steve within Clinical Services. We meet regularly to share Kathy's and Steve's enthusiasm for the work we do and to tackle the day-to-day challenges of helping CHI achieve its mission. There is genuine affection among these exceptional women, *as we have developed into a team that shares leadership rather than a group of people with similar jobs.*

He and a physician were paired to co-lead a family practice clinic. "There was no education for us and no coaching, guidance, or even advice as to how to *do* this new leadership 'thing.' On top of that, the physician had no management experience, and no stomach for 'upsetting' any of his former Family Practice peers. After the two of us decided, together, that one of the doctors wasn't competent, and needed to leave the practice, I was flummoxed when we met with her. My co-leader didn't say a word. He let me do all the talking and appeared sympathetic toward the doctor. She probably left thinking he wasn't in agreement, even though he was the one who initiated the whole thing!" (Apparently, even if the physician thought he could continue with this good cop, bad cop routine and leave anything unpleasant to his partner, management wasn't really to his liking. Eighteen months after being named a management co-leader, the doctor left that role for a job where he didn't provide patient care and also didn't have to supervise anyone who did.) That Dyad experience was not transformational!

CHANGE

New ways of doing things may be transformational for one organization but simply "garden variety" change for another. That depends, of course, on where the organization started and where it ended up after the change. If systemwide Dyad leadership is transformational in Organization A, but followed by widely utilized shared leadership, the evolution to shared leadership may be less transformational than if shared leadership is implemented in Organization B, where all leaders were previously "singles."

Whether it's transformational or not, change is the cause of much angst for human beings and a subject for much research by sociologists, psychologists, economists, and organizational scientists. Various theories and models explain the steps which individuals and organizations must perform in order to change. Some *sound* simple, like Conner and Patterson's three-part change model: (i) Prepare, (ii) accept, (iii) commit. Others seem more complicated, like Buckley and Perkins' steps in Table 10-1.

Table 10-1 "Takes" on the Order of the Change Process	
Model Originators	**Model Description**
Buckley, K., & Perkins, D. (1984). *Managing the complexity of organization transformation.* Alexandria, VA: Miles River Press.	Seven *phases* of change: 1. Unconscious—recognize a need 2. Awakening—become willing to move 3. Recording—move toward change 4. Translation—integrate information 5. Commitment—support the change 6. Embodiment—become changed 7. Integrate—incorporate the change into the Whole
Kirkpatrick, D. L. (1985). *How to make change effectively.* San Francisco, CA: Jossey-Bass.	Seven *steps* of change: 1. Determine a need to change or solve something 2. Prepare tentative solutions 3. Analyze probable reactions to various solutions 4. Make final decisions of what will change 5. Set timetable for change 6. Communicate change to stakeholders 7. Implement change
Connor, D., & Patterson, R. (1981). *Building commitment to organizational change.* Atlanta, GA: O.D. Resources.	1. Prepare 2. Accept 3. Commit
Schaller, L. E. (1978). *The change agent.* Nashville, TN: Abingdon Press.	1. Define gap between now and ideal future 2. Form group to initiate change 3. Form group to support change and make suggestions 4. Implement action 5. Freeze change

Careful analysis shows they are all similar, *because* behind each step (even if there are only three steps listed!) there is a whole lot more thinking and doing going on. Assumptions are made about earlier decisions (*before* the change model is initiated) including analyses of what it would take to implement the decision.

Change theories may differ in how they are described, but their substance indicates a recognition by various theorists that change is in response to someone perceiving a need (the *why*); someone making a specific decision (the *what*); and someone planning an implementation of the decision (the *how*). These three steps are (hopefully) followed by communication, implementation, and follow-up actions to make change *stick*.

Recognizing the importance of this point, Schaller writes that the steps to change are to (i) define the gap between the present state and the ideal state (assuming someone has perceived a "why" before formulating the "what"); (ii) convene a group to initiate change (further defining the "what"); (iii) form another group to support the change and make suggestions (firming up the "how"); (iv) implement change; and (v) freeze the change (making sure the changes stick) (11).

Use of the word "freeze" to describe change that sticks is reminiscent of psychologist Kurt Lewin's long taught theory of change. Lewin described people as being "frozen" in a certain way at any moment in time. When a person changes, he must unfreeze (thaw out), change, and then refreeze. He is then frozen with new or altered sets of beliefs or behaviors, until something causes him to unfreeze again (12).

Borrowing from Kathy's earlier leadership book, we note that, "Life, then, is a series of learning experiences resulting in continual freezing, thawing, changing, and refreezing." With the number and rapidity of change faced by those of us who work in healthcare today, it seems as if there isn't enough time for one cycle to complete before another begins. We don't have time to refreeze before the next thaw. The result is a messy state of affairs that can be described as a state of slush. Those of us who are attempting to survive and thrive in this icy, unformed flux may feel like a generation of "healthcare slush puppies" (13). (For those who may know it by another name, Slush Puppie is a brand name of an ice and flavoring treat similar to others that are known as Slurpies, Icees, or shaved ice sno-balls.)

Kathy's frosty humor aside, the messiness of the healthcare environment and the changes occurring are welcomed by some, but dreaded and resisted by others. The chaos is resulting in real stress and discomfort for many individuals.

A large part of Dyad partnership work will be managing change. Understanding the steps to a change model (*whichever* you choose) is important for both leaders, because neither gets to opt out of the hard work of leading it. Every step into the next era of healthcare takes effort on the part of the Dyad partners *and* their teams.

Change is especially hard when it is imposed (from higher in the organization or from the government or a regulatory body). In fact, early researchers Blake and

Mouton say imposed change sometimes succeeds, but more often fails (14). Even when an individual or group initiates change for themselves, it is seldom simple and not always successful. Some of the mistakes we have personally observed among colleagues tasked with making changes in (or transforming) healthcare areas for which they are the formal leader include

▶ Not clearly thinking through and articulating the why, how, what, and *who*.
▶ Not communicating well at every step of a change process.
▶ Not including the right people at every step.
▶ Not prognosticating who will be affected and where, who and what the resistance will be, and not planning tactics to mitigate this resistance.
▶ Not thinking through what might be collateral effects (after the fact these are called unforeseen consequences).
▶ Not realizing that what seems simple, nonimportant, or inevitable to some *does not* feel that way to others.
▶ Not considering what Thora Kron pointed out in 1971 as three obstacles to change in healthcare: emotions, habits, and self-satisfaction (15). Emotions can trump reason. Habits can be hard to break. An individual or group's self-satisfaction with their place in the current world can cause active resistance to anything that endangers that status.

Our organization has practiced a defined change model for the last decade. We adopted the General Electric (GE) Change Acceleration Process (CAP) (16) as our facilitation tool for all organizational change. Our leadership team understands that change is *not* easy, even in the best of times. Foreseeing major upheavals in the healthcare world, an early decision was made to prepare the company for these. We purchased the CAP model, hired a national change team, and began educating change agents (leaders) throughout the system. Display 10-4 depicts the CAP methodology as it is practiced at CHI. In Display 10-5, Master Change Agent Jerri Brooks defines our organizational change management process.

As we mention above, there are a variety of change models, but most have similar steps. We are not advocating for a particular methodology, but do believe that an organization should select a model, educate formal leaders and employees on the steps to successful change, and insist that it is implemented and used throughout the company. Change will still be disruptive, but a defined way of proceeding with the disruption will minimize some of the chaos in these chaotic days.

Utilizing the steps of a change process as Dyads are introduced into the formal leadership hierarchy will make it more likely that this management model will be successfully adopted. The CAP steps we use illustrate this. In order to implement change that sticks, *every* step must be considered, planned for, and implemented. These include leading change, creating a shared need, shaping a vision, mobilizing commitment, making change last, monitoring progress, and changing systems and structures.

Display 10-4 The CAP Methodology as Used at CHI

Change is effective and efficient when all components of the methodology are done well. The seven components of the CAP as purchased and adapted from GE and used by CHI are shared below. Included are brief definitions and examples of how these apply to the implementation of our Strategic Initiatives.

▶ **Leading Change:** Visible, active commitment by sponsors/champions and team members is critical to success. Leading change includes having CHI market-based organization leaders kick off and "own" the implementation of changes within their local organization, aligning key leaders, managers, and stakeholders around each project's goals, and ensuring governance structures are in place to effectively lead the change.

▶ **Creating a Shared Need**: The reason for change is understood and shared. Through regular calls and meetings, both national and market-based organization leaders create understanding of the need for and shared benefits of the change.

▶ **Shaping a Vision:** The desired outcome of a change is clear, legitimate, widely understood, shared, and actionable. Market-based organization leaders develop their understanding of the vision and desired outcomes for successful project implementation. They then build common understanding and commitment through consistent communication within their local organizations.

▶ **Mobilizing Commitment:** Key stakeholders are identified, resistance is analyzed, and actions are taken to gain strong commitment. Onboarding sessions, ongoing assessments, training, communication, and site visits help gain the commitment of all stakeholders in the project implementation process.

▶ **Making Change Last:** Learnings are transferred throughout the organization, with consistent, visible, and tangible reinforcement of the change. Market-based organization leaders communicate successes and lessons learned during implementations, addressing stakeholders' feedback and questions.

▶ **Monitoring Progress:** Success is defined with metrics and benchmarks to ensure accountability. Leaders regularly monitor progress toward project milestones and assess go-live success using operational metrics.

▶ **Changing Systems and Structures:** Management practices are aligned to complement and reinforce change. Leaders ensure that all policies, systems, structures, and processes are redesigned and aligned as needed with new project systems and processes. Effects on roles are identified and necessary changes implemented.

Organizational Communications: For CHI, we added a component to underpin the CAP model, focused on the importance of organizational communications. Multiple venues are put in place to ensure Dyad leaders are communicating with, and hearing from, appropriate stakeholders early, often, and throughout an initiative so that plans can be dynamically modified, based on customer needs.

From Jerri Brooks, MA, PMP, MCA, and Marilyn Jones-Davis, MHS, JD, Master Change Agents. Adapted from The General Electric CAP Model.

Display 10-5 **Our Organizational Change Management Model**

The sheer amount of change that healthcare organizations are facing is continuing and will continue to increase. Therefore, building the competency to lead and manage change is imperative for organizational success. Because of this, CHI adopted and adapted GE's CAP to ensure the system has a common approach focused on the people side of change. Leaders have a robust change management competency to navigate, prepare, manage, and sustain the health of our business, communities, and patients. We define change management for Catholic Health Initiatives as a set of concepts, methods, and tools for leading and managing the people side of change. Through the use of CAP, we live out our core values of reverence, integrity, compassion, and excellence.

According to research from Prosci's "Best Practices in Change Management" published in 2007, the top five contributors to successful change are (i) active and visible executive sponsorship; (ii) structured change management; (iii) frequent and open communication around the need for change; (iv) dedicated resources for change management; and (v) employee participation (17).

Change management in our company:

▶ Increases the organization's capability for effective change
▶ Is applied by leaders and managers to help the organization and its employee's transition from a current state to a desired future state
▶ Delivers methods and tools to help redesign processes and solve specific problems
▶ Uses a flexible/nonlinear model throughout the change process
▶ Facilitates commitment and behavioral change through team dialogue and action
▶ Increases the odds for and speed of successful change.

From Jerri Brooks, MA, PMP, MCA, Master Change Agent and Trainer.

CHANGING THE LEADERSHIP PARADIGM: IMPLEMENTING SUCCESSFUL DYADS

Leading Change

There needs to be a true commitment to this new type of shared leadership. The top executives in the organization must believe that co-management is the right model for defined departments, projects, service lines, or processes. They need to understand what they want to accomplish by implementing this significant departure from historical healthcare silos and hierarchies. They need to be ready to withstand criticism, angst, and resistance, *even from those who voice unhappiness with the current lack of partnership between the silos.*

Executives who support co-leadership should examine their own ability to accept increased influence from individuals currently not involved in the executive silo. Even leaders at the top will not escape some of the discomfort that will accompany the blurring of organizational silo boundaries.

We wrote this book partly because of our observation that executive leaders across the country are voicing a desire to implement shared leadership. We've watched as so-called Dyads are hired without consideration of what sharing really means. In some cases (granted, this is from the outside, so we may have inaccurate perceptions), it seems that two leaders are simply named Dyads, without thought of how to build their relationship, define individual roles, or provide basic management education to partners who have never managed. There does not seem to be consideration of the need to confront issues of differences in socialization and professional culture and to support two individuals who are embarking on a major job change *during* the chaos of healthcare transformation.

This change will fail if it is put in place without thoughtful planning and deliberate interventions to disrupt past relationship dysfunctions. Dyads won't work, or at least won't fulfill their potential of transforming organizations, if they are simply window dressing to appease specific stakeholders. The struggle for power between cultures will derail partnerships so that they won't be able to lead the way to changing healthcare in America *for everyone.*

When executive leaders determine that Dyad leadership is a model to take their organizations into the next era, they must support it wholeheartedly. They show this support by verbalizing their belief in what Dyad leaders will be able to accomplish. They keep a close eye on, and are involved in, the change process steps. It's essential that the Dyad leaders, their teams, the various organization silos, and the organization's employees at all levels perceive that this is the top executive team's preferred model for at least some (defined) management positions.

Creating a Shared Need

Once executive team members are convinced and committed to Dyad leadership, they will need to address the importance of other's education about why the organization will benefit from co-leadership. Organizations possess an inertia that supports maintaining the status quo. This is true even when individuals or groups profess unhappiness or great discomfort with the way things are now. Kurt Lewin described resistance to change through a force field analysis, when he pointed out that the need to change (or perception of the need) must have greater force than the need to stay "frozen" the way we are now (12). Peter Senge reminded leaders that, "Although we are all interested in large scale change, we must change one mind at a time" (18). Since organizations have huge numbers of employees and stakeholders, this would be daunting if we believed every single person needed 1:1 convincing from executives. Fortunately, we agree with Malcolm Gladwell's assertion that change occurs at certain dramatic moments known as "tipping points" (19). The tipping point for Dyad management will occur when multiple partnerships are implemented well and when they demonstrate an ability to unite previously siloed groups into teams working on shared goals.

Creating a shared need in an organization requires a diffusion of information about why Dyads will help lead into the future. This may require education as well as acknowledgement of what our current dysfunctions are because we operate in silos. The diffusion model we use in our organization includes education of formal leaders as part of helping them grasp the need to change. We also rely heavily on *informal* leaders for virtually *every* type of change. This is done through designating individuals as champions in our local markets and ensuring that they have the information and resources to share the need for change to *their* closest stakeholders.

You are reading this book, so we assume you perceive a need to at least consider a shared leadership model within your organization. You must have a compelling reason to change the healthcare habit of working in silos. This is probably because you can see that our industry is fragmented, is too costly, and does not provide the highest quality of care. You may feel your hospital is not providing the high value (low cost, plus high quality) you *want* to provide. Safety of your consumers may be a concern. Customer satisfaction scores may not be where you believe they should be, and employee and physician satisfaction may not be either. You may think this is the best way to lead a Clinically Integrated Network (CIN). You may have problems with variation in care that requires multidisciplinary teamwork. You may be concerned about mounting evidence that this variation is not beneficial to patients, and that some treatments and diagnostics we use not only are *not always needed* but are costly, and even harmful to individuals. All of these concerns might lead you to consider Dyad management.

Your conclusion might match ours: our professional cultural differences need to be bridged so that we can bring together the best thinking of diverse leaders to address long-standing problems, and one way to do this is to learn to share formal leadership.

We've learned that additional rationale for Dyad teams can be helpful when addressing leadership concerns of particular groups. For example, clinical groups are interested in knowing when one Dyad leader comes from their ranks, *because they perceive that members of their profession have not previously been at tables where they believe they can and should influence change.* (We've been surprised at how many professionals feel that their groups have been disenfranchised and disregarded, while *other* professions perceive those groups as powerful and controlling, while perceiving that *their* tribe has been disempowered!)

Whatever need your organization wishes to fill with Dyad leadership, it must become a shared need throughout the organization. That requires a dissemination plan, complete with disciples willing to spread the word that this is a good thing for diverse stakeholders.

Shaping a Vision

It's important that leaders articulate what the organization will look like after Dyad leadership is implemented. If this isn't done, there is no shared destination that people can move toward. It can't be assumed that everyone sees the same picture of the future. *Resistance to change occurs when different individuals and groups form their own visions.*

These are actual comments we've heard from people when they first heard about this model in their organizations:

▶ "*Finally.* Doctors will be in charge, like we were when *we* started hospitals and before these MHAs were invented." (Our interpretation of this statement is that this individual sees Dyads as a way to eventually move to a hierarchy where physicians are actually the sole top leaders. Incidentally, he also has a flawed historical lens because, while physicians led early academic centers, nurses were usually the superintendents of early community hospitals.)

▶ "*Oh no.* Here we go again. This is just another way to pacify physicians or pay money to an influential doctor, so he'll support administration by swaying his peers. I'll get a so-called partner who will simply give me all the work to do while he causes me more headaches with his lack of management skill and need to order people around." (Our interpretation of this statement is that this manager is cynical about the organization's commitment to actually leading *together*.)

▶ "*This is great.* Clinicians have been pushed out of the business side over time, and by combining the Docs and the RNs in teams, we will get the power to be heard. I see the day when we lead everything." (Our interpretation is that this person sees benefit in *two* professional cultures working together but might not view the future as a place where teams, individual professionals, and leaders from *all* healthcare stakeholder groups are empowered to lead.)

While these comments illustrate views of the future through slightly different lenses, they have something in common. They envision the future leadership models as a "tweaking" of today's hierarchy or dysfunctional relationships. They imply that power is a limited resource and something to be gained through positioning or by taking it away from someone else.

Our long-term vision is that Dyad leadership is a step toward other shared leadership models. We see the evolution of a system where learning to lead as two partners eventually leads to learning to lead in larger partnerships, too. Because that future is difficult to paint (early sketches have to be completed before murals can be done!) we share this verbal portrait of Dyad leadership: two leaders, peers from different professions, with different but complementary skills, education, and experience leading and managing multiprofessional teams to accomplish goals in support of the organization's mission and vision.

Whatever *your* vision is for the formation of Dyads, it's important to share it. Otherwise, ideas like those expressed above could undermine your organization's journey toward a preferred future.

Mobilizing Commitment

Some people call this step "implementing an influence strategy." You probably utilize a common influence strategy already, and this should be deployed as this model of management is rolled out. We mobilize commitment through change agents and designated champions. Our change (CAP) leaders, educators, human resource leaders, communication resources, and internal coaching teams have a part in developing these new partnerships. Change leaders reminded us to use our CAP steps. Educators develop leadership programs and courses for Dyad leaders. Human resource professionals help us with job descriptions, selections, and assessment of potential Dyad managers. Communication partners include references to Dyad partnerships throughout their various communication tools. Coaches work with individuals and Dyad pairs to help them work through their new roles and relationships.

Making Change Last

Dyads have great potential to lead organizational transformation, but only if the change to this type of leadership takes root in the organization. It is our intent, with this book, to share knowledge we've gained as a starting point for those pursuing this model. We intend to continue to share our successful (and not so successful) implementations of co-leadership and sincerely hope that other systems will do the same. As an industry, we can share best practices as we all integrate leadership models that will bring us together to change healthcare locally, as well as nationally, in the interest of individuals and communities.

Monitoring Progress

Implementing a new management model without planning how to determine its effectiveness is a mistake. As with any organizational change, there is a reason (a "why") for deciding to lead differently. Co-leading is a departure from single-leader management. It isn't competent leadership to put individuals and organizations through the cost or the disruption of this departure from the past without expected improvements in *something* (quality, cost, job satisfaction, or patient satisfaction). Goals for implementing Dyads should be documented and understood from the beginning. If they aren't met, reasons for lack of progress should be analyzed, and appropriate interventions or changes must be made. On the other hand, when Dyad teams demonstrate that their partnership has met goals, or improved value to the organization, they should be emulated as best practice, and celebrated for their achievements.

Changing Systems and Structures

All healthcare organizations have systems and structures that support their current way of doing business. When Dyad leadership teams are initiated, these "underpinnings" of the company need to be examined and altered to support the new way of managing. If this isn't done, there is high probability that 6, 12, 18, 24, or more months after implementation, executive leaders will declare that co-leadership simply doesn't work, either as a concept or with the particular individuals selected to co-lead. New Dyad partners may be picked to replace the originals, *or* the model may be discontinued as an experiment that failed.

We've seen the latter occur and heard the statements:

▶ Well, we tried, but formal leadership just doesn't work with two people. There must be *one* accountable manager making final decisions for every process, project, or department.

▶ I knew physicians couldn't learn to do the hard work of management or figure out how to be part of a team.

▶ That was just the "flavor of the month," another hare-brained, follow-the-pack management idea.

Executives who believe that this model of leadership could bridge traditional cultural divides *must* invest time considering what environmental changes support or threaten its success. Then, they need to remove or mitigate any identified barriers to success.

We've identified the need for appropriate selection of partners, evaluation of individual strengths and weakness, availability of individual and Dyad education and coaching opportunities, importance of team building, and the need to openly address cultural differences, as well as the "little things" that can add up to an environment not conducive to partnership development. Every organization probably has other systems and structures that could pose challenges to Dyad leadership. Are there committee structures that need to change to allow appropriate Dyad participation? Will executive pay practices be perceived by designated "equal partners" as unfair, inequitable, or illogical? Will these cause resentment between co-leaders if not addressed or rationally explained? Are there hiring practices that discourage selection of people who could best succeed in these roles? Are there policies or rigid hierarchical-based procedures that will prevent Dyad leaders from making timely decisions or coordinated change implementations together? Are there cultural barriers executives need to address to "smooth the way" for Dyad leaders?

Implementation of formal Dyad leadership partnerships in the place of individual leaders should be considered like any major organizational change. This is the responsibility of executives who choose to put them into practice.

FROM CHANGE TO TRANSFORMATION

As we mentioned before, Dyad leadership as a management structure is a beginning step in transforming an organization. Transformation is *more* than "garden variety" change. Figure 10-1, adapted from a slide from the consulting firm Accenture, is an excellent illustration of how much change is necessary to actually transform an organization. As it depicts, change occurs continually in small increments to make short-term alterations. This is labeled "Business as Usual." A greater amount of change must occur when an organization is in a "turnaround" state.

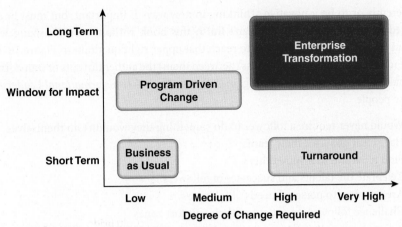

FIGURE 10-1 Types of transformation. (Adapted from Accenture with permission.)

It makes sense that turnarounds are also short term in their effect on an organization because the work done to help organizations survive is mostly transactional. Transactions, although important, do *not* make permanent transformation occur (see Chapter 2). More change (and better change management) is required to implement impactful modifications of how we do things based on program needs. The most change, which takes the most effort and time, but which *lasts the longest*, is transformation of the enterprise.

Hopefully, before this final chapter, we've been able to make the case for carefully planned, selected, and educated Dyads as important leaders for enterprise transformation. Two complementary managers make intuitive sense because of the cultural divides that must be crossed if organizations are to thrive in a new environment where the payment system and patient care system *will* change, even if some of us do not. If we either choose not to evolve or can't make major change (we lack the will or the ability), we, as individuals or organizations, will become obsolete.

We know individuals who are leaving or retiring early rather than deal with the changes coming. We read the prognostications that some healthcare organizations, particularly hospitals, will cease to exist. We've heard that, in a few years, our industry will be largely dominated by a few very large systems. Survivors will be those who think strategically, try new models and partnerships, and transform themselves into the organizations for the next era.

More on Transformation

New research continues to be shared in the management literature about *transformational leadership*. Consultants and executives alike have added these two words to their everyday vocabulary. Yet few express what it will take to move organizations all the way to transformation. Some talk, in general, about being willing to think differently or to be innovative. Thinking in new ways *is* important, but must be followed by implementation. We can't finish this book without reemphasizing what Dyad leaders *must* do if they are to reach that upper right quadrant in Figure 10-1.

First, the partners much possess (between them) the authentic traits of transformational leaders. According to R. Riggio (20), coauthor of *Transformational Leadership*, these people

▶ Would never require a follower to do something they wouldn't do themselves
▶ Have clear goals for their teams
▶ Find it natural to inspire others
▶ Celebrate the talents and successes of followers
▶ Are attentive to personal needs of followers
▶ Challenge followers to get out of their comfort zones
▶ Believe teamwork is the way to success
▶ Encourage followers to question their most basic ways of thinking
▶ Are told by followers that their enthusiasm and positive energy are infectious

Transformational Dyad leaders are relationship managers. They help diverse cultures question the biases developed through professional, gender, racial, ethnic, community, or other socialization. They respect the uniqueness of each team member and understand the power of diversity, including diversity of thought. They know that even the most brilliant strategies and comprehensive plans are of little value if they aren't put into practice.

Whether you are an executive responsible for implementing successful Dyads, leaders considering becoming a Dyad, *new* Dyad partners, or *experienced* Dyad partners, it's important to consider the hard work involved in learning together. *Before* Dyads can lead their teams and organizations effectively, the partners must

▶ Carefully consider and discuss what it will take to become equal co-leaders
▶ Explore the bias and perceptions each brings from his or her own cultures
▶ Understand their own and their partners' strengths and weaknesses
▶ Agree on division of labor, who will do what, when and how they will substitute or "stand in" for each other, and which responsibilities and accountabilities they share
▶ Determine a communication strategy, including how they will touch base regularly, when they will meet, what each needs or wants to know about the other's work, and preferences for emails, phone calls, or written notes
▶ Agree on what each needs and can expect from the other *and define* terms. (For example, what does *transparency* look like between us? What behaviors do I mean when I say I expect *support* from you? What does an *equal* partnership look like when we are meeting together or with others? What is our plan for avoiding *triangulation*? Will we *evaluate* individuals on our team together?)

- Discuss the "little" things (see Chapter 5) that can undermine the development of a partnership and how these will be addressed by both partners
- Agree on the Dyad's mission, vision, and goals
- Agree on how the partners will confront problems or perceived issues between themselves
- Share thoughts on development needs and how the partnership will increase leadership skills either separately or as a pair *learning together*
- Seek education and learning about management and leadership
- Regularly evaluate together, the state of the partnership, progress toward goals, and how to continually make the Dyad stronger, more effective, and a source of workplace pride and joy for *both* partners

Traditional families and Dyad Teams, as discussed earlier, are similar in many ways. When there is more than one formal family leader (two parents) or more than one formal team leader (Dyad partners), the family or team will mirror the functioning of the leaders. Organizations don't need dysfunctional Dyads.

After the Dyad partners are functioning well together is the right time for them to begin their other work: bringing their multiprofessional, multicultural teams together to transform their organizations.

THE FUTURE FOR DYADS AND OTHER MANAGEMENT MODELS

While Dyads are a promising leadership structure for helping organizations get ready for the next era of healthcare, many management positions will continue to be filled by "single" formal leaders. Our bias is that the successful singles will not be leading alone. They will be surrounded and supported by teams. They, too, will be transformational when they share leadership with others.

In Chapter 9, we mentioned that some systems appear to have skipped over Dyads to a form of Triad leadership teams. Within our organization, there are a variety of conversations occurring about different mini-teams of leaders configured to accomplish tasks, some of which are semipermanent because of the ongoing nature of shared work. Whatever leadership configurations evolve in the future, they will require individuals who are able to cross historical boundaries to work in new teams. This will be as true at the top of the organization as at the point of customer care.

As clinicians, we believe in evidence-based practice. We also believe in evidence-based management. That means innovations or experiments in leadership must be evaluated for effectiveness. We've begun discussions about more rigorous or "scientific" research on Dyad leadership, as we get better at it over time. In the meantime, more pressing than adding to management theory is the need to meet our goal of transforming healthcare. It's a huge challenge. It will take courageous leaders who understand we can't just tinker with current systems. These are the leaders who won't ignore the practices and cultures that must be disrupted before we can build a preferred future for all of our stakeholders.

Harvard Business School Professor John Kotter claims that we need people at the top who encourage others to leap into the future while helping them overcome their natural fears. He encourages us to expand our leadership capacity because by doing this we are providing "a profoundly important service for the entire human community" (21).

Kevin Lofton, CEO of Catholic Health Initiatives and a past chairman of the American Hospital Association Board, says, "The next era of healthcare will only be achieved with leaders who understand that transformation of the healthcare delivery system is an imperative. We have a moral calling to serve the people and communities who entrust their lives to us and expect providers will coalesce around their health and well-being. This is our mission, our motivation, and our resolution. It's fundamental to our shared success that we form strong partnerships through innovative management structures."

As you plan *your* part in healthcare transformation of the next era, we are glad you are exploring the possibility of Dyad leadership. We wish you well on your journey.

CHAPTER SUMMARY

Healthcare is changing rapidly, and models of leadership, like models of care, will evolve quickly, too. As executive leadership teams plan for the next era of healthcare, they must understand that resilience is as important for them as it is to clinicians and other members of the team.

Transformation is needed to take us into a thriving future, and Dyad leadership is a natural model to increase the organization's skill and comfort with change. Company executive leaders who recognize that traditional silo management has not resulted in ideal team work will benefit from exploring this way to lead in specific areas of their companies. They will challenge old paradigms in which there is an expressed preference for hierarchies of *individuals*. Healthcare executives must help others in the organization understand why we need to consider new leadership models, what some of these partnering models could be, and how Dyads can help lead and develop productive multiprofessional teams. They must select appropriate Dyad partners who exhibit the transformational traits listed in this chapter. Then, they must support the changes necessary for new leaders to succeed, including cultural change. This can only occur when people in power positions increase their own understanding of the difference between transactional change and transformational change.

A planned change is only as successful as its implementation. We advocate for this form of leadership as a method for increasing leadership skill. We see it as a step to expanding leadership capacity through new, engaged, cooperative teams led by a variety of leaders with complementary skills.

Dyads in Action

HOW TWO BECAME "WE"

Renae N. Battié and Peter Buckley

This is the story of how we (a nurse leader and physician leader) got to know each other and how we forged a sound working relationship that metamorphosed into a cordial and supportive relationship. That relationship then became our tool to spearhead the planning, opening, and running of a major new development in our institution's surgical services.

BACKGROUND

Both of us had a substantial background in the OR, and at the time we began to work together, we had both worked within an academic health center system for about 20 years, usually in separate locations. That is to say, we knew of each other, had a vague idea of each other's roles, but we did not really know each other.

Renae began her career as a full-time OR RN for several years, and then worked in a part-time capacity in a variety of staff/educator roles, all within the Medical Center (MC), while raising kids. She returned to school to acquire a Master's degree and, after completing that, became interested in developing and implementing new projects. In 2006, she successfully advocated for and became the new "special projects manager" for the Executive Director of Surgical Services and worked within the OR Management Committee. In that role, Renae led a variety of projects. She directed the move from paper to electronic charting, established short-term action teams to develop efficiencies with ambulatory ortho cases, improving data analytics, and led remodeling and quality projects. In 2001, her role transitioned to Perioperative Service Line Manager, where she focused on the ambulatory services development. Renae moved into the formal Ambulatory Surgery Manager role in 2003.

Peter's background was in OR anesthesia. He had extensive experience within the University system. Outside of the medical center, he had developed and run Acute Pain Services at a trauma center and a cancer center. His appointment at UWMC was as Deputy Chief of Anesthesia, to fill in for the Chief of Anesthesia, who was going on sabbatical, and to take on tasks as assigned by the Chief or the Surgical Services Committee (SSC).

HOW WE CAME TO WORK TOGETHER

Our initial contacts and interactions began as a consequence of our membership of, and attendance at, the weekly meeting of the SSC. The SSC managed the surgical services on a day-to-day basis, but also dealt with longer-term strategic issues and developments. The membership of the SSC was multidisciplinary and comprised the Executive Director of Surgical Service, the Operating Room (OR) Manager, Project Manager (Renae), OR Business manager, Chief of Surgery, Chief of Anesthesia, and Deputy Chief Anesthesia (Peter). This group developed into a more formal committee structure after recommendations from an outside consultant. We believe that the relative newness of this mode of governance, the fact that the leader had position authority due to being at the MC Executive level (indicating that Surgical Services is an important element of the system), the personality of the leader, and her leadership style, fostered a sense of common identity. The Executive Director's style included letting everyone have his or her say on issues, a "no shame, no blame" culture, clear assignment of specific tasks, follow-up on task completion, and a significant amount of irreverence and humor. As a result of these factors, we became a new kind of SSC. We were a team, not individuals differentiated as MDs, RNs, or Administrators. The team was cross-disciplinary, collaborative, and cooperative. In this environment, we were able to watch each other work, observe our interactions with others, and begin to establish a personal connection.

A few months into our membership on the SSC, our first opportunity to work together came as a consequence of us both volunteering to work on the "Surgical Block" challenges. Surgical blocks were defined as sectioned hours of time from the beginning of the day (defined time) to the end of the day (when the last patient of the day left the OR). Statistics for OR times were tracked by the OR computer system. All the available blocks in the available 14 ORs were fully assigned. There was one block per day for the various surgical specialties. There were no vacant blocks and, in consequence, there was significant interest on the part of surgical departments to acquire more "blocks" in order to do more cases. They also wanted "bragging rights." In other words, surgical block time was very much the coin of the realm, very highly prized, and much schemed over.

To manage the use and distribution of this scarce and much coveted block time, there were "rules" about "block use and distribution/redistribution," which had been developed and were, allegedly, applied to block usage. For example, if a service was unable to use a certain "block" (due to surgeon absence or a lack of booked cases), the service could relinquish (release) the block up to the day prior to surgery and not have that "released" block be part of the equation of the service's block use. This resulted in an inefficiency issue when block time was released the day before it was available. (It was then essentially useless to another service or the system.) In a 3-month epoch, a service was supposed to use at least 70% of its unreleased block. The formula for describing this is: (Used block/(Total block − Released block) × 100 >70%). If this metric was not met, the service was at risk of losing block time, which would then be reassigned to another service.

Block measurement, use, calculation, and the rules about these matters were a significant hot and contentious topic for the SSC, the institution, and the surgeons. Until we got involved with the block numbers, block had not really been much of a focus issue for the SSC, other than being the target of complaints from surgeons. There had been minimal loss/acquisition/reassignment of block in the previous 2 years. Our task was to jointly acquire and collate block use, block release, and block "no use" on a consistent basis; to present that information to the system; and to make recommendations (based on the block "rules") on how to proceed. We did this by jointly working with the OR computer guru, acquiring the data on a time-sensitive basis and meeting at least weekly to interpret the data. We explored different ways of presenting and interpreting the data and derived new indices that could give insights into OR functionality. We assembled the data into a form useful for presentation and action and then jointly presented our work to the SSC on a weekly basis.

We recognized early in this process that we were dealing with a data set and an initiative (beginning to enforce the "block rules") that was likely to be controversial, be called into question, and be attacked. We both recognized the importance of our data and presentation being credible, consistent, and accurate. If the data were missing any of these characteristics, our individual and joint credibility would be called into question. Therefore, a particular focus issue at our weekly meetings was to ensure that we had a joint and consistent understanding of the interpretation of the data. We planned to use a jointly developed single presentation. We are both strong individuals, with our own opinions, so these weekly conversations often revealed differing individual views. We expressed these with vigor! We were able to combine and mix those differing views and develop our joint "public" data set and presentation. In other words, we expressed our disagreements in private but presented a united front in public—after coming to joint agreements.

We planned this unity to prevent us from giving inconsistent answers when questioned individually. It also allowed either of us to present our information publicly and stand in for each other. When we began to go "public" with the data and presentations to the SSC, our forecasting of challenges proved to be correct. Our task and the data produced were assailed from both administration and surgeons in a number of different ways. We heard these statements: "How can you rely on a computer system that often breaks down?" "Your programmer and your data extraction person don't know what they're doing." "The system gives you faulty data and the data don't reflect reality." "The rules aren't fair."

To the credit of our leaders, the executives weighed in on our side and deflected and defused inappropriate attacks. Certainly the data set we produced initially was not perfect, but we massaged it based on our own perceptions and the criticisms of others. We just kept plugging doggedly away at the system and the data, as we attempted to iron out any kinks and anomalies.

At the end of several months, we believed that we had an accurate and functional system that numerically represented how OR time was used. Much of the criticism of the data acquisition, the data itself, and data accuracy wound down. However, there was still the undercurrent, from the surgeons, with statements like these: "the rules aren't fair." "The rules shouldn't apply to my service because—" Despite the existence of agreed upon "block rules," the hospital administration was reluctant to enforce them, based on the data we produced. Their lack of action was a source of frustration for us.

In spite of this early nonvictory, these circumstances helped contribute to the molding of our joint persona. We had the opportunity to work with each other and see each other in action (as part of the SSC) in noncompeting and nonthreatening ways before we began to work together on specific projects. We were operating in an environment that facilitated and fostered interdisciplinary cooperation and work. We were given a circumscribed data-based task and, while given some specific directions, were allowed significant latitude about how we used the data. We both recognized the need to really get accurate data and to work at our mutual understanding of the information, its interpretation and presentation. We believe that the contentious nature of the responses to the data (and the topic), as well as the "outside attacks" that were made on what we had produced and presented, pushed us into working closely and cooperatively. In a way, we were "a Dyad born of adversity."

Observing the opposition to what we were espousing was helpful in making our Dyad more functional and durable. When encountering opposition, we sometimes came away with differing views of what was said and why it was voiced. Our interpretation of the motives behind what was being said differed. Our discussions of our opposing views were helpful in organizing our joint front to others and helped each of us appreciate the perception capabilities of the other person. Paradoxically, even the frustration that we felt at the lack of institutional action to our recommendations served to reinforce our belief in our actions and effort, hence reinforcing the Dyad partnership.

DEVELOPING A NEW UNIT

The prevailing culture of the OR was to deal with any case, anytime, anywhere, with no limits. This is an analogous situation to owning a full service Mercedes dealership where the company can do all manner of tasks from a simple oil changes to very complex replacement of transmissions. Such a system certainly works, but it is cumbersome, expensive, and not in the least agile.

The Outpatient surgery workload of the system was significant, comprising about 40% of all cases. Despite the large number of outpatients every day, there was little or no provision built into the system to accommodate them. All patients came into, and exited, the system by the same routes, utilizing the same mechanisms and the same staff. There was no unified effort or system to manage outpatients differently from inpatients. Ostensibly, the system had made *some* provision for outpatient cases. Three ORs were designated as "ambulatory." These were very small, very cramped, and out of the way. They were staffed out of a general OR staffing pool of both RNs and anesthesiologists. There was no separate patient flow from the rest of the main OR. In other words, these were outpatient facilities in name only. Their lack of functionality and their similarity to the inpatient OR lead to the attitudes of RNs and MDs that outpatient procedures were to be treated no differently than inpatient surgeries. This view was perceived as a significant barrier to the institution's success as an ambulatory facility.

Renae was asked to lead a project to remodel a pain clinic/procedure room in an off-site clinic building to serve as the organization's first true ambulatory surgery center. The new off-site center offered the potential of providing a separate and distinct ambulatory patient flow while developing an ambulatory surgical "mindset" within the organization. This involved finalizing the remodeling plans, coordinating project details, and hiring a new team. The new model was to include the first surgical technicians, as the main OR had functioned with an exclusive all-RN staffing model.

Peter was the identified chief for ambulatory anesthesia, so we began to work together in developing some of the patient care and flow plans. Peter's background in delivering anesthetics in off-site areas was an important expertise for creating a safe place for care in this new facility.

We quickly found that while our roles were not intended to be what we would now call a "Dyad" (there really wasn't a precedent for that at the time, at least in our institution), the decisions we needed to make for this work were interdependent. Existing RN and anesthesia staff had functioned almost exclusively within the "full service," resource-rich environment of the Main OR. Many staff members, of both stripes, were very uncomfortable leaving a known and secure environment for an unfamiliar location. We recognized this mindset, so we lobbied for, and were allowed to hand pick and recruit our staff. We both had input on the qualities best suited for this new environment and shared our views and observations with each other during the process of choosing the best candidates. We had each worked with these candidates, so it was helpful to share the different perspectives our personal roles gave us on colleagues, as we reviewed the potential new team members. We wanted individuals who were experienced but flexible, positive, and constructive. We sought individuals who were not afraid of trying new things and who would be resilient when things didn't go as planned. We needed flexible team members because they would need to perform multiple roles in a facility without many support personnel. We wanted a "can do" attitude from everyone, because this was important for the creation of new workflows and new ideas.

We used our experience with block and surgical practices change management to develop the best options for potential surgeons in the environment. We met with the surgeons together to share the vision and expectations of this new unit. Peter described this as the attempt to go from a "Mercedes" to a "jiffy lube" mentality. This is difficult to do in a traditional academic institution where things are often seen as slow and plodding, versus the efficient focused process we wanted! In academics, because of a research mindset, it can be difficult to change quickly and to try new things without extensive testing and "proving" the evidence. Our motto became "Perfect Is the Enemy of the Good" as we set out to overcome the traditional inertia.

We opened in January 2002 with a brand new staff team, including handpicked anesthesia providers to develop our institutional ambulatory expertise. Coordinating schedule issues together as an administrative/clinical team cemented our "we" persona that became our mantra. Dealing with a variety of issues caused by being an off-site center was another source of "adversity" that brought us together.

Renae spoke with the anesthesia providers herself when they had concerns, knowing either of us could speak for both of us. Peter pulled Renae's staff aside when behaviors were not in line with our vision. Anything that compromised functionality was a risk for the success of the center and became something that was important to address, whether it was a technical skill or a behavioral issue. We became both cheerleaders and parents of the team! It was a great learning lab for us. We realized how important the esprit de corps was to the high-level functioning of the unit. We had a thin margin of the "right" people for this new venture, but these were people who could be flexible in their roles and good with problem solving. We had to walk the walk of the concept ourselves becoming, "Jack and Jill" of all trades. This included picking up mops and answering phones. Following our lead, even the surgeons took part in whatever needed to be done!

Early on, we experienced an incident with a high-volume surgeon. He had thrown a phone across the room (and broke it) in the OR. This physician was known to have a volatile personality, and he was our biggest customer. We set up a meeting with him together to address the behavior. It was a very respectful, well-received conversation. The power of doing this together as a partnered MD-RN leadership team was an eye opener for us. The ability to accomplish more together was not because one person wasn't capable, but because our strength together was more than we had as individuals. As we drove away from our meeting with the surgeon, we reflected on how well the discussion had gone. It was then that we began to realize we were really a team. After that, we began to speak more and more with the vocabulary of partnership. We talked of "our" vision and "our" service line.

The ambulatory project we did together (known as the Roosevelt project) was the pilot for a large new ambulatory facility being built adjacent to the current hospital. There was to be a floor dedicated to perioperative services, including 11 ORs, as well as 42 pre-/post-/overnight beds. It was to be the front door for all main campus surgical patients, regardless of their ambulatory status, so the importance of first impressions was paramount. We were able to take on the learnings about ambulatory flow that had been honed at the off-site facility and translate them into a different workflow for the new facility. The goal was to create a high-efficiency, high-tech environment that supported lean concepts, standardization, preparation, and patient readiness while making it easy for the staff to do the right things. The bigger challenge for this project was its adjacency to the main OR, the traditional inpatient facility with all the "how we've always done it" culture that was present there. The prevailing attitude was still that managing outpatient cases and outpatient case flows was pretty much the same as managing inpatients. Our difficulty was not in new ideas, but escaping the old ones! By this time, we had worked hard to become the ambulatory experts and were recognized as such by the surgical team. We were given a lot of latitude so that we could make the new facility work as well as the Roosevelt facility.

We were in agreement on what we wanted in terms of design, and were able to lobby effectively for the priorities we felt were important. We felt it was essential for staff morale that any break room was not closeted within the interior of the building, but had some view of the outside world. It took some rearranging of rooms, but we were able to finalize a large shared staff room with a wall of windows. To minimize hallway clutter, we planned inset bays for OR gurneys outside each room, with plenty of storage for OR equipment in spaces that didn't have doors to knock around.

This time, we worked together to develop the vision for the new facility and to set expectations around patient flow and culture. We met as a team with the potential surgeons to set the tone. We introduced the concept of using more technicians. We worked together with the new team to underscore the importance of a new culture. We had to hold the line on surgical schedules to retain a focus on outpatients. We found ourselves saying "no" quite a bit in order to protect the priority of the outpatient focus. Of course, with a new set of ORs, all surgeons wanted to work there, regardless of the type of cases they had! They pushed to utilize outpatient ORs for their inpatients. We faced resistance and arguments over the limited duration of the surgical day (we close at 1700—rather than staying open to an indefinite hour). We opened with six ORs in October 2003. Five unused ORs were shelled in for future expansion, but not equipped. We then worked together as co-leaders, until Renae left to join another organization, in June 2006.

We have been asked to do presentations on how we developed an ambulatory care model within an organization. It was fun to go back and revisit some of the work that we had done and reflect on how "we" had developed our shared vision along the way. One of our speaking engagements was an all-day seminar for a conference of OR managers that we presented together. Sharing the work and the stories was truly a pleasure, and we definitely gave a better presentation than if either had presented the same material alone.

PERSONALITIES/STYLES THAT FACILITATED THE FORMATION OF A DYAD

We share certain characteristics which we believe contributed toward our successful performance as a Dyad. We doubt that these characteristics were taken into account in placing us in our positions. It was circumstantial that we were "paired" to meet the organization's goals. Nonetheless, we believe that these common characteristics contributed to our willingness to form a Dyad and to perform as one. Age and maturity was important to our successful relationship. We were both well beyond the stage in our careers where we were focused upon acquiring and mastering the necessary technical proficiencies. We were able to take a wider view of our classical roles and explore how those might contribute to the success of a venture. We were willing to step into new roles outside of traditional jobs assigned to OR RNs (scrub/circulate) and anesthesiologists. We were willing to change locations. We were willing to continue to change every few years. We both have significant energy. We both have personal time-consuming interests outside the work place. We support change and new things and were willing to work toward those. We both were able to challenge the status quo in our quest for improvement. We both had a willingness to step out of our comfort zones to try new processes and new roles. We both enjoy an irreverent sense of humor. (For example, when we were visiting a well-run, efficient, and highly regarded Ambulatory Facility, we asked the Head RN about operative or postdischarge nausea and vomiting [PONV] problems. She answered that PONV was a minimal/nonexistent problem for her facility. Right then, from behind a curtain, came what almost amounted to a caricature of loud and ostentatious retching/vomiting. We had a hard time not bursting into laughter.) We both like to laugh and enjoy the work we do, and we can both laugh at ourselves. This is an important skill when doing new things that aren't perfect! We both are fairly contemplative, keen observers, and we like to share our observations. Sometimes we differ, but both are willing to thoughtfully consider changing our viewpoint as well as what adjustments or actions are needed as a result. We both have an affinity to the business side of surgery and a willingness to get into the details to understand processes. We both like a fair amount of independence and trust from our bosses and have a drive to perform at high levels of expertise and regard. We were both comfortable without a lot of structure and in creating structure for ourselves, which was important for this type of role.

WHAT MADE IT A GREAT PARTNERSHIP?

We knew we were in it together. Our success was interdependent. We really trusted each other to watch out for "our" work, and to speak up as one voice. We would check things out with each other. We could laugh together. We could lean on each other for encouragement. Each respected the other as individuals and for his or her accomplishments. There was no precedent for our project or for the shared leadership role, which gave us a great deal of latitude in developing our own version. We didn't formally divide work, but because we knew each other's strengths and clinical expertise, we generally tended to share work along those lines. We disagreed and disputed each other in private, but presented as one in public.

WHAT HELPED US GEL?

Our shared projects and challenges helped us to bond. We had major shared goals; first, the block project; then the pilot Ambulatory Surgery Center (ASC); then the larger facility development and opening. These brought us together, as the success or failure of each became a shared responsibility. This helped us create something we both had confidence and investment in. The shared risk created the sense of team, making us think about how members of a sports team need each other. We both play team sports and understand the interdependence of individual skills and team behavior, so this is a good analogy! There is less focus on one play, one inning or one mistake, knowing that winning the game is a combination of many activities. Peter has been a referee for rugby, which was also a useful background for dealing with all the issues we encountered! In perioperative services, a different team often is together each day, so we had a lot of experience in what makes the case go well and what does not.

Creating our vision together (as our leadership allowed us to do) helped us create something new that was *ours*, not something that one of us had done previously. We were not struggling with a preconceived form. That seems to have given us a higher sense of ownership.

We had leadership that supported us with a lot of trust and freedom. We had leaders to back us when we needed it. We worked to continue to earn that trust with a high level of accountability and responsiveness to all concerns. It probably helped that we both had built trust and a reputation as individual clinicians prior to this, so we could more easily build on that reputation in our new roles.

WHAT WOULD WE DO DIFFERENTLY, OR WHAT WE WOULD HAVE LIKED TO KNOW AHEAD OF TIME?

Our experiences occurred before "Dyads" were very common, so we certainly didn't expect to become as close as we did. The project evolved as we evolved, and the partnership grew with the increasing challenges and demands. Our ability to create a culture versus just building a new unit was the result of walking the talk of a new interdependent team. Sometimes thinking about how big a project is can be overwhelming, so being able to tackle the off-site project first was a great hands-on experience for the larger project.

It would have been helpful if our bosses had identified the Dyad potential and pushed us to more formal inquiry and learning about how to become a Dyad partnership, and what that entails. Perhaps, we should have negotiated conditions for some of the things that we did (the block stuff) so that we had an assurance that the data we produced and presented were going to get acted upon. Having said that, the adversity and frustration produced by the lack of action were a factor in the "bonding through adversity," which built some of our interdependence on each other.

WHEN AND WHY DID THE DYAD BREAK UP?

Our organization didn't formalize this model as a way we could lead into the future. Once the OP surgery suite was up and running, our Dyad function continued for about 18 months. Then, as sometimes happens, the organization's administration changed the administrative structure of Surgical Services. They eliminated the Executive Director of Surgical Services position and reverted to a model managed by the OR Director. The Chief of Anesthesia was approaching retirement and was less invested in the system and making it work. He subsequently retired and was replaced by a new chief. It was perceived that "block usage" work and data were less needed because there were more ORs. The new thought was, "Why bother with running the system tightly for the purpose of efficiency when you can just open up the available unused ORs?" The SSC did not work or function in its previous fashion and became less of an attractive proposition for team members. Renae was recruited across town to another large organization with an advanced job opportunity. Peter edged toward part-time and retirement.

We have stayed in touch over the years, and laughter and stories still come easily when we get together. We believe we became strong partners even without education or formalized recognition and support of this type of management. We weren't an official formalized Dyad on the organizational chart, but we accomplished great things together, and for that, both of us are proud and grateful.

REFERENCES

1. Klein, K., & Bowman, E. (October 2013). Building resilience: "Real" ways to thrive during tough times. *Wharton Work Newsletter*. Philadelphia, PA: University of Pennsylvania.
2. Autry, J. (1991). *Love and profit: The art of caring leadership*. New York, NY: Avon Books.
3. Brockner, J. (1988). *Self esteem at work: Research, theory and practice*. Lexington, MA: D.C. Heath and Company.
4. Yukl, G., & Van Fleet, D. (1982). Cross-Situational, multi-method research on military leader effectiveness. *Organizational Behavior and Human Performance, 30*, 87–108.
5. Avolio, B., & Bass, B. (1991). *Full-range of leadership development*. Binghamton, NY: Bass, Avolio & Associates.
6. Gruner, C. R. (1977). *The game of humor: A comprehensive theory of why we laugh*. New Brunswick, NJ: Transaction Publications.
7. Duncan, W. (1982). Humor in management: Prospectus for administrative practice and research. *Academy of Management Review, 7*, 136–142.
8. Ryan, K., & Oestreich, D. (1998). *Driving fast out of the workplace*. San Francisco, CA: Jossey-Bass.
9. Buckley, K., & Perkins, D. (1987). Transformative change. In D. L. Kirkpatrick (Ed.), *How to manage change effectively* (pp. 45–63). San Francisco, CA: Jossey-Bass.
10. Drinka, T., & Clark, P. (2000). *Health care teamwork: Interdisciplinary practice and teaching*. Westport, CT: Auburn House.
11. Schaller, L. E. (1978). *The change agent*. Nashville, TN: Abingdon Press.
12. Lewin, K. (June 1947). Frontiers in group dynamics: Concepts, methods, and reality in social science, social equilibrium and social change. *Human Relations, 1*, 5–41.
13. Sanford, K. (1998). *Leading with love*. Olalla, WA: Vashon Publishing.
14. Blake, R., & Mouton J. (1982). *Productivity: The human side*. New York, NY: Amacom.
15. Kron, T. (1971). *Management of patient care*. Philadelphia, PA: WB Saunders.
16. Becker, B., Huselid, M., & Ulrich, D. (2001). *The HR scorecard; Linking people, strategy and performance*. Boston, MA: Harvard Business School Press.

17. Corporate author. (2007). Best practices in change management. Loveland, CO: *Prosci Research*.
18. Senge, P. (1990). *The art and practice of the learning organization*. New York: Doubleday Currency.
19. Gladwell, M. (2002). *The tipping point: How little things can make a big difference*. New York: Little, Brown and Company.
20. Bass, B., & Riggio, R. (2006). *Transformational leadership*. (2nd ed.). Mahwah, NJ: Lawrence Erlbaum Associates.
21. Kotter, J. (1996). *Leading change*. Boston, MA: Harvard Business School Press.

Index